W9-AXJ-564

Contemporary Higher Education

International Issues for the Twenty-First Century

Series Editor

Philip G. Altbach
Boston College

A GARLAND SERIES

Contents of the Series

Organizational Studies in Higher Education

Edited with an introduction by

Ted I.K. Youn and Patricia B. Murphy
Boston College

GARLAND PUBLISHING, INC.
A MEMBER OF THE TAYLOR & FRANCIS GROUP
New York & London
1997

Library of Congress Cataloging-in-Publication Data

Organizational studies in higher education / edited with an
introduction by Ted I.K. Youn and Patricia B. Murphy.
p.   cm. — (Contemporary higher education ; 3)
Includes bibliographical references.
ISBN 0-8153-2664-5 (alk. paper)
1. Education, Higher—Social aspects. 2. Organizational sociology.
3. Universities and colleges—Sociological aspects. 4. Universities
and colleges—Management. I. Youn, Ted I. K. II. Murphy, Patricia B.
III. Series.
LC191.074 1997
378.1—dc21   97-22505
                                                      CIP

Printed on acid-free, 250-year-life paper
Manufactured in the United States of America

Contents

Volume Introduction

by Ted I.K. Youn and Patricia B. Murphy

Organizational Studies of Higher Education: A Review

Over the past thirty years, there have been significant developments in theories of organizations, yet there remains much debate among theorists as to how best to approach the study of highly specialized organizations such as arts organizations (DiMaggio 1977), mental health service organizations (Scott and Black 1986), and educational organizations (Bidwell 1986). While it is not at all clear how to develop a distinctive theory of *academic* organizations, it appears evident that studies on academic organizations have developed in conjunction with the general theoretical development in organizational studies. We believe, therefore, that one fruitful way to develop a broad framework for studying academic organizations might be to identify a number of fundamental constructs or themes from organizational studies that correspond to the development in studies of academic organizations. This broad framework could then be used to place the recent developments in organizational studies of higher education, presented in the subsequent sections of this volume, into the broader context of organizational theory. In this vein, this introductory essay briefly summarizes the development of organizational studies and the key theoretical traditions that have influenced studies of academic organizations.

The Development of Organizational Studies in Higher Education

Reviewing the history of organizational studies, Bidwell (1986) concludes that the history of organizational theory is the "history of efforts, only partly realized, to build on and surpass Weberian theories of organization." Studies of academic organizations were also built upon the classical Weberian idea, which takes the closed-system perspective of organizations, and have gradually moved toward more diverse and open perspectives that hold increasingly macrocosmic orientations. It is important to state that in recent decades three theoretical schools have influenced the development of the contemporary literature on academic organizations: the Carnegie school, the institutional school, and the proponents of resource and power dependence theory. The following paragraphs briefly describe how the main tenets of the Weberian closed-system perspective and these three distinctive perspectives have advanced our understanding of academic organizations. Finally, this essay concludes with the possibility of how diverse streams of theory development are seen as a form of renewed interest in institutions among emerging perspectives.

The Weberian Closed-System Perspective

The history of organizational theory originated from the Weberian model of organizations (Weber, 1947). When an organization is analyzed as a closed-system, it is viewed as if it were a machine or technical system. To account for the existence of this technical system, the early Weberian theorists assumed that organizations were tightly bounded, that stability was essential, and that organizational form was largely shaped by the managerial or formal authority. Weber's model, however, was limited to explaining variations in organizational forms, as it focused on the study of structural properties of formal organization. This overemphasis on structures left process in organizations largely unexplained.

The writings of Blau (1973), Gross (1968), and Etzioni (1961) represent the Weberian perspective of academic organizations. While Blau's academic organizations in varying degrees are understood according to structural attributes of the organizational machine, Gross and Etzioni emphasize organizational form as a solution to the problem of goals and compliance of members in organizations. Thus, in order to explain the variations in organizational form, these theorists were generally restricted to the study of relationships among structural attributes, such as the division of labor, and the structural effects of the size and composition of organizations.

Moreover, the closed-system perspective of the Weberian model forced these researchers to hold a narrow perspective of an organization's structures. A more dynamic and broad perspective, developed in response to the limitations of the Weberian model, was followed by the Carnegie school scholars. Rather than viewing organizations as rational and technical machines where the role of central actors are more implicit, the Carnegie school perspective conceives of organizations as systematically related to actors and events in their environments.

Contributions of the Carnegie School

Herbert Simon's (1962) view of the impact of human nature and the architecture of complexity on organizations had a great influence on several notable organizational studies during the 1960s and 1970s. The first of these was Cyert and March's work (1963) on behavioral theory of the firm, which opened up the possibility of political analysis of organizational control by recognizing that an organization is composed of fractured institutions where parochial interests dominate. Thus, organizational goals are often ambiguous and subject to multiple sources of influence. The second of these notable studies was led by Karl Weick's (1976) study of educational organizations. Weick presented an idea of educational organizations as complex and decomposable systems. Weick's holistic approach to organizational analysis introduced a new way to examine the environment as a source of information and organizational regularities. The environment remained an essential source of information and structural differentiation.

Weick's idea of the decoupled form of organization opens up the possibility that ambiguity of goals and uncertainty posed by the environment lead to a "garbage can" model of decision making (March and Olsen, 1976). In the context of environmental uncertainty, March and Olsen saw organizational decision-making behavior as a variety of logics of action and symbolic forms of action.

Simon, March, Cyert, and Weick developed a number of rich insights that students of organization now regard as foundational elements. For example, their skepticism toward rational-actor models of organizations, the habits and routines of formal organizations that are fundamentally important to how attention is directed, and their insights that follow the view of decision making as a political process involving multiple actors and ambiguous preferences are important contributions to organizational theory. By focusing on the structure of environments in explaining the theory of action, the recent development of organizational theory owes a considerable debt to the Carnegie school. In particular, the work of Simon, March, Weick and their colleagues profoundly influenced the institutionalists' approach to the study of organizations.

The Contribution of the Institutional School

While there are many approaches to institutional theory (DiMaggio and Powell, 1983), the institutional school basically holds the natural systems view of formal organizations, stressing that institutions are end products of random variation, selection, and retention. No doubt, this school takes the environment seriously and views institutionalization as a state-dependent process that makes organizations less instrumentally rational. Institutional histories of distinctive colleges (Clark, 1972), cultural rites of elite education (Kamens, 1987), and ritualized routines among historical single-sex colleges (Youn and Loscocco, 1991), therefore, become sources of normative obligations for formal organizations, and they are taken for granted in organizational life. These institutionalists argue that while there is an inescapable degree of diversity in organizations, each organization somehow develops its inner logic and life that are not necessarily shaped by those who appear to control it. The institutional school, therefore, points to a variety of institutionalizations as the theory of organizational action. A question among theorists is: does the action mean commitment to institutional values or responsiveness to environmental influences?

Debates between the Carnegie school and the institutionalists of old and new on how formal organizations relate to their environment have left diverse streams of unresolved theoretical issues. What is now clear, however, is that the development of theory reflects a more macro-level analysis of organizations (Meyer and Scott, 1983). Some even point to the view that organizations are increasingly prone to create or enact their environment deliberately rather than await the judgment of the environment. Organizations have the quality of "distinctive competence" in relating to the environment, as the argument goes (Weick, 1976). More importantly, it is argued by the followers of these debates that organizational strategic policies change the environment in which organizations operate. This notion of how strategies lead to structural changes seems to invite the idea of institutions as the prime shapers of interests and politics in organizations (Pfeffer, 1981). Therein lies the possibility of a power model in organizational analysis.

The Power Model: A Renewed Interest in Institutions

One of the Carnegie school's key contributions has been its focus on organizational rules and routines, taken-for-granted aspects of organizational life. Routines in organizations are important tools for the reduction of uncertainty, while they must not be seen as a purely passive form of behavior. Moreover, routines rationalize power relations among actors in an organization. While the work of March and his colleagues on the "garbage-can model" of organizational decision making raises the importance of complexity, it deepens our understanding of power and political institutions in organizations.

Some recent institutional theorists, while renewing their commitment to the study of institutional order in formal organizations, present a somewhat different interpretation of how power relations work. While organizational usage of power in facing competition for resources and uncertainty is an explanation for an organization's relation to the environment, Meyer and Scott (1983), for example, treat the powerful action taken by any organization as myths that are often rationalized by formal organizations. Symbolism, in particular, and culture, in general, are never meant to be politically neutral. They are created by political and economic elites and serve these elites well in organizations. Symbolism and culture become sources of pressure that make weaker organizations in the same field imitate seemingly successful organizations in order to achieve similar success (DiMaggio and Powell, 1983; Youn and Loscocco, 1991).

While sharing an open-system perspective of organizations, each of the emerging perspectives in organizational studies emphasizes different themes for explaining organizational actions. Nevertheless, there is a renewed focus on the importance of institutions of group interests and political orders in organizations among diverse theoretical groups. Interestingly, for this deepening interest in political institutions, we find the traces of Weber's theory of bureaucracy and his emphasis on the role of rules in reducing uncertainty and rationalizing power relations in organizations.

Conclusion and Implications for Higher Education

During the past three decades, theoretical models in organizational studies have developed from a closed-systems perspective toward a treatment of organizations as open systems, from a bounded view of organizations toward a recognition of the importance of environments and institutionalization, and from a focus on structures toward an exploration of institutionalized processes. These theoretical developments are mirrored in the literature on academic organizations. Studies of higher education now emphasize environments, power, organizational culture, and internal political processes.

This development in the literature on academic organizations must also be understood in the context of the dramatic changes that we observe in higher education. American colleges and universities have become increasingly complex organizations, closely connected to and influenced by their external environments. Increasing dependence on the federal government for funding, pressures for technological development and human resource training from industry, changing demands from students acting as "consumers," and increased competition among institutions for resources have placed enormous external constraints on academic organizations. In addition, institutions of higher education now fulfill many ambiguous and often conflicting roles in our society, which creates a continual state of confusion and divisiveness within academic organizations and places internal constraints on organizational leadership and decision making. Thus, academic organizations must relate to both internal and external constraints in trying to adapt and change.

These changes in higher education have rendered the Weberian closed-system perspective inadequate to explain the complexity of modern academic organizations. While acknowledging that organizational structure is still important, it is no longer possible to ignore the influence of external environments or the effect of internal processes on organizations. Recent theoretical models from the open-system perspective emphasize the role of various aspects of environments and processes in organizations. These models as presented in this essay should, thus, provide a broad framework for approaching the study of academic organizations. In addition, the readings in this volume have been organized to highlight the key themes critical for understanding how colleges and universities function as organizations in order to enable practitioners to manage academic organizations effectively.

References

Bidwell, C.E. 1986. On Organizational Studies. In *The Contributions of the Social Sciences to Educational Policy and Practice: 1965-1985*, edited by J. Hannaway and M.E. Lockheed. Berkeley, Calif.: McCutchan Publishers.

Blau, P.M. 1973. *The Organization of Academic Work*. New York: John Wiley and Sons.

Clark, B.R. 1972. "Organizational Saga in Higher Education," *Administrative Science Quarterly* 17.

Cyert, R.M. and James G. March. 1963. *A Behavioral Theory of the Firm*. Englewood Cliffs, N.J.: Prentice-Hall.

DiMaggio, P.J. 1977. "Market Structures, the Creative Process, and Popular Culture," *Journal of Popular Culture* 11: 436–52.

DiMaggio, P.J. and W.W. Powell. 1983. "The Iron Cage Revisited: Institutional Isomorphism and Collective Rationality in Organizational Fields." *American Sociological Review* 48 (April): 147–60.

Etzioni, A. 1961. *A Comparative Analysis of Complex Organizations: On Power, Involvement and Their Correlates*. New York: Free Press.

Gross, Edward. 1968. "Universities as Organizations: A Research Approach." *American Sociological Review* 49: 323–34.

Kamens, David. 1987. "Legitimizing Myths and Educational Organizations—Relationship Between Organizational Ideology and Formal Structure." *American Sociological Review* 42: 208–19.

March, J.G. and Herbert A. Simon. 1958. *Organizations*. New York: Wiley.

March, J.G. and J.P. Olsen. 1976. *Ambiguity and Choice in Organizations*. Bergen, Norway: Universitetsforlaget.

Meyer, J.W. and W.R. Scott. 1983. *Organizational Environments: Ritual and Rationality*. Beverly Hills, Calif.: Sage.

Pfeffer, Jeffrey. 1981. *Power in Organizations*. Boston: Pitman Press.

Scott, W.R. and Bruce L. Black, ed. 1986. *The Organization of Mental Health Services: Societal and Community Systems*. Beverly Hills, Calif.: Sage.

Simon, H.A. 1962. "The Architecture of Complexity." *Proceedings of American Philosophical Society* 106: 467–82.

Weber, M. 1947. *The Theory of Social Economic Organization.* Edited and translated by A.M. Henderson and
    T. Parsons. Glencoe, Ill: Free Press.
Weick, K. 1976. "Educational Organizations as Loosely Coupled Systems." *Administrative Science Quarterly*
    21: 1–19.
Youn, T.I.K. and Karyn A. Loscocco. 1991. "Institutional History and Ideology: The Evolution of Two
    Women's Colleges." *History of Higher Education Annual* 11: 21–44.

The Genesis and Evolution
of Organizational Forms

Continental and British Modes
of Academic Organization

The general structure of academic organization on the Continent combines faculty guild and state bureaucracy. Each of these forms has a long history. The understructure of guild-like faculty clusters originated in the medieval period; the university began as a guild, or more accurately a confederation of guilds, at a time when the guild was the common form for the organization of work in cities (Rashdall 1936; Haskins 1957; Thrupp 1968; Baldwin and Goldthwaite 1972). Instructors, and in some cases students, borrowed this form as a way of collectively implementing a common interest. In the process they acquired certain rights and privileges, established self-government, and developed means of defense against adverse actions of other groups. When a king or a pope initiated the enterprise, ordinarily he would charter a group as a recognized guild. Also academicians drifted into the guild style of self-regulation themselves, where a group of masters jointly controlled a territory of work, elected one of their own as head, took oaths of obedience and fealty, and, in smaller domains, individually exercised personal control over journeymen and apprentices. The guild form ultimately became the primary organizational base for the university, and provided a controlling mechanism and sturdy foundation that has endured for eight centuries and still appears in modern higher education (Reeves 1970; Ashby 1974; Clark forthcoming (a)).

The superstructure of state administration developed at about the same time as city-states and other local authorities attempted to regulate academic bodies. However, its genuine strength developed later when the national state emerged as the primary source of political authority and learned to use modern administrative methods. In one country after another on the Continent, building a nation meant encapsulating higher education in a public bureau. There was either the full nationalization of higher education, in which nearly all units were placed under one or more ministries of the national government, as for example in France after Napoleon or in Italy after unification in 1870; or there was a complete governmental embrace at a lower level, as in Germany where the universities came within a ministry of a *Land* government. Most important, the emerging governmental framework did not have the benefit of initiating new educational

3

systems but had to administratively embrace existing faculties and universities that had retained guild properties. The chaired professor in the European university of the last several centuries was a direct descendant of the guild master of old, in that he held a permanent appointment, exercised great personal power over assistants and students, and, together with other chairholders, monopolized decisions about what would be done within the university as well as in such major subunits as the faculty and the institute, especially regarding determination of faculty membership and curriculum. Thus guild authority was maintained by combining personal and collegial rule at the same time as faculties were changing from voluntary associations related to government to formal parts of government (Clark forthcoming (a)). The understructure continued to serve the interests of senior faculty. Not only was it supported by traditions that had been developed since twelfth-century Bologna and Paris, but it was also bolstered by the ideologies of each age. Indeed, *the* leading educational ideal of the nineteenth century, that of the German research-centered university, provided the rationale for rule by professors (Turner 1972, Chapter 4). While allowing for a ministerial framework, the reforms proposed by Wilhelm von Humboldt and others in Berlin in the 1810's stressed the necessity of freedom in research and teaching if scholarly progress and national advance were to be served. The eminence of German academic science during the rest of the century gave worldwide credence to a system of organization in which the autonomy and prerogatives of chairholders were central. These nineteenth-century ideals were congruent with baronial power and collective self-rule.

Guild organization that combined personal and collegial rule generally disappeared from eighteenth- and nineteenth-century industry and commerce. Marx ascribed this withering away of guild organization to the spread of capitalistic modes of production; Weber ascribed it to the spread of bureaucratic organization (Marx 1965; Weber 1950). Although elements of guild organization survive in modern craft unions and professional associations, the question of continuity between the old guilds and the new forms remains unanswered by historians (Thrupp 1968). But private entrepreneurship did not penetrate the arenas of Continental higher education, nor, in general, the realms of state activity and public administration in which there was no profit-seeking activity. The important result was that the guild-like university never had to face this competitive form.

4

As the state and national governments erected their administrative superstructures, bureaucratic forms grew stronger, although they had only partial control over the entrenched academic guilds. While ministries established national rules in such policy sectors as budget, admission, curriculum, and personnel, except during occasional periods of authoritarian suppression, they did not actively enforce them, because to do so would improperly invade the rights of guild self-determination and, later, the acquired rights of professors to freedom of teaching and research. "Bureaucratic" systems of higher education characteristically made many rules but enforced them weakly and encouraged much evasion. As chairholding professors became protected civil servants, their right to rule was usually enacted into state law and codified in state administration. Thus even the rules of the state often strengthened personal rule and collegial monopoly at the operating levels. In this climate, university-level administration had little opportunity to develop. The professors did not want it; the ministry took care of overhead services; and the "administrative directors" and other agents of the ministry located at the universities generally had only partial control over the professors and their elected deans and rectors.

Compared to the United States system, the Continental structure, which combines faculty guild and national ministry, minimizes institutional competition and the play of market forces. Such nationalized structures as those of France and Italy have attempted to equalize institutions: for example, the university degree is an award of the national system and not of the individual institution, and to study law at one university is the formal equivalent of studying law at another. Faculty are appointed within a single national personnel system, and promotion involves movement from one civil-service rank and salary to another. Uniform standards deter the separate institutions from competing for talent or emphasizing distinctive approaches. This uniform approach has had the unanticipated consequence of inducing faculty members to transfer their guild forms of authority, originally meant and still appropriate for small-scale organization, to the large-scale organization of national systems (or, in Germany, to a subnational or provincial level) in order to protect themselves against politicians and bureaucrats. Committees of senior professors often end up as a systemwide academic oligarchy. The guild as well as the bureaucracy prefers to control a domain of work.

Thus European academic organization has fostered excessive order, with institutions inclined toward unity and uniformity. New forces,

5

plans, and organizational forms have had great difficulty in penetrating such structures. As a result, the main thrust of recent reforms in the nationalized systems increasingly has been to counteract this uniformity. As these systems have attempted to move from elite to mass higher education within modern, complex economies, they have had to face more heterogeneous demands from ever greater numbers of students of diverse interests and backgrounds as well as from industry and government for highly trained manpower. They face the problem of creating diverse programs and approaches within the heavy constraints of structures that are uncomfortable with planned or unplanned diversity. Adaptiveness then becomes a very great problem: neither the deliberate action of planners nor the unplanned interaction of competitive institutions is a powerful force compared to the institutional strength of academic oligarchs and ministerial bureaucrats. Major efforts in reform may be mounted occasionally by central authorities under such extraordinary conditions of crisis as existed in France in 1968. But such efforts apparently have lasting impact only insofar as they disperse control and otherwise open up the domains long monopolized by the forms. A central edict may disperse control, with the commander disbanding old units and turning the troops loose to experiment and regroup. The post-1968 French reform, officially disbanding faculties and allowing instructors to regroup in new units of education and research (UERs), has moved in this direction (Patterson 1972; 1975; Fomerand 1975; Furth and Van de Graaff, forthcoming). More fundamental reform in the nationalized systems will probably stem from efforts by many countries to regionalize government. Shifting toward decentralized government and administration would increase regional and local influences on the character forms, encourage institutional responsibility and ambition, and inject some elements of competition. Reform is leaning in these directions, as a reaction to the old uniform system, but its potential effect remains questionable in face of the structural and ideological forces that favor centralization in modern government.

The British mode of academic organization is also historically rooted in guilds, but the British superstructure enfolds a very different combination of vested interests from those on the Continent. The British state bureaucracy has played a considerably lesser role (Berdahl 1959; Ashby 1966; Briggs 1970; Reeves 1970; Halsey and Trow 1971; Scott 1973; Moodie and Eustace 1974; Annan 1975). As chartered corporations composed of chartered colleges that could and did accumulate their own endowments, Oxford and Cambridge, dating from the thirteenth century, developed extensive autonomy from

6

the controls of local and national departments of government. The four Scottish universities—St. Andrews, Glasgow, Aberdeen, and Edinburgh—originating in the fifteenth centuries, also were independent of governmental bureaucracy. In the nineteenth century, after six centuries of an Oxbridge monopoly, England developed civic universities in industrial cities such as Manchester and Birmingham and a unique academic holding company for the nation and the Empire, in the form of the University of London, which had affiliated colleges in India and Ceylon, Africa and the West Indies, as well as in England. Again, the mechanism of a chartered autonomous corporation was used instead of the Continental device of placing the university within a governmental bureau and teachers within the civil service. Autonomy meant that each institution was free to admit its own students, arrange its own courses, hire its own faculty, own its own property, largely raise its own income, and pay its own bills.

Guild control flourished in this British pattern of remote state supervision, especially in the two oldest universities, whose historical primacy and prestige have subtly defined for all other universities a towering British style of academic control. Immensely elaborate and only partly codified rules and norms of personal privilege and collegial hegemony developed among a welter of chairs, departments, facilities, colleges-within-universities, senates, councils, and courts. But guild authority was not the only form of authority within the autonomous individual university. Especially outside of Oxford and Cambridge, laymen systematically have been included in an upper tier of academic government (the "Council"), and a key administrative post has been provided in the form of the vice-chancellorship. These participants have not been completely dependent on the professors, nor have they operated as functionaries of the state. Since they, and especially the Vice-Chancellor, are responsible for the welfare of the institution as a whole, they have helped tilt the guild interests of the professors toward a sense of corporate identity.

In short, compared to academic organization on the Continent, the British universities, responsible for their own administration, have developed different forms of participation. Infused with the old autocratic and collegial rights of the professoriate, bureaucratic and trustee authority has had a local role—a major role compared to the Continent, a minor one compared to the United States. Compared to the concentrations of power found at the top and at the bottom in the Continental systems, the British system has a weaker top but a strengthened middle at the level of the university. British faculty clusters have had to work with administrators and laymen who hold

7

university-level responsibility rather than with officials in a government bureau.

The professor's control beyond his autonomous institutions is more subtle and elaborate in Britain than in the United States. The practice of "external examiners," by which students are tested by professors from other institutions (and hence by which their own teachers are indirectly and informally assessed), has served to connect institutions. When such connections became standard, a whole "interorganizational field" may develop conformity by mutual tacit agreement; a set of norms grounded in basic consensus may evolve (Warren, Rose, and Bergunder 1974; Clark 1965). Such controls as are elaborated from the bottom up can be more compelling than the formal regulations of national systems. Their power in Britain helps to explain why that country seemed to have a system long before it had a formal system and why uniform practice and a shared commitment to certain standards may be more prevalent in a system of autonomous institutions than in a system of nationalized administration. Collegial pressure can be more cohesive than bureaucratic pressure among institutions as well as within them.

University autonomy has been so strong in Britain that we can speak of the bottom controlling the top of the national "system" until after World War II. The University Grants Committee (UGC), created in 1918 as a way of funneling increasing amounts of government money to the universities, has consisted mainly of university professors who have received money directly from the British Treasury and doled out lump sums to the individual universities. As formerly independent organizations became parts of an emerging national system, this "buffer" mechanism was heralded internationally as an excellent way of preserving institutional autonomy (Berdahl 1959). It was also, of course, a grand case of national academic oligarchy, one in which traditional commitment to high standards of performance became institutionalized. But increasingly during the 1950's and the 1960's, growing national financial support has brought with it more direction from the top. The autonomy of the University Grants Committee was considerably diminished in the late 1960's when it was placed under the national Department of Education and Science. The Department has become a formidable instrument of government policy, able, for example, to pump monies into a nonuniversity sector at the expense of the universities, particularly those universities considered bastions of privilege. The Department and the UGC now operate as policy centers in a national system; they determine not only salary scales but the direction in which the universities are encouraged

8

to move. The British now have moved toward the Continental mode in which nearly all units of higher education fall under a single national bureau. Traditional autonomy still remains a force and resists this nationalizing movement. Yet nationlization is proceeding at a time when the central government has modern administrative methods for achieving integration, as well as a compelling need to economize in a high-cost sector, and at least some of the time, the ideological inclination to eliminate private enterprises and to seek equality and equity through the administrative arms of the central state. In a system in which there has been much voluntary convergence, centering on emulation of the academic styles of Oxford and Cambridge and the subtle connections forged by external examiners, nationalized administration has induced even more convergence.

9

The Historical Emergence
of American Academic Organization

The general structure of academic organization in the United States is a mixture of forms of organization and types of authority, a unique combination that has resulted from the conditions under which different sectors have emerged, the development of vested interests, and the impact of earlier forms on later ones. The first institutional type to emerge was *not* the university, as in Europe, but the small independent college now known as the private liberal arts college. That form was organized from the top down, as Protestant groups in the colonial period established boards of managers, drawn primarily from outside academic life and from outside governmental authority, to hire and fire teachers, appoint and dismiss a president, and otherwise be responsible for the enterprise (Hofstadter and Metzger 1955; Rudolph 1962; Whitehead 1973). Trustee authority thus preceded either administrative or faculty authority; this method of governing later became customary even in the public sector. There was little or no guild organization among either faculty or students. The small private colleges multiplied rapidly during the westward expansion of the nineteenth century, spurred especially by civic and denominational competition (Tewksbury 1932; Naylor 1973). Although many of these voluntary associations without state support did fail, some 900 were in existence by 1900, and as a whole they were firmly fixed in the country's educational structure.

The university form of organization came late to America: the first university to be established as such, Johns Hopkins, dates only from 1876. Other older institutions had evolved from college into university: Yale developed "graduate work" in the 1850's and awarded the first American Ph.D. in 1861, and Harvard established a graduate department in the 1870's (Hofstadter and Metzger 1955; Storr 1953; Storr 1973). Other universities soon followed, and the important, prestigious, *private* university sector was well established by the turn of this century. At the same time, a public university sector was also emerging. The first universities supported by individual state governments date from the 1780's and 1790's, but it was not until after the Civil War and toward the end of the nineteenth century that they developed fully, due in part to the greater resources provided the states by the national government through the famous land-grant

10

legislation of the Morrill Act (Hofstadter and Metzger 1955; Veysey 1965; Storr 1953).

The emergence of the university after the institutionalization of the four-year college meant that a two-tier structure developed; advanced specialization was pursued in graduate and professional schools, which, as distinctive components of the university, were superimposed on the college structure. If the German university had been borrowed in its entirety, the American university would have accepted students directly out of high school as qualified to enter directly into the professional and graduate schools. But the borrowed idea of the research-centered university had to be adapted to established American expectations and the vested interests of the undergraduate college (Jencks and Risesman 1968). Thus a new comprehensive university emerged that included general education at the bottom and specialized education at the top. The general education offered by the state university served as its main basis of appeal for support from the state population and authorities. The undergraduate college of the private university served as an analogous basis of appeal for support from alumni and for effective competition against the hundreds of colleges that did not become universities. On the graduate level, the scientific disciplines and the research scholar were preeminent.

The device of a trustee board was carried over from the private colleges into both public and private universities: by the first half of the nineteenth century it was the chief American mechanism for bridging the gap between public accountability and professional autonomy, in sharp contrast to the assumption on the Continent and elsewhere that a governmental ministry was the appropriate mechanism. With trustees given formal responsibilies, no superior administrative bodies—a state department of higher education or a bureau in the state bureaucracy—developed. Instead, campus administration was subordinate to the trustees. In private universities and even more so in public universities, a separate group of administrators developed, headed by a president who was appointed and delegated authority by the trustees. Presidential leadership came into its own during the latter part of the nineteenth century. The presidents were swash-buckling captains of erudition in the eyes of Thorstein Veblen (Veblen 1954). Bureaucratic administration located within the institution itself, rather than within a higher state ministry, became by the turn of the century another distinctive feature of the American mode (Veysey 1965).

Then, too, the setting in which trustees and administrators operated was always inherently competitive within and among the major

11

sectors and the individual states. The competitive dynamism of the small colleges accelerated in the last quarter of the nineteenth century as the autonomous private universities and the state-supported public universities set out in descending order of preference: to become great research universities; to become well-regarded American universities that brought honor to supporters; or to establish themselves firmly enough so that students would continue to appear, the faculty would not leave, and the bills would be paid. Much of the present structure of American higher education is a result of the system's openness, which was typified in the nineteenth century by combining private initiative and voluntary association with a multistate fragmentation of public control, where numerous governmental authorities originated and developed public higher education under conditions that varied greatly according to time of settlement and regional differences within the large continental territory. No national office played any continuing role in this unplanned aggregation of institutions, as it did in the French central-administration version of the European mode; no state dominated the others, or even set the pace, as in the Prussian influence on the other *Länder* in the German federal-structure version of the European style. Instead, the American conditions led to dispersed control, unparalleled institutional diversity, and marked institutional competition.

If the university came late to America, guild forms of academic control came even later. Faculty claims of authority were preceded by the trustee mechanism and by strong university administration. As forms of faculty control emerged, they were conditioned by and blended with trustee and administrative control within the framework of a local legal entity. In contrast to the Continent, where academic organization began as a confederation of guilds, the original American building block was the unitary college. Then, when the college required formal subdivision to handle increased specialization, it was the academic department and not the European chair that emerged as the lower operating unit. The department existed at Harvard by 1825 and was firmly in place throughout the country by 1900 (Duryea 1973). As we will show in the following section, this organizational form allowed both for a certain amount of personal rule in specialized fields and for collegial decisions in certain matters about which professors cared the most, much in the style of the chairholding professors on the Continent. An ideological claim to guild-like rule was also gradually elaborated, particularly in the latter part of the nineteenth century and the early part of the twentieth, which drew on the oldest traditions of the university, the great nineteenth-century

12

German model of the research university, and the concept of academic freedom. But the American department developed within the hierarchy of an established administrative superstructure. Professors had to win the right to decide matters of curriculum and personnel selection within a context of a young administration that was itself subordinate to the powers of lay trustees.

Faculty influence has varied considerably among the major and minor institutional sectors of the diverse American system, correlating generally with the age and prestige of the particular types of institutions. For example, faculty influence has been higher in leading private and public universities and in the leading private colleges than in the less prestigious institutions in each of these sectors. And it has been relatively low in two sectors that emerged late, in which origins and development grew out of extant modes of administration in American elementary and secondary education. One of these sectors began to develop in the last half of the nineteenth century in the form of "normal schools" for training elementary school teachers. In the first decades of this century, these evolved into "teachers colleges" that awarded the bachelor's degree and prepared secondary as well as elementary school personnel; still later these evolved into "state colleges," public comprehensive colleges, and recently in some cases they have assumed the title and even the competence of "state universities." This sector's historical association with state boards of education who were responsible for lower schools permitted patterns of heavy dominance by trustees and administrators that were more characteristic of lower than higher education. Such control has been even stronger in the community college sector, a twentieth-century phenomenon that predates World War II but did not flower across the country until the great expansion in mass higher education of the 1950's and 1960's. This form originated and developed as an upward reach of systems of secondary education. Community colleges have been staffed extensively by secondary school administrators and teachers and governed either by local boards of citizens, who also govern the lower schools, or by boards built on this model.

It has been primarily in the community colleges and secondarily among the state colleges that instructors have been inclined to join faculty unions, a new form of faculty influence (Garbarino 1975). The relative powerlessness of these teachers has been further increased by the growth of an organizational structure that increasingly separates those at the top from those at the bottom. Unionization is yet another experiment in combining collegial and bureaucratic rule. And now union officials are added to the set of interest groups.

13

All of the major sectors identified above contain so many different mixtures of purposes, programs, and clientele that we must classify additional subtypes. The private sector, which now has only one student to the public sector's three, remains enormously varied. The private university contains at least three important subtypes: the research-centered university, highest in prestige and national in orientation (for example, Chicago, Columbia, Yale); the secular urban-based university, lower in prestige and more local in orientation (for example, Boston University, New York University, George Washington University, University of Cincinnati); and the Catholic municipal university, less prestigious, oriented both to locality and Catholicism (for example, University of Portland, University of Dayton, Seton Hall University, St. John's University). The 800 private colleges have shown equally great variations in quality and commitment: the secular, elite liberal arts college, competitive with the top universities (for example, Swarthmore, Reed, Amherst); the middle-rank institution that usually maintains a modest religious connection (for example, St. Olaf, Baldwin-Wallace, Westminster); and the rear-guard places struggling to gain or retain marginal accreditation and in some cases still completely dominated by a denominational board or an autocratic president (for example, Oral Roberts, St. Joseph, Bob Jones). The institutions at the tail end of the academic procession, inferior to the best high schools, are "colleges only by grace of semantic generosity" (Riesman 1956). And similarly in each of the public sectors—university, state college, community college—dispersed public control has produced a great range in the mixture of purpose, program, and academic quality: the University of Mississippi qualitatively differs from Berkeley; Western Kentucky University differs extensively from Brooklyn College or San Francisco State University; and suburban Foothill Community College (Los Altos, California) is an academic showpiece differing radically from such downtown community colleges as Chicago Loop College and Los Angeles City College, both of which, with more than 20,000 students, face large numbers of poor students from minority backgrounds and offer dozens of one- and two-year terminal programs along with the academic courses that permit later transfer to four-year institutions.

The development of so much variance among and within the major sectors led long before World War II to an unparalleled national *diversity*. This primary characteristic of American higher education has developed along with a second: marked *competition* among institutions striving to enhance their own position in an unmanaged market of producers, each in search of financial resources, personnel,

14

and clientele. The privately controlled institutions competed not only with one another but also with the public campuses as they developed. Competitiveness extended even to public institutions within the same state system: to wit, the rivalry between Michigan State University and the University of Michigan, UCLA and Berkeley in California, Southern Illinois and the University of Illinois. A third distinctive feature of American higher education is the *hugeness* of some major parts as well as the whole. After a quarter-century of rapid development following World War II, official statistics in 1970 counted more than 2,500 institutions and eight million students. By the mid-1970's, New York had a huge state system of 64 institutions and 325,000 students; New York City operated a separate system of its own, with 11 institutions and 250,000 students. This placed the total scale of operations for the entire state of New York second only to the huge public system in California, with its nine state university campuses (enrollment 122,000), 19 state colleges (291,000), and 103 community colleges (957,000), with total enrollment for the state in excess of 1,-372,000 (American Council on Education 1974; State University of New York 1974; Lee and Bowen 1971).

Especially from a cross-national and historical perspective, the size and internal complexity of the American "system" are staggering. Generalizing about *the* American mode of academic control is thus extremely difficult. One method is to establish levels of organization that potentially can be applied to all nations (Van de Graaff, editor, forthcoming), and then to compare the nature of authority at each level in the United States with what we know about the Continental and British modes. This approach will bring us face-to-face with contemporary structure and the ways that the interests of various groups are rooted in it.

15

Organizational Levels
in the American National System

We will speak primarily about the state university and the state college, although much of what we say bears also on the other major sectors. We will also occasionally discuss the American system as if we were foreign observers somewhat taken aback by the odd ways exhibited by those of another land.

At the lowest level of organization, the department is the standard unit. In comparison with the chair and its often-related institute, the department distributes power more widely: first, among a group of full professors, then, reduced portions to associate and assistant professors. The chairmanship of the department is an impersonal position in the sense that it commonly rotates on a three-year term among the senior faculty rather than remaining the fixed possession of one person. The incumbent must consult with other members, full professors and perhaps tenured associate professors, on some issues, and, on other issues must consult with the entire faculty. In such meetings, majority vote has been the common device for decision making. Thus, the department has been primarily a collegial body, unified in its common interest in a discipline and also somewhat hierarchical in the ranking of full professor, associate professor, assistant professor, and instructor (Clark 1961; Demerath, Stephens, and Taylor 1967; Ben-David 1971; Baldridge 1971; Blau 1973; Epstein 1974).

But the department is also a bureaucratic unit. The chairman is not only a spokesman for his colleagues to higher levels of authority, but is also the lowest representative of general academic management. He or she is responsible to one or more deans and one or more campus officials (president, academic vice-president, provost) and to a much greater degree than the chaired professor, the incumbent is accountable "up" an organizational hierarchy as well as "down" to colleagues of equal or near-equal status. He is often appointed by the administration, after consultation with department members, and serves at the pleasure of the central campus officials. Therefore, at the level in chair systems where the personal rule of the professor is strong, the American department system blunts the authority of the chairman by bureaucratic and collegial controls. The department sometimes can be particularistic in its decision making, through the

16

efforts of a towering figure in its midst or by heavy politicking in the voting of a collective body. But such tendencies are damped by the combination of lateral control within a collegial body and vertical control of higher officials. The situation of dual authority also induces the collegial body and the bureaucratic staff to watch one another. In this way, nearby administrative officials serve to check arbitrary power within the department. The tensions of the system fall most heavily on the chairman, because he is in the middle, placed between faculty and administration, and expected to assume responsibility on an ambiguous foundation of authority.

The next level up in the American university structure is the college (for example, the college of arts and sciences), or the school (for example, the school of medicine, law, or business). The college of arts and sciences commonly includes the basic disciplines—all the departments of the humanities, social sciences, and natural sciences. This central college also commonly has hegemony over undergraduate and graduate education, over everything, that is, other than the professional schools, which now operate almost exclusively on an advanced, post-graduate level. This is in contrast to the European system where professional study begins immediately after the secondary level and is organized in faculties that are parallel to the faculties for the humanistic and scientific disciplines. The basic college or similar units commonly have a dean for the undergraduate and one for the graduate realm. The department staff at most universities teaches at both levels and hence falls within both of these two major administrative jurisdictions. The deans are usually appointed by top officials of the university and operate more as true members of the central administration than do the department chairmen. The deans of the professional schools are somewhat more autonomous, although they usually are appointed rather than elected, and have the status of administrative officer. Each deanship is an administrative office staffed with assistant deans and other supporting personnel, a base of administrative power independent of faculty bodies and superior to constituent departments.

The college or school also has one or more collective bodies; for example, the faculty of arts and sciences, the faculty of the undergraduate college, and the faculty of the graduate school, which meet occasionally, hear reports from their own committees and the deans, and decide by collective voting. There is thus a dual structure within which the administrative officials and the faculty bodies must devise ways of separating and joining jurisdictions. Typically, the administration controls the budget, the teaching staff supervises the cur-

17

riculum, and both oversee student conduct. There are many dual-membership committees, and certain professors develop administrative capacities and relations of mutual trust with certain administrators, and thus serve as a bridging oligarchy. On most campuses, the broad academic collective bodies have little to say in the crucial area of personnel. The hiring, promoting, and firing of teaching staff falls to the individual department, which does the basic personnel work and usually has primary influence in junior appointments. The higher administrative officials and committees of professors appointed by the administration must approve all appointments and exercise this power (and the funding of requisite positions), which has serious consequences in the case of expensive, tenured personnel.

The relationship of administrators and academics at this level of organization may be characterized as a bureaucratized federation of collegial groups. As in the chair-based systems, where the counterpart unit is the faculty, the American college or school is a relatively flat structure comprising a number of formally equal collegial bodies, the departments, which may total fifty or more in the central college (arts and sciences) on large campuses. But it also has an administrative office that is hierarchically superior to the departments and is clearly a part of a large administrative framework. Bureaucratic authority is here much stronger than in the traditional systems of the Continent, which systematically intrude upon the power of subordinate groups and are interested in applying common standards.

At the third level of the university campus as a whole, the American structure exhibits a complex blending of the authority of trustees, administrators, and professors. The laymen who serve on the board of trustees (or regents) that is formally at the apex of control are supposed to guide the long-term development of the institution in the name of broad interests of the larger society. In public universities, they are usually appointed by the state governor, who is the head of the financing of the public sector, and hence may represent one or another political point of view, usually conservative. In private universities, they are largely elected by the existing trustees, with perhaps some participation by alumni, and tend to become self-perpetuating boards of relatively well-to-do and conservative businessmen (Veblen 1954; Beck 1947; Rauh 1967; Hartnett 1970). Like such boards in other sectors, they are part-time and amateur, meeting perhaps once a month, or as seldom as three or four times a year, although certain members (the chairman or the members of an executive committee) will meet more often and devote much time to the institution. As their most important power, the trustees appoint the

18

administrative head, the president or chancellor, and officially delegate much to him, while retaining residual powers and ultimate legal control.

Of course, what is delegated has been defined broadly by the historical evolution of respective powers of the boards and the administration, with a gradual drift from close trustee supervision to management by professional administration. Formal administration increasingly came into its own at the campus-wide level of organization beginning with the reign of the strong institution-building presidents (Veysey 1965). Here utterly unlike Continental systems and chair-based systems around the world, a large class of administrators has developed who are neither of the faculty and controlled by it nor of a state ministry of education and directed by it. As experts in such specialties as student admission, recordkeeping, personnel policy, physical plant management, library operations, budgeting, public relations, alumni affairs, and university planning, they compose an administrative structure within which they work for and at the pleasure of the president, the vice-president, the treasurer, and the business officer. Their specialized roles and training dispose them to points of view different from those of trustees, faculty, and students (Otten 1970; Lunsford 1970). They are generally grouped together in a large administration building that physically reinforces their mutual contact and interest.

At the same time, the academics have some collective and representational bodies operating across the campus and at major segments of it, for example, in the form of an academic senate or a board of permanent officers. But the faculty grasp tends to be weaker than that of the administration and trustees. The professional-school bodies are usually split off from the inclusive ones of the central "liberal arts faculty" of the undergraduate college and the graduate school. All-university committees that embrace every school and college are commonly appointed by and report to the chief administrative officer.

The American structure at this level thus differs considerably from other countries by combining the presence of laymen as trustees, responsible for general policy and holding ultimate responsibility and power, with the operation of an administrative corps answerable to the trustees and holding delegated authority, jurisdiction, and responsibility. As of the lower levels, the campus-wide structure is relatively flat and considerably federative, because the many departments, colleges, and schools retain impressive powers and degrees of influence in many sectors of decision making, particularly over personnel and curriculum. But the structure is also clearly hierarchical, with central

19

administrators and trustees superior. As a result, day-to-day activity entails an intermingling of the respective forms of authority of professors, bureaucrats, and trustees. In sum, *the control structure of the American university is a federation of collegial groups that is bureaucratically ordered and supervised by laymen.*

As we have the single campus and move up to wider administrative levels, the patterns of control become more divergent. The private university largely drops from view because it is not formally part of larger webs of organization. Its own trustees are the highest point of control. Traditional supervision of the conduct of private institutions has indeed been light, consisting largely of periodic evaluation by regional voluntary associations for general institutional "accreditation" and by professional associations for specific professional and scientific programs (discussed below) that pose little threat to any except marginally qualified institutions.

In the public sector, the years since World War II have seen a set of arrangements emerge at essentially a fourth level of organization, a coordinating structure for sets of universities within multicampus state universities. The University of California, for example, which at one time was virtually synonymous with the Berkeley campus, became a nine-campus system of institutions formally equal to Berkeley. In addition, sets of state colleges and community colleges also became, as nonuniversity sectors, more strongly organized as multicampus state systems (Lee and Bowen 1971). The controlling board of trustees moved from the single campus to the state level, and a "state-wide university administration" was created on top of the existing, and growing, campus administration. The central administrative staff rapidly became an imposing force, allocating resources and controlling the decisions of campus administrators by its power to establish uniform categories and to enforce compliance. Central multicampus administration is less accountable to the teaching staff than campus administration is to the trustees. A new division of interest has emerged as campus administrators and faculty unite to protect their own welfare against university-wide administrators who have a responsibility for the whole and a view from the top that is shared only with the trustees. With this elaboration of administrative superstructure, control has moved even further away from the dominant modes of chair systems, where the collegial control of professors has tended to dominate all levels up to that of state or national ministry of education. In the first level above the campus, professors have only minor places: in general, the higher the level, the lower the participation of professors.

20

Because education in the United States from earliest times was made the responsibility of state rather than national government, a fifth level of organization is important in the American structure. It has been to the state executive branch (the governor, the governor's budget and finance officers, and sometimes the department of education) and to the state legislature that the trustees and chief administrative officers of the universities and emerging university systems must turn for support—a situation that remains despite the great increase in federal grants of the postwar period. At this level, American higher education becomes a segment of public administration in the form of a large set of subgovernments within the separate states. The degree of integration into state government has varied considerably, given the different traditions, politics, and administrative structures of the states—from specific approval of narrow items in university budgets, such as faculty travel or the purchase of typewriters, to constitutional autonomy and lump-sum allocation that set higher education apart from all other governmental activities.

Also at this level, but apart from the regular offices of government, may superboards recently have been established for the purpose of coordinating all units of higher education supported by the state, thus bringing state colleges, community colleges, and universities together under one loose administrative framework. In attempting to map this organizational territory, recent research has pointed to four types of situations that vary in degree of central control and in proportion of members drawn from the public compared to members drawn from institutions (Berdahl 1971). The first type, with no state coordinating board at all, was found in as many as seventeen states as late as 1959 but in only two states a decade later. The second type, a board voluntarily organized by member organizations, also decreased in the same period from seven states to two. The third type, a formal coordinating board, spread from ten to twenty-seven states; and the fourth and most rigorous type, a "consolidated governing board," increased from sixteen to nineteen in number. Thus, the shift was clearly to the third type, which is essentially a formally mandated superboard placed over the existing boards of trustees that top the institutional sectors at our fourth level of organization. And within that type, there has been a trend toward boards that have a public majority and advisory powers—from three to eleven states—and boards that had a public majority *and* regulatory powers—from five to fourteen states. In these high councils, professors have virtually no role. "Faculty representation at the level of the 'superboard' is likely to be minimal or nonexistent" (Garbarino

1975, p. 11). Groups of professors may make occasional presentations, but they must turn to the officialdom of their own professional associations and, increasingly, their own unions to effect systematic purchase on state-level control.

To make matters even more complicated, this fifth level of state and regional academic organization in the American system also finds a set of nongovernmental associations playing a special role in accreditation: the awarding of legitimacy to institutions and the degrees they confer. Six regional voluntary associations judge whole institutions, among them, the North Central Association of Colleges and Secondary Schools or the New England Association of Colleges and Schools (Shelden 1960). Supported by annual fees paid by member institutions, each association has its own headquarters and small administrative staff. It draws on professors from within its own area, and sometimes from the outside, to compose the ad hoc committees that visit, evaluate, and report on various institutions, commonly on a five-year cycle. The operation of these associations permits a mild degree of professorial supervision and encourages consensus across a large domain of organizations. And the occasion of the accreditation visit calls for a self-assessment of weaknesses as well as strengths by the administration and faculty of an institution. But the accrediting association is an important pressure only on institutions that hover around a low threshold of quality—or, occasionally, an experimental college whose ways deeply offend established academic canons (Koerner 1970). Notably, these associations do not attempt to administer institutional equality and they do not serve as a private counterpart to the European ministry of education, which, as in Italy and France, attempts to equate the work at various institutions within the framework of state-certified national degrees. Nor are they equivalent to the English external examiners with their institutional commitment to the uniform maintenance of high standards. Rather the associations arose in the American context of dispersed control as a device for ensuring minimal competence and for establishing rudimentary norms of acceptable behavior. They do not have the power to stop already-qualified institutions from doing largely as they please. That power resides with the state agencies that top the individual state systems. The peculiar subsidary role given to the accreditation associations seems to have developed historically as a compensatory mechanism in a national system characterized by so much dispersed control, institutional diversity, and competition. Their role is congruent with considerable institutional inequality.

In international persepective, the sixth or national level of or-

22

ganization in the United States has been uncommonly weak. The foreign observer searching for order in American higher education could find no ministry of education, no formal structure that reached out from Washington, D.C., to embrace universities and colleges. Nor did any standing voluntary committees, councils, or commissions play a significant coordinating role. As late as the 1950's, the national Office of Education gathered statistics, administered a few categorical aid programs such as vocational education for the public schools, but dared not disturb state superintendents of public instruction, much less presidents of universities. Leaving aside special wartime efforts centered on scientific research, the nearest thing to systematic federal intervention was the "GI Bill" administered by the Veterans Administration, which gave financial support to veterans of World War II and later wars. In the 1950's, the National Science Foundation and the National Institutes of Health began to influence scientific research and teaching in the universities in voluntary rather than mandatory fashion. However, professional schools of medicine and scientific departments at some universities have gradually become heavily dependent on national funds, essentially becoming federal-grant units within state and private universities (Babbidge and Rosenzweig 1962; Orlans 1962; Kerr 1964; Wilson 1965). The Office of Education became a major enterprise in the 1960's, administering major grants for higher education as well as elementary and secondary schools and developing the resources, personnel, and orientations that permit it to behave more like a European national bureaucracy.

The funds of the national government now come to universities and colleges in several forms. One is student-centered funding, by which the government makes grants and loans to individuals who in turn can purchase their education anywhere they want, including private institutions. This form plays heavily on the market features of American higher education, relying on consumer choice to guide development in a disorderly system. A second form is institution-centered, by which funds flow directly from the government to the institution. As in national systems in other countries, such funds vary from categorical allotment for specific programs to broad lump sums for general institutional support. A third form is discipline-centered, by which funds for research and, on occasion, teaching are distributed to specific departments, research centers and individual professors.

An increasing amount of indirect manipulation by various bureaus and central councils of the national government has resulted from national funding. The early 1970's saw the emergence of direct influence when the Department of Health, Education, and Welfare together with the Department of Labor decided to withdraw all federal funds from an institution that failed to present an effective affirmative action plan for employing women and minorities. Other such direct interventions, not possible ten or twenty years ago, appear on legislative and executive agendas (for example, the requirement that medical schools set targets and quotas for training certain types of doctors, in the name of national medical manpower policy, as a condition for the continuation of federal funding).

However, it remains the case that American universities and colleges do not think of themselves as part of a nationally administered system, and, in comparative perspective, they are not. The basic institutionalized lines of influence found at the national level in Italy, France, and now even Britain remain strongest in the United States at the level of the fifty states. Although the federal lines grow in importance, they remain uneven and secondary. And some national policies are designed to enhance control of the individual states: to wit, a national law enacted in 1972 required all states to have some type of planning group ("1202 Commissions," named after the number of the law) for all public higher education, thus prompting super-board influence at the state level.

Thus, in formal organization, the United States has at best a quasi-system of largely indirect influences at the broadest level of control and coordination. Compared to the situation that existed before World War II, there is more of a formal system; compared to what obtains nationally in most countries of the world today, there is little. The private sector, topped in stature by such universities as Chicago, Columbia, Harvard, Princeton, Stanford, and Yale, remains independent and strong. The public sector is still essentially composed of the fifty states, within which individual public universities and colleges control personnel selection and compete with one another and with the private schools for students and faculty. Among the major advanced systems of the world, the American system remains the one structured to be most disorderly and to approximate a market of freely interacting competitive units (Ben-David 1972). It remains the most heavily influenced by the unorganized decision making that can be seen as "social choice"; it is at the opposite end of the continuum from unitary bureaucracy (Banfield 1961; Clark 1965; Warren 1967). The trend is clearly toward administered order, with some coordination provided by voluntary associations of administrators and professors headquartered in Washington, D.C. (Bloland 1969; Bloland and Bloland 1974), as well as by the increasing influence of a number of federal agencies. But market conditions remain the basic element.

24

The national level of control is still not tightly structured and has only fragmented influence over an assortment of universities that vary greatly in purpose and ethos as well as in size and resources. Fragmentation remains strong relative to the forces of system building.

To summarize the nature of academic control in the United States from an international perspective: the national center still possesses relatively little formal authority but is much stronger than it was a decade or two ago; the middle levels of organization (state, multi-campus system, and campus) are strongly organized, with the authority of trustees and administrators predominating over faculty prerogatives; and the lower levels (colleges and department) retain impressive decision-making powers in the areas of personnel and curriculum, areas in which professors care most about exercising collegial and personal rule. The various levels and the several major forms of authority constitute not only a division of powers but also a set of countervailing forces. In organization and authority, the "system" is not only inordinately large and complex but also fundamentally unsystematic.

The voice of students remains weak in all levels of formal councils despite the great attention paid in the 1960's to student protest and student participation in governance. It remains true in the United States that students vote mainly with their feet: they have much choice in where to attend and what field to pursue. They can choose not only what unit to enter but also can make the "exit" decision, moving from one organization to another (on exit and voice, see Hirschman 1972). With so much initial choice and later exiting, the viability of many individual colleges and universities depends on either adaptive response to clientele or the establishment of an ideology of unique performance. Since distinctiveness lays claim to clients in a way that sameness does not, many institutions attempt to develop a special character instead of passively accepting a uniform role (Clark 1970; Clark, Heist, McConnell, Trow, and Yonge 1972).

When we compare the distribution of authority across six levels of organization in the American system with those of the Continent, we see that powers usually found at the top elsewhere are located here at middle levels. Provincial and national ministries of education in other systems have taken care of the administrative overhead services involved in making appointments, paying salaries, running the physical plant, and supporting students. Little administration was considered necessary immediately above the domains of the professors, and, in any case, their strong guild organization did not permit it. Weak administrative structure at the university level thus became characteristic. But in the United States the tradition of institutional

25

autonomy demanded the handling of overhead services at the college and university itself, and the required government and administration became fixed in trustee and administrative authority that was separate from and above the domains of the professors. As administration became located *on campus,* the emerging class of university officials developed a vested interest in keeping it there, fighting against a shift that would move jurisdiction to the staff of state authorities.

In summary, the forces for change in the 1960's and early 1970's have affected this complicated control structure in the following ways: growth has led to increase in unit size at all levels, deepening the need for coordination within and between units and thereby favoring the development of more and larger administrative groups. Campus-wide administration has grown measurably and has become increasingly professionalized, with administrators even tending to use scientific management techniques in attempting to improve central assessment and effective intervention; administrative systems have grown larger and stronger at the level of state government; and new ones have developed at a level between the university and the state in the form of multi-campus university systems. The first major outcome of modern trends is ascendance of administration at these three levels. Administrators are so important that they overwhelmingly make up the membership of commissions, private or public, national or state, that advise on educational policy, in comparison to similar European commissions, which contain mostly prestigious professors. The growth of "federal intervention," itself important, remains a minor phenomenon compared to the administrative strength of the university-to-statehouse levels of the American system. Within these levels, the tilt has been definitely upward, toward a centralization of authority and administration.

Second, these three levels have come under greater public scrutiny and political pressure. The student discontent of the 1960's caused a wide range of specific publics to watch university affairs more closely, a rise in concern that was also propelled by escalating costs, growing interest in access, and the greater visibility of a larger enterprise. Even without the organized student actions, the increased interest would have brought about more political attention: and with the hostile public reaction to radical tactics on campus, intervention by external political forces was ensured at the levels that are primarily in the grasp of system administrators, boards of trustees, and state officials. A second major outcome therefore has been a growing entanglement of administration with the politics of the general political arena.

26

However, below these administrative levels are the academic domains whose drift is by no means determined solely by high administration and external political forces. The work of teaching and research is still done in the department, and in such auxiliary units as the research institute and the interdisciplinary program, and much policy directly relevant to the basic work is decided largely at the second level of college and school. At the levels where higher education is a structure of disciplines, collegial control remains strong, challenged mainly by bureaucratic authority of the campus administration. The disciplinary understructure is thick and tough and resistant to externally imposed change; to their frustration, political groups are usually not able to penetrate these levels. The governor of a state, as in California recently, may fume about the little time that faculty devote to teaching in the state university, but the faculty continues to find ways to save time for research, often shielded by a campus administration interested in attracting and holding faculty talent.

The growth in knowledge and the demand for experts that has typified recent decades has reinforced the strength of the disciplines inside the organizational mass of ever larger educational systems. Increased specialization in scientific and other academic fields, as well as in the upper reaches of the general labor force, strengthens the influence of those whose authority is rooted in expertise (Parsons 1968; Jencks and Riesman 1968). Administrators in the 1970's are less qualified than in the past to judge the work of personnel in the many specialized sectors, and hence must depend heavily on the judgments made by professional peers. Thus, a third major outcome of recent social trends is a strengthening of the disciplines that crosscut institutions and the creation of a national system of higher education organized along lines of occupational specialty. With the increased strength of diverse clusters of experts, organizational structure is pressed toward greater differentiation and decentralization.

The market conditions under which institutions have long been operated still prevail. Private colleges and universities still make their way by individually raising funds, recruiting faculty, and attracting students. Public institutions, although operating within administered systems and more accountable to higher bodies, also still have to face the competition generated when more than 2,500 institutions operate under dispersed control. Strengthened state coordination has not eliminated the market. The growing power of administrative staffs during the 1960's was congruent with enhanced competition in the affluent higher education economy of those years. The *nouveau riche*

27

among the state systems, for example, Texas, Florida, and Arizona, eagerly sought to buy and stock faculty talent on newly built or greatly expanded campuses. Developing campuses in the New York State system such as Stony Brook and Buffalo tried to lure professors from Michigan and UCLA, Princeton and Chicago. The financial downturn of the early 1970's did reduce this competitive zeal, but the basic structure and established custom of the national system continues to promote a level of competition that is different in kind from that of apparently all other countries of the world.

Some observers have been predicting homogenization of higher education under greater control by the state (Newman 1971; Hodgkinson 1971), but any trend in that direction is slight when seen in a cross-national perspective, and it may actually be the reverse, toward greater diversity in controls. The combination of huge size and decentralization seems to be bringing about an increased number of modal patterns for the distribution and combination of forms of control. An enlarged division of labor in matters of academic control also makes possible the simultaneous growth of divergent forms of authority. As a general approximation, we may say of the American system that the professional authority of faculty has increased at the lower levels, the bureaucratic authority of administrators has increased at the middle levels, and the public authority of trustees and other citizens has increased at state and national levels. American higher education as a whole demonstrates an organizational evolution that is simultaneously unilinear and multilinear (Kaufman 1971): The unilinear evolution is toward ever larger systems, with more power for high public officials and senior administrators and more scope for planners; the multilinear movement is toward greater diversity within systems, a looseness within which various professorial and professional groups can vest their interests in slices of the educational domain. Academic control in America is part of the broader modern problem of how general policy makers, administrators, and professional experts will all be able to express and combine their legitimate interests in systems of ever growing complexity.

28

Academic Power:
Concepts and Perspectives

Imbedded in the foregoing sections of this report and the related literature are a number of concepts and perspectives useful in the analysis of academic power. Our purpose is to aid future reflection and research by pulling together in one place many of the analytical ideas now available. Since modern national systems of higher education, especially the American, are among the most complex enterprises ever evolved, researchers need all the conceptual help they can get to penetrate the confusion and disentangle the strands of control. Many of the following conceptions have been drawn from the general literature in organizational studies, public administration, and political science, and are based on the broadest treatments of authority available in modern thought, such as Max Weber's classic treatment of traditional, bureaucratic, and charismatic forms of authority (Weber, translated by Henderson and Parsons 1947). Yet in no sense do these concepts constitute a "theory" and they are not presented as such. Instead they offer a battery of possibilities: each idea may apply heavily, moderately, lightly, or not at all to a particular empirical case; some of the ideas offer alternative ways of viewing particular situations. Enough is already known to warrant tentative judgments about their application to the American structure and we have presented only those that already have been found useful. But there is considerable variation in the American structure that further research can better identify. Thus we can foresee having both more specific conceptual statements and modifications of the more general concepts.

Forms of Authority

If we start from the bottom of national systems of higher education and work our way up to the highest levels, what types of legitimate rule might we observe? What is the minimal vocabulary for discussing the prime ingredients in various compounds of academic authority? We have identified the following ten forms of authority.

1. *Personal rulership (professorial)*—All modern complex organizations, usually portrayed globally as "bureaucratic," seem to contain much personalized and arbitrary rule of superiors over subordinates (Weber, translated by Henderson and Parsons 1947; Roth 1968). Systems of higher education are saturated with this form of rule; profes-

sors have acquired extensive leeway in personally supervising the work of students and sometimes the activities of junior faculty. The personal rule of the professors has many sources: it is historically linked to the dominance of the master in the early academic guilds; it is ideologically supported by doctrines of freedom in teaching and research, which in practice have been interpreted to mean that senior professors should be free to do largely as they please; and it is functionally based on expertise and the conditions that often promote creativity and scientific advance. Then, too, as professors acquire fixed slots in a bureaucracy, personal rule is often strengthened by the rights they acquire, an outcome that is the opposite of the intention of bureaucratic order. Such personal rule has been extremely high in chair-based academic systems, particularly when collegial supervision becomes nominal and state supervision is too remote from the operating sites of academic work to be effective. It exists in lesser degrees in department-based systems, such as the American, where power is formally held by an impersonal unit and spread within it among a plurality of permanent professors. But even there it exists, most noticeably in advanced research and teaching: for example, the supervision of the graduate student in dissertation research. Personalized authority is always potentially subject to abuse, but systems of higher education apparently cannot function effectively without it and hence it would have to be invented if it did not already exist.

2. *Collegial rulership (professorial)*—Collective control by a body of peers is a classic form of traditional authority (Weber, Gerth and Mills 1958). In the academic world from the twelfth century to the present, collegial rule has been widespread. It has exceedingly strong ideological support in academic doctrines of community of scholars and freedom of teaching and research. It is also based on expertise; the growth of specialization in recent decades has increased collegial rule in ever more specialities and subfields, outside of as well as inside higher education. In chair-based academic systems, collegial rule has often monopolized coordination at faculty and university levels of organization. It is also strong in department-based systems as the professors' preferred way to run the department and, if possible, the larger units of college, school, and university. In the American system it is generally but one element in a local compound of authority (see below).

3. *Guild authority*—This type of authority is a compound of the first two, blending collegiality with autocracy. The individual master has a personal domain within which he controls subordinates; the

30

masters come together as a body of equals (one person, one vote) to exercise control over a larger territory of work (Thrupp 1968). This combination never disappeared from certain cultures, and they were predominantly academic systems. Systems of higher education have continued to be guild-like at their operating levels, and the combination of personal rulership and collegial authority commonly dominates the substructure of national systems. The guild simply moved inside the bureaucracy (Clark, *Academic Power in Italy,* forthcoming (a)).

4. *Professional authority*—This concept, related to the three above, remains ambiguous and problematic in application. Professions are large occupational groups whose work involves the development and application of esoteric knowledge. Until recently, professional authority has been treated in social science literature as based in expertise, "technical competence," in contrast to bureaucratic authority, which is rooted in a formal position based on "official competence" (Parsons 1968). In practice professionals exercise authority in a host of ways—personally, collegially, and even bureaucratically—and therefore their actual exercise of power falls under one of the other categories. Much authority in such professions as medicine and law, as in the case of academic authority, began in guild organization and demonstrates the persistence and resilience of guild forms even when they are placed within large administrative frameworks, as they have been in the twentieth century. In large professions controls within and on the group are generally weak and depend considerably on the operation of personal and collegial rule. That rule may be particularistic as well as universalistic, oriented to short-run profit as well as to long-run service to society, and used to dominate clients and allied personnel as well as to serve ultimate professional ideals (Freidson 1970).

5. *Bureaucratic authority (institutional)*—As the best-known idea in the twentieth-century analysis of organizations, the concept of bureaucracy needs little explanation. It refers to formal hierarchy, formal delegation of authority to positions, formal written communication and coordination, and impersonality in judging individual worth and deciding what will be done. It is the antithesis of personal rule and collegial control.

Our earlier cross-national comparisons and discussion of organizational levels made clear the importance of distinguishing who "the bureaucrats" are and where they are located. In the chair systems of the Continent they have been largely found in central ministries, where they attempt to coordinate a national (or regional) system. In

31

these systems university-level bureaucracy has been relatively weak. In U.S. higher education, bureaucracy grew first at the institutional level, where it constrained the guild-like ways of faculty control, and it was until recently much weaker at "ministerial" levels of governmental coordination. The American pattern has put bureaucratic authority in the service of local ambition and need and helped to build identity and loyalty at institutional levels. Even more than professors, campus officials are likely to be boosters of their own institutions, because their job rewards and career successes depend directly on the success of the entire institution. Their perspectives and interests commonly will be different from those of officials in central offices.

In short, it is not the case that a bureaucracy is a bureaucracy is a bureaucracy. Bureaucratic authority can be hooked to different chariots. It functions in different ways in different systems, depending on the organizational level at which it operates. Only a few systems, preeminently the American, have placed bureaucracy at the institutional level and there given it a primary role of institution-building.

6. *Charismatic authority (institutional)*—The concept of charismatic authority refers to the willingness of a group of people to follow a person and accept his or her commands because of unusual personal characteristics—in the extreme, "a gift of grace" (Weber, translated by Henderson and Parson 1947; Shils 1968). The authority of such a leader is not basically made legitimate by position in an administrative structure or by established rights in traditional line of descent; rather authority is established by personal qualities. However, the exercise of charismatic authority is commonly compounded with bureaucratic or traditional position. In U.S. higher education, charisma has appeared most often in the college or university presidency, with the leader thereby drawing authority from both personal and structural sources. Charismatic authority, like all other forms, is situational: the personal qualities of the leader must be perceived *and* valued by would-be followers and subordinates. The authority disappears when followers are disillusioned even if magnetic personal qualities persist.

In American higher education during the late nineteenth century and early twentieth century, charismatic university presidents had considerable leeway in institution-building. In this period rule by amateur trustees was partially giving way to more systematic direction, guild forms were not yet elaborate, and many presidents were responsible for building administrative staffs as well as faculties. In

32

comparison, present-day higher education seems lacking in such openings for charisma, except that crisis situations as well as situations of new organization often beckon the person who seemingly has personal gifts of leadership. Even stable, established contexts occasionally open up to such personal intervention, as when a college or a professional school or a department becomes ambitious to be better or different and invites in a "builder." Charismatic authority apparently still occurs, serving certain needs of leadership, mission clarification, and change (Shils 1968).

7. *Trustee authority (institutional)*—Like bureaucracy, trusteeship is such a common form of legitimate authority in American higher education that it needs little additional identification. It is important, however, to recognize that it is a weak, or totally nonexistent form of authority in other national systems. Its basic role in this country is a fundamental part of what is different about the American system. Developed under the special conditions of institution-building and system coordination that we reviewed earlier, the board of trustees became a natural part of American academic governance, backed by law and assumed to be a necessary and correct way of organizing and supervising colleges and universities. Most important, this key form of authority became positioned not at national, provincial, or state levels of government but instead as an intrinsic part of operating institutions. There, like the institutional bureaucracy, it has served in part as an instrument of institutional aggrandizement, linking the partcipation of some influential citizens to the welfare of the individual college or university. It, too, has helped make the middle levels of the American "national system" relatively strong, building corporate identity and pride at the level of the campus. It has served to link specific segments of the general public to specific institutions, for example, Lutheran families and church bodies in the upper Midwest to a Lutheran college in Minnesota. In its many variations of public and private boards, it may be considered as dispersed public control, with specific publics, as narrow as a few families or as wide as the population of a state, represented in different institutions. In non-trustee systems, the general public, through its elected representatives and public bureaus, participates more diffusely and indirectly in the control of a large set of institutions. Dispersed public control allows for much ad hoc, uneven development, and for the particularisms of small-group preferences. Since each institution needs financial resources and roots in a sustaining social base, trustee membership is heavily weighed toward those who have money and useful connections.

33

The current trend toward the integration of control in multi-campus trusteeship, superboard coordination, state planning, and stronger oversight by the executive and the legislature in the fifty state systems, makes problematic the continued strength of trustee authority at the institutional level. If trustees move up from the campus to the multicampus system, and if some of their former powers are assumed at higher levels of system coordination, their role in sustaining distinctive institutional identities and institutional diversity will weaken.

8. *Bureaucratic authority (governmental)*—Wherever government assumes some responsibility for the provision of higher education, certain executive agencies will become the loci of administrative implementation. The involvement and the extent of participation of agency staffs can vary widely, of course, depending on the historical relation of the state to higher education and how that traditional relationship has been expressed in recent policy. For example, in the first quarter-century (approximately 1920-1945) of the existence of Great Britain's University Grants Committee, when monies flowed from the national treasury to the universities via a mediating mechanism, bureaucratic involvement was minimal. The UGC, controlled largely by persons from the university, had an extremely small staff, and was not located within the jurisdiction of a regular governmental department. In sharp contrast, high bureaucratic involvement has been presupposed and exercised in the European systems that use ministries of education as embracing frameworks.

Both the British and the American systems have been evolving toward the Continental model—the British at the natonal level and the American at both the state and national levels—and recent governmental policies in both countries have leaned heavily toward the build-up of bureaucratic staffs. Public officials are responding to problems of equity, accountability, and duplication by enacting laws —nearly all of which require larger central offices to disperse funds, to check on compliance with stated requirements, and otherwise to implement public policy. Reform brings bureaucratic accretions, a steadily augmented permanent staff that itself becomes an interest group with vested rights and self-sustaining points of view. Like other groups in the power equation, the permanent public educational officials need allies and supportive exchanges. Thus they develop tacit agreements with key legislators and staffs of legislative committees, political appointees in executive agencies, peers in bordering agencies, trustees and administrators at lower levels, and sometimes even professors. In small traditional European systems, the

34

ministerial staffs have had to trade principally with the most important senior professors within the systems, the superbarons who often have been able to dominate central staff. But in the large, modern American system, with its strong institutional bureaucracy and institutional trusteeship, the growing staffs in central public offices have a place in the division of control that is sharply separated from the teaching personnel (Lee, Eugene and Bowen 1971). They must relate primarily to the levels of academic organization immediately above and below them, especially because, of all the groups holding significant authority in the system, they are the most bureaucratic in nature and they are the ones most likely to accept the logic of hierarchical control. Largely overlooked in research thus far, these central administrative staffs should be seen as bureaucratic groups that are distinct from the administrative staffs located at colleges and universities. It is they who have system-wide, rather than local, duties, responsibilities, and concerns.

9. *Political authority*—From its very beginnings in Bologna and Paris some eight centuries ago, European higher education faced the problem of relating to the larger controls of state and church. As the nation-state increased its strength, it became the dominant framework; throughout the world today, higher education is primarily an organizational part of national government. It is thus conditioned by the nature of the legislative, executive, and judicial branches of government and is affected by the exercise of political authority in each government. Weak coalitional national governments are hard put to enact major legislation, but rather must move by studied indirection and incremental adjustment to safeguard a precarious consensus, as in Italy, whereas a dominant state authority can push through a big bill promising extensive reform, as in France under DeGaulle in 1968, even if implementation is slowed and attenuated by countervailing forces.

Research on higher education in the United States has thus far paid little attention to the effect of state and national political arenas in the determination of what is done in higher education. Due to traditions of private sector, campus-level control, and institutional autonomy, there has been a strong reluctance to recognize higher education as a definite part of government. Appropriate conceptualization has also been restrained by the long-standing academic differentiation between the study of public administration and policies, which is located in political science departments and schools of administration, and the study of school and college administration, which is usually located in schools of education. Still, today, of all the social sciences, political science remains the least involved in the study of educational organization. The lack of careful research on the role of general political authority in the governance of higher education has left a near-vacuum that invites easy speculation on the dominance of particular elites, with rightists charging that leftist faculty are in control, and leftists claiming that conservative cabals of trustees, administrators, and faculty rule the campuses. Such stereotypes of academic power will be corrected only as the intricate webs of political relationships found at the highest levels of state and national systems, as well as the distribution of authority at lower levels, are considered in the analysis of authority. Such analysis can be aided considerably by concepts drawn from comparative public administration and comparative politics—concepts such as those of political centralization, administrative centralization, bureau balkanization, and clientelism.

10. *National academic oligarchy*—Research on European systems of higher education has shown that under certain conditions professors are capable of transferring local oligarchical power to the national level (Clark, *Academic Power*, forthcoming (a)). Operating as the major professional group within a ministry of education, they have had privileged access to central councils and offices and have been the most important constituency for top bureaucratic and political officials. The situation has been otherwise in the United States, because of the lack of a formal national system and the strong role of bureaucratic and trustee forms of authority at campus- and state-wide levels. Still, some important American professors have had means of influencing policy relevant to their most important perceived interests in the national as well as the state capital. Disciplinary national associations have been important tools, national academies and associations of scientists have advised government, and in most years since World War II, a science advisory committee has operated within the White House. Peer review by committees of professors and scientists has become standard operating procedure in major governmental agencies that dispense funds for different segments of research and education—for example, the National Institutes of Health for the health field, the National Science Foundation for the natural and social sciences, and the National Endowment for the Humanities for the humanities. The need to use specialists is very great. Thus as part of a regular process, relatively small numbers of professors esteemed in their own disciplines play a national role. The legitimate part that academic oligarchs play in determining na-

36

tional (and state) allocations as well as broad policies ought to be explored more thoroughly in research on American academic authority.

Levels Analysis

The ten forms of authority identified above could easily be extended into a longer list in further efforts to escape the ambiguity of such general concepts as bureaucracy and collegiality and to specify terms that might be closer to reality and more helpful in research. Realistic conceptualization will be aided especially by a clearer awareness of the many levels of organization at which authority should be explored and the great variations in forms of authority at different levels. Cross-national analysis has revealed the necessity of attention to levels: To what units of organization in France and Germany does one compare the American department? To what governmental level in the United States does one compare the operations of a ministry of education in a German *Land*? Even a minimal awareness of levels can help analysts avoid such simple mistakes as comparing higher education in France to higher education in California. France is a whole country with a unified national system, whereas California is a segment of a country, a part that has extensive interchange with other parts in a national complex characterized by extensive institutional competition and high personnel mobility.

The power of decision making in areas such as finance, admissions, curriculum, and personnel selection is often distributed at different levels of organization and in different degrees at several levels and it is therefore differentially influenced by the forms of authority characteristic of those levels. For example, personnel selection tends to be the prerogative of the lower levels, influenced heavily by the collegial rule of professors, whereas budget determination has gravitated upward, influenced more than in the past by governmental bureaucracy and political authority. To progress in the analysis of academic power in the United States we will need to delineate more sharply the many levels of organization that stretch from the classroom and the laboratory to the Congress and the White House.

Integration Analysis

Organized social systems vary greatly in degree and form of internal integration, and organizational analysis has had great difficulty in grappling with those that are not tightly linked. Analysts have preferred to study single organizations, rather than networks of organizations, and to approach the unitary system as a problem of bureaucracy and heirarchy. These analytical biases have been particularly inappropriate for the study of academic authority, because, even in the single unit, organization may be inordinately loose and the legitimate exercise of power is often decidedly nonbureaucratic. Fortunately, during the last decade organizational analysis has increasingly recognized the problems of coordination and exchange among units that are loosely connected and not bounded by a unitary hierarchical structure (Levine and White 1961; Clark 1965; Warren 1967; Terreberry 1968; and Evans 1971). First, analysts have studied the problem of how individual organizations relate to their environments; then they have examined the relations among organizations (Thompson and McEwen 1958; Thompson 1967); most recently they have tackled whole sets or "fields" of organizations as the units of analysis rather than the individual organizations themselves (Warren 1967; Warren, Rose, and Bergunder 1974, Chapters 2 and 8). There is a sense that the older conceptions of coordination in formal organizations are increasingly inadequate for the understanding of how organized social units relate to one another in ever larger and more complicated webs of organization, and analysts are attempting to devise new ways to think about "organized social complexity" (e.g., LaPorte, editor, 1975).

Certain parts of the literature on system linkages are increasingly pertinent to the study of complex state and national systems of higher education, even if the descriptive materials are centered on health organizations or urban renewal agencies. Elementary classifications are available that help us go beyond such arguments as whether the university is really a bureaucracy or a community or a political system. One such framework has been provided by Warren (1967) in a typology of contexts in which organizational units interact in making decisions. His four types, containing six dimensions, range roughly along a general continuum from tight to loose connection: a unitary context, in which the units are parts of an inclusive structure; a federative context, in which the units primarily have disparate goals but some formal linkage for the purposes they share; a coalitional context, in which disparate goals are so paramount that there is only informal collaboration among the parts; and a social-choice context, in which there are no inclusive goals and decisions that are made independently by autonomous organizations. The latter three types—federative, coalitional, and social choice—are found frequently in systems of higher education. A university that is complex and internally fragmented may actually operate as a federative rather than an hierarchical bureaucracy; a peak higher education association, such as the American Council on Education, may operate largely as a coalitional organization, with some tendency to evolve toward a tighter federative arrangement in order to represent higher education more effectively to the national government (Bloland 1969; Bender and Simmons 1973); and many autonomous private universities and colleges, freely competing and interacting with one another and with public campuses, may constitute an interorganizational field that is mainly social-choice or market-like in nature, but perhaps with some subtle systematic linkage provided by mutual tacit agreements that develop over time and hence edge the whole set of organizations toward minimal coalitional arrangements, *and* even some regularized contact, for example, that of a league, that provides bits of a federation.

As research grapples with the exercise of power and authority in large academic systems, such important differences in type and degree of integration will have to be explored.

Developmental Analysis

Everyone agrees that we should learn from history to avoid repeating errors of the past *and* to sense better what road we are on, *and* . . . etc. But systematic approaches to that task are hard to come by and we generally leave the history books untouched or attempt to absorb their lessons as bedtime reading. One way to use the past systematically to help explain the present and predict the future is to take seriously the historical origin and development of the major forms of organization and control that comprise and characterize the present structure of higher education of a nation or state. The units of analysis are current components, and the search is for a developmental answer to the questions of why they exist and how likely they are to persist. The more we engage in cross-national comparisons, the more insistent become the historical questions.

For developmental analysis, three questions may be posed: (1) Why did a certain present-day form originate? (2) Once it was initiated, why did the form persist into the present, sometimes enduring over centuries of marked turmoil and change? (3) How did earlier forms condition later ones as they emerged? The question of persistence is the central one. Persistence may be rooted in apparent effectiveness: a given type of college or form of control seems to remain a more efficient tool than its possible competitors. Or, persistence may stem from lack of competition: the form in question may have developed a protected niche in higher education and has never had to face an open battle against other forms that may be equally or more effective. Or, persistence may follow basically from a set of sociological forces that turn an organizational form into an end in itself, a veritable

39

social institution. "Tradition" makes the establishment form into a valued way of doing things that is unconsciously assumed to be correct; participants become interested in perpetuating a form that serves and protects them and together become a vested collective interest as they develop legitimated rights, and appropriate ideologies develop that justify the traditionalized ways and the vested interests (Stinchcombe 1965). These sociological phenomena are seemingly at the heart of organizational persistence. They help to establish protection against possible competitors and thereby make irrelevant the rational question of comparative effectiveness. They help give certain types of colleges and universities and certain forms of academic control a stubborn capacity to survive all types of pressure, including the efforts of powerful reformers, and to project old ways into the future.

40

Consequences of Different
National Structures

Power can be studied for its own sake, but it becomes more interesting in both theory and practice if we identify its consequences. What difference does it make for certain intentions and outcomes of education whether the authority structure of a national system of higher education takes one form or another? It is always possible that teaching, learning, and research will go on about the same, relatively untouched by the structures of control that encase day-to-day activities. But there is reason to suspect that this is not the case, since structured power gives influence to certain groups, systematically backs certain values and points of view while subordinating others, and determines whether activities will be affected by monopolized or pluralistic participation.

Seen against the backdrop of European and British modes of academic organization, our earlier accounts of the historical production and organizational levels of the American system pointed to certain key characteristics of the American mode: dispersed control, institutional diversity, competition, and a major role given to trusteeship and institutional administrative authority. Four main consequences of this set of authority characteristics may be hypothesized.

1. *The persistence of institutional inequalities*—Local control that is responsive to specific demands and special clienteles will produce unlike institutions, compared to central control responding to nationally or regionally-articulated demands and interests. Dispersed control leads toward diverse institutions that present different programs, attract different mixes of students, and develop different aggregations of faculty and financial resources. There will be rich institutions and poor ones, "noble" ones and "less-noble" places. In short, there will be extensive stratification of institutions, and equal treatment of students across institutions will not be possible in the sense of a promise of similar quality of training and value of degree.

Of course, fragmented and dispersed control is correlated with institutional inequality. Systems of concentrated authority may attempt to plan diversity for the parts under their control. Conversely, insitutions operating under dispersed control may move toward uniformity, rather than diversity, through voluntary imitation of leading institutions. This type of institutional drift has been often noted

41

in the countries characterized in past years by a high degree of institutional autonomy from central control. Yet the basic tendency seems to be that concentrated control leads toward uniformity, dispersed control toward diversity. Reformers who value mainly equality of opportunity and treatment will usually prefer increased central control, wanting to use mandates of the state to lessen institutional inequality, while reformers who value diversity and choice will prefer continuation of dispersed control.

2. *The formation of corporate identities*—The fundamental characteristics of the authority structure of American higher education encourage the development of organizational identity at the level of the college or university. In contrast, identity formation at this level is damped in systems of concentrated control, since fundamental responsibilities are lodged at a higher, all-system level. Under dispersed control, many institutions must take considerable responsibility for their own survival and viability; under competition, they must guard their own advantages and seek to reduce their competitive disadvantages. The locating of trustee and administrative authority at the campus level historically in the American system also puts two powerful groups to work on the construction and protection of the identity of the individual institution. As a result, the problem of distinctive organizational character has been given relatively high priority in American academic administration.

3. *The facilitation of scientific progress*—The American authority structure seems conducive to scientific advance, particularly in the leeway granted young scientists to move among institutions in search of individual autonomy, collegial support, and resources. Such individual mobility depends considerably on dispersed control and competition among autonomous institutions. In contrast, mobility is restrained in national unitary authority structures, where all academics are members of a single corps, and uniform civil service procedures stress seniority over merit and also prevent institutions from making differential offers. In addition, chair-based systems have been noted for the power of individual professors and the dependency of younger academics on the wishes and inclination of a patron. Ben-David has hypothesized that the leading role of the German and American systems of higher education in scientific productivity in different historical periods has been related to the considerable amount of institutional competition they have allowed (Ben-David 1968; Ben-David 1971).

Numerous features of higher education and society will influence scientific progress. Thus, it is possible that centralized control may

42

provide less favorable conditions. Current research in the history and sociology of science is likely to soon provide more insight in this important matter.

4. *The maintenance of system flexibility and innovation*—In comparative perspective, the American structure of academic power favors adaptation and innovation. Financial support comes from many sources, rather than the national treasury alone; autonomous private institutions adapt to different, specific clienteles; state colleges and universities reflect state and regional differences. Institutions are relatively exposed to market forces—e.g., changing consumer interests, and competition from other colleges and universities. Dispersed control has included a differentiation of sectors, and what one sector will not do, another will. Thus, the conservatism of leading research universities in innovations in teaching and learning does not block other types of institutions from experimenting in those activities. The overall "system" is able to respond to a host of competing and often contradictory demands, needs, and interests, as its parts move in different directions. In short, the general structure happens to be appropriate for the heterogeneity of function that is implied in mass higher education.

Bibliography

The ERIC Clearinghouse on Higher Education abstracts and indexes the current research literature on higher education for publication in the National Institute of Education's monthly *Resources in Education* (RIE). Readers who wish to order ERIC documents cited in the bibliography should write to the ERIC Document Reproduction Service, Post Office Box 190, Arlington, Virginia 22210. When ordering, please specify the ERIC document number. Unless otherwise noted, documents are available in both microfiche (MF) and hard/photocopy (HC).

Altbach, Philip G. *Comparative Higher Education.* ERIC Higher Education Research Report No. 5, 1973. ED 082 623. MF-$0.76; HC-$4.73.

Annan, Lord. "The University in Britain." In *Universities For a Changing World,* edited by Michael D. Stephens and Gordon W. Roderick. Newton Abbot, England: David & Charles, 1975. Chapter 1: 19-33.

Archer, Margaret Sootford, ed. *Students, University and Society: A Comparative Sociological Review.* London, England: Heinemann Education Books, 1972.

Armytage, W. H. G. *Civic Universities.* London: Ernest Benn Limited, 1955.

Ashby, Eric. *Universities: British, Indian, African: A Study in the Ecology of Higher Education.* Cambridge, Mass.: Harvard University Press, 1966.

————. *Any Person, Any Study: An Essay on Higher Education in the United States.* New York: McGraw-Hill, 1971.

————. *Adapting Universities to a Technology Society.* San Francisco: Jossey- Bass, 1974.

Bachrach, Peter, and Baratz, Morton S. "Two Faces of Power." *The American Political Science Review* 56 (1962): 947-952.

Baldridge, J. Victor. *Power and Conflict in the University: Research in the Sociology of Complex Organizations.* New York: John Wiley & Sons, 1971.

————, ed. *Academic Governance: Research on Institutional Politics and Decision Making.* Berkeley, Calif.: McCutchen Publishing Co., 1971.

44

—————. *Models of University Governance: Bureaucratic, Collegial, and Political.* Palo Alto, California: Stanford University, School of Education, 1971. ED 060 825. MF-$0.76; HC-$1.79.

—————, and Burnham, Robert. *Adoption of Innovations: The Effect of Organizational Size, Differentiation, and Environment.* Palo Alto, California: Stanford University, Center for Research and Development in Teaching, 1973. ED 077 147. MF-$0.76; HC-$2.15.

Baldwin, J. W., and Goldthwaite, R., eds. *Universities in Politics: Case Studies from the Late Middle Ages and Early Modern Period.* Baltimore: The Johns Hopkins Press, 1972.

Banfield, Edward C. *Political Influence.* New York: The Free Press, 1961.

—————. "Ends and Means in Planning." In *Concepts and Issues in Administrative Behavior,* edited by Mailick and Van Ness. Englewood Cliffs, New Jersey: Prentice-Hall, 1962.

Barton, Allen H. *Organizational Measurement and Its Bearing on the Study of College Environment.* New York: College Entrance Examination Board, 1961.

Beck, Hubert Park. *Men Who Control Our Universities.* New York: King's Crown Press, 1947.

Ben-David, Joseph, and Zloczower, Abraham. "The Idea of the University and the Academic Market Place." *Archives of European Sociology II,* 1961: 303-314.

Ben-David, Joseph. "Universities." *International Encyclopedia of the Social Sciences.* New York: The Macmillan Company and The Free Press, Vol. 16, 1968: 191-199.

—————. *Fundamental Research and Universities.* Paris: OECD, 1968.

—————. "The Universities and the Growth of Science in Germany and the United States." *Minerva* (1968-69): 1-35.

—————. *The Scientist's Role in Society: A Comparative Study.* Englewood Cliffs, New Jersey: Prentice-Hall, Inc., 1971.

—————. *American Higher Education: Directions Old and New.* New York: McGraw-Hill, 1972.

Bender, Louis W., and Simmons, Howard L. *One Dupont Circle: National Influence Center for Higher Education.* Tallahassee, Florida: Center for State and Regional Leadership, Florida State University, 1973. ED 086 054. MF-$0.76; HC-$3.62.

Berdahl, Robert O. *Statewide Coordination of Higher Education.* Washington: American Council on Education, 1971.

—————, and Altmore, George. *Comparative Higher Education: Sources of Information.* New York: International Council for Educational Development, 1972. ED 070 390. MF-$0.76; HC-$5.99.

45

————. *British Universities and the State.* Berkeley, California: University of California Press, 1959.

Blau, Peter M., and Scott, W. Richard. *Formal Organizations.* San Francisco: Chandler Publishing Co., 1962.

————, and Schoenherr, Richard A. *The Structure of Organizations.* New York: Basic Books, 1971.

————. *The Organization of Academic Work.* New York: John Wiley & Sons, 1973.

Bloland, Harland G. *Higher Education Associations in a Decentralized Education System.* Berkeley: Center for Research and Development in Higher Education, University of California, Berkeley, 1969. ED 029 619. MF-$0.76; HC-$9.98.

————, and Bloland, Sue M. *American Learned Societies in Transition: The Impact of Dissent and Recession.* New York: McGraw-Hill Book Co., 1974.

Boyle, Edward, and Crosland, Anthony. *The Politics of Education.* Middlesex, England: Penguin Books Limited, 1971.

Briggs, Asa. "Development in Higher Education in the United Kingdom: Nineteenth and Twentieth Centuries." In *Higher Education: Demand and Response,* edited by W. R. Niblett. San Francisco: Jossey-Bass, Inc., 1970. Chapter 5: 95-116.

Burns, Barbara et al. *Higher Education in Nine Countries: A Comparative Study of Colleges and Universities Abroad.* New York: McGraw-Hill, 1971.

Caplow, Theodore, and McGee, Reece J. *The Academic Marketplace.* New York: Basic Books, Inc., 1958.

The Carnegie Commission on Higher Education. *Governance of Higher Education.* New York: McGraw-Hill Book Company, 1973.

Clark, Burton R. "Interorganizational Patterns in Education." *Administrative Science Quarterly* 10 (September 1965): 224-237.

————. "Organizational Adaptation to Professionals." In *Professionalization,* edited by Howard M. Vollmer and Donald L. Mills. Englewood Cliffs, New Jersey: Prentice-Hall, Inc., 1966: 282-291.

————. *The Distinctive College: Antioch, Reed, and Swarthmore.* Chicago, Illinois: Aldine Publishing Co., 1970.

————. "Belief and Loyalty in College Organization." *Journal of Higher Education* 42 (June 1971): 499-515.

————; Heist, Paul; Trow, Martin; McConnell, T. R.; and Yonge, George. *Students, and Colleges: Interaction.* Berkeley, Calif.: Center for Research and Development in Higher Education, 1972.

————. *Academic Power in Italy: A Study of Bureaucracy and*

46

Oligarchy in a National System of Higher Education, forthcoming (a).

————. "The United States." In *Power in Academia: Changing Patterns in Seven National Systems,* tentative title, edited by John H. Van de Graaff, forthcoming (b).

Clark, Terry N. "Institutionalization of Innovations in Higher Education: Four Models." *Administrative Science Quarterly* 13 (1968): 1-25.

————. *Prophets and Patrons: The French University and the Emergence of the Social Sciences.* Cambridge, Mass.: Harvard University Press, 1973.

Coleman, James S. "The University and Society's New Demands Upon It." In *Content and Contest: Essays on College Education,* edited by Carl Kayen. New York: McGraw-Hill Book Co., 1973.

Corson, John J. *Governance of Colleges and Universities.* New York: McGraw-Hill Book Co., 1962.

Crozier, Michel. *The Bureaucratic Phenomenon.* Chicago, Illinois: University of Chicago Press, 1964.

————. *The Stalled Society.* New York: The Viking Press, 1970.

Dahl, R. A. "The Concept of Power." *Behavioral Science* 2 (1957): 201-215.

Demerath, Nicholas J.; Stephens, Richard W.; and Taylor, R. Robb. *Power, Presidents, and Professors.* New York: Basic Books, Inc., 1967.

Duff, Sir James, and Berdahl, Robert O. *University Government in Canada.* Toronto: University of Toronto Press, 1966.

Duryea, E. D.; Fisk, Robert, and Associates. *Faculty Unions and Collective Bargaining.* San Francisco: Jossey-Bass, Inc., 1969.

————. "Evolution of University Organization." In *The University as an Organization,* edited by James A. Perkins. New York: McGraw-Hill Book Company, 1973: 15-37.

Engel, Arthur Jason. "From Clergyman to Don: The Rise of the Academic Profession in Nineteenth Century Oxford." Unpublished Ph.D. dissertation, Princeton University, 1975.

Epstein, Leon D. *Governing the University.* San Francisco: Jossey-Bass Publishers, 1974.

Etzioni, Amitai. *A Comparative Analysis of Complex Organizations.* New York: The Free Press of Glencoe, 1961.

Evan, William M. "The Organization-Set: Toward a Theory of Interorganizational Relations." In *Readings in Organization Theory: Open Systems Approach,* edited by John C. Maurer. New York: Random House, 1971: 33-45.

Flexner, A. *Universities: American, English, German.* New York: Teachers College Press (Columbia University), 1967.

Fomerand, Jacques. "Policy Formulation and Change in Gaullist France: The 1968 Orientation Act of Higher Education." *Comparative Politics* 8 (October 1975): 59-89.

Freidson, Eliot. *Professional Dominance.* New York: Atherton Press, 1970.

Furth, Dorotea and Van de Graaff, H. "France." In *Power in Academia: Changing Patterns in Seven National Systems,* tentative title, edited by John H. Van de Graaff, forthcoming.

Garbarino, Joseph W. *Faculty Bargaining: Change and Conflict.* New York: McGraw-Hill Book Co., 1975.

Geiger, Roger L. "Reform and Restraint in Higher Education: The French Experience, 1865-1914." A Working Paper published by the Institution for Social & Policy Studies, Yale University, New Haven, Conn., 1975.

Gerth, H. H., and Mill, C. Wright. *From Max Weber: Essays in Sociology.* New York: Oxford University Press, 1946.

Gilpin, R. *France in the Age of the Scientific State.* Princeton: Princeton University Press, 1968.

Gouldner, Alvin. "Organizational Analysis." In *Sociology Today,* edited by Robert K. Merton *et al.* New York: Basic Books, 1959: 400-428.

Gross, Edward, and Grambsch, Paul V. *University Goals and Academic Power.* Washington, D.C.: American Council on Education, 1968. ED 028 692. MF-$0.76; HC-$8.62.

————, and Grambsch, Paul V. *Changes in University Organization, 1964-1971.* New York: McGraw-Hill, 1974.

Hage, Jerald, and Aiken, Michael. *Social Change in Complex Organizations.* New York: Random House, 1970.

Hagstrom, Warren D. *The Scientific Community.* New York: Basic Books Inc., 1965.

Hall, Richard H. "The Concept of Bureaucracy: An Empirical Assessment." *The American Journal of Sociology* 69 (July 1963): 32-40.

————. "Professionalization and Bureaucratization." *American Sociological Review* 33 (February 1968): 92-104.

Halsey, A .H. and Trow, Martin A. *The British Academics.* Cambridge, Mass.: Harvard University Press, 1971.

Hartnett, Rodney T. "College and University Trustees: Their Backgrounds, Roles, and Educational Attitudes." In *The State of University: Authority and Change,* edited by C. E. Kruytbosch and Sheldon L. Massinger. Beverly Hills, Calif.: Sage Publishers, 1970.

48

Haskins, C. H. *The Rise of the Universities.* Ithaca, New York: Cornell University Press (Great Seal Books), 1957.

Hayward, Jack, and Watson, Michael. *Planning, Politics and Public Policy: The British, French, and Italian Experience.* London: Cambridge University Press, 1975.

Henderson, A. M., and Parson, Talcott, eds. *Weber: The Theory of Social Economic Organization.* New York: The Free Press, 1947.

Hirschman, Albert O. *Exit, Voice, and Loyalty.* Cambridge, Mass.: Harvard University Press, 1970.

Hodgkinson, Harold L. *Institutions in Transitions: A Profile of Change in Higher Education.* New York. McGraw-Hill Book Co., 1971.

Hodgkinson, Harold L., and Meeth, L. Richard, eds. *Power and Authority.* San Francisco: Jossey-Bass, 1971.

Hofstadter, Richard, and Metzger, Walter P. *The Development of Academic Freedom in the United States.* New York: Columbia Press, 1955.

Jencks, Christopher, and Riesman, David. *The Academic Revolution.* Garden City, New York: Doubleday and Company, Inc., 1968.

Kagan, Richard L. *Students and Society in Early Modern Spain.* Baltimore, Maryland: The Johns Hopkins University Press, 1974.

Kaufman, Herbert. *The Limits of Organizational Change.* University: The University of Alabama Press, 1971.

————, and Serdman, David. "The Morphology of Organizations." *Administrative Science Quarterly* 15 (December 1970): 439-451.

Keeton, Morris. *Shared Authority on Campus.* Washington, D.C.: American Association for Higher Education, 1971.

Kerr, Clark. *The Uses of the University.* Cambridge, Mass.: Harvard University Press, 1964.

————. "Governance and Functions." *Daedalus* (Winter 1970): 108-121.

Koerner, James D. *Parson's College Bubble: A Tale of Higher Education in America.* New York: Basic Books, Inc., 1970.

Kornhauser, William. *Scientists in Industry.* Berkeley, Calif.: University of California Press, 1962.

Kruybosch, Carlos E., and Messinger, Sheldon L., eds. *The State of the University: Authority and Change.* Beverly Hills, Calif.: Sage Publications, 1970.

La Porte, Todd R., ed. *Organized Social Complexity: Challenge to Politics and Policy.* Princeton, New Jersey: Princeton University Press, 1975.

Lee, Eugene C., and Bowen, Frank M. *The Multicampus University.* New York: McGraw-Hill Book Company, 1971.

49

Levine, Sol, and White, Paul E. "Exchange as a Conceptual Framework for the Study of Interorganizational Relationships." *Administrative Science Quarterly* 5 (March 1961): 583-601.

Lipset, Seymour M. and Ladd, Everett C. *Professors, Unions, and American Higher Education*. New York: McGraw-Hill Book Company, 1972.

Litwak, Eugene, and Hylton, Lydia F. "Interorganizational Analysis: A Hypothesis on Co-Ordinating Agencies." *Administrative Science Quarterly* 6 (March 1962): 395-420.

Livingstone, Hugh. *The University: An Organizational Analysis*. Glasgow and London: Blackie, 1974.

March, James G., and Simon, Herbert A. *Organizations*. New York: John Wiley & Sons, 1958.

————, and Cohen, Michael D. *Leadership and Ambiguity: The American College President*. New York: McGraw-Hill Book Company, 1974.

Marx, Karl. *Pre-Capitalist Economic Formations*. Translated by J. Cohen and edited by E. J. Hobsbaun. New York: International Publishers, 1965.

Mayhew, Lewis B. *The Carnegie Commission on Higher Education*. San Francisco: Jossey-Bass, 1973.

McConnell, T. R., and Mortimer, Kenneth P. *The Faculty in University Governance*. Berkeley: Center for Research and Development in Higher Education, University of California, Berkeley, 1971. ED 050 703, MF-$0.76; HC-$11.25.

McKenna, John F. "Partisans and Provincials: The Political Milieu of Illinois Public Higher Education 1870-1920." A Working Paper published by the Institution for Social and Policy Studies, Yale University, New Haven, Conn., 1976.

Millett, John D. *The Academic Community*. New York: McGraw-Hill, 1962.

Moodie, G. C., and Eustace, R. *Power and Authority in British Universities*. Montreal: McGill-Queen's University Press, 1974.

Naylor, Natalie. "The Ante-Bellum College Movement: A Reappraisal of Tewksbury's Founding of American Colleges and Universities." *History of Education Quarterly* 260 (Fall 1973): 261-274.

Newman, Frank et al. *Report on Higher Education*. Washington, D.C.: U.S. Government Printing Office, 1971. ED 049 718. MF-$0.76; HC-$7.34.

Otten, C. Michael. *University Authority and the Student: The Berkeley Experience*. Berkeley, Calif.: University of California Press, 1970.

50

Parsons, Talcott. "Professions." In *International Encyclopedia of the Social Sciences*. New York: The McMillan Company and The Free Press, 1968.

————, and Platt, Gerald M. *The American University*. Cambridge, Mass.: Harvard University Press, 1973.

Patterson, Michele. "French University Reform: Renaissance or Restoration?" *The Comparative Education Review* 16 (June 1972): 281-302.

————. "Conflict Power and Organization: The Reform of the French University." Unpublished Ph.D. dissertation, Yale University, New Haven, 1975.

Perkins, James A., ed. *The University as an Organization*. New York: McGraw-Hill Book Company, 1973.

————, and Israel, B. B., eds. *Higher Education: From Autonomy to Systems*. New York: International Council for Educational Development, 1972.

Perrow, Charles. "The Analysis of Goals in Complex Organizations." *American Sociological Review* 26 (December 1961): 854-866.

Rashdall, Hastings. *The Universities of Europe in the Middle Ages*. Vols. 1 and 2. Oxford: Oxford University Press, 1936.

Rauh, Morton A. *The Trusteeship of Colleges and Universities*. New York: McGraw-Hill, 1969.

Reeves, M. "The European Universities from Medieval Times, with Special Reference to Oxford and Cambridge." In *Higher Education: Demand and Response*, edited by W. R. Niblett. San Francisco: Jossey-Bass, Inc., 1970: 61-84.

Riesman, David. *Constraint and Variety in American Education*. Lincoln, Nebraska: University of Nebraska Press, 1956.

Ringer, Fritz K. *The Decline of the German Mandarins: The German Academic Community, 1890-1933*. Cambridge, Mass.: Harvard University Press, 1969.

Roth, Guenther, "Personal Rulership, Patrimonialism and Empire Building in the New State. *World Politics* 20 (1968): 194-206.

Rudolph, Frederick. *The American College and University*. New York: Alfred A. Knopf, 1962.

Scott, John H. MacCallum. *Dons and Students: British Universities Today*. London: The Plume Press Limited, 1973.

Seidman, Harold. *Politics, Position, and Power: The Dynamics of Federal Organization*. New York: Oxford University Press, 1970.

Selznick, Philip, *Leadership in Administration: A Sociological Interpretation*. New York: Harper and Row Publishers, 1957.

51

Shelden, W. K. *Accreditation: A Struggle Over Standards in Higher Education*. New York: Harper, 1960.

Shils, Edward. "Charisma." In *International Encyclopedia of the Social Sciences*, Vol. 2. New York: McMillan Co. and The Free Press, 1968: 386-390.

Simon, Herbert. *Administrative Behavior: A Study of Decision-Making Process in Administrative Organization*. New York: The Free Press, 1965.

Smelser, Neil J., and Almond, Gabriel, eds. *Public Higher Education in California*. Berkeley, California: University of California Press, 1974.

Stinchcombe, Arthur L. "Bureaucratic and Craft Administration of Production: A Comparative Study." *Administrative Science Quarterly* 4 (1959): 169-187.

————. "Social Structure and Organizations." In *Handbook of Organizations*, edited by James G. March. Chicago: Rand McNally & Co., 1965: 142-193.

Stone, Laurence, ed. *The University in Society: Europe, Scotland and the United States from the 16th to the 20th Century*, Volume II. Princeton, New Jersey: Princeton University Press, 1974.

————, ed. *The University in Society: Oxford and Cambridge from the 14th to the Early 19th Century*, Volume I. Princeton, New Jersey: Princeton University Press, 1974.

Storr, Richard J. *The Beginnings of Graduate Education in America*. Chicago: University of Chicago Press, 1953.

————. *The Beginning of the Future: A Historical Approach to Graduate Education in the Arts and Sciences*. New York: McGraw-Hill Book Co., 1973.

Stroup, Herbert H. *Bureaucracy in Higher Education*. New York: The Free Press, 1966.

Terreberry, Shirley. 'The Evolution of Organizational Environments." *Administrative Science Quarterly* 12 (1968): 590-613.

Tewksbury, Donald G. *The Founding of American Colleges and Universities Before the Civil War: With Particular Reference to the Religious Influences Bearing Upon the College Movement*. New York: Teachers College, Columbia University, 1932.

Thompson, James D. *Organizations in Action*. New York: McGraw-Hill Book Co., 1967.

————, and McEwen, William J. "Organizational Goals and Environments." *American Sociological Review* 23 (1958): 23-31.

Thompson, Victor A. "Bureaucracy and Innovation." *Administrative Science Quarterly* 10 (June 1965): 1-20.

52

Thrupp, S. L. "Gilds." In *International Encyclopedia of the Social Sciences*. New York: The Macmillan Company and The Free Press, 1968: 184-187.

Touraine, Alain. *The Academic System in American Society*. New York: McGraw-Hill Book Co., 1974.

Turner, R. Steven. "The Prussian Universities and the Research Imperative, 1806 to 1848." Unpublished Ph.D. dissertation, Princeton University, 1972.

Udy, Stanley H., Jr. "The Comparative Analysis of Organizations." In *Handbook of Organizations*, edited by James G. March. Chicago: Rand McNally & Co., 1965: 678-709.

Van de Graaff, John H., ed. *Power in Academia: Changing Patterns in Seven National Systems*, tentative title, forthcoming.

Veblen, Thorstein. *The Higher Learning in America*. Stanford, Calif.: Academic Reprints, 1954.

Veysey, Laurence. *The Emergence of the American University*. Chicago: University of Chicago Press, 1965.

Warren, Roland L. "The Interorganizational Field as a Focus for Investigation." *Administrative Science Quarterly* 12 (December 1967): 396-419.

———, Rose, Stephen M., and Bergunder, Ann F. *The Structure of Urban Reform*. Lexington, Mass.: D. C. Heath and Company (Lexington Books), 1974. Chapter 2, "The Interorganizational Field," and Chapter 8, "Implications for Interorganizational Theory and Research."

Weber, Max. *General Economic History*. Glencoe, Illinois: The Free Press, 1950.

Whitehead, John S. *The Separation of College and State, Columbia, Dartmouth, Harvard and Yale, 1776-1876*. New Haven: Yale University Press, 1973.

Wildavsky, Aaron. *The Politics of the Budgetary Process*. New York: Little, Brown and Company, 1964.

———, and Heclo, Hugh. *The Private Government of Public Money: Community and Policy Inside British Politics*. Berkeley, California: University of California Press, 1974.

Wilensky, Harold L. *Organizational Intelligence: Knowledge and Policy in Government and Industry*. New York: Basic Books, 1967.

Wilson, Logan. *The Academic Man*. New York: Oxford University Press, 1942.

———, ed. *Emerging Patterns in American Higher Education*. Washington, D.C.: American Council on Education, 1965.

2. Evolution of University Organization

by E. D. Duryea

It has become customary in histories of American higher education to begin with a description of medieval origins. In general, there is good basis for looking back to those distant and turbulent days. The idea of a university itself as a formal, organized institution is a medieval innovation, which contrasts to the Greek schools and to the rudimentary organizational precedents in ancient Alexandria and in the Byzantine and Arabian cultures. The medieval universities instituted the use of many contemporary titles such as *dean, provost, rector,* and *proctor.* They initiated the idea of formal courses and of the curriculum leading to the baccalaureate and the master's and doctor's degrees. Our commencements are graced annually by the color and distinction of medieval garb. Fascinating anecdotes confirm that student violence has early precedents.

The point is, of course, that complex institutions such as universities do not appear full-blown at a particular point in time. They evolve through that complicated process by which men and cultures mingle over a history fraught with traditions and happenstance. Contemporary Western culture itself originated in the centuries that followed the "dark ages," and the university has served as one of the major institutions by which this culture has been transmitted over the years.

Within this context, certain aspects of the university's organization do have some important medieval precedents. Other aspects of its organization reflect the more direct influence of the English colleges of the sixteenth and seventeenth centuries. A history of American colleges and universities must be written also with due recognition of that educational revolution which took place in this country during the four decades following the Civil War. As Laurence R. Veysey (1965, p. 2) comments in his detailed interpretation of that era, "The American university of 1900 was all but

55

unrecognizable in comparison to the colleges of 1860." The contemporary system of higher education dominated by the large,
multifunctional university stands as a heritage of those years.
Organizationally as well as educationally, its form and function
were set by the time of the First World War. Its history during this
century is primarily a chronicle of expansion and consolidation.

Reflecting these major historical influences, the following analysis examines the evolution of university organization from three
major perspectives. The first deals with (1) the origins and use of
the corporate form by which authority was granted to lay governing
boards and (2) how their legal control has been modified by alumni
and faculty influences that go back well into the nineteenth century.
The second views the origins and expansion of the organizational
structure of universities, an evolution epitomized by the comment
that the old-time college president has all but disappeared behind
a bureaucracy of academic and administrative offices and councils.
In this sense the transition from the small, struggling colleges of
the past to the large multiversity with its complex administration
is first of all the history of the presidency. The third views the
twentieth-century period of organizational expansion and consolidation. A concluding section identifies very briefly the evidences of
dysfunction that have emerged in recent years.

CORPORATE
ORIGINS

By the twelfth century in Europe the church not only reigned supreme as a ruler of man's conscience but also exercised great
temporal power over his mundane affairs. Rare were the individuals
who would, when threatened with excommunication, choose to
face an uncertain future in the hereafter. As the arbitrator of an
ultimate destiny which included the possibility so vividly described
in Dante's *Inferno* and as the only effective organization for all
Europe, the church entered into the total life of the culture. But
early in the thirteenth century, the more astute popes began to feel
the rumblings of a shift of temporal power to political states and
kings. The remote threat of hell began to give way to the more
tangible thrust of the sword. As a result, the church hierarchy
moved to bring its scattered organizations—religious orders,
cathedral chapters, and universities—under more effective papal
control. To this end, canon lawyers looked back to Roman law and
its concept of corporations as fictitious legal entities. Their learned
investigations led to a number of papal statements in the first
decades of the thirteenth century and in 1243 to the famous bull or

proclamation of Pope Innocent IV. The central idea in the Innocentean doctrine was that each cathedral chapter, collegiate church, religious fraternity, and university constituted a *Universitas,* i.e., a free corporation. Its corporate personality, however, was not something natural in the sense of a social reality but rather "an artificial notion invented by the sovereign for convenience of legal reasoning," existent only in the contemplation of law. This was a theoretical conception but nonetheless a very real one, since the corporation thereby derived its right to exist from an external authority and not from the intrinsic fact of its being (Brody, 1935, pp. 3–4).

The efforts of the papacy, the need of universities for protection against the immediate threats to their freedom from local bishops and townspeople, and the fact that the kings also intruded on their sovereignty—all these supported the corporate idea. The theory of corporate existence meant ultimately the end of the guild system and, for universities, of the idea of an independent association of scholars. The history of this development is complex and detailed, certainly beyond the scope of this particular analysis. It is sufficient to note that Emperor Frederick II rivaled Pope Gregory IX during the later years of the thirteenth century in the issuance of grants of authorization to universities, which in turn did not hesitate to strengthen their own hand by playing off pope against king (Rashdall, 1936, vol. 1, pp. 8–9). As national states gained dominance, however, universities ultimately had to look solely to kings for their charters, and what the king gave the king could take away.

The concept of corporations which served as precedent for the early colleges in this country matured in England during the fifteenth and sixteenth centuries. It provided an effective legal means by which the king and later parliament could delegate in an orderly way authority for designated activities, not only to universities but to municipalities, trading companies, charitable establishments, and various other institutions. Charters provided for perpetual succession and the freedom for corporate bodies to set up and maintain the rules and regulations which in effect constituted internal or private governments. They also carried the right of supervision and visitation by representatives of the state. They established, in addition, legal protections associated with the rights of individuals in the sense that the corporation existed as an artificial or juristic individual. This conception of governmental grant of authority served also as the basis for the charters and statutes of the colleges of the English universities, which in general included provisions for external visitors or overseers, a head elected by the teaching staff or fellows, and a formal body constituted of these fellows which "exercised the legislative powers" (Davis, 1961, pp. 303–305).

The influence of this English college model was evident in the founding of the first two colonial colleges, Harvard (1636) and William and Mary (1693). For example, the language of the 1650 charter for Harvard is very similar to that of the royal charters for the colleges of Oxford and Cambridge (Morison, 1935, p. 10). Both these institutions were formed with governing councils composed of internal members (the presidents and teaching fellows) in tandem with external supervising boards that held final approval powers and the right of visitation.[1]

Another medieval precedent, however, came to the colonies with the early settlers and caused a significant modification of the English practice. In place of immediate control of the colleges by the teachers or professors, the practice evolved of granting complete corporate power to governing boards composed of external members. The origins of the use of external control lie in the medieval universities of northern Italy. Initially guilds of students who hired their professors, universities proved good for local business. The Italian towns competed for their presence in part by subsidizing salaries of outstanding teachers. The inexorable result was a blunting of student economic power and the establishment of municipal committees, in effect the first lay governing boards, to guard their financial interests (Rashdall, 1936, vol. 2, p. 59). Again, the detailing of the history of this tradition goes beyond the scope of this chapter. The lay board of control proved an appropriate mechanism for the direction of advanced education under the Calvinists at Geneva in the early sixteenth century, at the

[1] These arrangements for the College of William and Mary were stated in a manner that led to conflicts between the two boards during its early years, although essentially they remained in effect until it became a state institution shortly after 1900. At Harvard, however, practice nullified the apparent intent of the 1650 charter, so that by the eighteenth century the immediate governing council (the Corporation) had passed into the hands of external members. The practice was disputed from time to time by tutors until an 1825 vote of the Overseers finally and formally stated that "the resident instructors of Harvard University" did not have any exclusive right to be chosen members of the Corporation (Quincy, 1860, vol. 2, p. 324).

Dutch University of Leyden a few years later, at the Scottish universities of that same era, and finally at the Protestant Trinity College in Dublin. It was in part from these Dutch, Scottish, and Irish sources that the concept of lay boards came to the colonies (Cowley, 1964; 1971).

The English pattern of internal control by academics which was followed by Harvard and William and Mary did not set the precedent for university government in this country. That distinction fell to Yale College, established in 1701. Whether because of direct influences from the European Calvinistic practices noted above or simply because of parallel sectarian desires to maintain religious orthodoxy, the founders of Yale petitioned for a single nonacademic board of control. As a consequence, the colonial legislature of Connecticut granted authority to a board of "Trustees, Partners, or Undertakers" to "erect a collegiate school." Renamed in the revised 1745 charters as the "President and Fellows of Yale College," it continued as an external board with the right of self-perpetuation and with final control of the affairs of the institution (*The Yale Corporation*, 1952; see also Brody, 1935, Ch. 1).

Meanwhile, yet another deviation from English precedents also had begun to emerge. The right of the king and parliament to grant a charter carried with it an equal right to withdraw this charter. In fact, during the times of religious conflict in England this did occur, as first a Protestant and then a Catholic sovereign reconstituted the organization of the English universities in terms of religious biases. In the eighteenth century a new philosophy, that formalized by John Locke, gained acceptance, especially in the American colonies so strongly committed to a separation of church and state. This view stressed the nature of government as a compact among individuals, with sovereignty held by the people. In these terms of reference, having legal status as a person in law, although a fictitious or juridical person, corporations gained protection from legislative intrusions associated with the rights of individuals. Early in the nineteenth century court decisions began to interpret charters as contracts equally as binding upon the state as upon their recipients. The first intimation of this position regarding corporate autonomy appeared in the 1763 statement of President Clap of Yale to the colonial legislature. He was protesting a threatened legislative visitation of the college on the grounds that such action would be contrary to the nature of the charter and the private

59

legal nature of the institution.[2] Clap's position was novel in his day, but after the turn of the eighteenth century support of a judicial theory which interpreted charters to private corporations as contracts or compacts between the state and the founders began to appear. This point of view received its legal, judicial confirmation in the famous Dartmouth College case decision of the Supreme Court under Chief Justice Marshall. In that decision, the Court viewed the college as a private institution and interpreted its charter as a contract binding upon the state of New Hampshire as well as the trustees, "a contract, the obligation of which cannot be impaired without violating the constitution of the United States" (Wright, 1938, p. 45).

The Dartmouth College decision led to a reexamination of the state-college relationship. Faced with a loss of control, legislators understandably questioned the award of public funds to private corporations. As a result there emerged in subsequent decades a number of public or state colleges, but not as agencies of state government under ministers of education in the continental tradition. Rather, the early public colleges took the form of public corporations parallel in their general organization to the private colleges. In the nineteenth century, it became common practice for legislatures to delegate governing power over state institutions to boards of control established as public corporations.[3] These boards received authority to control property, contracts, finances, forms of internal governance, and relationships with internal personnel — students, faculty members, and administrative employees (Brody, 1935, Ch. 6).[4]

---

[2] Yale historians apparently have tended to credit Clap with a successful defense. Recent investigation of this incident by Professor W. H. Cowley, however, discloses that a visitation was made the following year, about which one of the visitors later observed that "we touch'd them so gently, that till after ye Assembly, they never saw they were taken in, that we had made ourselves Visitors, & subjected them to an Annual Visitation" (a point made in correspondence with this author).

[3] This precedent has undergone modification in more recent decades as state budget bureaus, civil service commissions, and coordinating boards have intruded directly into the internal affairs of public institutions.

[4] Exceptions to these rights do exist, particularly in connection with the control of property and the borrowing of monies. Frequently special corporations are set up within the control of state universities to handle private funds. Actual practice varies among the states, some of which limited the powers of boards in the founding legislation.

MODIFICATION
OF BOARD
CONTROL:
FACULTY AND
ALUMNI PAR-
TICIPATION Whatever the legal authority inherent in lay governing boards, continuing modification of their actual power is documented by a history of university organization. Early in the nineteenth century, accounts of the administration of Jeremiah Day at Yale College attest to the influence of faculty members with whom Day conferred regularly on policy decisions. Students, while rarely a direct component of government until recent years, have traditionally participated as alumni.

Earlier precedents than Yale exist. Professor W. H. Cowley (1964, Ch. 7) has uncovered a number of such instances. Overall, it is clear from his analysis and from histories of the leading universities that faculties greatly expanded their influence over academic affairs during the nineteenth century. The period from 1869 to 1900 illustrates the gradual but decisive involvement of professors in academic policies (Morison, 1930, p. xxxiv). The trustees at Cornell in 1889, for example, established a University Senate of the president and full professors (Kingsbury, 1962, pp. 263–264). Similar arrangements existed at Michigan, Illinois, Wisconsin, and other Midwestern institutions. At Johns Hopkins and Chicago, professors were accepted as the guiding force for all matters concerned with education and research. Faculty influence reached the point that, by the 1890s, President Jacob G. Schurman of Cornell saw his influence in educational affairs limited to final approval of appointments and his role as "the only man in the University who is a member of all boards, councils and organizations" (Kingsbury, 1962, p. 323).

By the turn of the century the trend to faculty participation was definite in the larger universities and major colleges. The decades that followed have chronicled the extension of faculty control over academic affairs, a development influenced by the policies and pressures of the American Association of University Professors subsequent to its founding in 1915.[5]

During the nineteenth century, alumni also entered actively into the government of colleges and universities. In doing this, they had well-established precedents in both England and Scotland,

---

[5] In recent decades the growth in academic status and influence of the disciplines and professional departments and schools has further strengthened faculty power within institutions. The status associated with productive scholarship and research has given faculty members a greatly improved position vis-à-vis administration in internal affairs, a condition documented by Theodore Caplow and Reece J. McGee in their classic study, *The Academic Marketplace*, 1958.

though little evidence exists to support a causal relationship. It is probably more accurate to explain alumni participation as the result of a unique commitment epitomized by the spirit of alma mater and reinforced by recollections of campus camaraderie. The college class has constituted a primary social as well as academic unit which, early in the history of the colleges, led to campus reunions and thus served regularly to reinforce the loyalty of graduates. In turn, it was natural for the members of governing boards and leaders of state governments to look to graduates of colleges for service on these boards when openings occurred. "From the very beginnings," Professor Cowley (1964, Ch. 10, p. 10) has written, "alumni have contributed to the support of private colleges and universities; and as legislators, lobbyists, and moulders of public opinion they have strategically influenced the subsidizing of civil institutions." Formal representation by means of elected members to governing boards first appeared at Harvard in 1865, a pattern that was followed by many other institutions in the subsequent decades.[6]

In summary, university government had coalesced into the pattern we know today by shortly after the turn of the century. It reflected a continuation of medieval and English precedents whereby institutional autonomy received a high degree of protection, modified perhaps in American higher education by a more overt sense of commitment to societal needs. Private colleges and universities had the protection afforded them by their status as corporations under law.[7] In practice, public institutions obtained much of this same autonomy through their status as public corporations under the control of boards established by state constitution or

[6] Amherst in 1874, Dartmouth in 1875, Rutgers in 1881, Princeton in 1900, Columbia in 1908, Brown in 1914. (In the 1865 modification of its charter, Harvard adopted a plan whereby alumni gained the right to elect all new members to the Board of Overseers, the body with ultimate responsibility for that institution.)

[7] Little attention is given, unfortunately, to the uniquely significant role of the governing board in this country as the agency that both has protected internal autonomy and intellectual freedom and has served as a force to keep institutions relevant to the general society. This history badly needs doing. Despite occasional intrusions into internal affairs and matters related to academic freedom, the governing board has served as a point of balance for that essential dualism between institutional and academic autonomy and public accountability which has characterized American higher education. Current forces pressing for greater internal participation on the one hand and increased public control on the other need tempering by the experience of the past in this connection.

legislative law. But even before the end of the nineteenth century, evidences of growing restrictions upon the actual power of governing boards had begun to emerge. Over and above any incipient faculty militance, the practical result of growing size and complexity necessitated the delegation of some policy-making and managerial responsibilities to presidents and faculties.

Finally, the unique role and influence of presidents during this era require recognition. In contrast to earlier periods when presidents served more as principals responsible for campus conduct and morality—of professor and student alike—and trustees sat importantly at commencements to examine graduating seniors, by 1900 presidents had become a positive force. Every university to rise to major status did so under the almost dominating influence of such presidential leaders as Charles W. Eliot at Harvard, Andrew D. White at Cornell, Daniel Coit Gilman at Johns Hopkins, Charles R. Van Hise at Wisconsin, William Rainey Harper at Chicago, David S. Jordan at Stanford, and Benjamin Ide Wheeler at California. The office of president emerged as the central force that has given United States higher education a distinctive character among systems of higher education in the world. Whether one viewed the president as the alter ego of boards or as a discrete unit in institutional government had little bearing on practice. Whatever faculty voices may have been raised to the contrary, university government by the twentieth century centered upon the office of the president.

ADMINIS-TRATIVE STRUCTURE In his history of Williams College, *Mark Hopkins and the Log* (1956), Frederick Rudolph vividly portrays a typical college from 1836 to 1872. President Hopkins presides as the paternal head of a small and personal college family, responsible for the character of its children, the students. The curriculum was fixed and limited. In any event, what the students studied was secondary to the quality of personal moral life. In contrast, the "new education" of the last half of the nineteenth century reflected the new morality of the times, a turning away from Christian theology as the basis for life's judgments and toward values oriented far more to the marketplace and material success. In the words of Veysey (1965, Ch. 2), "discipline and piety" gave way to "utility" as the hallmark of a college education. Specialized knowledge replaced the "disciplining of the mind and character" as the raison d'être for higher education. Adherents of reform rallied to elective ideas which supported, to a degree at least, the rights of students to choose their subjects and thus to open the universities to the new studies of science and technology and of specialization in the humanities, all of which stressed the advancement of knowledge and a utilitarian commitment. By 1900 graduate studies, professional schools, and professors whose careers rested upon their published research rather than upon their role as teachers were moving to positions of the highest status in the academic hierarchy. Harvard University offered good evidence of the impact of this influence upon the curriculum. The 1850 catalog described the entire four years of undergraduate study on four pages; in 1920, 30 times that number of pages were required to list the courses offered at the university.

Two shifts in organizational structure inevitably followed. On the one hand, by the turn of the century departments and professional schools had become the basic units for academic affairs. The academic structure of the university coincided with the structure of knowledge. On the other hand, the impact of this "new education" fitted the times. In contrast to the declining enrollment of the 1840s and 1850s, the latter half of the nineteenth century marked the beginning of what has become a constantly increasing rate of college attendance. More students meant more professors, more buildings, more facilities and equipment, and, above all, more money from private and public sources. As chief executive, the president inherited the responsibility both for securing this support and for coordinating and managing the inevitable internal complexities that resulted. Initially, a vice-president and a few professors who served as part-time registrars, bursars, and librarians assisted him. By 1900, however, such staffs proved insufficient; the managerial burden of the president had begun to necessitate what has become a burgeoning administrative bureaucracy.

Academic Organization Some intimations of the specialized departments and professional schools which have become the basic organizational units of universities do appear in the early colleges. The University of Virginia, for example, opened in 1825 with eight schools, each headed by a professor and each offering a program of studies. In that same year, the statutes reorganizing Harvard College established nine "departments" for instruction, each of which (in the pattern already set for medicine, law, and divinity) would be "governed by a board of its full professors" (Cowley, 1964, Ch. 7, p. 4). The use of departments appeared also in 1826 at the University of Vermont, a decade later at Wisconsin, and at Michigan in 1841. But these departments served only as progenitors of the disciplinary and professional units that fashioned the academic organization of universities later in the century.

The appearance of departments as organizational entities accompanied the expansion of knowledge — particularly scientific and technological — and the elective system, by means of which the adherents of specialized study forced their point of view into institutions with traditions of a fixed, classical curriculum. But the reason for the association of departments of scholars in this country (in contrast to the chair held by one professor in foreign universities) has not been documented historically. That they had become the established structural units by 1900 is evident nonetheless in the histories of all major universities.[8]

A similar development occurred in the various professional studies, which appeared with few exceptions first as departments and later as schools, which in turn procreated their own departments. Certainly by 1900 professional specializations in more than a dozen areas were well established, ranging from the traditional trinity of medicine, law, and theology to such new areas as business administration, veterinary medicine, journalism, librarianship, and architecture.

The departmental structure that followed in the wake of specialized knowledge was accompanied by other evidence of disciplinary and professional segmentation, such as journals and national societies. Professors, as the authorities for their respective specializations, assumed more and more control over academic affairs. This revolutionary change from the earlier colleges had evolved by 1910 to the extent that a study of physics departments complains about their having "too much autonomy." The report describes the department as "usually practically self-governing" in control of its own affairs — that is, its students, staff, and curriculum (Cooke, 1910).

---

[8] For example, Harvard established 12 divisions, each including one or more departments, in 1891; Chicago had 26 departments in three faculties in 1893; Cornell, Yale, Princeton, Johns Hopkins, and Syracuse, among others, all reveal the trend toward departmentalization during the decade of the 1890s (Forsberg & Pearce, 1966).

Administrative Organization Responding to the pressures of office work, travel, supervising new construction, employing new faculty, and initiating educational programs, in 1878 President Andrew Dickson White of the new Cornell University appointed a professor of modern languages and history, William C. Russel, as vice-president. Russel functioned as a kind of executive associate—hiring and dismissing junior faculty members, answering correspondence, and carrying out routine responsibilities as well as acting as institutional head in White's absence. The same year, a presidential colleague at Harvard, Charles W. Eliot, appointed Professor Ephriam W. Gurney as dean of the college faculty. In contrast to Russel's initial tasks, Dean Gurney's primary responsibility was to relieve the president of the burden of contacts with students.

These appointments at two major universities signaled the beginning of a trend. For the college growing into a large and complex university, the office of the president quickly ceased to be a one-man job. Those part-time assistants, usually professors, who served as librarian, bursar, or registrar had by 1900 turned into full-time administrative officers, and by the 1930s they were supervising large staffs. A 1936 study by Earl J. McGrath documents the trend. The author charts the growth from a median of three or four administrative officers in the 1880s to a median of nearly sixty for the larger universities by 1930. As noted previously in this chapter, the decades from 1890 to 1910 proved to be the turning point. The lines on McGrath's chart after 1890 turn upward abruptly, showing a doubling of these officers from an average of about 12 in that year to 30 in 1910.

What brought about this transformation of American universities into complex administrative systems, especially in contrast to the much simpler organization of European universities? Many determinants exerted influence, of course. In large part, administrative expansion responded to the need to coordinate and, to a degree, control the expansion of the academic structure. In part, it grew out of a relationship with the general society, unique to this country, which imposed on the university the task of securing financial support from both public and private sources and concurrently of attending to public relations. In part, the enlarged administration implemented an intricate credit system for student admissions and educational accounting.

Fundamentally, however, the administrative organization of

universities resulted from the managerial role of the American college president, the coincidental result of the fact that early founders looked to the colleges of the English universities for their patterns. In doing this they carried over the concept of a permanent headship, designated in the English colleges as *warden, master, provost, president,* or *rector* (Cowley, 1971, Ch. 11, p. 10; Davis, 1961, p. 304).[9] In contrast to the English custom of election by the fellows of the college, the presidents in this country from the very beginning have been appointed by governing boards. Thus, the presidents of the early colleges had responsibilities as executives for boards. For the first two centuries this constituted a relatively simple and personal, almost paternal, relationship with student and teachers. When, after the Civil War, colleges ceased to be small and universities appeared with expanded enrollments, academic fragmentation, and diversified relationships with the external society, presidents found their responsibility elaborated and their need for staff assistance imperative.

By 1900 it could be said that the general administration had developed something like its full measure of force in American higher education. In 1902, President Nicholas Murray Butler assumed the presidency of Columbia complete with clerical staff, abetted by well-established offices for the registrar and bursar (Veysey, 1965, p. 307). Probably typical of its times, the University of North Carolina administration included a registrar, bursar, librarian, and part-time secretary for the university. The office of alumni secretary was not unknown by 1900 (McGrath, 1936). Although largely a product of this century, business officers commonly served as bursars or collectors of fees. By the turn of the century, librarians had established themselves on a full-time basis and had begun to employ assistants—in contrast with the rudimentary condition of these services 40 years previously. The first press bureau appeared at the University of Wisconsin in 1904 (Seller, 1963, p. 3). The office of registrar was nearly universal. The office of vice-president, usually assigned to handle specific functions such as university relations, academic affairs, medical affairs, or similar constellations of administrative services, had appeared in some numbers by the First World War.

[9] Actually, the first head of Harvard had the title of *master* and that of Yale, *rector.* The Harvard custom lasted two years, that at Yale about forty. Both colleges shifted to the title of *president.*

Concurrently, presidents turned to the title of *dean* to further delegate their academic responsibilities. By 1900 this title was used for the heads of professional schools, especially medicine and law, and of schools or divisions of arts and sciences. The office of dean served in smaller colleges to designate the "second in command." In an 1896 reorganization at Cornell, for example, President Schurman appointed deans of academic affairs and of graduate studies. All the universities and two-thirds of the colleges included in the McGrath study had academic deans by 1900. The designation of the title of *dean* for student affairs also has precedent in the late nineteenth century. At Harvard, Eliot's appointment of Dean Gurney, as noted above, was a response to the pressures of his responsibilities for students. Similar appointments were made at Swarthmore, Oberlin, and Chicago in the 1890s. The same forces that had fragmented the unitary curriculum of the early colleges in support of specialized knowledge made the orientation of faculty members more intellectual and pushed into secondary or tertiary importance their concern with students. Into this void came the forerunners of contemporary student personnel services. Deans of women began to meet annually in 1903; directors of student unions appeared in 1914; the National Association of Deans of Men was organized in 1917.

In summary, then, the organizational structure of American universities was etched clearly enough by the first decade of this century. Its two mainstreams flowed to and from the offices of presidents: one an academic route to deans and thence to departmental chairmen; the other a managerial hierarchy. Whatever the organizational charts designated, as early as 1910 it had become apparent that initiative on the academic side had begun to rest heavily at the departmental level.

TWENTIETH-CENTURY EXPANSION If the late nineteenth century constitutes the formative years of American higher education, the present century has been an era of growth and consolidation. During the decades following the Civil War, colleges began their search for a personality appropriate to the times and to their position in society. As the years of maturity approached, each found its particular role in what has become a spectrum from small, unitary schools to large, complex universities which set the pace and pattern for the whole system. Diversity became the pervasive quality of the new era—diversity among institutions and within the major universities.

Expansion in this century has led to colleges and universities that number faculty members in the hundreds and thousands and students in the thousands and tens of thousands. Society's commitment to send youth to college as a major preparation for adult roles is evident in the steady increase from 52,000 students in 1869 to 2,650,000 in 1949 to more than double this by the 1970s. The less than 2 percent of the age group who attended college at the close of the Civil War has grown to more than 40 percent and approaches 50 percent. This expansion in numbers has carried with it a similar expansion in functions. By the early 1960s Clark Kerr, then president of the University of California, could comment that his university employed more people "than IBM . . . in over a hundred locations, counting campuses, experiment stations, agricultural and urban extension centers, and projects abroad involving more than fifty countries." He pointed to "nearly 10,000 courses in its catalogues; some form of contact with nearly every industry, nearly every level of government, nearly every person in its region" (Kerr, 1966, pp. 7–8). The "multiversity" has proved to be the ultimate outcome for the "new university" of 70 years ago.

Since 1900 no radical departures have altered the form of university organization or changed in any substantial way its function. In the retrospect of the last 60 years, the major thrusts that have characterized this era are the following: first, the expansion in numbers of both personnel and of units of the administrative structure, both academic and managerial; second, the consolidation of departmental control over academic matters; and, third, the diffusion of participation in government with a concurrent lessening of the influence of boards and presidents.

Administrative Expansion

Aside from the study by McGrath (1936) and a recent article by David R. Witmer (1966), little documentation exists to delineate the specifics of administrative expansion in this century. But the outward manifestations are obvious. What university of any size today lacks that imposing administration building located near the center of the campus? Within its walls dozens and even hundreds of clerks, typists, secretaries, bookkeepers, accountants, staff assistants, and a variety of administrative officers labor diligently over correspondence and reports, accounts and records, and a variety of managerial services—frequently in a high degree of efficient isolation from the classroom, laboratory, and library across the campus. In addition, one finds a plethora of service positions ranging from dietitians and delivery men to personnel for institutional research.

Paralleling the managerial services, the academic organization has had its own expansion of new functions and offices appended to departments and professional schools. It takes only a quick glance at the telephone directory of a major university to spot such activities as the animal facilities, athletic publicity and promotion, black studies program, carbon research, program in comparative literature, council for international studies, continuing education division, cooperative urban extension center, and creative craft center at the top of the alphabet through to technical research services, theater program, upward bound project, urology studies, and urban studies council at the bottom. Each of these activities has its director or head who reports to a chairman, a dean, or a vice-president. Each has a professional staff of one to a dozen individuals aided by secretaries and research assistants. The totality presents a bewildering complex of functions requiring administrative coordination and control.

As one looks over charts for the period, what stands out clearly is the steady, inexorable increase in administrative personnel and services paralleling the increase in numbers of students and faculty members.

Departmental Influence Specialization of knowledge has its counterpart in specialization of departments. But more than this it has led to what amounts to a monopoly of the expert. This specialization has left the university-wide administrators, and at times deans as well, unable to do more than respond to initiative on matters of personnel, facilities, teaching, curriculum, and research. Authors Paul L. Dressel and Donald J. Reichard (1970, p. 387)[10] observed in their historical overview that the department "has become a potent force, both in determining the stature of the university and in hampering the attempts of the university to improve its effectiveness and adapt to changing social and economic requirements." As early as 1929 a study of departments in small colleges demonstrated that they exercised a major influence in matters related to teaching, curriculum, schedule, and promotion (Reeves & Russell, 1929). More recent studies confirm the trend toward departmental autonomy and control over

[10] This report anticipated a more complete study by Dressel, Marcus, and Johnson entitled *The Confidence Crisis,* Jossey-Bass, Inc., San Francisco, 1970.

its own affairs (Caplow & McGee, 1958), evidenced by what David Riesman (1958) has called an academic procession in which the less prestigious institutions have followed the leadership of the major, prestigious universities.

This departmental autonomy has come as a logical outgrowth of size and specialization and of the pressing necessity to delegate and decentralize if major administrators were not to find themselves overwhelmed. A new kind of professor, the specialist and expert and man of consequence in society, has replaced the teacher and has augmented his (the specialist's) influence with a national system of professional and disciplinary societies. Together they have set the standards and the values, both oriented to productive scholarship, that dominate the universities.

Diffusion of Government Following hard on the downward shift of academic power, governing boards have withdrawn extensively from active involvement in university affairs. This condition was incipient in 1905, as noted by James B. Munroe, industrialist and trustee at Massachusetts Institute of Technology. The trustees, he observed then, "find less and less opportunity for usefullness in a machine so elaborate that any incursion into it by those unfamiliar may do infinite harm" (Munroe, 1913). Fifty years later, in the same vein, the 1957 report on *The Role of Trustees of Columbia University,* (Columbia University, 1957) stated flatly that, while governing boards may hold final legal authority, their actual role in government leaves them removed from the ongoing affairs of their institutions. And as Trustee Ora L. Wildermuth, secretary of the Association of Governing Boards of State Universities, commented in 1949: "If a governing board contents itself with the selection of the best president available and with him develops and determines the broad general principles . . . and then leaves the administration and academic processes to the administrative officers and the Faculty, it will have done its work well." It serves best to select a president, hold title to property, and act as a court of last appeal, he summarized (Wildermuth, 1949, p. 238).

Pressing up from a departmental base, faculty members have moved into governmental affairs via the formalization of a structure of senates, councils, and associated committees. Evidence supports the contention that by 1910 professors were not hesitant to refer to their "rightfully sovereign power" (Veysey, 1965, p. 392). President Harper of Chicago formally stated in his decennial report

71

that it was a "firmly established policy of the Trustees that the responsibility for the settlement of educational questions rests with the Faculties" (Bogert, 1945, p. 81). During the first half of this century the precedent of the major universities slowly carried over to other institutions. In 1941 a survey of 228 colleges and universities by the AAUP (American Association of University Professors) Committee T on College and University Government led to the comment that "in the typical institution the board of trustees appointed the president, the president appointed deans, and the deans in turn designated executives. . . . Consultation concerning personnel and budget . . . took place between administrative and teacher personnel through departmental executives" ("The Role of Faculties . . . ," 1948). A decade later, however, the same committee reported an increase in faculty communication with trustees, participation in personnel decisions, influence on personnel policies, consultation about budgetary matters, and control of academic programs ("The Place and Function . . . ," 1953). By the late 1960s the basic position of the AAUP had the strength of general tradition; in the eyes of a new breed of faculty radicals it had become a conservative force. In essence, the AAUP's position was based upon five principles: (1) that faculties have primary responsibility over educational policies; (2) that they concur through established committees and procedures in academic personnel matters; (3) that they participate actively in the selection of presidents, deans, and chairmen; (4) that they are consulted on budgetary decisions; and (5) that appropriate agencies for this participation have official standing.

Precedents for student involvement in university and college government (distinct from extracurricular campus activities) have gained a new force, although their roots lie deep in the history of higher education. Professor Cowley (1964, Ch. 11, p. 16) has described the abortive two-year "House of Students" at Amherst in 1828 as a legislative body concerned with security on campus, study hours, and similar matters. In this century, something of the same spirit has appeared sporadically. At Barnard during the academic year 1921–22, students carried out a sophisticated analysis of the curriculum. At Dartmouth in 1924, a committee of 12 seniors submitted a critical review of the education program. At Harvard in 1946, following the publication of the faculty report *General Education in a Free Society* (Harvard Committee, 1946), students published an equally formidable document. Overall, as

Cowley (1964, Ch. 11, p. 47) observes, "American students have continuously and sometimes potently affected the thinking and actions of professors, presidents, and trustees." Historically their influence has been an informal one. Their drive for direct participation on the governing councils and boards of colleges and universities generated real potency only during the late 1960s.[11] Its effectiveness remains conjectural, although the evidence suggests that the student drive for participation will tend to dissipate further the influence of boards and presidents.

Alumni have maintained their traditional voice in government, although one can perceive an undermining of the spirit of alma mater and the significance of financial contributions so long associated with their institutional commitments. This participation was substantiated by a 1966 survey of 82 public and private universities and colleges which reported that 31 of the institutions have elected alumni trustees and an additional 24 have trustees nominated by alumni. Nearly all had alumni on their boards, however.[12] Cornell University's situation is typical of private institutions. In a 1966 letter the president of the Alumni Association noted that "a trustee is not required to be an alumnus of the University unless he is elected by the alumni. At present, however, of the 40 members, 35 are alumni."

In retrospect, then, higher education is moving into the final decades of the twentieth century with a pattern of organization similar in its major dimensions to that with which it entered the century. The question readily comes to mind whether this form will continue to prove effective.

CONCLUSION That the American university, the hallmark of the American system of higher education, has flourished as an institution uniquely fitted to its times stands without question. Its commitment to the

---

[11] In his 1970 book, *Should Students Share the Power?* Earl J. McGrath reports a survey of existing practice, noting that more than 80 percent of 875 institutions admit some students to membership in at least one policy-making body. In the same year the University of Tennessee admitted students to its trustee committees. A House bill submitted in 1969 in the Massachusetts legislature proposed an elected student member of each of the governing boards of public universities.

[12] Conducted by Howard University with the sponsorship of the American Alumni Council. The questionnaire was mailed to 112 institutions, from which 82 usable responses were received.

expansion of knowledge and its application are emulated throughout the world. Similarly, its organizational arrangements have grown out of and suited well its particular kind of educational enterprise. Inevitably governing boards and presidents had to delegate as institutions expanded. That they did so in a manner that enhanced the effectiveness of the academic endeavor has proved to be no minor achievement. Departments, in turn, have served well by translating the essence of specialized knowledge into workable organizational forms. Student personnel administrators, in their turn, have filled that void between individual and organization left by the impersonalism inherent in a faculty preeminently concerned with the extension of knowledge. A faculty governing structure has given an organizational channel to the exercise of professorial influence, in turn an academically essential counterbalance to the authority of governing boards and external constituencies. In sum, universities have proved an effective organizational means by which scholarship and learning could flourish within the confines of large, complex organizations.

Yet, as the decade of the 1970s unfolds, a sense of uncertainty about just how well universities do perform has begun to settle over the campuses of the nation. Students in large universities, and even to a degree in smaller institutions, find themselves caught in a complex of increasingly impersonal relationships and an educational endeavor which enhances advanced study and research more than student learning. Both influences tend to dull any sense of intellectual awakening or of personal meaning for life on the part of students. Most faculty cling hard to the traditional fields of knowledge and to specialization despite a societal need for synthesis and application of what is known. As, historically, cultures and nations in their greatest flowering have begun to show their inherent weaknesses, so the university in the last few decades has provided evidence of its limitations. The changing nature of the social order, as it too reaches a pinnacle of scientific-technological achievement, amplifies these weaknesses.

A historical survey such as this would be inadequate indeed if it did not at least suggest some clues to the future. In conclusion, therefore, we note three pervasive organizational inadequacies. One can be attributed to size and complexity, a second to specialization and departmentalization, and the third to the shifting pattern of institutional government. All were incipient but generally underway as higher education emerged from the First World War.

The size and complexity of United States universities seem to dictate that they have become large bureaucracies. Actually, however, one finds two bureaucracies. On the one hand, over the past 50 years faculties have created a hierarchy of departments, schools, and senates or executive councils well larded with a variety of permanent and temporary committees. This bureaucracy claims rights of control over the totality of the academic function. On the other hand, administrators have formed a separate hierarchy to grapple with the immense tasks of management of essential yet supportive services which maintain the university, not the least of which are budget and finance. The lines of relationship between the two bureaucracies have become tenuous. The different attitudes and values associated with each have driven a psychological wedge between faculty members and administrators. Faculty remain committed to a traditional ideal of the university as an integrated community, at the same time giving constant evidence that they fail to grasp its real operational nature and managerial complications. Administrators find their managerial tasks so consuming that they become forgetful of the nature of the academic enterprise.

The second evidence of dysfunction stems from the nature of the department as the organizational unit for disciplinary and professional specialization. The commitment to specialization energizes centrifugal forces that tend to push faculty loyalties out from the universities. Thus the university is often merely a base, temporary or permanent, from which the scholar pursues his primary concern with research activities. Specialization has produced a similar tendency toward fragmentation of the academic organization. While exercising a dominant influence on instruction, curriculum, research, and other academic matters, schools and departments show a low regard for university values and a high concern for disciplinary and professional values. Despite many evidences to the contrary during the student disruptions of the last few years, this condition is reinforced by academic condescension toward administrators, who are viewed as servants rather than leaders of the professoriate. It reflects what one might call a faculty schizophrenia which categorizes administrators as minions while condemning them for failure to stand firmly as defenders of the academic faith in times of crisis.

75

At times this divergency threatens an atrophy in leadership for large universities in an era when leadership is of utmost importance. The remedy, however, inevitably must lie beyond the bounds of organizational factors. Forms of government serve only as well as they are supported in the general values and commitments of those affected by them. Any rectification of this condition, therefore, must stem from deep within the higher education enterprise. In particular, there must be some resolution of the conflict between the clear and direct rewards that accompany achievement in scholarship and research and the nominal recognition, despite societal expectation, accorded to the education of students. From this base line one moves into explorations of reward systems that conform to stated purposes. One also has to reflect upon organizational systems that prove responsive to changing conditions as against those that support existing arrangements.

The third problem—the shifting power in institutional government—was anticipated in 1903 by President Schurman of Cornell when he characterized his role as that of a mediator. Sixty years later Clark Kerr made the same observation with greater force. Presidential deference to faculty expertise in academic affairs is only one facet of the situation, however. The history of university organization in the twentieth century has been an account of the disintegration of the traditional form of government conceived in terms of formal authority granted to governing boards, which have exercised it through the president as executive officer.

The diffusion of government by means of dissipation of boards and presidential influence and dispersion of operating control to departments, administrative offices, and faculty governing bodies has been accompanied by the intrusion of external forces. Professional and disciplinary associations, accrediting agencies, agencies of the federal government for all institutions and state executive offices for public ones—all have tended to bypass presidents and boards. It appears that higher education has experienced one of those historic circles. Governing boards today serve much the way the original visitors or overseers did. What is lacking is a new corporation in the sense of a controlling or managerial council to fill the vacuum. As one English observer phrased it, organizationally American universities have tended to become "confederations of largely autonomous departments." It adds up to what he has characterized as "the hole in the centre" (Shils, 1970).

As universities enter the decade of the 1970s, the pressures on the established organization are evidenced in student dissent and the public reaction to it. The movement toward decentralization of control over educational and administrative functions has begun to come up against external demands for more forceful central authority to the end not only of "law and order" but of a "more efficient use of resources." Mass higher education and the possibility of almost universal higher education exacerbate the problems. More fundamentally, one finds growing evidences of academic inadequacies in the face of the need for new kinds of education and scholarship. These must relate to the role of the university in a society pressed by ecological and social dislocation stemming from scientific and technological achievement. One readily suspects that the organizational forms effective in 1900 may serve but poorly for the year 2000.

Emerging Theories
and Models

The Review of Higher Education
Fall 1982, Volume 6, No. 1
Pages 1 to 18

EMERGING DEVELOPMENTS IN THE STUDY OF ORGANIZATIONS

James G. March

An invitation to speak on emerging developments in any active research field is an invitation to pretense; and my observations will, I fear, be substantially less comprehensive than might be wished. Recent studies of organizations encompass enough variety to assure that the parochial interests and competence of a speaker will color considerably the portrait that is painted, and I am no exception. Thus, a small introduction in the spirit of full disclosure. I intend to talk about a few developments in that small corner of the study of organizations having to do with decision-making, change, information, and the like. Within this domain of organizational research, I intend first to provide a little background, a quasi-history of the development of ideas; second, to list a few recent developments; third, to note some implications of those developments for some basic questions about organizations; and fourth, to comment on a few prospects and needs for additional research. My concern that such a relatively narrow focus may be inadequately responsive to your invitation is ameliorated by a conviction that it is necessary and an awareness that others have looked at different corners of the field in recent review articles that are readily available (Nystrom and Starbuck, 1981; Cummings, 1982; Faucheux, Amado, and Laurent, 1982).

Background

The canonical beginning for students of organizations is a view of organizations as hierarchial systems for taking consequential action in a compre-

This paper was delivered at the annual meetings of the Association for the Study of Higher Education, Washington, D. C., March 3, 1982. The paper reports work done jointly with a number of colleagues, most notably Michael D. Cohen, Martha Feldman, Scott Herriott, Daniel LeVinthal, Johan P. Olsen, Guje Sevon, and Zur Shapira. The research has been supported by grants from the Spencer Foundation, the Stanford Graduate School of Business, and the Hoover Institution.

James G. March is professor of management, Stanford University

hensible world. Although everyone knows that such a characterization can be profoundly misleading, it is a frame for much of our thinking about organizational life. Modern theories of organizational decision-making can be viewed as attempts to modify that conception in two simple ways. First, there has been considerable effort devoted to examining the consequences of the ways in which organizations, and the people in them, act on the basis of a limited comprehension of the world. They are boundedly rational rather than completely rational. They have incomplete information and modest capacities for processing information. These observations have led to development of theories of limited rationality, satisficing, attention, search, and organizational slack.

The basic ideas are well-known. Decision-makers are assumed to have aspiration levels against which they evaluate performance. When goals are not achieved, the organization searches for new alternatives and new information. The search continues until it reveals an alternative that satisfies the currently evoked goals. New alternatives are sought in the neighborhood of old ones. The key scarce resource is attention; and theories of limited rationality are, for the most part, theories of the allocation of attention. They are also theories of organizational slack. When aspirations are achieved, search for new alternatives is assumed to be modest, slack accumulates, and aspirations rise. Conversely, when performance falls below aspiration, search is stimulated, slack is decreased, and aspirations delcine. These changes in aspirations, search, and slack tend to keep performance and aspiration resonably close; and the process serves to buffer the organization somewhat from fluctuations in the environment.

Second, it has been observed that organizations are not simple hierachies. They are political systems with unresolved, or partially resolved, conflicts of interest. Awareness of conflicts of interest in organizations has led to an elaboration of theories of coalitions, bargaining power, the quasi-resolution of conflict, and implementation. These basic ideas are also well-known. It is assumed that individuals enter a decision arena with preferences and resources; the resources are used to pursue personal advantages measured in terms of the preferences. Disputes are settled by some process that does not assume agreement on objectives. The usual metaphors are those of combat, exchange, or alliance. In the combat metaphor, collective decisions are weighted averages of individual desires, where the weights reflect the power distribution among individuals. In an exchange metaphor, collective decisions are reached through a mutually acceptable structure of trades. Markets facilitate cross-section trading (e.g., bribery, blackmail) and encourage the pursuit of resources with high exchange value (e.g., the taking of hostages). In an alliance metaphor, disputes are settled by forming teams and then engaging in combat. The coalition structure is developed through exchange agreements and side payments. Within such political visions of organizations, attention is a scarce resource, so mobilization is important; information is an instrument of strategic actors, so its veracity is problematic; alliances are based on trades over time, so often depend on informal understandings and expectations; decisions are executed by different people than those who make them, so implementation is a potential problem.

It is testimony to the power of the ideas, or the persuasiveness of their proponents, that these two elementary notions have spawned substantial elaboration. They have stimulated significant developments in behavorial decision theory (Kahneman, Slovic, and Tversky, 1982), and in economic theory where, under the labels of information economics, agency theory (Hirschleifer and Riley, 1979), and transaction costs (Williamson, 1975), they represent a large fraction of the work in microeconomics over the past ten years. The elaboration can be illustrated by examining the way in which the simple search model suggested by theories of limited rationality has been developed within organization theory.

Several studies confirm that organizations search for new alternatives in the face of adversity (Staw and Szwajkowski, 1975; Manns and March, 1978). They discover efficiencies previously ignored; they economize. At the same time, however, it is clear that innovation, in general, cannot be explained in terms of problem-oriented search. Necessity is not the only mother of invention. Although the mechanisms involved are by no means well-understood it is possible to identify several complications. The first is the prevalence of solution-driven search. Solutions look for problems to which they might be imagined to be answers, and innovations depend not only on the intensity with which problems search for solutions, but also on the intensity with which solutions look for problems. A second complication is what might be called risk satisficing. There is some evidence, taken mostly from studies of individual behavior, that choices tend to be risk avoiding where expected outcomes are favorable, but risk seeking where expected outcomes are unfavorable. The result is consistent with a view of satisficing that assumes an organization seeks to maximize the probability of an outcome that exceeds its aspiration level, rather than maximize expected reward.

Risk satisficing is, however, qualified by a third complication, decentralization and slack search. Under conditions of plenty, organizational decisions tend to become more decentralized, more diffuse, less tightly linked to a coordinated organizational strategy. Consequently, although central decisions may tend to become risk avoiding during good times, decentralization increases the significance of slack search. Under conditions of success, search occurs as a part of the slack activities of an organization. It reflects the professional preferences of highly qualified workers and the wandering of loosely controlled subunits. From the point of view of the central authorities in the organization, slack search increases the level of risk taken. Thus, fluctuations in slack move an organization from a situation (high slack) where central authorities are relatively cautious, but slack search and decentralization introduces significant levels of risk, to a situation (low slack) in which central decisions are more risk-seeking but slack search and local autonomy are more constrained.

A fourth complication involves the slack reservoir of ideas. Under good conditions, slack search generates ideas, many of them too risky for adoption. When conditions change, such ideas are available as potential solutions to new problems. An organization is able to meet brief periods of decline by drawing on discoveries generated, but overlooked, during better times. A prolonged period of adversity, or of exceptional efficiency in avoiding slack, depletes the reservoir and leaves the organization vulnerable. The result of these elaborations is a considerably more complicated understanding of the relations among success, search, slack, and organizational decisions. The elaborations have the usual costs of making it more difficult to unravel the net effects.

Some New Directions

Recent work on organizations has gone beyond ideas of limited rationality and conflict to consider the ways in which organizations are filled with ambiguity, confusions, and complexity. The argument is that focusing only on cognitive limitations of human actors and on explicit conflicts of interest is likely to lead to understanding the problems of coherence in organizations. In particular, the work has emphasized the ambiguities and complexities of preferences, experiences, and technology (Cohen and March, 1974; March, 1978). In classic treatments of decision-making in organizations, preferences are not problematic. They are assumed to drive action, to be stable, consistent, and precise, and to be exogenous to the decision problem. In classic treatments of learning in organizations, experience is not problematic. Organizations, and the individuals in them, learn from their experience, discovering the consequences of their actions and modifying subsequent behavior to improve it. The casual inferences of experiences are assumed to be easy to make. In classic treatments of technology in organizations, technology is not problematic. Technological coherence is assured through means-ends chains, division of labor, and hierarchy. The revelance of a solution for a problem is well defined, and the problems of consistency are solved through allocation of responsibility and the making of policy.

Observations of organizations suggest that although organizations exhibit impressive elements of coherence and coordination, they cannot be fully comprehended in terms of clear objectives, experiences, and technologies.

Organizational goals seem to be unclear, changing, and in conflict. Actions in one part of an organization appear often to be only loosely linked to actions in another. Solutions seem often to have only modest connections to problems. Policies often aren't implemented. Decision-makers seem often to wander in and out of decision arenas. The whole process has been described as a funny soccer game played on a round soccer field (March and Romelaer, 1976). Many different people (but not everyone) can join a game (or leave it), depending on what other things they have to do. Some people can throw balls into the game or remove them. Individuals while they are in the game can kick whatever ball comes near them in the direction of whatever goal they choose, and away from goals they wish to avoid. And the whole field is sloped so that some goals are more easily scored than others.

Organizational action in such an ambiguous and confusing world is perplexing. It is not immediately obvious how organizations act and survive, even thrive, under such conditions. Or how we might think about them. Indeed, the apparent disorderliness of many things that are observed in organizations has led some people to argue that there is very little order to organizational decision-making, that it is best described as chaos. A more conservative position, however, is that the order in organizations is less hierarchical and less a collection of means-ends chains than is anticipated by traditional theories. There is order, but it is not the conventional order.

Temporal Orders

It has been argued that understanding decisions requires an appreciation of how decision-making fits into the lives of decision-makers. Any decision process involves individuals and groups who are simultaneously involved in other things. Problems, solutions, and decision-makers come together because they are available at the same time and the same place. Thus, from this perspective, decisions depend on an ecology of attention. Since some factors important to the flow of problems, solutions, and decision-makers are exogenous to any specific decision process, the process will appear to be quite disorderly if the attention context is ignored.

From this point of view, the loose coupling that is observed in a particular organization is a consequence of a shifting intermeshing of the demands on the attention and lives of the whole array of actors. It is possible to examine any particular decision as the seemingly fortuitous consequence of combining different moments of different lives, and some effort has been made to describe organizations in something like that cross-sectional detail (Krieger, 1979). A more limited version of the same fundamental idea focuses on the allocation of attention. The idea is simple. Individuals attend to some things, thus do not attend to others. The attention devoted to a particular· decision by a particular potential participant depends not only on the attributes of the decision but also on alternative claims on attention. Since those alternative claims are not homogeneous across participants and change over time, the attention any particular decision receives can be both quite unstable and remarkably independent of the properties of the decision. The same decision will attract much attention, or little, depending on the other things that possible participants might be doing. The apparent erratic character of attention is made somewhat more explicable by placing it in the context of multiple, changing claims on attention.

Such ideas have been used to deal with flows of solutions and problems, as well as participants. In a garbage can decision process (Cohen, March & Olsen, 1972; Padgett, 1980), choice opportunities are seen as connecting solutions, problems, and decision-makers not only in terms of rules of access that might reflect beliefs about the casual connections among problems and solutions and the legitimacy of decision-maker participation, but also in terms of their simultaneous availability. In the model, it is assumed that there are exogenous, time-dependent arrivals of choices, problems, solutions, and decision-makers. Problems and solutions are attached to choices, and thus to each other, not because of their inherent connections in a means-ends sense but because of their temporal proximity. The specific collection of decision-makers, problems, and solutions that comes to be associated with a particular choice opportunity is orderly—but the logic of the ordering is temporal and contextual rather than hierarchial or consequential. At the limit, almost any solution can be associated with almost any problem—provided they are contemporaries.

Rules and Routines

Much of the decision-making behavior observed in an organization reflects the routine way in which people do what they are supposed to do. Most of the time, people follow organizational operating procedures. They follow rules even when it is not obviously in their self-interest to do so. The proposition that organizations follow rules—that much of the behavior in an organization is specified by standard operating procedures—is a common one in the bureaucratic and organizational literature. To describe behavior as driven by rules is to see action as a matching of behavior with a position or situation. The criterion is appropriateness rather than consequential optimality. The terminology is one of duties and roles rather than anticipatory decision-making. Search involves an inquiry into the nature of a particular situation, and choice involves matching a situation with behavior that fits it. Rule following can be described as obligatory action (though the idea of obligation may suggest an overly narrow conception), as contrasted with consequential action. The behavior can be viewed as contractual, an implicit agreement to act appropriately in return for being treated appropriatedly, and to some extent there certainly is such a "contract". But socialization into rules and their appropriateness is ordinarily not a case of willful entering into an explicit contract. It is a set of understandings of the nature of things, of self-conceptions and of organizational images.

Rules are fundamental to understanding both the ways in which organizations maintain stability and the ways in which they change. On the one hand, the existence and persistence of rules, combined with their relative independence of the preferences and beliefs of individual participants, makes it possible for organizations to function reasonably reliably and reasonably consistently in complex worlds. At the same time, change in organizations is closely linked to mundane rules. Rules are efficient and effective devices for allowing complex organizations to respond to variations in conditions. Moreover, organizations adapt to their environments by changing rules, though the processes of such change are slower than the routine adaptation to changing conditions within the rules. Current rules store information generated by previous organizational experiences and analyses, even though the information cannot easily be retrieved in a form amenable to systematic current evaluation.

Interpretation, Rituals, and Symbols

Most theories of organizations assume that an organizational process is to be understood primarily in terms of its outcomes, that participants enter an organization in order to affect outcomes, and the point of life is choice. The emphasis is instrumental; the central conceit is the notion of decision significance. It is possible, however, to see the central phenomena of organizations not as the making and implementing of choices, or the execution of tasks, though those may be important, but as the search for order in the face of confusion and complexity. Like students of organizations and decision-making, individuals within and outside an organization try to understand what is going on, to interpret their lives and to help each other develop beliefs that make the incomprehensibilities of existence tolerable.

From such a point of view, decision-making is an arena for symbolic action, for developing and enjoying an interpretation of life and one's position in it (Feldman and March, 1981). The rituals of choice infuse organizations with an appreciation of the sensibility of organizational arrangements and behavior. They tie routine organizational events to beliefs about the nature of things. The rituals give meaning, and meaning controls life. Thus, understanding organizations involves recognizing that organizational outcomes may often be less significant than the ways in which organizational processes provide meaning in an ambiguous world. The meanings involved may be as grand as the central ideology of a society committed to reason and participation. They may be as local as the ego needs of individuals or groups within the organization.

Some treatments of symbols in organizations treat them as perversions of decision processes. They are portrayed as ways in which the gullible are misled into acquiescence. In such a portrayal, the witch doctors of symbols use their tricks to confuse the innocent, and the symbolic features of choice are viewed as simple opiates. Although there is no question that symbolic action is often taken strategically, few students of organizations accept such a picture of unrelieved malevolence. Effective decision-making in organizations depends critically on the legitimacy of the processes of choice and their outcomes, and such legitimacy is consistently problematic in a confusing, ambiguous world. Confidence in the legitimacy and adequacy of decisions is part of the context of organizations that work. And that confidence cannot be assumed to be automatic.

As a consequence, organizations orchestrate the process of choice in a way that legitimizes the choices, the choosers, and the organization. In most cases, the orchestration tries to assure an audience of two essential things: First, that a choice has been made intelligently, that it reflects planning, thinking, analysis, and the systematic use of information. Organizations plan, gather information, develop analyses, consult authorities, and perhaps reports partly in order to discover the correct choice. But those performances are also ways by which an organization reassures itself and its audiences that it is a proper organization, and that it makes proper decisions. Second, that a choice is sensitive to the concerns of relevant people, that the right people have been influential in the process. Defining the "right" people is, of course, itself a complicated issue, partly affected by the orchestration of decision. For example, part of the drama of decision is used to reinforce the idea that managers (and managerial decisions) affect the performance of organizations. Such a belief is, in fact, difficult to confirm using the kinds of data routinely generated by a confusing world. But it is important to the functioning of a hierarchical system. Executive compensation schemes and the mythology of executive careers are used to reassure executives (and others) that an organization is controlled by its leadership, and appropriately so.

To see the symbolic structure of decision-making as serving an important instrumental function in establishing the legitimacy of decisions and decision-makers is, however, to see organizational ritual in a subordinate way. It becomes a possibly necessary limitation on the purity of life. Some students of organizational choice would make a stronger claim. Life is not primarily choice. It is interpretation. Outcomes *are* generally less significant than process. It is the process that gives meaning to life, and meaning is the core of life. The reason organizations and the people in them devote so much time to symbols, myths, and rituals is that they (appropriately) care more about them. From this point of view, choice is an elegant construction that finds justification in its elegance, and organizational decision-making should be understood and described in approximately the same way we would understand and describe art or poetry.

Some Implications

Earlier work on decision-making in organizations, as well as much current work, emphasizes understanding how organizations deal with uncertainity and conflict in making choices. As a result of that work, our understanding of organizations and the ways in which we act in them have changed in significant ways. The work I have sketched emphasizes understanding ambiguity, confusion, and complexity; it asks how organizations bring order to confusing worlds, or act without conventional order. The research has some implications for how we think about some key aspects of organizational action.

Understanding Management Information Systems

In standard treatments of information, the value of information depends on the way in which it contributes to improving decisions; information has value to the extent to which it can be expected to affect a decision; a rational decision-maker will invest in information as long as the marginal expected return exceeds the marginal expected cost; and a proper management information system assembles and displays information that meets such criteria. Much of the information that managers seek and exchange in organizations is hard to rationalize in such terms. Much managerial information appears to be idle talk from the point of view of decision theory perspectives on information. It has no apparent relevance to managerial decisions.

If, however, management is seen less as choice and more as discovering new objectives, developing myths and interpretations of life, and modifying the diffuse beliefs and cultural understandings that make organizational events comprehensible and life enjoyable, then it is not obvious that the best management information system is a decision support system. Intelligent managers might pay more for, and attend more to, a system designed to develop interpretations of events and understandings of history rather than to help make choices.

Intelligent choice often presumes understanding, of course, and it is possible to see the interpretation of history as instrumental to the action (choices) by which we seek to control our fate. It can, however, be seen as more fundamental than that. Perhaps interpretation is more a primary feature of human behavior than a servant of choice. From such a perspective, information is sought and considered because it contributes to understanding what is going on in life; and understanding what is going on is important independent of any purpose to which the knowledge might be put. Perhaps we can better understand the uses of information in organization if we see information, and decision-making, as part of an effort to comprehend and appreciate human existence, as driven by elementary curiosity as much as a hope for instrumental advantage. We can see organizations as having been designed (or evolved) around some problems of developing, enjoying, and sharing interpretations of reality, communication in organizations as tied to the discovery, clarification, and elaboration of meaning, and the process of decision-making in organizations as a performance within which individuals and groups construct an interpretation of experience that can be shared meaningfully and enjoyably (March and Sevon, 1982).

In order to use such ideas in the design of management information, we require some notion of the value of alternative information sources that is less tied to a prior specification of a decision (or class of decisiosn) than to a wide spectrum of possible decisions impossible to anticipate in the absence of the information; less likely to show the consequences of known alternatives for existing goals than to suggest new alternatives and new objectives; less likely to test old ideas than to provoke new ones; less pointed toward anticipating uncertain futures than toward interpreting ambiguous pasts. It would be a collection of pieces of information of doubtful relevance.

In fact, a view of information and life not far from the one we have sketched is a quite traditional one, associated classically with literature, art and education; and if there are appropriate models for a management information system of this sort, perhaps they lie in discussions of the nature and design of education rather than in modern theories of decision. Perhaps management information designers could profit from some attention to the ancient and modern discussions of the linkage between education and life, the arguments over the relevance of "relevance" in thinking about a curriculum, and the efforts of art and literary criticism to explicate the expression of meaning.

To be sure, there are differences between an organization and a society and between managers and educators or artists. Many of those differences involve the relative specificity of activities and objectives in organizations, compared with the relative diffuseness of broader social relations. The differences make the leap from the analysis of education to the analysis of organizational information a large and possibly treacherous one. But not entirely foolish. As we discover the elements of loose coupling and ambiguity in organizations, the role of symbols in decision-making and information processing, the place of myths, stories, and rituals in management, and the significance of beliefs in the transformation of organizations, some of the distances between the properties of organizations and the properties of art and education seem to grow smaller.

To describe organizational management in such terms is, of course, to glorify it. It suggests that office memoranda might be viewed as forms of poetry and staff meetings as forms of theater, and we may perhaps wonder whether it would be better to admit distinctions between the activities of accountants and an abstract painting—if only to assure that each may achieve its unique qualities. The dangers are real; but to a glorified view of idle talk and memoranda, we can add a romantic view of the possibilities for artistry in organizational engineering. Perhaps, with a little imagination here and there, educational philosophy and literary criticism could be used to point management information systems in the direction of a useful quality of irrevelance.

Understanding Organizational Leadership

An understanding of organizational leadership is ordinarily built around two fundamental, interrelated, and subjectively very compelling beliefs. The first is a belief in the efficacy of leadership. The belief depends on the idea that life is choice, that indivduals and institutions make decisions on the basis of an awareness of the consequences of action for goals. The efficacy of such goal-oriented choice is, then, dependent on the power of the individual or institution involved. In short, it is assumed that things happen in organizations and society because some people want them to happen and have the power to make them happen. Organizational leaders are seen as individuals who make decisions (e.g., "the buck stops here"). And because of their position and the resources they control, their decisions are seen as efficacious. As a result, the great actions of leaders are, appropriately, based on great hopes for consequences. Leaders are seen as important.

The second basic belief underlying much of our talk about organizational leadership is a belief in the meaningfulness of differential success among leaders. We generally believe that managerial careers are the result of managerial performance, and that managerial performance is a reliable reflection of individual capabilities for meeting the demands of the job. In some cases, we may believe that the demands of the job involve some socially irrelevant criteria (e.g., familial ties); but we generally assert that the differences in performance that are reflected in differences in careers are reliable, that they stem from some underlying differences in managers. In short, we believe not only that leadership makes a difference but also that different leaders produce different outcomes, that leadership success is a consequence of individual attributes.

It is not easy to examine beliefs that so deeply condition our observations and our inferences. We can to ask, however, whether it is possible that such beliefs might be mistaken or misleading. Consider two simple arguments: First, there are some reasons, drawn from our research on organizations, to question our beliefs in the efficacy of leadership action and the reliability of leader success. As has been suggested above, organizing our thinking around decision-making may easily mislead us. Frequently it is unclear who made a decision, what a decision is, and when a decision is made. Calling organizational action a result of a decision may obscure the nature of a process that is more imitative or rule-following. And the relationship between organizational decisions and organizational outcomes is often obscure. In such a situation, the consequences (if any) of leader action are likely to be substantially confounded with other factors, and the problems of reliably assessing the quality of leaders are likely to be considerable.

These problems are particularly acute as we approach the top of an organization, where goals tend to be somewhat less simple and casual relations somewhat less clear. Moreover, they are accentuated by the fact that as we move toward the top of a hierarchy of managers promoted on the basis of performance, we find a pool of managers that is increasingly homogeneous with respect to attributes that produce reliable success. It is entirely possible that these two processes—the filtering of managers through peformance on the way to the top and the increasing ambiguity of managerial evaluation (or at least its connection to managerial action)—combine to make the error variance in the measurement of performance greater than the variation in the pool of potential leaders (March and March, 1977, 1981). Under such a circumstance, you could not (reliably) distinguish among vice-presidents in selecting a president. Different vice-presidents would look different, of course; they would have different records of apparent success; but the differences would not be reliable.

Second, there are some familiar processes of human inference that would lead us to such beliefs and to considerable subjective confidence in them, even if they were not true. When we look at recent efforts to understand the way human beings form inferences about their experience, four features of inference-processing seem particularly relevant to leaders.

(1) *Conservation of belief.* We seem to be more accepting of evidence that confirms prior beliefs than we are of disconfirming evidence. We tend to distort evidence to make it conform to our beliefs. The confidence of experts, as well as others, appears to be substantially independent of the correctness of their beliefs.

(2) *Belief in determinacy.* We seem not to believe in the possibility of chance events. Anything that suggests a situation involves skill will make humans treat it as a situation involving skill, even though outcomes are determined by a chance process.

(3) *Anthropocentrism.* We seem systematically to overestimate the role of individual intentions and dispositions in determining events we observe, and systematically to underestimate situational and unintentional factors. We believe that people make things happen.

(4) *Success bias.* Particularly in important tasks, personal success tends to accentuate the inclination to make explanations of events that attribute outcomes to personal intentions and actions. Successful people tend to think they produce the effects (success) they experience.

Leaders in organizations are successful. That is how they become leaders. They operate within a social norm that attributes considerable importance to leaders. As result, we would expect them to exaggerate the importance of individual actions, and specifically their own actions, on events. They would come to believe in their control over organizational outcomes, even if they had very little actual control; and their subjective beliefs would be reinforced by their (subjectively plausible) interpretations of their experience.

What this suggests is not that leadership is unimportant. Rather, the argument is that there are reasons for suspecting that reliable discrimination among leaders at the top may be difficult and for suspecting that even if we couldn't make such discriminations we would come to believe that we could. Our confidence in the significance of individual variation among leaders is, in short, no evidence for the veracity of the belief. It seems likely that the difference between a successful leader and an unsuccessful leader is less than we believe, and it seems possible that we may want to question the conventional idea that great leader action should be built on great expectations for the consequences of action.

Understanding Organizational Change

Insofar as action can be viewed as rule-following, decision-making is not willful in the normal sense. It does not stem from the pursuit of interests and the calculation of future consequences of current choices. Rather it comes from matching a changing set of contingent rules to a changing set of situations. The intelligence of the process arises from the way rules store information gained through learning, selection, and contagion, and from the reliability with which rules are followed. Understanding the broader intelligence of the adaptation of rules depends on a fairly subtle appreciation of how rules develop, thus how organizations change.

Most discussions of change in organization grow out of a concern for making them do what we want them to do. As a result, many theories of change in organizations emphasize planned, intentional, anticipatory change. They imagine situations in which individuals or groups choose future directions and then try to lead an organization. These observations may lead us to confuse organizational resistance to change with organizational resistance to *arbitrary* change. In fact, organizations adapt routinely and easily to their experience, though they rarely do exactly what they are told to do by proper authorities or managers. They follow rules that are contingent on the environment in such a way as to produce large changes without great difficulty. Since adaptation occurs at several levels simultaneously and in a confusing and changing world, sensible adaptive processes sometimes produce surprises (March, 1981). As a result, understanding organizational change may be not as much a matter of looking for unique change processes as one of looking for the ways routine procedures and ordinary behavior both facilitate easy adaptation and result in occasional surprises.

It is possible to find numerous elaborations of this theme. I will limit myself to a few. First, it is possible to see technological change in an organization as a result of a simple adaptive process in which organizations learn and modify search investment decisions. That is, they learn to have a reasonable level of aspiration. At the same time, suppose they gain competence in search through experience at it. The more they search in a particular way, the higher the expected return from that kind of search. Finally, suppose they learn how to allocate effort to different search alternatives as a consequence of experience with the outcomes of past allocations. Explorations of such learning processes indicate that they are sensitive to the relative speed of the three kinds of learning and to the fortuitous outcomes of probabilistic events (Levinthal and March, 1982). Thus, very similar processes operating in (probabilistically) identical environments produce considerable variation in organizational change, and rapid learning is not always the best.

It is also possible to view organizational change as occurring through a process of selection. By building on observations of the importance of standard operating procedures and decision rules, Winter (1971) and Nelson and Winter (1973) portray organizations as evolving collections of invariant rules. The mix of rules observed in a family of existing organizations reflects the differential growth and survival of organizations that follow different rules in a particular environment. A similar perspective, but focusing on selection of organizational forms rather than rules is found in Hannan and Freeman (1977).

Conceptions of organizations as evolving mixes of inexplicably sensible rules and structures have been appealing to students of organizations who would like to assume that organizations act in an optimal way even though the processes they use seem far from rational calculation. Information about past experience is stored (irretrievably) in the rules and forms that survive. The argument is an interesting one, but it assumes that selection processes are rapid enough or general enough to be insensitive to rates of change in the environment. Under such conditions, the equilibrium properties of the processes are of considerable interest. Behavioral students of organizations have generally been less interested in emphasizing the equilibria of adaptive processes then they have been in describing the time-paths of movement under conditions of environmental instability and uncertainty, and in identifying some of the conditions under which the information content of rules or organizational forms will be less (or greater) than the information content of explicitly rational procedures. The latter issue is, of course, a classic one in the ideology of social change.

A theme that runs through several treatments of organizational change as an adaptive process is the problem of foolishness in organizations. The discussion of foolishness has emphasized two main concerns. On the one hand, organizations that focus too narrowly on achieving present objectives reduce their chances for inadvertant discovery of alternative goals through experience. In a world in which preferences are discovered through action, there is some need for experimenting with actions that cannot presently be justified. On the other hand, organizations are systems that are adapting at several levels, and actions that are optimal from the perspective of one level are unlikely to be optimal from the perspective of another. It is likely, for example, that optimizing on the survival prospects of an organization will be inconsistent with optimizing at the individual level. Of greater interest in recent work, however, had been the potential for conflict between the survival needs of individual organizations and the needs of larger systems of organizations. For example, it is often wiser for any individual organization to wait for another organization to experiment with innovations and then adopt those that seem to work. But since that is true of every organization, there is a system problem of producing the "foolishness" that sometimes leads to new discoveries. Since, on average, such foolishness has a negative expected value, we require a process of decision that (in effect) reduces the likelihood of survival for the individual organization making the decision, but makes the conditions for other organization more benign.

Some organizational processes have evolved that accomplish this. They are not conscious strategies by which organizations enter into contracts to share the costs and benefits of risky innovative adventures. Rather they are rules of behavior within organizations that stimulate, or tolerate, foolishness. These include responses to organizational slack. Under favorable conditions, organizations seem systematically to reduce the tightness of controls over subgroups and individuals. As a consequence, they encourage activities that are justified on the sub-organizational level but are probably suboptimal at the organizational level. Similarly, organizations encourage (or are led to accept) rules of professional conduct that are, from the organization's point of view, foolish. For example, managers are encouraged to "make their marks", to make changes. It is doubtful that the expected value of a random managerial change is positive. So most efforts by managers to leave some sign of their existence are probably mistakes. But the rule encourages the kind of experimentation that (at some cost to the organization) leads to occasional discovery of practices that are generally useful. Since individual organizations are probably somewhat more enamored of individual organizational survival than would be optimal for the system of organizations, these "unconscious" rules protect sensible (system-wide) behavior from the predations of rational organizational analysis.

Prospects and Needs

I think the study of organizations, and particularly the study of decision-making in organizations, seems rich in possibilities for future research. We know a little. We would like to know a little more. The theoretical ideas sketched above are invitations to more theoretical development. We need

better models of organizational learning and evolution, and a better understanding of the kinds of surprises that may arise from a mostly sensible learning
or evolutionary process. We need better models of garbage can decision
processes and of supply-side (i.e., solution driven) problem-solving in organizations. We need better understanding of how individuals and organizations process preferences, how we can imagine decision-making in situations
in which preferences are changing, inconsistent, and endogenous to choice.
We need better ideas for the analysis of symbolic action in organizations,
something that goes beyond the simple observation that it is important.

Theoretical ideas in organizational decision-making are, however, heavily
dependent on the effectiveness with which we stimulate, and honor, the
difficult work of observing the ways in which real organizations function.
Many recent theoretical developments have been essentially attempts to comprehend the richly contextual, historical case studies of organizational decision-making. In a more than usual way, theories of organizational decision-
making are dependent on acutely sensitive observers of natural decision processes, observers who can report events without a premature commitment to
an interpretation of events, who have the patience to watch what is happening,
and who have the subtle minds of serious ethnographers. Those people are
rare people.

A significant number of recent developments in the theoretical analysis of
organizational decision-making have come from the study of institutions of
higher education. This is, no doubt, partly an accident of the fact that many
of the contributors to the field inhabit colleges and universities, and to the
problematics of university governance after the student unrest of the 1960's.
But such happy accidents are often the basis for happy traditions; and as we
look ahead to the next decade of research, it may not be entirely unreasonable
to hope that students of higher education will contribute as much to our
understanding of organizations in the next ten years as they have in the past
ten years.

References

Cohen, M. D., and March, J. G. *Leadership and ambiguity: The american college president.*
    New York: McGraw-Hill, 1974.
Cohen, M. D., March, J. G., and Olsen, J. P., A garbage can model of organizational choice.
    Administrative Science Quarterly, 1972, 17, 1–25.
Cummings, L. L. Organizational behavior. *Annual Review of Psychology.* 1982, *33,* 541–579.
Faucheux, C. Amado, G., and Laurent, Andre Organizational development and Change. *Annual
    Review of Psychology,* 1982, *33,* 343–370.
Feldman, Martha S., and March, James G., Information in organizations as signal and symbol.
    Administrative Science Quarterly 1981, *26,* 171–186.
Hannan, M. T., and Freeman, J. The population ecology of organizations. *American Journal
    of Sociology,* 1977, *82,* 929–966.

Hirschleifer, J., and Riley, J. G. The analytics of uncertainty and information—An expository survey. *Journal of Economic Literature* 1979, *17*, 1375–1421.

Kahneman, D., Slovic, P., and Tversky, A., eds. *Judgment under uncertainty: Heuristics and biases.* Cambridge: Cambridge University Press, 1982.

Krieger, S. *Hip capitalism.* Beverly Hills, CA: Sage, 1979.

Levinthal, D., and March, J. G. A model of adaptive organizational choice. *Journal of Economic Behavior and Organization,* forthcoming, 1982.

Manns, C., and March, J. G. Financial adversity, internal competition, and curricular change in a university. *Administrative Science Quarterly,* 1978, *23,* 541–552.

March, J. G. Bounded rationality, ambiguity, and the engineering of choice. *Bell Journal of Economics,* 1978, *9,* 587–608.

March, J. G. Footnotes to organizational change. *Administrative Science Quarterly* 1981, *26,* 563–577.

March, J. C., and March, J. G. Almost random careers: The Wisconsin school superintendency, 1940–1972. *Administrative Science Quarterly,* 1977, *22,* 377–409.

March, J. C., and March, J. G. Performance sampling and weibull distributions. *Administrative Science Quarterly,* 1981, *26,* 90–92.

March, J. G., and Romelaer, P. Position and presence in the drift of decisions. In J. G. March and J. P. Olsen, *Ambiguity and choice in organizations.* Bergen: Universitetsforlaget, 1976.

March, J. G., and Sevon, G. Gossip, information, and decision making. To appear in L. S. Sproull and P. D. Larkey, eds., *Advances in information processing in organizations,* Vol. I Greenwich, CT: JAI Press, forthcoming, 1982.

Nelson, R. R., and Winter, S. G. Towards an evolutionary theory of economic capabilities. *American Economic Review,* 1973, *63,* 440–449.

Nystrom, P. C., and Starbuck, W. H. *Handbook of organizational design.* Oxford: Oxford University Press, 1981.

Padgett, J. F. Managing garbage can hierarchies. *Administrative Science Quarterly,* 1980, *25,* 583–604.

Staw, B. M., and Szwajkowski, E. The scarcity-munificence component of organizational environments and the commission of illegal acts. *Administrative Science Quarterly,* 1975, *20,* 345–354.

Williamson, O. E. *Markets and hierarchies.* New York: Free Press, 1975.

Winter, S. G. Satisficing, selection, and the innovating remannt. *Quarterly Journal of Economics,* 1971, *85,* 237–261.

Educational Organizations as Loosely Coupled Systems

Karl E. Weick

In contrast to the prevailing image that elements in organizations are coupled through dense, tight linkages, it is proposed that elements are often tied together frequently and loosely. Using educational organizations as a case in point, it is argued that the concept of loose coupling incorporates a surprising number of disparate observations about organizations, suggests novel functions, creates stubborn problems for methodologists, and generates intriguing questions for scholars. Sample studies of loose coupling are suggested and research priorities are posed to foster cumulative work with this concept.[1]

Imagine that you're either the referee, coach, player or spectator at an unconventional soccer match: the field for the game is round; there are several goals scattered haphazardly around the circular field; people can enter and leave the game whenever they want to; they can throw balls in whenever they want; they can say "that's my goal" whenever they want to, as many times as they want to, and for as many goals as they want to; the entire game takes place on a sloped field; and the game is played as if it makes sense (March, personal communication).

If you now substitute in that example principals for referees, teachers for coaches, students for players, parents for spectators and schooling for soccer, you have an equally unconventional depiction of school organizations. The beauty of this depiction is that it captures a different set of realities within educational organizations than are caught when these same organizations are viewed through the tenets of bureaucratic theory.

Consider the contrast in images. For some time people who manage organizations and people who study this managing have asked, "How does an organization go about doing what it does and with what consequences for its people, processes, products, and persistence?" And for some time they've heard the same answers. In paraphrase the answers say essentially that an organization does what it does because of plans, intentional selection of means that get the organization to agree upon goals, and all of this is accomplished by such rationalized procedures as cost-benefit analyses, division of labor, specified areas of discretion, authority invested in the office, job descriptions, and a consistent evaluation and reward system. The only problem with that portrait is that it is rare in nature. People in organizations, including educational organizations, find themselves hard pressed either to find actual instances of those rational practices or to find rationalized practices whose outcomes have been as beneficent as predicted, or to feel that those rational occasions explain much of what goes on within the organization. Parts of some organizations are heavily rationalized but many parts also prove intractable to analysis through rational assumptions.

It is this substantial unexplained remainder that is the focus of this paper. Several people in education have expressed dissatisfaction with the prevailing ideas about organizations supplied by organizational theorists. Fortunately, they have

1

This paper is the result of a conference held at La Jolla, California, February 2–4, 1975 with support from the National Institute of Education (NIE). Participants in the conference were, in addition to the author, W.W. Charters, Center for Educational Policy and Management, University of Oregon; Craig Lundberg, School of Business, Oregon State University; John Meyer, Dept. of Sociology, Stanford University; Miles Meyers, Dept. of English, Oakland (Calif.) High School; Karlene Roberts, School of Business, University of California, Berkeley; Gerald Salancik, Dept. of Business Administration, University of Illinois; and Robert Wentz, Superintendent of Schools, Pomona (Calif.) Unified School District. James G. March, School of Education, Stanford University, a member of the National Council on Educational Research, and members of the NIE staff were present as observers. This conference was one of several on organizational processes in education which will lead to a report that will be available from the National Institute of Education, Washington, D.C. 20208. The opinions expressed in this paper do not necessarily reflect the position or policy of the National Institute of Education or the Department of Health, Education, and Welfare.

also made some provocative suggestions about newer, more unconventional ideas about organizations that should be given serious thought. A good example of this is the following observation by John M. Stephens (1967: 9–11):

[There is a] remarkable constancy of educational results in the face of widely differing deliberate approaches. Every so often we adopt new approaches or new methodologies and place our reliance on new panaceas. At the very least we seem to chorus new slogans. Yet the academic growth within the classroom continues at about the same rate, stubbornly refusing to cooperate with the bright new dicta emanating from the conference room . . . [These observations suggest that] we would be making a great mistake in regarding the management of schools as similar to the process of constructing a building or operating a factory. In these latter processes deliberate decisions play a crucial part, and the enterprise advances or stands still in proportion to the amount of deliberate effort exerted. If we must use a metaphor or model in seeking to understand the process of schooling, we should look to agriculture rather than to the factory. In agriculture we do not start from scratch, and we do not direct our efforts to inert and passive materials. We start, on the contrary, with a complex and ancient process, and we organize our efforts around what seeds, plants, and insects are likely to do anyway . . . . The crop, once planted, may undergo some development even while the farmer sleeps or loafs. No matter what he does, *some* aspects of the outcome will remain constant. When teachers and pupils foregather, some education may proceed even while the Superintendent disports himself in Atlantic City.

It is crucial to highlight what is important in the examples of soccer and schooling viewed as agriculture. To view these examples negatively and dismiss them by observing that "the referee should tighten up those rules," "superintendents don't do that," "schools are more sensible than that," or "these are terribly sloppy organizations" is to miss the point. The point is although researchers don't know what these kinds of structures are like but researchers do know they exist and that each of the negative judgments expressed above makes sense only if the observer assumes that organizations are constructed and managed according to rational assumptions and therefore are scrutable only when rational analyses are applied to them. This paper attempts to expand and enrich the set of ideas available to people when they try to make sense out of their organizational life. From this standpoint, it is unproductive to observe that fluid participation in schools and soccer is absurd. But it can be more interesting and productive to ask, how can it be that even though the activities in both situations are only modestly connected, the situations are still recognizable and nameable? The goals, player movements, and trajectory of the ball are still recognizable and can be labeled "soccer." And despite variations in class size, format, locations, and architecture, the results are still recognized and can be labeled "schools." How can such loose assemblages retain sufficient similarity and permanence across time that they can be recognized, labeled, and dealt with? The prevailing ideas in organization theory do not shed much light on how such "soft" structures develop, persist, and impose crude orderliness among their elements.

The basic premise here is that concepts such as loose coupling serve as sensitizing devices. They sensitize the observer to notice and question things that had previously been taken for granted. It is the intent of the program described here to develop a language for use in analyzing complex organizations, a language that may highlight features that have previously gone unnoticed. The guiding principle is a reversal of the common assertion, "I'll believe it when I see it" and

100

presumes an epistemology that asserts, "I'll see it when I believe it." Organizations as loosely coupled systems may not have been seen before because nobody believed in them or could afford to believe in them. It is conceivable that preoccupation with rationalized, tidy, efficient, coordinated structures has blinded many practitioners as well as researchers to some of the attractive and unexpected properties of less rationalized and less tightly related clusters of events. This paper intends to eliminate such blindspots.

THE CONCEPT OF COUPLING

The phrase "loose coupling" has appeared in the literature (Glassman, 1973; March and Olsen, 1975) and it is important to highlight the connotation that is captured by this phrase and by no other. It might seem that the word coupling is synonymous with words like connection, link, or interdependence, yet each of these latter terms misses a crucial nuance.

By loose coupling, the author intends to convey the image that coupled events are responsive, *but* that each event also preserves its own identity and some evidence of its physical or logical separateness. Thus, in the case of an educational organization, it may be the case that the counselor's office is loosely coupled to the principal's office. The image is that the principal and the counselor are somehow attached, but that each retains some identity and separateness and that their attachment may be circumscribed, infrequent, weak in its mutual affects, unimportant, and/or slow to respond. Each of those connotations would be conveyed if the qualifier loosely were attached to the word coupled. Loose coupling also carries connotations of impermanence, dissolvability, and tacitness all of which are potentially crucial properties of the "glue" that holds organizations together.

Glassman (1973) categorizes the degree of coupling between two systems on the basis of the activity of the variables which the two systems share. To the extent that two systems either have few variables in common or share weak variables, they are independent of each other. Applied to the educational situation, if the principal-vice-principal-superintendent is regarded as one system and the teacher-classroom-pupil-parent-curriculum as another system, then by Glassman's argument if we did not find many variables in the teacher's world to be shared in the world of a principal and/or if the variables held in common were unimportant relative to the other variables, then the principal can be regarded as being loosely coupled with the teacher.

A final advantage of coupling imagery is that it suggests the idea of building blocks that can be grafted onto an organization or severed with relatively little disturbance to either the blocks or the organization. Simon (1969) has argued for the attractiveness of this feature in that most complex systems can be decomposed into stable subassemblies and that these are the crucial elements in any organization or system. Thus, the coupling imagery gives researchers access to one of the more powerful ways of talking about complexity now available.

But if the concept of loose coupling highlights novel images heretofore unseen in organizational theory, what is it about these images that is worth seeing?

101

COUPLED ELEMENTS

There is no shortage of potential coupling elements, but neither is the population infinite.

At the outset the two most commonly discussed coupling mechanisms are the technical core of the organization and the authority of office. The relevance of those two mechanisms for the issue of identifying elements is that in the case of technical couplings, each element is some kind of technology, task, subtask, role, territory and person, and the couplings are task-induced. In the case of authority as the coupling mechanism, the elements include positions, offices, responsibilities, opportunities, rewards, and sanctions and it is the couplings among these elements that presumably hold the organization together. A compelling argument can be made that *neither* of these coupling mechanisms is prominent in educational organizations found in the United States. This leaves one with the question what *does* hold an educational organization together?

A short list of potential elements in educational organizations will provide background for subsequent propositions. March and Olsen (1975) utilize the elements of intention and action. There is a developing position in psychology which argues that intentions are a poor guide for action, intentions often follow rather than precede action, and that intentions and action are loosely coupled. Unfortunately, organizations continue to think that planning is a good thing, they spend much time on planning, and actions are assessed in terms of their fit with plans. Given a potential loose coupling between the intentions and actions of organizational members, it should come as no surprise that administrators are baffled and angered when things never happen the way they were supposed to.

Additional elements may consist of events like yesterday and tomorrow (what happened yesterday may be tightly or loosely coupled with what happens tomorrow) or hierarchial positions, like, top and bottom, line and staff, or administrators and teachers. An interesting set of elements that lends itself to the loose coupling imagery is means and ends. Frequently, several different means lead to the same outcome. When this happens, it can be argued that any one means is loosely coupled to the end in the sense that there are alternative pathways to achieve that same end. Other elements that might be found in loosely coupled educational systems are teachers-materials, voters-schoolboard, administrators-classroom, process-outcome, teacher-teacher, parent-teacher, and teacher-pupil.

While all of these elements are obvious, it is not a trivial matter to specify which elements are coupled. As the concept of coupling is crucial because of its ability to highlight the identity and separateness of elements that are momentarily attached, that conceptual asset puts pressure on the investigator to specify clearly the identity, separateness, and boundaries of the elements coupled. While there is some danger of reification when that kind of pressure is exerted, there is the even greater danger of portraying organizations in inappropriate terms which suggest an excess of unity, integration, coordination, and consensus. If one is nonspecific about boundaries in defining elements then it is easy—and careless—to assemble these ill-defined elements and talk about integrated organizations. It is not a trivial issue explaining how elements persevere over time. Weick, for example, has argued (1974: 363–364) that elements may appear or disappear and may merge or become separated in response to need-deprivations within the individual, group, and/or organization. This means that specification of elements is not a one-shot activity. Given the context of most organizations, elements both appear and disappear over time. For this reason a theory of how elements become loosely or tightly coupled may also have to take account of the fact that the nature and intensity of the coupling may itself serve to create or dissolve elements.

The question of what is available for coupling and decoupling within an organization is an eminently practical question for anyone wishing to have some leverage on a system.

STRENGTH OF COUPLING

Obviously there is no shortage of meanings for the phrase loose coupling. Researchers need to be clear in their own thinking about whether the phenomenon they are studying is described by two words or three. A researcher can study "loose coupling" in educational organizations or "loosely coupled systems." The shorter phrase, "loose coupling," simply connotes things, "anythings," that may be tied together either weakly or infrequently or slowly or with minimal interdependence. Whether those things that are loosely coupled exist in a system is of minor importance. Most discussions in this paper concern loosely coupled systems rather than loose coupling since it wishes to clarify the concepts involved in the perseverance of sets of elements across time.

The idea of loose coupling is evoked when people have a variety of situations in mind. For example, when people describe loosely coupled systems they are often referring to (1) slack times—times when there is an excessive amount of resources relative to demands; (2) occasions when any one of several means will produce the same end; (3) richly connected networks in which influence is slow to spread and/or is weak while spreading; (4) a relative lack of coordination, slow coordination or coordination that is dampened as it moves through a system; (5) a relative absence of regulations; (6) planned unresponsiveness; (7) actual causal independence; (8) poor observational capabilities on the part of a viewer; (9) infrequent inspection of activities within the system; (10) decentralization; (11) delegation of discretion; (12) the absence of linkages that should be present based on some theory—for example, in educational organizations the expected feedback linkage from outcome back to inputs is often nonexistent; (13) the observation that an organization's structure is not coterminus with its activity; (14) those occasions when no matter what you do things always come out the same—for instance, despite all kinds of changes in curriculum, materials, groupings, and so forth the outcomes in an educational situation remain the same; and (15) curricula or courses in educational organizations for which there are few prerequistes—the longer the string of prerequisties, the tighter the coupling.

POTENTIAL FUNCTIONS AND DYSFUNCTIONS OF
LOOSE COUPLING

It is important to note that the concept of loose coupling need not be used normatively. People who are steeped in the conventional literature of organizations may regard loose coupling as a sin or something to be apologized for. This paper takes a neutral, if not mildly affectionate, stance toward the concept. Apart from whatever affect one might feel toward the idea of loose coupling, it does appear a priori that certain functions can be served by having a system in which the elements are loosely coupled. Below are listed seven potential functions that could be associated with loose coupling plus additional reasons why each advantage might also be a liability. The dialectic generated by each of these oppositions begins to suggest dependent variables that should be sensitive to variations in the tightness of coupling.

The basic argument of Glassman (1973) is that loose coupling allows some portions of an organization to persist. Loose coupling lowers the probability that the organization will have to—or be able to—respond to each little change in the environment that occurs. The mechanism of voting, for example, allows elected officials to remain in office for a full term even though their constituency at any moment may disapprove of particular actions. Some identity and separateness of the element "elected official" is preserved relative to a second element, "constituency," by the fact of loosely coupled accountability which is measured in two, four, or six year terms. While loose coupling may foster perseverance, it is not selective in what is perpetuated. Thus archaic traditions as well as innovative improvisations may be perpetuated.

A second advantage of loose coupling is that it may provide a sensitive sensing mechanism. This possibility is suggested by Fritz Heider's perceptual theory of things and medium. Heider (1959) argues that perception is most accurate when a medium senses a thing and the medium contains many independent elements that can be externally constrained. When elements in a medium become either fewer in number and/or more internally constrained and/or more interdependent, their ability to represent some remote thing is decreased. Thus sand is a better medium to display wind currents than are rocks, the reason being that sand has more elements, more independence among the elements, and the elements are subject to a greater amount of external constraint than is the case for rocks. Using Heider's formulation metaphorically, it could be argued that loosely coupled systems preserve many independent sensing elements and therefore "know" their environments better than is true for more tightly coupled systems which have fewer externally constrained, independent elements. Balanced against this improvement in sensing is the possibility that the system would become increasingly vulnerable to producing faddish responses and interpretations. If the environment is known better, then this could induce more frequent changes in activities done in response to this "superior intelligence."

A third function is that a loosely coupled system may be a good system for localized adaptation. If all of the elements in a large system are loosely coupled to one another, then any one element can adjust to and modify a local unique contingency without affecting the whole system. These local adaptations can be swift, relatively economical, and substantial. By definition, the antithesis of localized adaptation is standardization and to the extent that standardization can be shown to be desirable, a loosely coupled system might exhibit fewer of these presumed benefits. For example, the localized adaptation characteristic of loosely coupled systems may result in a lessening of educational democracy.

Fourth, in loosely coupled systems where the identity, uniqueness, and separateness of elements is preserved, the system potentially can retain a greater number of mutations and novel solutions than would be the case with a tightly coupled system. A loosely coupled system could preserve more "cultural insurance" to be drawn upon in times of radical change than in the case for more tightly coupled systems. Loosely coupled systems may be elegant solutions to the problem that adaptation can preclude adaptability. When a specific system fits into an ecological niche and does so with great success, this adaptation can be costly. It can be costly because resouces which are useless in a current environment might deteriorate or disappear even though they could be crucial in a modified environment. It is conceivable that loosely coupled systems preserve more diversity in responding than do tightly coupled systems, and therefore can adapt to a considerably wider range of changes in the environment than would be true for tightly coupled systems. To appreciate the possible problems associated with this abundance of mutations, reconsider the dynamic outlined in the preceding discussion of localized adaptation. If a local set of elements can adapt to local idiosyncracies without involving the whole system, then this same loose coupling could also forestall the spread of advantageous mutations that exist somewhere in the system. While the system may contain novel solutions for new problems of adaptation, the very structure that allows these mutations to flourish may prevent their diffusion.

Fifth, if there is a breakdown in one portion of a loosely coupled system then this breakdown is sealed off and does not affect other portions of the organization. Previously we had noted that loosely coupled systems are an exquisite mechanism to adapt swiftly to local novelties and unique problems. Now we are carrying the analysis one step further, and arguing that when any element misfires or decays or deteriorates, the spread of this deterioration is checked in a loosely coupled system. While this point is reminiscent of earlier functions, the emphasis here is on the localization of trouble rather than the localization of adaptation. But even this potential benefit may be problematic. A loosely coupled system can isolate its trouble spots and prevent the trouble from spreading, but it should be difficult for the loosely coupled system to repair the defective element. If weak influences pass from the defective portions to the functioning portions, then the influence back from these functioning portions will also be weak and probably too little, too late.

Sixth, since some of the most important elements in educational organizations are teachers, classrooms, principals, and so forth, it may be consequential that in a loosely coupled system there is more room available for self-determination by the actors. If it is argued that a sense of efficacy is crucial for human beings, then a sense of efficacy might be greater in a loosely coupled system with autonomous units than it would be in a tightly coupled system where discretion is limited. A futher comment can be made about self-determination to provide an example of the kind of imagery that is invoked by the concept of loose coupling.

It is possible that much of the teacher's sense of—and actual—control comes from the fact that diverse interested parties expect the teacher to link their intentions with teaching actions. Such linking of diverse intentions with actual work probably involves considerable negotiation. A parent complains about a teacher's action and the teacher merely points out to the parent how the actions are really correspondent with the parent's desires for the education of his or her children. Since most actions have ambiguous consequences, it should always be possible to justify the action as fitting the intentions of those who complain. Salancik (1975) goes even farther and suggests the intriguing possibility that when the consequences of an action are ambiguous, the stated *intentions* of the action serve as surrogates for the consequences. Since it is not known whether reading a certain book is good or bad for a child, the fact that it is intended to be good for the child itself becomes justification for having the child read it. The potential trade-off implicit in this function of loose coupling is fascinating. There is an increase in autonomy in the sense that resistance is heightened, but this heightened resistance occurs at the price of shortening the chain of consequences that will flow from each autonomous actor's efforts. Each teacher will have to negotiate separately with the same complaining parent.

Seventh, a loosely coupled system should be relatively inexpensive to run because it takes time and money to coordinate people. As much of what happens and should happen inside educational organizations seems to be defined and validated outside the organization, schools are in the business of building and maintaining categories, a business that requires coordination only on a few specific issues—for instance, assignment of teachers. This reduction in the necessity for coordination results in fewer conflicts, fewer inconsistencies among activities, fewer discrepancies between categories and activity. Thus, loosely coupled systems seem to hold the costs of coordination to a minimum. Despite this being an inexpensive system, loose coupling is also a nonrational system of fund allocation and therefore, unspecifiable, unmodifiable, and incapable of being used as means of change.

When these several sets of functions and dysfunctions are examined, they begin to throw several research issues into relief. For example, oppositions proposed in each of the preceding seven points suggest the importance of contextual theories. A predicted outcome or its opposite should emerge depending on how and in what the loosely coupled system is embedded. The preceding oppositions also suggest a fairly self-contained research program. Suppose a researcher starts with the first point made, as loose coupling increases the system should contain a greater number of anachronistic practices. Loosely coupled systems should be conspicuous for their cultural lags. Initially, one would like to know whether that is plausible or not. But then one would want to examine in more fine-grained detail whether those anachronistic practices that are retained hinder the system or impose structure and absorb uncertainty thereby producing certain economies in responding. Similar embellishment and elaboration is possible for each function with the result that rich networks of propositions become visible. What is especially attractive about these networks is that there is little precedent for them in the organizational literature. Despite this, these propositions contain a great deal of face validity when they are used as filters to look at educational organizations. When compared, for example, with the bureaucratic template mentioned in the introduction, the template associated with loosely coupled systems seems to take the observer into more interesting territory and prods him or her to ask more interesting questions.

METHODOLOGY AND LOOSE COUPLING

An initial warning to researchers: the empirical observation of unpredictability is insufficient evidence for concluding that the elements in a system are loosely coupled. Buried in that caveat are a host of methodological intricacies. While there is ample reason to believe that loosely coupled systems can be seen and examined, it is also possible that the appearance of loose coupling will be nothing more than a testimonial to bad methodology. In psychology, for example, it has been argued that the chronic failure to predict behavior from attitudes is due to measurement error and not to the unrelatedness of these two events. Attitudes are said to be loosely coupled with behavior but it may be that this conclusion is an artifact produced because attitudes assessed by time-independent and context-independent measures are being used to predict behaviors that are time and context dependent. If both attitudes and behaviors were assessed with equivalent measures, then tight coupling might be the rule.

Any research agenda must be concerned with fleshing out the imagery of loose coupling—a task requiring a considerable amount of conceptual work to solve a few specific and rather tricky methodological problems before one can investigate loose compling.

By definition, if one goes into an organization and watches which parts affect which other parts, he or she will see the tightly coupled parts and the parts that vary the most. Those parts which vary slightly, infrequently, and aperiodically will be less visible. Notice, for example, that interaction data—who speaks to whom about what—are unlikely to reveal loose couplings. These are the most visible and obvious couplings and by the arguments developed in this paper perhaps some of the least crucial to understand what is going on in the organization.

An implied theme in this paper is that people tend to over-rationalize their activities and to attribute greater meaning, predictability, and coupling among them than in fact they have. If members tend to overrationalize their activity then their descriptions will not suggest which portions of that activity are loosely and tightly coupled. One might, in fact, even use the presence of apparent overrationalization as a potential clue that myth making, uncertainty, and loose coupling have been spotted.

J.G. March has argued that loose coupling can be spotted and examined only if one uses methodology that highlights and preserves rich detail about context. The necessity for a contextual methodology seems to arise, interestingly enough, from inside organization theory. The implied model involves cognitive limits on rationality and man as a single channel information processor. The basic methodological point is that if one wishes to observe loose coupling, then he has to see both what is and is not being done. The general idea is that time spent on one activity is time spent away from a second activity. A contextually sensitive methodology would record both the fact that some people are in one place generating events and the fact that these same people are thereby absent from some other place. The rule of thumb would be that a tight coupling in one part of the system can occur only if there is loose coupling in another part of the system. The problem that finite attention creates for a researcher is that if some outcome is observed for the organization, then it will not be obvious whether the outcome is due to activity in the tightly coupled sector or to inactivity in the loosely coupled sector. That is a provocative problem of interpretation. But the researcher should be forewarned that there are probably a finite number of tight couplings that can occur at any moment, that tight couplings in one place imply loose couplings elsewhere, and that it may be the *pattern* of couplings that produces the observed outcomes. Untangling such intricate issues may well require that new tools be developed for contextual understanding and that investigators be willing to substitute nonteleological thinking for teleological thinking (Steinbeck, 1941: chapt. 14).

Another contextually sensitive method is the use of comparative studies. It is the presumption of this methodology that taken-for-granted understandings—one possible "invisible" source of coupling in an otherwise loosely coupled system—are embedded in and contribute to a context. Thus, to see the effects of variations in these understandings one compares contexts that differ in conspicuous and meaningful ways.

Another methodological trap may await the person who tries to study loose coupling. Suppose one provides evidence that a particular goal is loosely coupled to a particular action. He or she says in effect, the person wanted to do this but in fact actually did that, thus, the action and the intention are loosely coupled. Now the problem for the researcher is that he or she may simply have focused on the wrong goal. There may be other goals which fit that particular action better. Perhaps if the researcher were aware of them, then the action and intention would appear to be tightly coupled. Any kind of intention-action, plan-behavior, or means-end depiction of loose coupling may be vulnerable to this sort of problem and an exhaustive listing of goals rather than parsimony should be the rule.

Two other methodological points should be noted. First, there are no good descriptions of the kinds of couplings that can occur among the several elements in educational organizations. Thus, a major initial research question is simply, what does a map of the couplings and elements within an educational organization look like? Second, there appear to be some fairly rich probes that might be used to uncover the nature of coupling within educational organizations. Conceivably, crucial couplings within schools involve the handling of disciplinary issues and social control, the question of how a teacher gets a book for the classroom, and the question of what kinds of innovations need to get clearance by whom. These relatively innocuous questions may be powerful means to learn which portions of a system are tightly and loosely coupled. Obviously these probes would be sampled if there was a full description of possible elements that can be coupled and possible kinds and strengths of couplings. These specific probes suggest, however, in addition that what holds an educational organization together may be a small number of tight couplings in out-of-the-way places.

ILLUSTRATIVE QUESTIONS FOR A RESEARCH AGENDA

Patterns of Loose and Tight Coupling: Certification versus Inspection

Suppose one assumes that education is an intrinsically uninspected and unevaluated activity. If education is intrinsically uninspected and unevaluated then how can one establish that it is occurring? One answer is to define clearly who can and who cannot do it and to whom. In an educational organization this is the activity of certification. It is around the issues of certification and of specifying who the pupils are that tight coupling would be predicted to occur when technology and outcome are unclear.

If one argues that "certification" is the question "who does the work" and "inspection" is the question "how well is the work done," then there can be either loose or tight control over either certification or inspection. Notice that setting the problem up this way suggests the importance of discovering the distribution of tight and loosely coupled systems within any organization. Up to now the phrase loosely coupled systems has been used to capture the fact that events in an organization seem to be temporally related rather than logically related (Cohen and March, 1974). Now that view is being enriched by arguing that any organization must deal with issues of certification (who does the work) and inspection (how well is the work done). It is further being suggested that in the case of educational organizations there is loose control on the work—the work is intrinsically uninspected and unevaluated or if it is evaluated it is done so infrequently and in a perfunctory manner—but that under these conditions it becomes crucial for the organization to have tight control over who does the work and on whom. This immediately suggests the importance of comparative research in which the other three combinations are examined, the question being, how do these alternative forms grow, adapt, manage their rhetoric and handle their clientele. Thus it would be important to find organizations in which the controls over certification and inspection are both loose, organizations where there is loose control over certification but tight control over inspection, and organizations in which there is tight control both over inspection and over certification. Such comparative research might be conducted among different kinds of educational organiza-

109

tions within a single country (military, private, religious schooling in the United States), between educational and noneducational organizations within the same country (for example, schools versus hospitals versus military versus business organizations) or between countries looking at solutions to the problem of education given different degrees of centralization. As suggested earlier, it may not be the existence or nonexistence of loose coupling that is a crucial determinant of organizational functioning over time but rather the patterning of loose and tight couplings. Comparative studies should answer the question of distribution.

If, as noted earlier, members within an organization (and researchers) will see and talk clearly about only those regions that are tightly coupled, then this suggests that members of educational organizations should be most explicit and certain when they are discussing issues related to certification for definition and regulation of teachers, pupils, topics, space, and resources. These are presumed to be the crucial issues that are tightly controlled. Increasing vagueness of description should occur when issues of substantive instruction—inspection—are discussed. Thus, those people who primarily manage the instructional business will be most vague in describing what they do, those people who primarily manage the certification rituals will be most explicit. This pattern is predicted *not* on the basis of the activities themselves—certification is easier to describe than inspection—but rather on the basis of the expectation that tightly coupled subsystems are more crucial to the survival of the system and therefore have received more linguistic work in the past and more agreement than is true for loosely coupled elements.

Core Technology and Organizational Form

A common tactic to understand complex organizations is to explore the possibility that the nature of the task being performed determines the shape of the organizational structure. This straightforward tactic raises some interesting puzzles about educational organizations. There are suggestions in the literature that education is a diffuse task, the technology is uncertain.

This first question suggests two alternatives: if the task is diffuse then would not any organizational form whatsoever be equally appropriate *or* should this directly compel a diffuse form of organizational structure? These two alternatives are not identical. The first suggests that if the task is diffuse then any one of a variety of quite specific organizational forms could be imposed on the organization and no differences would be observed. The thrust of the second argument is that there is one and only one organizational form that would fit well when there is a diffuse task, namely, a diffuse organizational form (for instance, an organized anarchy).

The second question asks if the task in an educational organization is diffuse then why do all educational organizations look the way they do, and why do they all look the same? If there is no clear task around which the shape of the organization can be formed then why is it that most educational organizations do have a form and why is it that most of these forms look indentical? One possibile answer is that the tasks of educational organizations does not constrain the form of the organization but rather this constraint is imposed by the ritual of certification and/or the agreements that are made in and by the environment. If any of these nontask possibilities are genuine alternative explanations, then the general literature on organizations has been insensitive to them.

One is therefore forced to ask the question, is it the case within educational organizations that the technology is unclear? So far it has been argued that loose coupling in educational organizations is partly the result of uncertain technology. If uncertain technology does not generate loose coupling then researchers must look elsewhere for the origin of these bonds.

Making Sense in/of Loosely Coupled Worlds

What kinds of information do loosely coupled systems provide members around which they can organize meanings, that is, what can one use in order to make sense of such fleeting structures? (By definition loosely coupled events are modestly predictable at best.) There is a rather barren structure that can be observed, reported on, and retrospected in order to make any sense. Given the ambiguity of loosely coupled structures, this suggests that there may be increased pressure on members to construct or negotiate some kind of social reality they can live with. Therefore, under conditions of loose coupling one should see considerable effort devoted to constructing social reality, a great amount of face work and linguistic work, numerous myths (Mitroff and Kilmann, 1975) and in general one should find a considerable amount of effort being devoted to punctuating this loosely coupled world and connecting it in some way in which it can be made sensible. Loosely coupled worlds do not look as if they would provide an individual many resources for sense making—with such little assistance in this task, a predominant activity should involve constructing social realities. Tightly coupled portions of a system should not exhibit nearly this preoccupation with linguistic work and the social construction of reality.

Coupling as a Dependent Variable

As a general rule, any research agenda on loose coupling should devote equal attention to loose coupling as a dependent and independent variable. Most suggestions have treated loose coupling as an independent variable. Less attention has been directed toward loose coupling as a dependent variable with the one exception of the earlier argument that one can afford loose coupling in either certification or inspection but not in both and, therefore, if one can locate a tight coupling for one of these two activities then he can predict as a dependent variable loose coupling for the other one.

Some investigators, however, should view loose coupling consistently as a dependent variable. The prototypic question would be, given prior conditions such as competition for scarce resources, logic built into a task, team teaching, conflict, striving for professionalism, presence of a central ministry of education, tenure, and so forth, what kind of coupling (loose or tight) among what kinds of elements occurs? If an organization faces a scarcity of resources its pattern of couplings should differ from when it faces an expansion of re-

111

sources (for instance, scarcity leads to stockpiling leads to decoupling). Part of the question here is, what kinds of changes in the environment are the variables of tight and loose coupling sensitive to? In response to what kinds of activities or what kinds of contexts is coupling seen to change and what kinds of environments or situations, when they change, seem to have no effect whatsoever on couplings within an organization? Answers to these questions, which are of vital importance in predicting the outcomes of any intervention, are most likely to occur if coupling is treated as a dependent variable and the question is, under what conditions will the couplings that emerge be tight or loose?

Assembling Loosely Connected Events

Suppose one assumes that there is nothing in the world except loosely coupled events. This assumption is close to Simon's stable subassemblies and empty world hypothesis and to the idea of cognitive limits on rationality. The imagery is that of numerous clusters of events that are tightly coupled within and loosely coupled between. These larger loosely coupled units would be what researchers usually call organizations. Notice that organizations formed this way are rather unusual kinds of organizations because they are neither tightly connected, nor explicitly bounded, but they are stable. The research question then becomes, how does it happen that loosely coupled events which remain loosely coupled are institutionally held together in one organization which retains few controls over central activities? Stated differently, how does it happen that someone can take a series of loosely coupled events, assemble them into an organization of loosely coupled systems, and the events remain both loosely coupled but the organization itself survives? It is common to observe that large organizations have loosely connected sectors. The questions are, what makes this possible, how does it happen? What the structure in school systems seems to consist of is categories (for example, teacher, pupil, reading) which are linked by understanding and legitimated exogenously (that is, by the world outside the organization). As John Meyer (1975) puts it, "the system works because everyone knows everyone else knows roughly what is to go on . . . . Educational organizations are holding companies containing shares of stock in uninspected activities and subunits which are largely given their meaning, reality, and value in the wider social market." Note the potential fragility of this fabric of legitimacy.

It remains to be seen under what conditions loosely coupled systems are fragile structures because they are shored up by consensual anticipations, retrospections, and understanding that can dissolve and under what conditions they are resilient structures because they contain mutations, localized adaptation, and fewer costs of coordination.

Separate Intending and Acting Components

Intention and action are often loosely coupled within a single individual. Salancik (1975) has suggested some conditions under which dispositions within a single individual may be loosely coupled. These include such suggestions as follows.

(1) If intentions are not clear and unambiguous, then the use of them to select actions which will fulfill the intentions will be imperfect. (2) If the consequences of action are not known, then the use of intention to select action will be imperfect. (3) If the means by which an intention is transformed into an action are not known or in conflict, then the coupling of action to intention will be imperfect. (4) If intentions are not known to a person at the time of selecting an action, then the relationships between action and intention will be imperfect. This may be more common than expected because this possibility is not allowed by so-called rational models of man. People often have to recall their intentions after they act or reconstruct these intentions, or invent them. (5) If there exists a set of multiple intentions which can determine a set of similar multiple actions, then the ability to detect a relationship between any one intention and any one action is likely to be imperfect. To illustrate, if there is an intention A which implies selecting actions X and Y, and there is also an intention B which implies selecting actions X and Y, then it is possible that under both presence and absence of intention A, action X will be selected. Given these circumstances, an observer will falsely conclude that this relationship is indeterminant.

The preceding list has the potential limitation for organizational inquiry in that it consists of events within a single person. This limitation is not serious *if* the ideas are used as metaphors or if each event is lodged in a different person. For example, one could lodge intention with one person and action with some other person. With this separation, then all of the above conditions may produce loose coupling between these actors but additional conditions also come into play given this geographical separation of intention from action. For example, the simple additional requirement that the intentions must be communicated to the second actor and in such a way that they control his actions, will increase the potential for error and loose coupling. Thus any discussion of separate locations for intention and action within an organization virtually requires that the investigator specify the additional conditions under which the intending component can control the acting component. Aside from the problems of communication and control when intention and action are separated there are at least two additional conditions that could produce loose coupling.

1. If there are several diverse intending components all of whom are dependent on the same actor for implementing action, then the relationship between any one intention and any one action will be imperfect. The teacher in the classroom may well be the prototype of this condition.

2. The process outlined in the preceding item can become even more complicated, and the linkages between intention and action even looser, if the single acting component has intentions of its own.

Intention and action are often split within organizations. This paper suggests that if one were to map the pattern of intention and action components within the organization these would coincide with loosely coupled systems identified by other means. Furthermore, the preceding propositions begin to suggest conditions under which the same components might be at one moment tightly coupled and at the next moment loosely coupled.

CONCLUSION: A STATEMENT OF PRIORITIES

More time should be spent examining the possibility that educational organizations are most usefully viewed as loosely coupled systems. The concept of organizations as loosely coupled systems can have a substantial effect on existing perspectives about organizations. To probe further into the plausibility of that assertion, it is suggested that the following research priorities constitute a reasonable approach to the examination of loosely coupled systems.

1. Develop Conceptual Tools Capable of Preserving Loosely Coupled Systems

It is clear that more conceptual work has to be done before other lines of inquiry on this topic are launched. Much of the blandness in organizational theory these days can be traced to investigators applying impoverished images to organizational settings. If researchers immediately start stalking the elusive loosely coupled system with imperfect language and concepts, they will perpetuate the blandness of organizational theory. To see the importance of and necessity for this conceptual activity the reader should reexamine the 15 different connotations of the phrase "loose coupling" that are uncovered in this paper. They provide 15 alternative explanations for any researcher who claims that some outcome is due to loose coupling.

2. Explicate What Elements Are Available in Educational Organizations for Coupling

This activity has high priority because it is essential to know the practical domain within which the coupling phenomena occur. Since there is the further complication that elements may appear or disappear as a function of context and time, this type of inventory is essential at an early stage of inquiry. An indirect benefit of making this a high priority activity is that it will stem the counterproductive suspicion that "the number of elements in educational organizations is infinite." The reasonable reply to that comment is that if one is precise in defining and drawing boundaries around elements, then the number of elements will be less than imagined. Furthermore, the researcher can reduce the number of relevant elements if he has some theoretical ideas in mind. These theoretical ideas should be one of the outcomes of initial activity devoted to language and concept development (Priority 1).

3. Develop Contextual Methodology

Given favorable outcomes from the preceding two steps, researchers should then be eager to look at complex issues such as patterns of tight and loose coupling keeping in mind that loose coupling creates major problems for the researcher because he is trained and equipped to decipher predictable, tightly coupled worlds. To "see" loosely coupled worlds unconventional methodologies need to be developed and conventional methodologies that are underexploited need to be given more attention. Among the existing tools that should be refined to study loose coupling are comparative studies and longitudinal studies. Among the new tools that should be "invented" because of their potential relevance to loosely coupled systems are nonteleological thinking (Steinbeck, 1941), concurrence methodology (Bateson, 1972: 180–201), and Hegelian, Kantian, and Singerian inquiring systems (Mitroff, 1974). While these latter methodologies are unconventional within social science, so too is it unconventional to urge that we treat unpredictability (loose coupling) as our topic of interest rather than a nuisance.

4. Promote the Collection of Thorough, Concrete Descriptions of the Coupling Patterns in Actual Educational Organizations

No descriptive studies have been available to show what couplings in what patterns and with what strengths existed in current educational organizations. This oversight should be remedied as soon as possible.

Adequate descriptions should be of great interest to the practitioner who wants to know how his influence attempts will spread and with what intensity. Adequate description should also show practitioners how their organizations may be more sensible and adaptive than they suspect. Thorough descriptions of coupling should show checks and balances, localized controls, stabilizing mechanisms, and subtle feedback loops that keep the organization stable and that would promote its decay if they were tampered with.

The benefits for the researcher of full descriptions are that they would suggest which locations and which questions about loose coupling are most likely to explain sizeable portions of the variance in organizational outcomes. For example, on the basis of good descriptive work, it might be found that both tightly and loosely coupled systems "know" their environments with equal accuracy in which case, the earlier line of theorizing about "thing and medium" would be given a lower priority.

5. Specify the Nature of Core Technology in Educational Organizations

A suprisingly large number of the ideas presented in this paper assume that the typical coupling mechanisms of authority of office and logic of the task do not operate in educational organizations. Inquiry into loosely coupled systems was triggered partly by efforts to discover what *does* accomplish the coupling in school systems. Before the investigation of loose coupling goes too far, it should be established that authority and task are not prominent coupling mechanisms in schools. The assertions that they are not prominent seem to issue from a combination of informal observation, implausibility, wishful thinking, looking at the wrong things, and rather vague definitions of core technology and reward structures within education. If these two coupling mechanisms were defined clearly, studied carefully, and found to be weak and/or nonexistent in schools, *then* there would be a powerful justification for proceeding vigorously to study loosely coupled systems. Given the absence of work that definitively discounts these coupling mechanisms in education and given the fact that these two mechanisms have accounted for much of the observed couplings in other kinds of organizations, it seems crucial to look for them in educational organizations in the interest of parsimony.

It should be emphasized that if it *is* found that substantial coupling within educational organizations is due to authority of office and logic of the task, this does not negate the agenda that is sketched out in this paper. Instead, such discoveries would (1) make it even more crucial to look for patterns of coupling to explain outcomes, (2) focus attention on tight and loose couplings within task and authority induced couplings, (3) alert researchers to keep close watch for any coupling mechanisms other than these two, and (4) would direct comparative research toward settings in which these two coupling mechanisms vary in strength and form.

6. Probe Empirically the Ratio of Functions to Dysfunctions Associated with Loose Coupling

Although the word "function" has had a checkered history, it is used here without apology—and without the surplus meanings and ideology that have become attached to it. Earlier several potential benefits of loose coupling were described and these descriptions were balanced by additional suggestions of potential liabilities. If one adopts an evolutionary epistemology, then over time one expects that entities develop a more exquisite fit with their ecological niches. Given that assumption, one then argues that if loosely coupled systems exist and if they have existed for sometime, then they bestow some net advantage to their inhabitants and/or their constituencies. It is not obvious, however, what these advantages are. A set of studies showing how schools benefit and suffer given their structure as loosely coupled systems should do much to improve the quality of thinking devoted to organizational analysis.

7. Discover How Inhabitants Make Sense Out of Loosely Coupled Worlds

Scientists are going to have some big problems when their topic of inquiry becomes low probability couplings, but just as scientists have special problems comprehending loosely coupled worlds so too must the inhabitants of these worlds. It would seem that quite early in a research program on loose coupling, examination of this question should be started since it has direct relevance to those practitioners who must thread their way through such "invisible" worlds and must concern their sense-making and stories in such a way that they don't bump into each other while doing so.

Karl E. Weick is a professor of psychology and organizational behavior at Cornell University.

REFERENCES

Bateson, Mary Catherine
1972 Our Own Metaphor. New York: Knopf.

Cohen, Michael D., and James G. March
1974 Leadership and Ambiguity. New York: McGraw-Hill.

Glassman, R. B.
1973 "Persistence and loose coupling in living systems." Behavioral Science, 18: 83–98.

Heider, Fritz
1959 "Thing and medium." Psychological Issues, 1 (3): 1–34.

March, J. G., and J. P. Olsen
1975 Choice Situations in Loosely Coupled Worlds. Unpublished manuscript, Stanford University.

Meyer, John W.
1975 Notes on the Structure of Educational Organizations. Unpublished manuscript, Stanford University.

Mitroff, Ian I.
1974 The Subjective Side of Science. New York: Elsevier.

Mitroff, Ian I., and Ralph H. Kilmann
1975 On Organizational Stories: An Approach to the Design and Analysis of Organizations Through Myths and Stories. Unpublished manuscript, University of Pittsburgh.

Salancik, Gerald R.
1975 Notes on Loose Coupling: Linking Intentions to Actions.

Unpublished manuscript, University of Illinois, Urbana-Champaign.

Simon, H. A.
1969 'The architecture of complexity." Proceedings of the American Philosophical Society, 106: 467–482.

Steinbeck, John
1941 The Log from the Sea of Cortez. New York: Viking.

Stephens, John M.
1967 The Process of Schooling. New York: Holt, Rinehart, and Winston.

Weick, Karl E.
1974 "Middle range theories of social systems." Behavioral Science, 19: 357–367.

117

Cultures and
Institutional Histories

Belief and Loyalty
in College Organization

BY BURTON R. CLARK

My premise is that there are ideational elements in complex organizations that do not lie outside of matters of governance but rather exist as basic sentiments that help determine the structures of governance and how they work.[1] In this approach, problems of governance are seen to vary with the quality of institutional self-conception. The key mediating elements in this relationship are loyalty and trust. In the causal flow, the organizational self-conception heavily determines the degree of loyalty and trust, which in turn affects in a major way the problems and forms of governance.

Sociologists commonly conceive of two broad dimensions of social bonding: the structural, consisting of patterns of relation and interaction of persons and groups, and the normative, consisting of shared beliefs, attitudes, and values. The two dimensions appear in complex organizations as organizational structure, including informal patterns, and "organizational culture." When we approach issues of governance in colleges and universities, we have an overwhelming tendency to fix on the

---

[1]My formulation of a basic relation between institutional beliefs and institutional governance has been stimulated by verbal and written comments of Albert J. Cohen of the University of Connecticut.

Burton R. Clark *is the chairman of the Department of Sociology at Yale University.*

499

dimension of structure. We look to see how much authority is located in the position of the president, how authority is delegated and otherwise caused to be located in various subunits, and how the committee system operates. We seek the mechanisms that allow faculty and administrative authority to exist simultaneously and provide a reasonable degree of peaceful effectiveness most of the time. When we want to improve things, we ask how to "restructure" the organization. My purpose here is to fix on the other dimension, that of organizational culture. I wish to dramatize the importance of normative bonding in the formal organization, so that we will always ask about its fundamental beliefs as well as its fundamental structures. This means that when we want to improve things, specifically governance, we will ask how to "re-norm" the organization or how to alter the basic beliefs of the personnel and other participants about the nature of the enterprise.

How does normative bonding occur in formal organizations? There are undoubtedly many ways, of which we have thus far dimly sensed only a few. I will concentrate here on one fundamental route, that of development of an institutional story. I will refer to this phenomenon as an organizational saga. In the following pages, I will first discuss the concept of a saga; then, drawing upon research on small colleges, describe the build-up of college sagas; and, thirdly, emphasize the consequences of a saga for loyalty and trust.[2] The last section of the paper speculates on the nature of belief and loyalty in large universities, as compared with small colleges, and attempts to specify the matter of governance as problems of a sense of the whole and the social conditions of trust.

An organizational saga is a collective understanding of unique accomplishment in a formally established group. Based on past exploits, the formal group develops a unitary sense of highly valuable performance and place. The group's definition of the situation, intrinsically historical, links stages of organizational development. The definition is also embellished: while based

[2]These sections draw upon Burton R. Clark, *The Distinctive College: Antioch, Reed, and Swarthmore* (Chicago: Aldine Publishing Company, 1970) and Burton R. Clark, "The Saga of the Formal Place," the revised version of a paper presented at the annual meeting of the American Sociological Association in September, 1970, at Washington, D.C.

500

on a past reality, it has, over time, through retelling and rewriting, become rounded and sentimental. The participants have added affect, an emotional loading that places the understanding between the affective coolness of rational purpose and manipulative doctrine and the capitulation to sentiment found in religion and magic. An organizational saga presents some administrative logic, some rational explanation of how certain means led to certain ends, but it also contains a sense of romance and mystery that turns a formal place into a deeply beloved institution. Participants are passionate to the point where we say they partake of the gospel of the organization.

Most organizations probably develop in time at least a weak legend for some segment of their personnel. Those who have together persisted for some years in one formal place will have had, at minimum, a thin stream of shared experience into which neither they nor anyone else can ever step again. Sensing that flow of common fate, they find cause to elaborate a plausible account of uniqueness. The story helps rationalize for the individual his commitment of time and energy for years, perhaps for a lifetime, to a particular enterprise. Even when weak, the belief can compensate in part for the loss of meaning in much modern work. If labor itself does not provide direct satisfaction, there is all the more reason to clutch the pleasure of the story that gives some cultural identity to one's otherwise routine instrumental efforts. By this reasoning, the loss of craftsmanship heightens the tendency to add value to one's involvement by tooling and retooling a symbolic expression, a minor legend of some sort. At the other end of the continuum, among the deviant cases of extreme expression, a saga engages the mind and the heart so intensely as to make one's immediate place overwhelmingly valuable.

Organizational sagas also vary in durability. We seem to find fragility in organizational legends that bloom quickly in relatively unstructured social settings, as in the case of professional sports organizations that operate in the volatile context of contact with large spectator audiences through the mass media. For example: the New York Mets professional baseball team created a rags-to-riches legend in a few months' time in the

501

123

summer of 1969, one that greatly excited millions of people. This instant saga, which gave so much life and unity and pride, was also highly fragile as an ongoing definition of the organization. For a variety of reasons, the story could be removed quickly from the collective understanding of the present (and future) and placed in memory of the concluded past. In such instances of the highly perishable organizational saga, "successful" performance is often unstable. The original events that set the direction of belief can be readily reversed by later opposite happenings, with the great winners becoming quickly just another bunch of habitual losers. The saga must then be seriously amended or replaced by a story of the fall from grace. Such cases, too, seem to entail an undependable structural connection between the organization and the base of believers. The large mass base is not anchored within the organization itself or in personal ties between insiders and outsiders, but rather floats at the end of the line of mass media mediation, away from firm control by the organization. Thus, in first approximation, such sagas continue to have direct effect only as the organization goes on repeating its earlier success and also keeps the mood of detached followers from straying to other sources of excitement and identification.

In contrast, we observe high durability in organizational sagas when they are built relatively slowly in relatively stable, highly structured social contexts. One such arena is the educational system, specifically for our purposes here the realm of liberal arts colleges in American higher education. Within a cohort of hundreds of small private colleges, the exciting story of special performance emerges not in a few months but at a minimum over a number of years and more likely in a decade or two. When the saga is firmly in place, it is embodied in many steady components of the organization, affecting the definitions and performances of the future and finding protection in the webbing of the institutional parts. The exciting story will erode sooner or later, but it has a stubborn capacity to continue. It is not here today and gone tomorrow; it can be relegated to the shelves of history only by years of attenuation or organizational decline into crisis.

502

How do strong and durable organizational sagas develop? The possibilities in college organization are illuminated by developments in three distinctive and highly regarded American colleges, Reed, Antioch, and Swarthmore.

We distinguish two stages in the building of an organizational saga, its initiation and its fulfillment. Initiation takes place under widely varying conditions and occurs within a relatively short period of time. Fulfillment converges on certain inescapable features of organization that are enduring and more predictable.

Sagas do not develop strongly in passive organizations, those tuned to adaptive servicing of demand or to the obedient filling of role dictated by higher authorities. The saga is initially strong purpose, born in an image of the future conceived and enunciated by a single man or a small cadre. The first task of the agents of change is to find a setting that is open, or can be opened, to a special effort. The most obvious setting is the autonomous new organization. In the new place, there is no established structure, no rigid custom. The environment may stand back for a while, especially if a deliberate effort has been made to establish initial autonomy and bordering outsiders are preoccupied with their old problems. A leader may also there have the notable advantage of building from the top down, appointing lieutenants and picking up recruits who like his banner and the sound of his drums.

Among liberal arts colleges, Reed College is heavily characterized by the phenomenon of a saga, and its embellished story of hard-won excellence and nonconformity began as strong purpose in a new organization. Its first president, William T. Foster, a thirty-year-old high-minded reformer, took himself from the sophisticated East of Harvard and Bowdoin to the untutored Northwest, to an unbuilt campus on land in suburban Portland in 1910 precisely because he did not want to be trapped in established institutions, all of which, including his alma mater Harvard, were to his mind corrupt in practice. The projected college in Oregon was clear ground, intellectually as well as physically, and he would there assemble the people and devise the practices that would finally give this country an

503

academically pure college, a Balliol for America. The later saga was initiated by a man with a mission, one stubborn to a fault, who took a new organization as his means of creating a distinctive college.

The second setting for initiation is the established organization in a crisis of decay. The deep crisis born of sustained decline is the great eraser of prior commitments. Those in charge, after years of attempting to muddle through with incremental adjustment, realize finally that they must either give up established ways or give up the organization. Preferring to survive, they may relinquish the helm with grudging gratitude to the one proposing a plan that promises revival and later strength, or they may even accept a man of utopian intent. Deep crisis in the established organization thus re-creates some of the conditions of the new organization. It suspends past practice; it forces some bordering groups to stand back a pace, to give the victim air, or even causes them to turn their backs and flee at the sight of the organizational mess; and it tends to catch the attention of the reformer who is looking for a great opportunity. As we have long known, crisis is the natural condition for charisma, and the institutional call goes out for the unusual man "who can save us."

Antioch College is a dramatic case in American higher education of the revolutionary overturn that leads to a saga. Started in the 1850's, its first seventy years were characterized by little money, weak staff, few students, and obscurity. Never too strong, the condition of the college worsened in the 1910's under the inflation and other strains of World War I, and in 1919 Antioch tottered on the edge of the grave. At that time, a charismatic utopian reformer, Arthur E. Morgan, came in contact with the college. He decided it was more advantageous to take over an old college, available for the asking, with buildings and a charter, than to start a new one. He grabbed hold, first as a trustee and then as president, and took off in the early 1920's in a fantastic bit of institutional renovation, overturning everything from the trustees on down. As president, he found it easy to push aside old, badly debilitated structures and usages. He elaborated a grand plan of general education in-

504

volving an unusual combination of work, study, and community participation, and he set about to devise the implementing tool. For a few years, even up to a decade, the place belonged to him. Crisis and charisma made possible a radical transformation out of which came "a second Antioch," a college soon characterized by a sense of exciting history, unique practice, and exceptional performance.

The third context of initiation is the established organization that is viable rather than in crisis, secure in person rather than collapsing from long decline, yet in a state of readiness for evolutionary change. This is the most difficult situation to illuminate and predict, having to do with degrees of rigidity in established successful organizations. In both ideology and structure, institutionalized colleges vary in openness to change. In those under church control, for example, the colleges of the more liberal Protestant denominations have been more hospitable than Catholic colleges, at least until recently, to educational experimentation. A college with a tradition of presidential power is more fertile ground than one where the trustees check the water fountains and the professors spin a tight collegial web around the president's office. Particularly promising is the college in a state of self-defined need for educational leadership: "We have just had for twenty years a good business-affairs man in the presidential chair, and now it is time for some leadership on the educational side." This is the opening for which some reformers watch. They seek neither the drama and danger of the new college nor the trauma of one deep in crisis, but the solid footing of the sound place that has some ambition to rise in academic stature.

Swarthmore is a case in point. Begun in the 1860's, it had become by 1920 a secure and stable college, prudently managed by Quaker trustees and administrators and solidly based in traditional support from nearby Quaker families in Pennsylvania, New Jersey, and Maryland. Such an organization would not usually be thought promising for reform, but Frank Aydelotte, who came to the presidency of Swarthmore in 1920, judged it ripe for change. At the time, Aydelotte was a promising, well-sponsored man in the marketplace of college adminis-

505

127

tration. Magnetic in personality, highly placed within the elite circle of former Rhodes Scholars, personally liked by important foundation officials, and recommended as a scholarly leader, he was offered other college presidencies. He picked Swarthmore as a decent place appropriate for an effort to jump to the first rank, open to change through a combination of financial health, liberal Quaker ethos, and some institutional ambition. His judgment proved correct, although the tolerance for his gradual changes in the 1920's and 1930's was narrow at times and a less forceful man might not have squeezed through. The point is that he perceived openness in a traditional setting and moved in with his mission, his plan for change. He began the gradual introduction of a modified Oxford honors program and a host of related changes, setting in motion a stream of events and noteworthy achievements that supporters were to identify later as the Swarthmore saga.

While the conditions of initiation of a legend vary, the means of durable embodiment are more predictable, converging on certain inescapable features of organization. There are, of course, unique features in each case and a host of detailed ways in which a unified sense of a special history is expressed. In a liberal arts college, one may find a patch of sidewalk or a coffee room partaking of a legend, evoking emotion among the believers. But such bits and pieces can be grouped analytically in major and minor categories and we can seek to assert, for broad classes of organization, the components that are at the center of the development of a saga. As a beginning, we identify in American colleges: the personnel core; the program core; the external social base; the student subculture; and the organizational ideology itself.

The personnel core. We have spoken of a saga as a story of a development, a story believed by an organized group which becomes more united by sharing the belief. In a college, the key group of believers is the senior faculty. When the senior men are hostile to an emerging theme, however it was introduced, its attenuation is ensured; when they are passive, its success is anemic; and when they are devoted to the idea, the making of a saga is probable. A single leader, a college presi-

506

dent, can initiate the change, but the organizational idea will not be expanded over the years and expressed in performance unless ranking and powerful members of the faculty swing into line and remain committed while the initiator is present and, especially, after he is gone. The leader is perishable; he is only one, and increasingly the implementing work is the work of others. As they invest themselves deeply, taking some credit for the change and seeking to insure its future, charisma is routinized in collegial authority. The faculty cadre of true believers, formed over years and potentially self-replacing for decades, helps to effect the legend, then to protect it against later presidents and other new participants who, less pure in belief, are ready to swing the organization in some other direction.

After ten to fifteen years of the effort to build distinctively, such faculty cadres were well developed at Reed, Antioch, and Swarthmore. In all cases, the senior faculty took over after the departure of the change agent or agents, with the succeeding president a man appropriate for consolidation or for the full working out of the experiment. The faculty believers also replaced themselves well, through socialization and selective recruitment and retention, passing the mantle in the 1940's and 1950's to a second generation. Meanwhile, new potential innovators had sometimes to be beaten back. In such instances, faculty power to protect faculty belief was the main means of shielding the distinctive effort against erosion or deflection. At Reed, for example, major clashes between president and faculty in the late 1930's and the early 1950's were precipitated by a new change-minded president, coming in from the outside, squaring off with a faculty proud of what had been done, attached deeply to what the college had become, and determined to maintain what was for them, the students, the alumni, and many outsiders—friend and foe—the distinctive Reed style. From the standpoint of creating a regional and national model of purity and severity in undergraduate education, the Reed faculty did on those occasions, in its own stubborn way, serve creatively while acting conservatively.

The program core. For a college to transform purpose into an exciting story of accomplishment, there must be visible practices

507

around which claims of distinctiveness can be elaborated. We find a celebration of innovative courses and requirements, special methods of teaching, and a climate of learning not duplicated elsewhere. On the basis of a few unique practices, the program becomes over time a set of communal symbols and rituals, rich with invested meaning. Academic men point to their decorated spears, their village totems, their bracelets signifying honor and beauty, as they speak proudly of the courses and curricula they have lovingly fashioned by hand and the trials they have devised for students to give great meaning to what otherwise would be only a paper credential. A simple thing like not reporting grades to the students becomes a symbol (as at Reed) that the whole college cares about learning for learning's sake. Thus inflated, mere instructional technique becomes part of a general legend.

In the three colleges at hand, the program was seen by insiders and outsiders alike as the heart of distinctiveness, the center of the exciting story. At Swarthmore, it was the special seminars and other practices of the honors program, capped by written and oral examination at the hands of teams of visiting outsiders in the last days of the senior year. At Antioch, it was the work-study cycle, the special set of general education requirements, and the legitimating of community involvement as a form of education. At Reed, it was the required freshman lecture-and-seminar courses, the junior qualifying examination, and the thesis in the senior year. Such practices became the core content of a belief that here things had been done so differently and to such a degree, against the mainstream and often against imposing odds, that the group had been party to a saga.

The social base. The institutional story becomes fixed also in the minds of some outside believers, a segment external to the physical boundaries of the campus, who have become deeply devoted to the institution. Usually the core of the external social base is the alumni of the changed institution. When a college saga is strong, this extended family is second to none in sentimental attachment to the general visions and the specific symbols of what the college has become. The alumni are the best located to hold beliefs enduringly pure. They are of the

508

institution, yet do not have to face directly the new problems generated by a changing environment or an evolving input of students. For them the embodied and exciting idea of the college can be everything, taking on the qualities of an untouchable saga.

The relatively liberal or radical alumni here become conservative, seeking to protect what they believe to be a unique liberal or radical institution from all the conservative forces of society which might change the college to pull it back in line, make it like other places. The alumni at Antioch, Reed, and Swarthmore all have exhibited this small paradox. At Reed, for example, dropouts as well as graduates constitute an alumni struck by the intellectual power of their small college, convinced that life on that tight little island has been unlike life anywhere else, and ready to conserve the practices that seem to sustain the mysterious power of the campus. Here, too, for a time, one might interpret conservative acts as contributing to an innovation, protecting a distinctive place while it attempts a full working out of the potential of a particular direction of effort.

The student subculture. The student body is the third group within which we find essential believers, not as overwhelmingly important as they in full pride are likely to think but still a necessary support for the legend. If the definitions of the dominant student subculture do not reflect the central theme of the institution, then that theme will weaken. To become and remain a legend, a change must be supported by the student subculture over decades, integrating significantly with the central ideas of the believing administrators and faculty. When the students define themselves as personally responsible for upholding what the college has become and are ready to take on enemies, real or imagined, then a design or plan has become to an important degree an organizational saga.

At Antioch, Reed, and Swarthmore, the student subcultures have been powerful mechanisms for carrying a developing legend from one generation to another over a long period. Reed students, almost from the beginning and extending at least to the early 1960's, were unexcelled believers in the uniqueness and

509

power of their campus, constantly on the alert for any action that would alter the place, even fearful that some men in the administration and faculty might succumb to pressures of the day and seek to make Reed into a college that would be just like all the others. Students at Antioch and Swarthmore also have long offered unstinting support for the respective institutional idea. Each student body steadily and dependably transfers campus ideals from one generation to another. Often socializing deeply, they help produce the graduate who never quite rids himself of the wish to go home again, that is, back to the campus. To marry such a graduate is to find that one has also married a college. A tiny place, of no account in the large affairs of society, observers might say, and yet there are clearly those who deeply love it.

The ideology. Finally, the invested institutional idea has self-sustaining capacity. Upheld by faculty, alumni, and students, expressed in the practices of the teaching encounter, the institutional theme is even more widely a generalized tradition expressed in statues and ceremonies, written histories and current catalogs, even in an "air about the place" felt by participants and some outsiders. The more special the empirical history and the more forceful the claim to a place in history, the more intensely cultivated are the ways of sharing memory and symbolizing the institution. The idea spills over everywhere, to be found on paper, in concrete, on the faces of men. Thus, so widely and deeply embodied, in so many linking parts, the legend is a strong self-fulfilling belief. Working through institutional self-image and public image, a saga is indeed a switchman, in Weber's famous phrase, helping to determine the tracks along which action is pushed by men's self-defined interests. In short, a developing ideology of a special history can help make a special history.

As a picture of the institution that is at once encompassing and sentimental, an organizational saga is an unparalleled means of unity. It forges links across internal divisions and organizational boundaries, as internal and external groups emotionally share their common belief. It binds together various operations of work and avenues of participation, emphasizing the

510

whole over the parts, as the specific forms are seen to have contributed to the making and expressing of the story. Most important, the saga deeply commits the individual to the organization. With deep emotional engagement, some believers significantly define themselves by their organizational affiliation. Their bondage to other believers is like that of comrades in a cause: they share an intense sense of the unique, knowing a beautiful secret. A symptom of a powerful saga is a feeling that there are really two worlds—the small blessed one of the lucky few and the large routine one of the rest. An emotional bond of this quality turns the membership into a community, even a cult. It maximizes for the individual the satisfaction of being associated with the organization which far surpasses the rewards of money and skill in the job. The organization becomes a model in a sense of what the individual wants to be: a social being with clear identity, a proven ability to cope, and a social definition of success. At the least, the individual has the satisfaction of playing a small part in a successful group effort.

An organizational saga is thus a valuable resource, created over a number of years out of the social components of the formal enterprise. As participants become ideologues, their common institutional definition becomes a foundation for trust, easing communication and cooperation. With little regard for the clock, they extend and intensify their efforts in what others call work. They are uncommonly happy when the organization is well and unusually sad when it is not. We find them loyal beyond reason. Such bonding has effects beyond that of enlarged effort and enhanced morale by giving the organization a competitive edge in recruiting and maintaining personnel. It is capital against the vicious circle of organizational decline in which some actual or anticipated erosion of organizational strength leads to the exit of some personnel, which leads to further decline and more exit. A high degree of loyalty causes individuals to stay with a system, to save and improve it rather than to exit to serve self-interest elsewhere. The genesis and persistence of loyalty is a key organizational and analytical problem. Enduring loyalty follows from a collective belief of

511

personnel and followers that their organization is special, that, at least for them, it is distinctive. That kind of belief comes from a credible story of uncommon effort, achievement, and form.

Pride in the organized group and pride in one's identity as taken from the group are personal returns that are in short supply in modern social involvement. The development of organizational legends is one way in which organizational man increases such rewards. The concept of the organizational saga, therefore, finally steers our attention to dimensions of pride and joy in organizational life. As we study the devotional ties of the formal institution we move closer to the fundamental differences among organizations in their capacity to enhance or diminish our lives. In the organization possessed by a saga, we find at least for a time a formal place in which men happily accept their bond and their condition. They would have it no other way.

Small colleges possessed by sagas can govern themselves somewhat differently from colleges of the same size that have only a weak self-belief. Among those sharing the deep emotional commitment in a saga-defined college, the felt commonality is the backbone of a sense of relationships firmly bridged. Differences and conflicts are seen as secondary, and solvable through informal exchange among comrades. Normative capital accumulates that can be spent in emergencies without incurring a normative deficit. With this source of linkage working overtime, the tendency lessens to seek new administrative structure as the solution to all problems. Those who are aggrieved argue the relevance of their actions for the institutional idea to which nearly all are committed. Due process and adjudicating procedure are given little weight. In contrast, the weaker normative bonding in the institutions of weak self-belief gives greater play to the factionalism and fragmentation inherent in the specialized commitments and orientations of the academic disciplines and the normal division of work into "administration" and "faculty" and "academic" and "business." As belief in the part ascends over belief in the whole, loyalty attaches to the part rather than the whole. Governance then calls for more

512

mediation among the parts, with a tendency to explicate the mediation in quasi-formal and formal rules of procedure. As normative bonding weakens, even in systems of small scope, one or more internal groups will develop a self-interest in having informal relations replaced by more discernible structure. Surely almost all of us at one time or another have been agents of this bureaucratic tendency. We seek to insure through rules what we feel is no longer reasonably provided through ties of sentiment and unified belief.

But in small educational systems, this tendency need not go very far. Administrators, faculty members, and students often encounter one another, spontaneously and informally—as well as deliberately and formally—as they enter the common mailroom, walk the paths between the few buildings, and share the tables in the cafeteria. So even if there is not much common belief, or the unified belief is only weak in expression, there is likely to be some capital of interpersonal trust on which to operate, some of which can be spent in handling the worst conflicts when they occur.

As we move from small colleges to modest-size universities and then to large multiversities, we not only tend toward formal structure but it also becomes exceedingly difficult to develop a credible story that embraces the whole. On ideational as well as structural grounds, belief in and loyalty to the whole will likely weaken. Moral or ideational capital will be in short supply and all too readily exhausted in time of conflict, crisis, or decline. The formal burdens of governance are thereby increased considerably, with little to resort to other than further elaboration of rules and due-process machinery of conflict resolution.

If the large campus becomes an administered political system of factions of divergent belief, solutions to problems of governance must tend basically in one of two directions: (1) to accept the general nature of the system and then seek to devise the best machinery for the formal representation of factions and the formal resolution of conflicts; or (2) to change the nature of the system in the direction of more unified belief and the reducing of factions. Most large campuses tend in the first direction.

513

135

Sensing that they are evermore like vast industrial conglomerates, held together by an administrative framework, they seek new or enlarged formal patterns that will channel conflict into peaceful streams. Much attention must go to the legitimation of such patterns, since the social conditions of trust here take the form of participants coming to believe they can get fair treatment in processes due them. No one particularly expects to turn out to work for the common interest since it is hard to know what the common interest is. There is little to fall back on, normatively, in times of stress. The best way to prepare for governmental stress in such settings is to build up a capital of formal procedure. If the procedures are prepared in depth, securely interlocked, and coated with acceptance, they may, we hope, hold us together in the worst of times.

Some large campuses attempt to solve the problem of governance by moving in the second direction, toward more unified self-belief and a reduction rather than an explication and formalization of factions. We usually call this move "decentralization." We try to make certain components of the whole relatively self-contained and autonomous, to create a confederation of units each small enough and sufficiently limited in its concerns to develop its own mission, its own culture and community, and even its own saga to some degree. One's organizational end-in-view is to create units of a size and scope appropriate for developing over time a sense of a distinctive whole. The social conditions of trust here reside in shared belief as well as the intimacy of interaction. Down this road, we teach ourselves to rely in governance on shared belief, informal influence, satisfaction, and loyalty.

One can make a powerful case for moving in either of the two directions discussed above. The overall size of the American system of mass higher education alone argues persuasively that the first direction is the primary route. With that many students, many very large campuses seem a practical necessity, particularly as we take into account the business and economic models that have long informed the definitions of the situation held by legislators and state officials. The decentralization ap-

514

proach then seems excessively romantic. On the other hand, the feeling will not down in nearly all campus circles that the first way is not the best way, that we must decentralize to create the units most conducive to education work. This route, too, at times seems a practical necessity, particularly as we take into account the collegial model that has long informed the faculty's definition of the situation and the expectations of students that they will be seen and treated as individuals. Decentralization may be the price of peace where these faculty and student definitions have not been met but remain enduringly strong.

The phenomenon of the organizational saga, observed in extreme form in Antioch, Reed, and Swarthmore, is a powerful argument for the second route. There are such rich personal and institutional returns from sagas as to argue strongly for those forms of academic organization that make them most likely. Even in modest strength, a saga adds much meaning to the work of administrators and faculty and the transitory participation of the students. When seen as a matter of degree, rather than all-or-nothing, we can encourage ourselves to create, even in adverse settings, those general conditions that are conducive to this and other forms of normative bonding. The normative build-up changes materially the nature of administration and governance.

Thus as we trace the effects of an organizational saga on belief and trust and then on the problems of governance, we turn our attention away from such structural changes as bicameralism and altered representation on committees and focus instead on the size and scope and mission of the entity that is to be governed. We return to the embodiment of goals in the historical development of an organization and what meaning is thus available to those who give so much of their lives there. In raising explicitly the matter of whether and how academic groups come to have rewarding collective representations of themselves, we perhaps in the end can even link matters of governance to the quality of life within the modern college and university.

515

J O U R N A L   O F   H I G H E R   E D U C A T I O N

C O M M E N T   B Y   R I C H A R D   C .   R I C H A R D S O N ,   J R .

Belief in and loyalty to an institutional saga are the least difficult to maintain when an institution is small and when those involved represent true believers in their own uniqueness. Increases in size and complexity reduce opportunities for interaction and hence attenuate the degree to which new faculty, students, and supporting constituencies can become imbued with the loyalty that is characteristic of the initiators of the saga. Hence it may be said that the greater the growth, the more difficult it will become to create or maintain the saga and its corresponding beliefs and loyalties.

The concept of normative bonding, the procedure through which belief and loyalty develop, is a critical one in that an organization can operate effectively only as long as a certain core of values is held in common. The critical question concerns the circumstances under which such bonding is likely to take place. It is quite apparent that within the complex institution it is highly unlikely that norms can be superimposed by the leader whose role seems to be increasingly defined in terms of establishing procedures through which conflict can be resolved. Values are likely to be held in common only as long as there continues to exist a high degree of interaction among constituent groups. For practical purposes, therefore, we must discount the likelihood that contrived values can either be established or maintained in the absence of the conditions of the restricted models described in Mr. Clark's paper.

It would appear that the development of an institutional story or saga as a source of belief and loyalty is dependent upon a number of variables that must come into being or exist concurrently. Among these variables may be included a strong and preferably charismatic leader, a receptive faculty, a viable and compelling ideology that lends a sense of purpose, limited size, relative isolation, and a period of grace or freedom from

RICHARD C. RICHARDSON, JR., *is the president of the Northampton County Area Community College at Bethlehem, Pennsylvania.*

516

138

the impingement of strong external influences. Such constellations of variables have occurred in the past, and may occur again in the future with respect to small private institutions. They are far less likely to occur in public institutions in general, and in large public institutions in particular. Therefore, we are left with a model which, if operational at all, can apply only to a limited segment of higher education.

These comments on the model are not intended to suggest any lack of faith in the importance of the normative dimension within institutions of higher education; rather, they are used to emphasize the importance of procedures through which norms may be developed and maintained in complex organizations where the saga, if it exists at all, is likely to be weak and subject to conflicting interpretations. Under such circumstances, belief in and loyalty to the uniqueness of an institution may be improbable. However, it may be possible to induce belief in and loyalty to the procedures through which the institution guarantees to individuals the right to their interpretation of the institutional saga.

Even if it were possible to develop an institutional saga in our larger institutions, we would need to raise the question of the implications of such a saga for adaptability when confronted with the need for change. A strong saga, as is pointed out in the paper, requires a high degree of internalization of values by all constituencies. As more faculty and students become involved, the question of what represents the true belief must inevitably occur with increasing frequency and intensity. Again, the small stable institution has a far greater chance to create and maintain the resistance to change characteristic of a strong institutional saga than does the large or rapidly growing institution with its constant need to adapt to ever varying circumstances.

To overcome these limitations, Mr. Clark raises the question of whether an institution can be both large and small simultaneously. In other words, can the process of decentralization create the conditions under which an institutional saga of sorts can be created and maintained, at least for the subunits of the

517

system. It is probable that this question can be answered in the affirmative. However, if the most common element of decentralization, the department, is to become the subunit, it is very apparent that the norms developed within such a subunit may bear little resemblance to what many perceive as the best interests of the larger system. It is this very tendency for decentralized units to develop norms that oppose the thrust of the larger system which causes the constant movement between centralization and decentralization which we can observe in most large systems. Since the need for autonomy can never be entirely satisfied without the destruction of the larger system, decentralization can proceed only to the point where the larger system is threatened. At that point, the interests of the larger system reassert themselves and an opposite movement in the direction of centralization takes place.

Another disadvantage of decentralization, at least as it can be observed among departments, is that the loyalty to such subunits replaces loyalty to the institution. While it can certainly be argued that there are viable units of decentralization other than the department, we must also recognize the difficulty of superimposing small units on a larger collectivity, especially where this is done as an alternative to dealing with basic issues.

If we reject the applicability of the institutional saga for large, complex institutions, we must still consider the need for loyalty and belief in such institutions as an integrating and perpetuating force.

Those who have studied the problems created by growth in size and increasing exposure to external constituencies have, as Mr. Clark points out, tended to stress one of two approaches. Some have emphasized restructuring, while others have emphasized re-norming through the use of decentralization or human relations approaches. Each group has tended somewhat to denigrate the efforts of the other, and to feel that it alone represents the true approach to the resolution of role conflict and the redefinition of institutional relationships and directions.

It is probable that the answer lies in a synthesis of the two approaches, since in large complex organizations the satisfac-

518

tion of the higher order needs of the participants requires structures that are considerably more sophisticated and sensitive than those that now exist. Arguments concerning the merits of centralization versus decentralization to reconcile the need for increased autonomy with the need for institutional coordination are the source of much of the confusion that currently permeates the efforts of practitioners to cope with these issues.

It can be argued that it may not be necessary to choose between the two; we may be able to achieve both simultaneously through the creation of structures which are based on a realistic comprehension of human motivation and which are oriented toward problem solving rather than coordination. It may well be necessary to create parallel structures to accomplish this task. We may need one structure for involving individuals in the process of problem solving and conflict resolution, while a separate structure may be necessary to coordinate the essential activities of the total organization. In the past, we have attempted to find individuals who can serve as leaders in the process of solving problems and as preservers of the institutional order simultaneously. Perhaps we need different kinds of individuals in our parallel structures so that the same person is not torn between his responsibility to support the larger goals of the institution as defined by the board of trustees and his responsibility to provide the kind of environment within which individuals and subunits may achieve the development of loyalty and trust.

In the final analysis, we must recognize the interrelatedness between structure and the maintenance of norms. Each is dependent upon the other. Without a structure which provides for "procedures prepared in depth, securely interlocked, and coated with acceptance" we cannot have the formal arrangements required by large institutions to create the conditions under which interaction essential to the maintenance of norms can take place. By the same token, if the norms that exist do not support the prevailing structure, then the lack of credibility will destroy the institution's capability of achieving that level of consensus necessary to maintain institutional integrity. It

519

is not a question of either restructuring or re-norming, rather it is a question of how the relative importance of these two interdependent variables can be recognized and interwoven to create belief and loyalty and, above all, a continuing sense of institutional purpose and direction.

520

The Review of Higher Education
Winter 1985, Volume 8, No. 2
Pages 157-168

ORGANIZATIONAL CULTURE IN THE STUDY OF HIGHER EDUCATION

Andrew T. Masland

The pervasive influence of organizational culture has recently recaptured the attention of those who study organizations. Ouchi's *Theory Z* (1981), Pascale and Athos' *The Art of Japanese Management* (1981), and Deal and Kennedy's *Corporate Cultures* (1982) describe how organizational culture profoundly influences managerial behavior. This paper first defines organizational culture and briefly examines how the concept has been applied to colleges and universities. It then describes possible approaches and techniques for uncovering the influence of organizational culture. Finally, the paper explores why the study of organizational culture is relevant to researchers and practitioners. Thus, the paper defines and illustrates the application of a useful perspective on higher education.

The literature has previously recognized that there is more to organizations than formal structure. The classic elements of organizational design such as hierarchical structure, formalization, rationality, and specialization are important (Tosi, 1975), but they do not fully explain organizational behavior. Leadership, for example, can transform an organization with a formal structure of rules and objectives into an institution that is a "responsive, adaptive organism" (Selznick, 1957, p. 5).

Pettigrew (1979) expands upon Selznick's study of organizations. Pettigrew views leadership and values as one part of a concept he calls organizational culture. He defines organizational culture as "the amalgam of beliefs, ideology, language, ritual, and myth" (1979, p. 572). Pettigrew argues that an organization is a continuing social system and the elements of culture exert a powerful control over the behavior of those within it. Organizational culture induces purpose, commitment,

Andrew T. Masland in the Center for the Study of Higher Education at The Pennsylvania State University.

and order; provides meaning and social cohesion; and clarifies and explains behavioral expectations. Culture influences an organization through the people within it.

The recent popular literature on Japanese management techniques highlights the influence of organizational culture. Pascale and Athos (1981) describe organizational culture as the glue that holds an organization together. It is a "bass clef" that conveys at a deep level what management really cares about. Theory Z (Ouchi, 1981) is a specific configuration of cultural beliefs and values. Ouchi asserts that this particular combination of cultural elements is largely responsible for the success of Japanese businesses. In contrast to Ouchi, Deal and Kennedy (1982) propose that a variety of corporate cultures can increase organizational effectiveness. A strongly articulated culture tells employees what is expected of them and how to behave under a given set of circumstances. The coherence of thought and action a strong culture produces thus enhances organizational success. Corporations with weak cultures do not have the sense of purpose and direction that is found in those with strong cultures, and are often less successful (Deal & Kennedy, 1982).

It is somewhat ironic that widespread interest in the interaction of culture and management grew out of studies of Japanese firms. As Chait (1982), Dill (1982), and Wyer (1982) note, traditional administrative practices common in American colleges and universities are similar to Japanese management styles. Shared governance and collegiality are participatory management. Academic departments, in discussions of future direction, quality control, and problem resolution, function like quality circles. Tenure traditionally provides the economic and psychological benefits of lifetime employment. Although colleges and universities have long benefited from these managerial practices, they have not been identified as "organizational culture."

The concept of organizational culture is not new to higher education, however. Clark (1980) notes that the lofty doctrines associated with colleges and universities elicit almost religious emotions. He defines four cultural spheres that affect academic life in this way. They are (a) the cultures of specific academic disciplines, (b) the culture of the academic profession, (c) institutional cultures, and (d) the cultures of national systems of higher education. These four elements reflect academic structures. This paper focuses on the third category, the cultures of specific institutions.

The strength of institutional culture depends on several factors (Clark, 1980). Primary among them is the scale of the organization. Small organizations tend to have stronger cultures than do large organizations. Second is the tightness of the organization. Colleges with highly interdependent parts have stronger cultures than those with autonomous parts. Third is the age of the organization. As discussed below, culture develops over time and an institution with a long history simply has a larger foundation upon which to build its culture. Finally, the institution's founding influences the strength of its culture. A traumatic birth or transformation, like a long history, provides a stronger base upon which to build cultural values and beliefs. In colleges with stronger cultures there is greater coherence among beliefs, language, ritual, and myth. Weak cultures lack this coherence.

Clark's description of organizational saga is a classic embodiment of academic culture. Saga is a "collective understanding of unique accomplishment in a formally established group" (Clark, 1972, p. 179). It is a set of beliefs and values tied together in a story about the institution's past. A saga strengthens the bond between the organization and students, alumni, faculty, and staff. A saga shapes social reality on the campus and thus helps control behavior. According to Clark saga intensifies organizational commitment and feelings of membership in a special community. The trust and loyalty a saga produces are valuable resources in preserving organizational strength.

At the institutional level culture affects many aspects of campus life. There is a long history of interest in student culture and its effects (see, for example, Feldman & Newcomb, 1969; Becker, Geer, Hughes, & Strauss, 1961). Similar to the study of student culture is research on organizational climate—the atmosphere or style of life on a campus (Pace, 1968). A wide variety of instruments measure climate, but they classify institutions by standard typologies and are heavily influenced by psychological constructs. Organizational culture, on the other hand, focuses on the shared values, beliefs, and ideologies which are unique to a campus. Thus measures of climate do not illuminate culture.

Organizational culture also affects curriculum and administration. Masland (1982), for example, demonstrates that organizational culture influences how academic computing fits into an institution's curriculum. As might be expected, a college that values a traditional liberal arts education is less apt to introduce a technical computing major. On the other hand, a college that primarily teaches business and management will want to introduce its students to the practical applications of computing that support business decisions. Along somewhat similar lines, an organization's culture affects the management of computer resources. A belief that students should have free access to computer resources in the same way that they have unlimited library resources is part of some campus cultures. But when computer resources are scarce, allocating them among competing users is a difficult task. This problem would not arise if institutional values did not stress unlimited access to educational resources.

Thus, the literature on higher education has begun to apply the concept of organizational culture—the implicit values, beliefs, and ideologies of those within an organization. In particular, research demonstrates that in higher education culture can affect student life, administration, and curriculum.

While organizational culture is becoming more widely used and accepted, it is still difficult to find clear and succinct methods of uncovering an institution's culture. Typical of the means given for discovering organizational culture is this description.

> All one has to do to get a feel for how the different cultures of competing businesses manifest themselves is to spend a day visiting each. . . . There are characteristic ways of making decisions, relating to bosses, and choosing people to fill key jobs (Schwartz & Davis, 1981, p. 30).

Although this may be true, the advice is rather vague for the researcher who wants to study organizational culture. The difficulty in studying culture arises because culture is implicit, and we are all embedded in our own cultures. In order to observe organizational culture, the researcher must find its visible and explicit manifestations (Schein, 1981).

Windows on Organizational Culture

Fortunately, there are methods available which uncover manifestations of organizational culture. Each involves looking for a specific influence of culture at work and from that evidence deducing something about the culture itself. Examination of organizational history, for example, often illuminates culture and its influences because culture develops over time through the actions and words of organizational leaders. Cultural manifestations can also be seen in current actions. The methods used to make decisions, agendas of meetings, and personnel policy are common arenas for cultural influences. To understand an organization's culture one must pay close attention to the details of daily life. There are a number of windows on organizational culture that make it easier to see both past and present cultural influences. This article focuses on four in particular: saga, heroes, symbols, and rituals. While there are a variety of ways to "see" culture, these four are particularly helpful, in part because they are easy to understand and apply. These four windows are closely related and may seem redundant, yet there are subtle differences among them.

Saga like heroes: Symbols and rituals

Saga (Clark, 1972) is the first window on organizational culture in higher education. A saga usually has its roots in an organization's history, and it describes a unique accomplishment of the organization. An institution's saga codifies what sets a college apart from others. Key faculty members, students, and alumni usually support an institution's saga, as do unique academic program elements and images about the institution. Clark uses Antioch, Swarthmore, and Reed as examples of three colleges with strong sagas. He demonstrates how the sagas at these schools profoundly influence institutional life. At Reed College, for example, the saga dates from the school's founding in 1910 by William T. Foster. The first president established a college known for "hard-won excellence and nonconformity" (Clark, 1972, p. 180). Antioch's saga arose from the influence of reformer Arthur E. Morgan who completely restructured Antioch and launched a saga based on combining work, study, and community participation.

Heroes

Organizational heroes or Saints (Deal & Kennedy, 1982; Dill, 1982) are a second window on organizational culture. Heroes are people who are important to an organization and often represent ideals and values in human form. They may play a central role in an institution's saga because heroes are people who have made crucial decisions or who exemplify behavior suitable to the college. They are role models, set standards, and preserve what makes the organization unique. People in an organization tell stories about heroes and the examples they set. The stories about heroes are another way to see organizational culture. They are passed down to newcomers in an organization as examples of successful behavior in the past.

Often, a college's founder is an organizational hero. The examples of Reed and Antioch cited above illustrate such heroes. Another example is a small college that has always combined liberal arts with career-oriented programs for women. Its founder stated that he wanted to provide women with an education that would make them self-sufficient. The college does this, and it did so long before the current trend towards career education began. The school's founder set an example personnel at the college endeavor to follow. A hero at a business college provides a final illustration. He was a long-time faculty member and administrator who fought for accreditation from an important agency. His long battle demonstrated and validated the value college personnel place on excellence.

Symbols

Symbols are a third window on organizational culture. A symbol can represent implicit cultural values and beliefs, thus, making them tangible. Personnel can point to a symbol as a concrete example much the same way that a hero personifies cultural values. Symbols also can serve an important external function. While heroes and stories may only be known to those within an organization, the public may recognize organizational symbols.

The business college mentioned above provides an excellent example of how a symbol gives insight into culture. The college has fairly extensive computer resources. It uses them to introduce students to the techniques and knowledge they will need in tomorrow's business environment. The desire to do this stems in part from the value the college places on leadership and excellence in business education. The computer facilities are a symbol of this value.

Metaphor is another type of symbol that is helpful in understanding organizational culture. The language people use when they talk about an organization reveals its culture. As with other symbols, metaphors make explicit normally implicit cultural values and beliefs (Beaudoin, 1981). Because metaphors help express that which usually is difficult to verbalize, they are an excellent key for unlocking culture. Masland (1982) examined a college that described its computer facilities as "supermarket computing." This is a vivid metaphor that invokes an image of practicality and value in the institution's approach to computing.

Rituals

Rituals are another means of identifying cultural values, beliefs, and ideologies. Rituals are a useful tool for uncovering culture because they translate culture into action. They provide tangible evidence of culture. An outstanding teaching award ceremony, for example, can demonstrate to an academic community the strength of the institution's values. Is such a ceremony taken seriously and the recipient seen as receiving a great honor, or is it dismissed as meaningless? If the institution values excellence in teaching, the former is more likely than the latter. Rituals provide continuity with the past. They demonstrate that old values and beliefs still play a role in campus life. Rituals also provide meaning. In an organization with ambiguous goals and uncertain outcomes, the annual convocation ceremony may provide a sense of meaning and direction for personnel. This kind of ritual reinforces the institution's culture. Moreover, daily rituals of interaction between faculty and administrators illustrate the relative importance of each group and the ideologies surrounding their roles.

Collecting Cultural Data

Saga, heroes, rituals, and symbols are means of exploring an organization's culture. In a strong culture they work in unison and illustrate the culture. But the researcher still needs specific methodologies to learn about each window. The common techniques described below are useful ways of examining the four cultural windows and thus culture itself.

Interviews, observation, and document analysis are three basic techniques. Of the three, interviews may be the most important. According to Gorden (1975), interviews are the most effective means of gathering data on beliefs, attitudes, and values. But because culture is implicit interview questions cannot ask about culture directly. Instead the researcher should probe the four cultural windows discussed above. Asking respondents what makes their college distinct or unique, or what makes it stand apart from similar schools a prospective applicant might consider, uncovers organizational saga. Similar questions focus on the school's educational philosophy and what is unique about its academic mission. Respondents draw upon their understanding of the institution's saga when answering such questions. They disclose what the college means to them. They also refer to the symbols and rituals that represent this meaning in a more tangible form. Thus listening carefully to responses in an interview is an excellent means of uncovering manifestations of organizational culture.

Interviewees may also respond positively to questions about organizational heroes, although referring to them as heroes may be counterproductive. It can be helpful to ask respondents to describe who the organization remembers and why they are remembered. Questions about organizational heroes are closely connected to questions about institutional history. Because cultural values and beliefs become institutionalized slowly over a period of time, their influence on past events is often apparent. Interviews are an excellent means of gathering such data.

Members of various campus constituencies such as faculty, students, administrators, and staff should be included in the interview sample. Snowball sampling (Murphy, 1980), in which one respondent suggests others who might also have valuable information, is one useful sampling method. With such a sampling plan the investigator can locate those individuals who have the greatest knowledge of the college.

Observation, a second useful technique, can be used concurrently with interviews. It is not simply classical observation of decision makers at work, committee meetings, or faculty members' teaching. Rather, it is also observing from many sources what is important in daily life on the campus. Through observation one can learn which issues receive careful attention and close scrutiny. Such issues are often central to the organization's culture.

Observation is a valuable means of learning more about cultural symbols, rituals, and heroes. As an outsider, an observer often sees symbols to which community members have become habituated. Thus, the observer may recognize the implicit meaning and importance of symbols that an insider takes at face value. As with symbols, an outsider may see rituals that insiders do not notice. These are the small, daily rituals that illustrate the relative value placed on different people or positions in the organization. Moreover, the memories of heroes are often immortalized in paintings, statues, or buildings.

A third technique is analysis of written documents. Document analysis is a useful means of filling in the gaps interviews and observation leave. It is also a valuable addition because documents are not subject to problems of selective recall and reinterpretation in light of the contemporary situation (Murphy, 1980).

Document analysis is an efficient method of gathering background information on the college. It is well suited for collecting data on institutional history. Historical accounts provide past examples of cultural influences while also illuminating the development of values, beliefs, and ideologies. Presidential annual reports often reference particularly important or traumatic events and decisions. Similarly, reports of blue ribbon committees may contain information about organizational culture. Campus newspapers may refer to key events and decisions. Those that create controversy often come closest to important cultural values and beliefs. Document analysis is also a means of learning more about the college's curriculum and its relationship to the campus culture. Worth noting are the unique features of a curriculum and why they exist. Finally, documents often highlight important and continuing rituals such as convocations or award ceremonies.

Several types of documents lend themselves to cultural analysis. These can include, but are not limited to, official college publications, correspondence, minutes of meetings, campus newspapers, and college histories. Institutional mission statements, planning documents, and self-studies for accreditation may also be useful. While such documents may seem trite (Chait, 1979), they are part of an organization's culture. Particularly in an organization with a strong culture, a mission statement reflects the institution's culture.

In summary, the use of interviews, observation, and document analysis encourages triangulation (Denzin, 1970). Each technique can confirm, disconfirm, or modify data obtained using the other two. Differences among the data must be investigated and the reasons for inconsistencies uncovered. In organizations with a strong culture, data from each source should confirm the other two because written statements, actions, and oral descriptions all form a coherent whole. Discrepancies among the data sources may indicate a weak or fractured culture.

Analysis of Cultural Data

Qualitative data collected while investigating organizational culture are usually complex and voluminous. Analysis begins and is concurrent with data collection. While gathering information, researchers may begin to see themes and trends in what people say about the organization and what they observe. These preliminary findings are then tested and further explored as the data collection process continues.

A basic technique for analyzing cultural data is thematic analysis— finding the recurrent cultural themes in the data (Schatzman & Strauss, 1973). Using this approach, the analyst structures and codes the data in order to distill important aspects of the organizational culture. Once researchers discover the underlying themes, they must determine how the themes fit together. Gradually, the analyst refines the principal ideas that recur throughout and begins to develop the central "story line" on the institution's culture. On a campus with a strong culture the analytic process is relatively straightforward because the data are consistent. If the culture is weak, the themes will not be as strong and the data may show discrepancies.

Consistency in cultural images takes several forms. Each respondent often refers to the same organizational heroes. Trends or problems which reappear over the history of the organization point to important cultural elements. Rituals and symbols support the culture. The clarity of values and the ways in which people act on them will be apparent. Another key to analysis is to look for the repeated use of symbols and rituals. Those repeated in many different contexts point to fundamental cultural features (Ortner, 1973). Important parts of the organization's culture are often associated with several different symbols or rituals.

151

Why Study Organizational Culture?

Over the past decade the perspectives on academic governance have expanded from the bureaucratic model to include political concepts and those of organized anarchies (Baldridge, 1971; Cohen & March, 1974). The concept of organizational culture may also provide valuable insight into colleges and universities. On a theoretical level, cultural analysis is another tool for researchers. Understanding the culture of a particular institution may further explain campus management because culture appears to influence managerial style and decision practices. Analysis of culture may expose conflicting cultural elements which could lead to ineffective behavior and plans. It might also help explain variations in curriculum and resistance to curricular change. Additional empirical research is needed to explore this area.

There is another argument that makes the study of organizational culture appear even more central to higher education. Organizational culture is what Leifer (1979) calls an unobtrusive organizational control. Unobtrusive controls operate in conjunction with two other levels of control mechanisms. Explicit controls (such as formal regulations and direct comments) and implicit controls (such as specialization and hierarchy) also influence organizational life. But when explicit and implicit controls are weak, the unobtrusive forces such as organizational culture become more important. A college or university campus is the classic example of an organization with weak explicit and implicit control mechanicms (Cohen & March, 1974; March & Olsen, 1976). Thus, it seems all the more appropriate to study organizational culture in higher education in greater depth.

Organizational culture is also useful on a practical level. Exploration of organizational culture may help explain how an organization arrived at its current state. Culture may explicate past influences on decisions and actions. It may provide an underlying rationale for institutional development. This understanding can then provide a better foundation for administrators' decision making (Smith & Steadman, 1981).

Finally, as colleges and universities confront the challenges of the eighties, a better comprehension of organizational culture may be vital at a broader level. As institutions and systems of higher education expand, academic culture fragments (Clark, 1980; Dill, 1982). Larger institutions, increased autonomy of institutional units, and specialization within disciplines contribute to what Clark calls the move from an "integrated academic culture" to "the many cultures of the conglomeration" (1980, p. 25). If, as this paper suggests, culture is a critical element of institutional life and management, it deserves careful attention. In fact, Dill (1982) argues that administrators must "manage" academic cultures during these times of decline because an institution derives strength from its culture. Institutional culture relieves some of the pressures and strains that decline puts on the social fabric of an organization. It does this because culture is a force that provides stability and a sense of continuity to an ongoing social system such as a college or university. Managing a force such as culture is a difficult task at best. The first step is acknowledging culture's existence and trying to understand the cultures of individual campuses. The techiques outlined above are useful in this respect.

In conclusion, exploring organizational culture is another means of learning more about colleges and universities. Traditional approaches to studying governance and decision making provide useful insights into why and how higher education works the way it does. But the perspective of cultural influences supplements the traditional approaches. It may further explain the variations found among colleges and universities. Although organizational culture is difficult to identify and study, it is worth the effort. Further investigation of organizational culture is needed to uncover its specific influence on the college and university campus. Before this is possible, however, culture needs to become part of the common parlance of researchers in higher education.

References

Baldridge, J. V. (1971). **Power and conflict in the university.** New York: John Wiley.

Beaudoin, D. B. (1981). **Presidents' metaphors and educational leadership.** Unpublished manuscript. Harvard University, Harvard Graduate School of Education, Cambridge.

Becker, H. S., Geer, B., Hughes, E. C., & Strauss, A. L. (1961). **Boys in white.** Chicago: University of Chicago Press.

Chait, R. P. (1979, July 16). Mission madness strikes our colleges. **The Chronicle of Higher Education,** p. 36.

Chait, R. P. (1982, March/April). Look who invented Japanese management! **AGB Reports,** pp. 3-7.

Clark, B. R. (1972). The organizational saga in higher education. **Administrative Science Quarterly, 17,** 179-194.

Clark, B. R. (1980, March). **Academic culture.** Working Paper, IHERG-42, Yale University, Higher Education Research Group.

Cohen, M. D., & March, J. G. (1974). **Leadership and ambiguity.** New York: McGraw-Hill.

Deal, T. E., & Kennedy, A. A. (1982). **Corporate cultures.** Reading, MA: Addison-Wesley.

Denzin, N. K. (1970). **The research act: A theoretical introduction to sociological methods.** Chicago: Aldine Publishing.

Dill, D. D. (1982). The management of academic culture: Notes on the management of meaning and social integration. **Higher Education, 11,** 303-320.

Feldman, K. A., & Newcomb, T. M. (1969). **The impact of college on students.** San Francisco: Jossey-Bass.

Gorden, R. L. (1975). **Interviewing: Strategy, techniques, and tactics.** Homewood, IL: Dorsey Press.

Leifer, R. (1979, June). **The social construction of reality and the evolution of mythology as a means for understanding organizational control processes.** Paper presented at the international meeting of the Institute of Management Science, Honolulu, Hawaii.

March, J. G., & Olsen, J. P. (1976). **Ambiguity and choice in organizations.** Bergen, Norway: Universitetsforlaget.

Masland, A. T. (1982). **Organizational influences on computer use in higher education.** Unpublished doctoral dissertation, Harvard University, Cambridge.

Murphy, J. T. (1980). **Getting the facts: A field guide for evaluation and policy analysis.** Santa Monica, CA: Goodyear Publishing.

Ortner, S. B. (1973). On key symbols. **American Anthropologist, 75,** 1338-1346.

Ouchi, W. (1981). **Theory Z: How American businesses can meet the Japanese challenge.** Reading, MA: Addison-Wesley.

Pace, C. R. (1968). The measurement of college environments. In R. Tagiuri & G. H. Litwin (Eds.), **Organizational climate** (pp. 127-147). Boston: Harvard University, Division of Business Research.

Pascale, R. T., & Athos, A. G. (1981). **The art of Japanese management.** New York: Simon & Schuster.

Pettigrew, A. M. (1979). On studying organizational cultures. **Administrative Science Quarterly, 24,** 570-581.

Schatzman, L., & Strauss, A. L. (1973). **Field research: Strategies for a natural sociology.** Englewood Cliffs, NJ: Prentice Hall.

Schein, E. H. (1981). Does Japanese management have a message for American managers. **Sloan Management Review, 23**(1), 55-68.

Schwartz, H., & Davis, S. M. (1981). Matching corporate culture and business strategy. **Organizational Dynamics, 10,** 30-48.

Selznick, P. (1957). **Leadership in administration.** New York: Harper & Row.

Smith, G. D., & Steadman, L. E. (1981). Present value of corporate history. **Harvard Business Review, 59**(6), 164-173.

Tosi, H. C. (1975). **Theories of organization.** Chicago: St. Clair Press.

Wyer, J. C. (1982). Theory Z—the collegial model revisited: An essay review. **The Review of Higher Education, 5**(2), 111-117.

Power in Academic
Organizations

THE CONCEPT OF POWER

by Robert A. Dahl

Department of Political Science, Yale University

What is "power"? Most people have an intuitive notion of what it means. But scientists have not yet formulated a statement of the concept of power that is rigorous enough to be of use in the systematic study of this important social phenomenon. Power is here defined in terms of a relation between people, and is expressed in simple symbolic notation. From this definition is developed a statement of power comparability, or the relative degree of power held by two or more persons. With these concepts it is possible for example, to rank members of the United States Senate according to their "power" over legislation on foreign policy and on tax and fiscal policy.

THAT some people have more power than others is one of the most palpable facts of human existence. Because of this, the concept of power is as ancient and ubiquitous as any that social theory can boast. If these assertions needed any documentation, one could set up an endless parade of great names from Plato and Aristotle through Machiavelli and Hobbes to Pareto and Weber to demonstrate that a large number of seminal social theorists have devoted a good deal of attention to power and the phenomena associated with it. Doubtless it would be easy to show, too, how the word and its synonyms are everywhere embedded in the language of civilized peoples, often in subtly different ways: power, influence, control, pouvoir, puissance, Macht, Herrschaft, Gewalt, imperium, potestas, auctoritas, potentia, etc.

I shall spare the reader the fruits and myself the labor of such a demonstration. Reflecting on the appeal to authority that might be made does, however, arouse two suspicions: First (following the axiom that where there is smoke there is fire), if so many people at so many different times have felt the need to attach the label power, or something like it, to some Thing they believe they have observed, one is tempted to suppose that the Thing must exist; and not only exist, but exist in a form capable of being studied more or less systematically. The second and more cynical suspicion is that a Thing to which people attach many labels with subtly or grossly different meanings in many different cultures and times is probably not a Thing at all but many Things; there are students of the subject, although I do not recall any who have had the temerity to say so in print, who think that because of this the whole study of "power" is a bottomless swamp.

Paradoxical as it may sound, it is probably too early to know whether these critics are right. For, curiously enough, the systematic study of power is very recent, precisely because it is only lately that serious attempts have been made to formulate the concept rigorously enough for systematic study.[1] If we take as our criterion for the efficiency of a scientific concept its usability in a theoretical system that possesses a high degree

[1] By demonstrating the importance of concepts such as power and influence, particularly in political analysis, and by insisting upon rigorous conceptual clarity, Harold Lasswell has had a seminal influence. Cf. especially Reference 3. A similar approach will be found in References 6, 7, 8, 10. For the approach of the present article I owe a particularly heavy debt to March, with whom I had countless profitable discussions during a year we both spent as fellows at the Center for Advanced Study in the Behavioral Sciences. I have drawn freely not only on our joint work but on his own published and unpublished writings on the

of systematic and empirical import, then we simply cannot say whether rigorous definitions of the concept of power are likely to be useful in theoretical systems with a relatively large pay-off in the hard coin of scientific understanding. The evidence is not yet in.

I think it can be shown, however, that to define the concept "power" in a way that seems to catch the central intuitively understood meaning of the word must inevitably result in a formal definition that is not easy to apply in concrete research problems; and therefore, operational equivalents of the formal definition, designed to meet the needs of a particular research problem, are likely to diverge from one another in important ways. Thus we are not likely to produce—certainly not for some considerable time to come—anything like a single, consistent, coherent "Theory of Power." We are much more likely to produce a variety of theories of limited scope, each of which employs some definition of power that is useful in the context of the particular piece of research or theory but different in important respects from the definitions of other studies. Thus we may never get through the swamp. But it looks as if we might someday get around it.

With this in mind, I propose first to essay a formal definition of power that will, I hope, catch something of one's intuitive notions as to what the Thing is. By "formal" I mean that the definition will presuppose the existence of observations of a kind that may not always or even frequently be possible. Second, I should like to indicate how operational definitions have been or might be modelled on the formal one for

subject. The comments of Jacob Marschak on this paper have also been most helpful. There are, of course, approaches radically different from the one employed here and in the works mentioned above. John R. P. French, Jr. (2), has developed a model that assumes "a unidimensional continuum of opinion which can be measured with a ratio scale," and he defines "the power of A over B (with respect to a given opinion) [to be] equal to the maximum force which A can induce on B minus the maximum resisting force which B can mobilize in the opposite direction." Game theory provides still another approach. Cf. References 4, 5, 9.

some specific purposes, and the actual or possible results of these operational definitions.

I should like to be permitted one liberty. There is a long and honorable history attached to such words as power, influence, control, and authority. For a great many purposes, it is highly important that a distinction should be made among them; thus to Max Weber, *"Herrschaft ist . . . ein Sonderfall von Macht,"* Authority is a special case of the first, and Legitimate Authority a subtype of cardinal significance (11). In this essay I am seeking to explicate the primitive notion that seems to lie behind *all* of these concepts. Some of my readers would doubtless prefer the term "influence," while others may insist that I am talking about control. I should like to be permitted to use these terms interchangeably when it is convenient to do so, without denying or seeming to deny that for many other purposes distinctions are necessary and useful. Unfortunately, in the English language power is an awkward word, for unlike "influence" and "control" it has no convenient verb form, nor can the subject and object of the relation be supplied with noun forms without resort to barbaric neologisms.

POWER AS A RELATION AMONG PEOPLE

What is the intuitive idea we are trying to capture? Suppose I stand on a street corner and say to myself, "I command all automobile drivers on this street to drive on the right side of the road"; suppose further that all the drivers actually do as I "command" them to do; still, most people will regard me as mentally ill if I insist that I have enough power over automobile drivers to compel them to use the right side of the road. On the other hand, suppose a policeman is standing in the middle of an intersection at which most traffic ordinarily moves ahead; he orders all traffic to turn right or left; the traffic moves as he orders it to do. Then it accords with what I conceive to be the bedrock idea of power to say that the policeman acting in this particular role evidently has the power to make automobile drivers turn right or left rather than go ahead. My intuitive idea of power, then, is something like this: A has power over B to the extent that he can get B to do something that B would not otherwise do. If Hume and his intellectual successors had never existed, the distinction between the two events above might be firmer than it is. But anyone who sees in the two cases the need to distinguish mere "association" from "cause" will realize that the attempt to define power could push us into some messy epistemological problems that do not seem to have any generally accepted solutions at the moment. I shall therefore quite deliberately steer clear of the possible identity of "power" with "cause," and the host of problems this identity might give rise to.

Let us proceed in a different way. First, let us agree that power is a relation, and that it is a relation among people. Although in common speech the term encompasses relations among people and other animate or inanimate objects, we shall have our hands full if we confine the relationship to human beings. All of the social theory I mentioned earlier is interesting only when it deals with this limited kind of relationship. Let us call the objects in the relationship of power, actors. Actors may be individuals, groups, roles, offices, governments, nation-states, or other human aggregates.

To specify the actors in a power relation— A has power over B—is not very interesting, informative, or even accurate. Although the statement that the President has (some) power over Congress is not empty, neither is it very useful. A much more complete statement would include references to (a) the source, domain, or *base* of the President's power over Congress; (b) the *means* or instruments used by the President to exert power over Congress; (c) the *amount* or extent of his power over Congress; and (d) the range or *scope* of his power over Congress. The base of an actor's power consists of all the resources—opportunities, acts, objects, etc.—that he can exploit in order to effect the behavior of another. Much of the best writing on power—Bertrand Russell is a good example—consists of an examination of the possible bases of power. A study of the war potential of nations is also a study of the bases of power. Some of the possible bases of a President's power over a Senator are his

patronage, his constitutional veto, the possibility of calling White House conferences, his influence with the national electorate, his charisma, his charm, and the like.

In a sense, the base is inert, passive. It must be exploited in some fashion if the behavior of others is to be altered. The *means* or instruments of such exploitation are numerous; often they involve threats or promises to employ the base in some way and they may involve actual use of the base. In the case of the President, the means would include the *promise* of patronage, the *threat* of veto, the *holding* of a conference, the *threat* of appeal to the electorate, the *exercise* of charm and charisma, etc.

Thus the means is a mediating activity by A between A's base and B's response. The *scope* consists of B's responses. The scope of the President's power might therefore include such Congressional actions as passing or killing a bill, failing to override a veto, holding hearings, etc.

The *amount* of an actor's power can be represented by a probability statement: e.g., "the chances are 9 out of 10 that if the President promises a judgeship to five key Senators, the Senate will not override his veto," etc. Clearly the amount can only be specified in conjunction with the means and scope.

Suppose now we should wish to make a relatively complete and concise statement about the power of individual A over individual a (whom I shall call the respondent) with respect to some given scope of responses. In order to introduce the basic ideas involved, let us restrict ourselves to the 2 by 2 case, where the actor A does or does not perform some act and the respondent a does or does not "respond." Let us employ the following symbols:

(A, w) = A does w. For example, the President makes a nationwide television appeal for tax increases.

$(A, \overline{w})$ = A does not do w.

(a, x) = a, the respondent, does x. For example, the Senate votes to increase taxes.

$(a, \overline{x})$ = a does not do x.

$P(u|v)$ = Probability that u happens when v happens.

Then a relatively complete and concise statement would be symbolized:

$$P(a, x|A, w) = p_1$$

$$P(a, x|A, \bar{w}) = p_2$$

Suppose now, that $p_1 = 0.4$ and $p_2 = 0.1$. Then one interpretation might be: "The probability that the Senate will vote to increase taxes if the President makes a nationwide television appeal for a tax increase is 0.4. The probability that the Senate will vote to increase taxes if the President does not make such an appeal is 0.1."

PROPERTIES OF THE POWER RELATION

Now let us specify some properties of the power relation.

1. A necessary condition for the power relation is that there exists a time lag, however small, from the actions of the actor who is said to exert power to the responses of the respondent. This requirement merely accords with one's intuitive belief that A can hardly be said to have power over a unless A's power attempts precede a's responses. The condition, obvious as it is, is critically important in the actual study of power relations. Who runs the XYZ Corporation? Whenever the president announces a new policy, he immediately secures the compliance of the top officials. But upon investigation it turns out that every new policy he announces has first been put to him by the head of the sales department. Or again, suppose we had a full record of the times at which each one of the top Soviet leaders revealed his positions on various issues; we could then deduce a great deal about who is running the show and who is not. A good bit of the mystery surrounding the role of White House figures like Sherman Adams and Harry Hopkins would also be clarified by a record of this kind.

2. A second necessary condition is, like the first, obvious and nonetheless important in research: there is no "action at a distance." Unless there is some "connection" between A and a, then no power relation can be said to exist. I shall leave the concept of "connection" undefined, for I wish only to call attention to the practical significance of this second condition. In looking for a flow of influence, control, or power from A to a, one must always find out whether there is a connection, or an opportunity for a connection, and if there is not, then one need proceed no further. The condition, obvious as it is, thus has considerable practical importance for it enables one to screen out many possible relations quite early in an inquiry.

3. In examining the intuitive view of the power relation, I suggested that it seemed to involve a successful attempt by A to get a to do something he would not otherwise do. This hints at a way of stating a third necessary condition for the power relation. Suppose the chances are about one out of a hundred that one of my students, Jones, will read *The Great Transformation* during the holidays even if I do not mention the book to him. Suppose that if I mention the book to him and ask him to read it, the chances that he will do so are still only one out of a hundred. Then it accords with my intuitive notions of power to say that evidently I have no power over Jones with respect to his reading *The Great Transformation* during the holidays—at least not if I restrict the basis of my action to mentioning the book and asking him (politely) to read it. Guessing this to be the case, I tell Jones that if he does not read the book over the holidays I shall fail him in my course. Suppose now that the chances he will read the book are about 99 out of 100. Assume further that nothing else in Jones's environment has changed, at least nothing relevant to his reading or not reading the book. Then it fully accords with my intuitive notions of power to say that I have some power over Jones's holiday reading habits. The basis of my power is the right to fail him in his course with me, and the means I employ is to invoke this threat.

Let me now set down symbolically what I have just said. Let

(D, w) = my threat to fail Jones if he does not read *The Great Transformation* during the holidays.

$(D, \overline{w})$ = no action on my part.

(J, x) = Jones reads *The Great Transformation* during the holidays.

Further, let

$p_1 = P(J, x|D, w)$ the probability that Jones will read *The Great Transformation* if I threaten to fail him.

$p_2 = P(J, x|D, \overline{w})$ the probability that Jones will read the book if I do not threaten to fail him.

Now let us define the *amount of power*. To avoid the confusion that might arise from the letter p, let us use the symbol M (from *Macht*) to designate the amount of power. Then, in accordance with the ideas set out in the illustration above, we define A's power over a, with respect to the response x, by means of w, as M, or, more fully:

$$M\left(\frac{A}{a} : w, x\right) = P(a, x \mid A, w)$$

$$- P(a, x \mid A, \overline{w}) = p_1 - p_2$$

Thus in the case of myself and Jones, M, my power over Jones, with respect to reading a book during the holidays, is 0.98.

We can now specify some additional properties of the power relation in terms of M:

a. If $p_1 = p_2$, then $M = 0$ and no power relation exists. The absence of power is thus equivalent to statistical independence.

b. M is at a maximum when $p_1 = 1$ and $p_2 = 0$. This is roughly equivalent to saying that A unfailingly gets B to do something B would never do otherwise.

c. M is at a minimum when $p_1 = 0$ and $p_2 = 1$. If negative values of M are to be included in the power relation at all—and some readers might object to the idea—then we shall have a concept of "negative power." This is not as foolish as it may seem, although one must admit that negative control of this kind is not ordinarily conceived of as power. If, whenever I ask my son to stay home on Saturday morning to mow the lawn, my request has the inevitable effect of inducing him to go swimming, when he would otherwise have stayed home,

I do have a curious kind of negative power over him. The Legion of Decency sometimes seems to have this kind of power over moviegoers. Stalin was often said to wield negative power over the actions on appropriations for foreign aid by the American Congress. A study of the Senate that will be discussed later suggested that at least one Senator had this kind of effect on the Senate on some kinds of issues.

Note that the concept of negative power, and M as a measure, are both independent of the *intent* of A. The measure does, to be sure, require one to assign a positive and negative *direction* to the responses of the respondent; what one chooses as a criterion of direction will depend upon his research purposes and doubtless these will often include some idea as to the intent of the actors in a power relation. To take a specific case, p_1 *could* mean "the probability that Congress will defeat a bill if it is contained in the President's legislative program," and p_2 could mean "the probability that Congress will defeat such a bill if it is not contained in the President's legislative program." By assigning direction in this way, positive values of M would be associated with what ordinarily would be interpreted as meaning a "negative" influence of the President over Congress. The point of the example is to show that while the measure does require that direction be specified, the intent of A is not the only criterion for assigning direction.

POWER COMPARABILITY

The main problem, however, is not to determine the existence of power but to make comparisons. Doubtless we are all agreed that Stalin was more powerful than Roosevelt in a great many ways, that McCarthy was less powerful after his censure by the Senate than before, etc. But what, precisely, do we mean? Evidently we need to define the concepts "more power than," "less power than," and "equal power."

Suppose we wish to compare the power of two different individuals. We have at least five factors that might be included in a comparison: (1) differences in the basis of their power, (2) differences in means of employing the basis, (3) differences in the

scope of their power, i.e., in type of response evoked, (4) differences in the number
of comparable respondents, and (5) differences in the change in probabilities, or M.

The first two of these may be conveniently
thought of as differences in properties of the
actors exercising power, and the last three
may be thought of as differences in the
responses of the respondents. Now it is
clear that the pay-off lies in the last three—
the responses. When we examine the first
two in order to compare the power of individuals, rulers, or states, we do so on the
supposition that differences in bases and
means of actors are very likely to produce
differences in the responses of those they
seek to control.

As I have already indicated, much of the
most important and useful research and
analysis on the subject of power concerns
the first two items, the properties of the
actors exercising power, and there is good
reason to suppose that studies of this kind
will be as indispensable in the future as they
have been in the past. But since we are
concerned at the moment with a formal
explication of the concept of power, and
not with an investigation of research problems, (some of these will be taken up later
on) it is important to make clear that
analysis of the first two items does not,
strictly speaking, provide us with a comparison of the power of two or more actors,
except insofar as it permits us to make
inferences about the last three items. If we
could make these inferences more directly,
we should not be particularly interested in
the first two items—at least not for purposes
of making comparisons of power. On the
other hand, given information about the
responses, we may be interested in comparing
the efficiency of different bases or means;
in this case, evidently, we can make a
comparison only by holding one or both of
the first two factors constant, so to speak.
In general, the properties of the power
wielder that we bring into the problem are
determined by the goals of one's specific
research. For example, one might be interested in the relative power of different
state governors to secure favorable legislative action on their proposals by means
of patronage; or alternatively, one might be

interested in the relative effectiveness of the
threat of veto employed by different governors.

In whatever fashion one chooses to define
the relevant properties of the actors whose
power he wishes to compare, strictly speaking one must compare them with respect to
the responses they are capable of evoking.
Ideally, it would be desirable to have a
single measure combining differences in
scope, number of comparable respondents
controlled, and change in probabilities.
But there seems to exist no intuitively
satisfying method for doing so. With an
average probability approaching one, I
can induce each of 10 students to come to
class for an examination on a Friday after-
noon when they would otherwise prefer to
make off for New York or Northampton.
With its existing resources and techniques,
the New Haven Police Department can
prevent about half the students who park
along the streets near my office from staying
beyond the legal time limit. Which of us has
the more power? The question is, I believe,
incapable of being answered unless we are
ready to treat my relationships with my
students as in some sense comparable with
the relations of the Police Department to
another group of students. Otherwise any
answer would be arbitrary, because there is
no valid way of combining the three variables—scope, number of respondents, and
change in probabilities—into a single scale.

Let us suppose, for a moment, that with
respect to two of the three variables the
responses associated with the actions of
two (or more) actors we wish to compare
are identical. Then it is reasonable to define
the power of A as greater than the power
of B if, with respect to the remaining variable, the responses associated with A's acts
are greater than the responses associated
with B's acts. It will be readily seen, however, that we may have jumped from the
frying pan into the fire, for the term "greater
than" is still to be defined. Let us take up
our variables one by one.

To begin with, we may suppose that the
probability of evoking the response being the
same for two actors and the numbers of
comparable persons in whom they can evoke
the response also being the same, then if the

scope of responses evoked by A is greater than that evoked by B, A's power is greater than B's. But how can we decide whether one scope is larger than another? Suppose that I could induce my son to bathe every evening and to brush his teeth before going to bed and that my neighbor could induce his son to serve him breakfast in bed every morning. Are the two responses I can control to be counted as greater than the one response my neighbor can control? Evidently what we are willing to regard as a "greater" or "lesser" scope of responses will be dictated by the particular piece of research at hand; it seems fruitless to attempt to devise any single scale. At one extreme we may wish to say that A's scope is greater than B's only if A's scope contains in it every response in B's and at least one more; this would appear to be the narrowest definition. At the other extreme, we may be prepared to treat a broad category of responses as comparable, and A's scope is then said to be greater than B's if the number of comparable responses in his scope is larger than the number in B's. There are other possible definitions. The important point is that the particular definition one chooses will evidently have to merge from considerations of the substance and objectives of a specific piece of research, and not from general theoretical considerations.

Much the same argument applies to the second variable. It is clear, I think, that we cannot compare A's power with respect to the respondents $a_1, a_2 \ldots a_n$ and B's power with respect to the respondents $b_1, b_2 \ldots b_n$ unless we are prepared to regard the two sets of individuals as comparable. This is a disagreeable requirement, but obviously a sensible one. If I can induce 49 undergraduates to support or oppose federal aid to education, you will scarcely regard this as equivalent to the power I would have if I could induce 49 Senators to support or oppose federal aid. Again, whether or not we wish to treat Senators as comparable to students, rich men as comparable to poor men, soldiers as comparable to civilians, enlisted men as comparable to officers, military officers as comparable to civil servants, etc., is a matter that can be de-

termined only in view of the nature and aims of the research at hand.

The third variable is the only one of the three without this inherent limitation. If scope and numbers are identical,[n] then there can be no doubt, I think, that it fully accords with our intuitive and common-sense notions of the meaning of power to say that the actor with the highest probability of securing the response is the more powerful. Take the set of Democratic Senators in the United States Senate. Suppose that the chance that at least two-thirds of them will support the President's proposals on federal aid to education is 0.6. It is fair to say that no matter what I may do in behalf of federal aid to education, if there are no other changes in the situation except those brought about by my efforts the probability that two-thirds of them will support federal aid will remain virtually at 0.6. If, on the other hand, Senator Johnson, as majority leader, lends his full support and all his skill of maneuver to the measure the probability may rise, let us say, to 0.8. We may then conclude (what we already virtually know is the case, of course) that Senator Johnson has more power over Democratic Senators with respect to federal aid to education than I have.

Earlier in defining the amount of power by the measure, M, I had already anticipated this conclusion. What I have just said is precisely equivalent to saying that the power of A with respect to some set of respondents and responses is greater than the power of B with respect to an equivalent set if and only if the measure M associated with A is greater than the measure M associated with B. To recapitulate:

$$M\left(\frac{A}{a} : w, x\right) = p_1 - p_2, \text{ where}$$
$$p_1 = P(a, x | A, w)$$

the probability that a will do x, given action w by A

$$p_2 = P(a, x | A, \overline{w})$$

the probability that a will do x, given no action w by A.

$$M\left(\frac{B}{b}:y, z\right) = p_1^* - p_2^*, \text{ where}$$

$$p_1^* = P(b, z/B, y)$$
$$p_2^* = P(b, z/B, \bar{y}).$$

Now if these two situations are *power comparable* (a notion we shall examine in a moment) then A's power is greater than B's if and only if

$$M\left(\frac{A}{a}:w, x\right) > M\left(\frac{B}{b}:y, z\right).$$

In principle, then, whenever there are two actors, A and B, provided only that they are power comparable, they can be ranked according to the amount of power they possess, or M. But if it is possible to rank A and B, it is possible to rank any number of pairs. And it is obvious from the nature of M that this ranking must be transitive, i.e.,

$$\text{if } M\left(\frac{A}{a}:w, x\right) > M\left(\frac{B}{b}:y, z\right), \text{ and}$$

$$M\left(\frac{B}{b}:y, z\right) > M\left(\frac{C}{c}:u, v\right), \text{ then}$$

$$M\left(\frac{A}{a}:w, x\right) > M\left(\frac{C}{c}:u, v\right).$$

In principle, then, where any number of actors are in some relation to any number of equivalent subjects, and these relations are regarded as power comparable, then all the actors can be unambiguously ranked according to their power with respect to these subjects.

There is, as everyone knows, many a slip 'twixt principle and practice. How can one convert the theoretical measure, M, into a measure usable in practical research? Specifically, suppose one wishes to examine the power relations among some group of people—a city council, legislature, community, faculty, trade union. One wants to rank the individuals in the group according to their power. How can one do so?

The first problem to be faced is whether given the aims, substance, and possible theoretical import of his study, one does in fact have *power comparability*. One of the most important existing studies of the power

structure of a community has been criticized because of what appears to have been a failure to observe this requirement. A number of leaders in a large Southern city were asked, "If a project were before the community that required *decision* by a group of leaders—leaders that nearly everyone would accept—which *ten* on the list of forty would you choose?" On the basis of the answers, individuals were ranked in such a way that a "pyramidal" power structure was inferred to exist in the city, i.e., one consisting of a small number of top leaders who made the key decisions, which were then executed by a larger middle-group of subordinate leaders. The significance of this conclusion is considerably weakened, however, if we consider whether the question did in fact discriminate among different kinds of responses. Specifically, suppose the leaders had been asked to distinguish between decisions over local taxes, decisions on schools, and efforts to bring a new industry to the community: would there be significant differences in the rankings according to these three different kinds of issues? Because the study does not provide an answer to this question, we do not know how to interpret the significance of the "pyramidal" power structure that assertedly exists. Are we to conclude that in "Regional City" there is a small determinate group of leaders whose power significantly exceeds that of all other members of the community on all or nearly all key issues that arise? Or are we to conclude, at the other extreme, that some leaders are relatively powerful on some issues and not on others, and that no leaders are relatively powerful on all issues? We have no way of choosing between these two interpretations or indeed among many others that might be formulated.

Let us define A and B as formally power comparable (in the sense that the relative magnitudes of the measure M are held to order the power of A and B correctly) if and only if the actors, the means, the respondents and the responses or scopes are comparable. That is,

the actor	A is comparable to	the actor	B;
A's respondent, a,	" " "	B's respondent, b;
A's means,	w " " "	B's means,	y; and
a's response,	x " " "	b's reponse,	z.

But this is not a very helpful definition. For the important question is whether we can specify some properties that will insure comparability among actors, respondents, means, and scopes. The answer, alas, is no. So far as an explication of the term "power" is concerned, power comparability must be taken as an undefined term. That is, power comparability will have to be interpreted in the light of the specific requirements of research and theory, in the same way that the decision as to whether to regard any two objects—animals, plants, atoms, or whatnot—as comparable depends upon general considerations of classification and theoretical import. To this extent, and to this extent only, the decision is "arbitrary"; but it is not more "arbitrary" than other decisions that establish the criteria for a class of objects.

To political scientists it might seem farfetched to compare the power of a British prime minister over tax legislation in the House of Commons with the power of the President of the United States over foreign policy decisions in the Senate. It would seem farfetched because the theoretical advantages of such a comparison are not at all clear. On the other hand, it would not seem quite so farfetched to compare the two institutional positions with respect to the "same" kind of policy—say tax legislation or foreign policy; indeed, political scientists do make comparisons of this kind. Yet the decision to regard tax legislation in the House of Commons as comparable in some sense to tax legislation in the Senate is "arbitrary." Even the decision to treat as comparable two revenue measures passed at different times in the United States Senate is "arbitrary." What saves a comparison from being genuinely arbitrary is, in the end, its scientific utility. Some kinds of comparisons will seem more artificial than others; some will be theoretically more interesting and more productive than others. But these are criteria derived from theoretical and empirical considerations independent of the fundamental meaning of the term power.

On what grounds, then, can one criticize the study mentioned a moment ago? Be-

cause the use of undiscriminating questions produced results of very limited theoretical significance. By choosing a relatively weak criterion of power comparability, the author inevitably robbed his inquiry of much of its potential richness. Considerations of comparability are, therefore, critical. But the criteria employed depend upon the problem at hand and the general state of relevant theory. The only way to avoid an arbitrary and useless definition of "power comparability" is to consider carefully the goals and substance of a particular piece of research in view of the theoretical constructs one has in mind. Thus in the case of the Senate, it may be satisfactory for one piece of research to define all Senate roll-call votes on all issues as comparable; for another, only votes on foreign policy issues will be comparable; and for still another, only votes on foreign policy issues involving large appropriations; etc. In a word, the researcher himself must define what he means by comparability and he must do so in view of the purpose of the ranking he is seeking to arrive at, the information available, and the relevant theoretical constructs governing the research.

APPLICATIONS OF THE CONCEPT OF POWER COMPARABILITY

Assuming that one has power comparability, the next problem is to rank every actor whose rank is relevant to the research. Here we run into practical problems of great magnitude.

Suppose we wish to rank a number of Senators with respect to their influence over the Senate on questions of foreign affairs. Specifically, the respondent and response are defined as "all Senate roll-call votes on measures that have been referred to the Foreign Relations Committee." To begin with, let us take two Senators. What we wish to find out is the relative influence on the Senate vote of the activities of the two Senators for or against a measure prior to the roll call. "For" and "against" must be defined by reference to some standard "direction." Passage of the measure is one possible "direction" in the sense that a Senator can be for passing the measure, against it, or without a position for or against passage. This is not, however, a particularly significant or meaningful direction, and one might wish to determine the direction of a measure by reference to the President's position, or by content, or by some other standard. For this discussion, I shall assume that "for" and "against" are defined by reference to the first standard, i.e., passing the measure.

Let us now assume that a Senator does one of three things prior to a roll-call vote. He works for the measure, he works against it, or he does nothing. (The assumption, although a simplification of reality, is by no means an unreasonable simplification). Let us further assume (what is generally true) that the Senate either passes the measure or defeats it. With respect to a particular Senator, we have the following conditional probabilities:

| | *The Senator* | | |
	Works For	Works Against	Does Nothing
Passes	p_1	p_2	p_3
Defeats	$1 - p_1$	$1 - p_2$	$1 - p_3$

The Senate (row label between Passes and Defeats)

Since the bottom row provides no additional information we shall, in future, ignore it. Following the earlier discussion of the concept M, the measure of power, it is reasonable to define

$$M_1 = p_1 - p_3.$$

$$M_2 = p_3 - p_2.$$

M_1 is a measure of the Senator's power when he works for a measure and M_2 a measure of his power when he works against a measure; in both cases a comparison is made with how the Senate will act if the Senator does nothing. There are various ways in which we might combine M_1 and M_2 into a single measure, but the most useful would appear to be simply the sum of M_1 and M_2. To avoid confusion with the earlier and slightly different measure which we are now approximating, let us call the sum of M_1 and M_2, M^*. Like M, it is at a maximum of 1 when the Senate always passes the bills a given Senator works for and always

defeats the bills he works against; it is at a minimum of -1 when the Senate always defeats the bills he works for and always passes the bills he works against; and it is at 0 when there is no change in the outcome, no matter what he does.

In addition, there is one clear advantage to M^*. It is easily shown that it reduces to

$$M^* = p_1 - p_2.$$

In a moment we shall see how advantageous such a simple measure is.

The theoretical problem, then, is clear-cut and a solution seems reasonably well defined. It is at this point, however, that practical research procedures begin to alter the significance of a solution, for the particular operational means selected to breathe life into the relatively simple formal concepts outlined so far can produce rather different and even conflicting results.

Let me illustrate this point by drawing on a paper by Dahl, March, and Nasatir (1) on influence ranking in the United States Senate. The aim of the authors was to rank thirty-four Senators according to their influence on the Senate with respect to two different areas, foreign policy and tax and economic policy. The 34 Senators were all those who had held office continuously from early 1946 through late 1954, a long enough period, it was thought, to insure a reasonably large number of roll-call votes. The classification of measures to the two areas was taken from the *Congressional Quarterly Almanac*, as were the votes themselves. Thus the subject was well defined and the necessary data were available.

No such systematic record is maintained of course, for the positions or activities of Senators prior to a roll-call vote, and what is more it would be exceptionally difficult to reconstruct the historical record even over one session, not to say over an eight-year period. Faced with this apparently insuperable obstacle, it was necessary to adopt a rather drastic alternative, namely to take the recorded roll-call vote of a Senator as an indication of his position and activities *prior to* the roll-call. While this is not unreasonable, it does pose one major difficulty: a vote is necessarily cast either for or against a measure and hence the roll-call provides no way of determining when a Senator does nothing prior to the roll-call. But the very essence of the formal concept of power outlined earlier hinges on a comparison of the difference between what the Senate will do when a Senator takes a given position and what it does when he takes no position.

It is at this point that the advantages of the measure M^* reveal themselves. For provided only that one is prepared to take the Senator's recorded vote as a fair indication of his prior position and activities, the data permit us to estimate the following probabilities, and hence M^*

	The Senator	
	Works For	Works Against
The Senate Passes	p_1	p_2

One could, therefore, estimate M^* for each of the 34 Senators and rank all of them.

The validity of this method ranking would appear to be greatest, however, when all Senators are ranked on precisely the same set of bills before the Senate. To the extent that they vote on different (although mostly overlapping) sets of bills, the comparability of M^* from one Senator to another will be reduced, conceivably to the vanishing point.

For a number of reasons, including a slightly different interpretation of the characteristics of an ideal measure, the authors chose a rather different approach. They decided to pair every Senator against every other Senator in the following way. The number in each cell is an estimate of the probability that the Senate will pass a proposal, given the positions of the two Senators as indicated; the number is in fact the proportion of times that the Senate passed a foreign policy (or tax) measure in the period 1946–54, given the recorded votes of the two Senators as indicated.

	S	
	Favors the motion	Opposes the motion
S Favors the motion	p_{11}	p_{12}
Opposes the motion	p_{21}	p_{22}

With 34 Senators, 561 possible pairs of this kind exist; but only 158 pairs were tabulated for foreign policy and 206 for tax and economic policy over the whole period. The measure used to enable comparisons to be made between the two Senators in each pair might be regarded as an alternative to M^*. This measure—let us call it M''—rests upon the same basic assumption, namely that we can measure a Senator's influence by the difference between the probability that the Senate will pass a measure the Senator opposes and the probability that it will pass a measure he supports. However, there are two important differences. First, the authors decided not to distinguish between "negative" and "positive" power; consequently they used absolute values only. Second, in estimating the probability of a measure passing the Senate, the positions of two Senators were simultaneously compared in the manner shown in the table. Thus the influence of S_1 over the Senate was measured as the difference between the probability that a bill will pass the Senate when S_1 favors it and the probability that it will pass when S_1 opposes it. However, this difference in probabilities was measured twice: (1) when S_2 favors the motions before the Senate; and (2) when S_2 opposes the motions. In the same way, S_2's influence was measured twice. Thus:

$$M_1''(S_1) = |p_{11} - p_{12}|,$$

that is, the change in probabilities, given S_2 in favor of the bill.

$$M_2''(S_1) = |p_{21} - p_{22}|,$$

that is, the change in probabilities, given S_2 in opposition to the bill. Likewise,

$$M_1''(S_2) = |p_{11} - p_{21}|$$

$$M_2''(S_2) = |p_{12} - p_{22}|.$$

The influence of S_1 was said to be greater than the influence of S_2 only if $M_1''(S_1) > M_1''(S_2)$ and $M_2''(S_1) > M_2''(S_2)$. That is, if

$$|p_{11} - p_{12}| > |p_{11} - p_{21}| \text{ and}$$

$$|p_{21} - p_{22}| > |p_{12} - p_{22}|.$$

Except for the rare case of what would ordinarily be regarded as "negative" power—which, as I have already said, this particular measure was not intended to distinguish from "positive" power—the absolute values are the same as the algebraic ones. Where the algebraic differences can be taken, and this will normally be the case, both inequalities reduce to

$$p_{21} > p_{12}.$$

In the ordinary case, then, using the measure M'' we can say that the power of Senator George is greater than that of Senator Knowland if the probability that the Senate will pass a measure is greater when Senator George favors a bill and Senator Knowland opposes it than when Senator Knowland favors a bill and Senator George opposes it.

TABLE 1

THIRTY-FOUR U. S. SENATORS RANKED ACCORDING TO "POWER" OVER SENATE DECISIONS ON FOREIGN POLICY, 1946-54

HIGH

Hayden	(tie) Magnuson
	Chavez
	Smith (N. J.)**
	George**
	Maybank
	Green**
	Hill*
Aiken	(tie) Wiley**
	Hoey
	Kilgore
	Ferguson*
	Murray*
	Knowland*
	Morse
Fulbright**	(tie) Saltonstall
	Johnston
	Cordon
	Hickenlooper**
	Ellender
Millikin	(tie) McClellan
	Eastland
	Russell
	Bridges*
	Johnson (Colo.)
	Byrd
	Butler (Nebr.)
	Langer*
	Young
	Capehart*
	McCarran

LOW

** member of Foreign Relations Committee five or more years
* member of Foreign Relatins Committee one to four years

The results, some of which are shown in Tables 1 to 3, are roughly consistent with expectations based on general knowledge.

Note how the formal concept of power has been subtly altered in the process of research; it has been altered, moreover, not arbitrarily or accidentally but because of the limitations of the data available, limitations that appear to be well-nigh inescapable even in the case of the United States Senate, a body whose operations are relatively visible and well recorded over a long period of time.

The most important and at first glance the most innocent change has been to accept the roll-call position of a Senator as an indication of his position prior to the roll-call vote. This change is for most practical purposes unavoidable, and yet it generates a serious consequence which I propose to call the problem of the chameleon. Suppose a Senator takes no prior position on any

TABLE 2

THIRTY-FOUR U. S. SENATORS RANKED ACCORDING TO "POWER" OVER SENATE DECISIONS ON TAX AND ECONOMIC POLICY, 1946-54

HIGH

	Georgett
	Millikintt
	Ellender
	Byrdtt
	Saltonstallt
	Cordon
	McCarran
	Young
	Hoeytt
	Maybank
Johnson (Colo.) tt	(tie) McClellan
	Hickenlooper
	Eastland
	Russell
	Smith (N. J.)
	Knowland
	Aiken
	Capehart
	Johnston
	Bridges
Hayden (tie) Chavez	
Butler (Nebr.)tt (tie) Wiley (tie) Ferguson	
Langer (tie) Hill (tie) Murray (tie) Magnuson	
(tie) Fulbright (tie) Green	
Morse (tie) Kilgore	

LOW

tt member of Finance Committee five or more years
t member of Finance Committee one to four years

TABLE 3

THIRTY-FOUR U. S. SENATORS CLASSIFIED ACCORDING TO 'POWER" OVER SENATE DECISIONS ON FOR-
EIGN POLICY AND TAX POLICY, 1946-54

Foreign Policy

		High influence	Medium influence	Low influence
	High influence	George**†† Hoey†† Maybank	Ellender Saltonstall† Cordon	Millikin†† Byrd†† McCarran Young Johnson (Colo.)†† McClellan
Tax and Economic Policy	Medium influence	Smith (N. J.)** Aiken* Hayden Chavez	Hickenlooper** Knowland* Johnston	Eastland Russell Capehart* Bridges*
	Low influence	Wiley** Hill* Magnuson Green**	Ferguson* Murray* Fulbright** Morse Kilgore	Butler (Nebr.)†† Langer*

** member of Foreign Relations Committee five or more years
* member of Foreign Relations Committee one to four years
†† member of Finance Committee five or more years
† member of Finance Committee one to four years

bill and always decides how to vote by guessing how the Senate majority will vote; then, if he is a perfect guesser, according to the ranking method used he will be placed in the highest rank. Our common sense tells us, however, that in this case it is the Senate that has power over the Senator, whereas the Senator has no influence on the votes of other Senators.

If the reader will tolerate an unnatural compounding of biological and celestial metaphors, a special case of the chameleon might be called the satellite. Although I have no evidence that this was so, let us suppose that Senator Hoey took no prior positions on issues and always followed the lead of Senator George (Table 3). Let us assume that on foreign policy and tax policy, Senator George was the most powerful man in the Senate—as indeed nearly every seasoned observer of the Senate does believe. By following George, Hoey would rank as high as George; yet, according to our hypothetical assumptions, he had no influence at all on George or any other Senator.

The problem of the chameleon (and the satellite) is not simply an artifact created by the method of paired comparisons employed. It is easy to see that ranking according to the measure $M*$ would be subject to, the same difficulties given the same data. The formal concept of power, that is to say, presupposes the existence of data that in this case do not seem to be available—certainly not readily available. If one had the kinds of observations that permitted him to identify the behavior of the chameleon or satellite then no serious problem would arise. One could treat chameleon activity as equivalent to "doing nothing" to influence the passage or defeat of a measure. Since, as we have seen, under the measure $M*$ the column "does nothing" is superfluous, the effect would be to ignore all cases of chameleon or satellite behavior and make estimates only from the instances where a Senator actually works for or works against various bills.

Thus the conceptual problem is easily solved. But the research problem remains. In order to identify chameleon behavior and separate it from actual attempts at influence, one cannot rely on roll-calls. One needs observations of the behavior of Senators prior to the roll-calls. But if it is true, as I have been arguing, that observations of this kind are available only with great difficulty, rarely for past sessions, and probably never in large numbers, then in fact the data needed are not likely to exist. But if they do not exist for the Senate, for what institutions are they likely to exist?

CONCLUSIONS: A DIALOGUE BETWEEN A "CONCEPTUAL" THEORETICIAN AND AN "OPERATIONALIST"

The conclusions can perhaps best be stated in the form of a dialogue between a "conceptual" theoretician and a strict "operationalist." I shall call them C and O.

C. The power of an actor, A, would seem to be adequately defined by the measure M which is the difference in the probability of an event, given certain action by A, and the probability of the event given no such action by A. Because the power of any actor may be estimated in this way, at least in principle, then different actors can be ranked according to power, provided only that there exists a set of comparable subjects for the actors who are to be ranked.

O. What you say may be true in principle, but that phrase "in principle" covers up a host of practical difficulties. In fact, of course, the necessary data may not exist.

C. That is, of course, quite possible. When I say "in principle" I mean only that no data are demanded by the definition that we cannot imagine securing with combinations of known techniques of observation and measurement. The observations may be exceedingly difficult but they are not inherently impossible: they don't defy the laws of nature as we understand them.

O. True. But the probability that we can actually make these observations on, say, the U. S. Senate is so low as to be negligible, at least if we want relatively large numbers of decisions. It seems to me that from a strict operational point of view, your concept of power is not a single concept, as you have implied; operationally, power would appear to be many different concepts, depending on the kinds of data available. The way in which the researcher must adapt to the almost inevitable limitations of his data means that we shall have to make do with a great many different and not strictly comparable concepts of power.

C. I agree with all you have said. In practice, the concept of power will have to be defined by operational criteria that will undoubtedly modify its pure meaning.

O. In that case, it seems wiser to dispense with the concept entirely. Why pretend that power, in the social sense, is a concept that is conceptually clear-cut and capable of relatively unambiguous operational definitions—like mass, say, in physics? Indeed, why not abandon the concept of power altogether, and admit that all we have or can have is a great variety of operational concepts, no one of which is strictly comparable with another? Perhaps we should label them: Power 1, Power 2, etc.; or better, let's abandon single, simple, misleading words like "power" and "influence", except when these are clearly understood to be a part of a special operational definition explicitly defined in the particular piece of research.

C. I'm afraid that I must disagree with your conclusion. You have not shown that the concept of power as defined by the measure M is inherently defective or that it is never capable of being used. It is true, of course, that we cannot always make the observations we need in order to measure power; perhaps we can do so only infrequently. But the concept provides us with a standard against which to compare the operational alternatives we actually employ. In this way it helps us to specify the defects of the operational definitions as measures of power. To be sure, we may have to use defective measures; but at least we shall know that they are defective and in what ways. More than that, to explicate the concept of power and to pin-point the deficiencies of the operational concepts actually employed may often help us to invent alternative concepts and research methods that produce a much closer approximation in practice to the theoretical concept itself.

REFERENCES

1. Dahl, R. A., March, J., & Nasatir, D. Influence ranking in the United States Senate.

Read at the annual meeting of the American Political Science Association, Washington, D. C. September 1956 (mimeo).

2. French, J. R. P. Jr. A formal theory of social power. *Psychol. Rev.*, 1956, 63, 181–194.

3. Lasswell, H. D., & Kaplan, A. *Power and society.* New Haven: Yale Univ. Press, 1950.

4. Luce, R. D. Further comments on power distribution for a stable two-party Congress. 1956 (September) (mimeo).

5. Luce, R. D., & Rogow, A. A. A game theoretic analysis of Congressional power distributions for a stable two-party system. *Behav. Sci.*, 1956, 1, 83-95.

6. March, J. G. An introduction to the theory and measurement of influence. *Amer. pol. Sci. Rev.*, 1955, 59, 431–451.

7. March, J. G. Measurement concepts in the theory of influence. *J. Politics*. (In press).

8. March, J. G. Influence measurement in experimental and semi-experimental groups. *Sociometry.* 1956, 19, 260–271.

9. Shapley, L. S. & Shubik, M. A method for evaluating the distribution of power in a committee system. *Amer. pol. Sci. Rev.*, 1954, 48, 787–792.

10. Simon, H. Notes on the observation and measurement of political power. *J. Politics*, 1953, 15, 500–516.

11. Weber, M. *Wirtschaft und Gesellschaft.* Tubingen: J. C. B. Mohr, 1925, 2 vols. (*Grundriss der Sozialekonomik*, Vol. 3).

(Manuscript received April 3, 1957.)

❧

─── CHAPTER 2 ───

ASSESSING
POWER IN
ORGANIZATIONS

As Pettigrew (1973: 240) has so aptly noted:

> *An accurate perception of the power distribution in the social arena in which he lives is . . . a necessary prerequisite for the man seeking powerful support for his demands.*

The assessment of power in organizations is important for several reasons. In the first place, the exercise and use of power is facilitated by an accurate diagnosis of the political situation confronted by the social actor. Strategies ranging from coalition formation to cooptation require an accurate diagnosis of the political landscape. Second, the measurement and assessment of power is important for those who would do research on the topic. If we are to assess whether or not power is correlated with other attributes, is stable over time, and across decision issues (March, 1966), then power will have to be measured. Third, as Pondy (1977) has suggested, one way of understanding what power is, is to consider how the concept can be examined and used. Thus, the assessment of power will help in the understanding of the concept.

Two tasks are required in assessing organizational political systems. In the first place, the principal organizational actors need to be identified on a meaningful basis. Then, the power of these various actors needs to be assessed. Both issues are covered in the discussion of the assessment of power in organizations which follows.

173

Identifying Political Actors

The first problem confronted by an analyst of organizational politics is to identify the relevant units for analysis. Organizations are, after all, comprised of people, who are grouped into subunits, which may be grouped into departments, divisions, etc. Furthermore, organizations are stratified by level of hierarchy as well as by horizontal grouping. The various people can be distinguished in terms of their race, sex, educational background, type of work, number of years with the company, and so forth. Are cohort groups, which are identified by the time they entered the organization, more important than departmental affiliation? As an illustration of this problem, the following different sets of groupings were among those used by my class for an assignment on diagnosing power within a school of business:

1) quantitative versus non-quantitative subjects

2) administration, faculty, and students

3) subject fields (finance, economics, accounting, management science, organizational behavior, marketing)

4) men and women

5) administration, tenured faculty, untenured faculty, doctoral students, MBA students, undergraduate students

Which are the most useful?

The solution to the problem is not simply a matter of judgment or intuition. What the analyst wants to do is to identify groupings which are as inclusive as possible and which are internally homogeneous with respect to preferences and beliefs on the issues being investigated. In a sense, it is a problem of clustering, in which the criterion is to cluster social actors together to maximize their homogeneity in opinions, preferences, and values which are relevant to the political issue being investigated, or which are the most salient and important in the organization at the time. If one had data on the preferences and opinions of all the various actors within the organization, such clustering would be readily accomplished by using available computational algorithms. However, in most cases it will require judgment to assess whether or not the appropriate units of analysis have been identified. In each instance, the questions to be asked are: is there relative homogeneity in the goals, preferences, and beliefs about technology within the categories of social actors identified; and are there differences among the preferences and beliefs of the

174

social actors so identified? This does not mean that every grouping is necessarily different from every other grouping; indeed, the building of coalitions requires finding areas of common interest. Rather, it is a judgmental decision which involves discerning whether or not there are differences between social actors on enough important issues to justify considering them as analytically separate. And, it is important to recognize that the identification of meaningful political units will change over time and be dependent on the particular set of issues at hand.

In identifying relevant political units, it is wise to start with the labels used in and provided by the organization. As Dearborn and Simon (1958) have noted, departmental identification, for instance, provides a frame of reference and exposure to information that may color one's perception of the world. The demarcations formally and persistently recognized within the organization come to create expectations for behavior which are self-fulfilling. Furthermore, the physical proximity which accompanies such identification, as well as the increased social interaction within such groups, contributes to the development of a common frame of reference which tends to reinforce their validity as distinct political units.

At the same time, it is important to recognize that in organizations, just as in the larger society, people have multiple memberships and interests that are cross-cut in a variety of different ways. A faculty member may be at once: untenured; a specialist in management science; interested in theory and research; opposed to consulting; have a preference to de-emphasize teaching, particularly as a criterion for promotion; and be one of eight persons who entered the organization at the same time. In a business firm, a person may be identified by: his or her disciplinary background (engineering, business, law, etc.); level of education; type of college attended (elite, Ivy League or state university); family social background; functional or departmental background (finance, marketing, consumer products, etc.); length of time in the organization; or age, and this is hardly an exhaustive list. Each one of these ways of characterizing an individual may be relevant in determining meaningful political groupings in the organization.

A HEURISTIC DEVICE

In assessing organizational political systems, the analyst faces the same problems confronted by one who seeks to understand organizational interdependence (Pfeffer and Salancik, 1978), and the problems become greater with the *more* localized knowledge possessed. The problems have to do with taking for granted what the relevant political units are, and thinking one understands when one doesn't what the important dimensions are that form the basis for political cleavage within the organization.

Thus, what analysts of organizational political systems require is some simple way of disciplining the analytical process to avoid overlooking important elements and to avoid reaching premature conclusions concerning the political landscape. One simple, easy to use device is to construct a matrix along the following lines:

Possible Political Actors

	A	B	C	D	....
1					
2					
3					
4					
.					
.					
.					

Relevant Issues or Topics, framed in terms of proposed actions or policies

For each issue or decision, ask yourself, is there likely to be homogeneity on this issue with respect to those persons or subunits grouped under each of the categories? If the answer is no, you have identified categories that fail to match the relevant political cleavages on the issues in question, and another way of identifying political units needs to be tried. If the answer is generally yes within each of the categories and across most or all of the issues, then you have a heuristically useful representation of the political scene. If two of the categories are perfectly correlated, in that their positions on all of the listed issues are likely to be identical, then they can be safely combined into one. The matrix, by the way, does not need to be filled in with great detail; a plus (+), zero (0), or minus (−) representing favor, neutral, and oppose on each of the proposed actions or policies will probably suffice for this part of the analysis.

Of course, by looking at similarities (correlations) among preferences across political actors, potential coalitions of interest can be identified. The more similar the structure of preferences is over a set of decision issues, the more easily the two actors can identify mutual interests and coordinate action. The framework can, of course, be further refined to consider the relative importance of the various issues or actions to the actors, and to consider the relative potency of the actors themselves.

When weighted by the potency of the various political actors, the matrix facilitates the prediction of what particular actions will be, in fact, adopted within the organization. Actions opposed by a majority of the potent actors will probably not be implemented. And, as we shall see in later chapters, the matrix also provides some insights into how to go about obtaining sufficient support in order to get a particular decision adopted.

AN EXAMPLE: CHANGE AT
NEW YORK UNIVERSITY

We can use Baldridge's (1971: Chapter 4) discussion of the change in educational orientation at New York University to illustrate the use of the kind of analysis we have been describing. The change was from one of virtually open enrollment and unlimited educational opportunity to one in which there were higher admissions standards, fewer part-time students, and a stronger emphasis on research and graduate education.

> *For many years NYU had a consistent interpretation of its role in New York's higher education. From its founding the university offered educational advantages to all types of people, including underprivileged minority groups. . . . this was to be "a different kind of institution" from the upper-class colleges that dominated American education in the early nineteenth century. As part of this philosophy NYU accepted students of relatively low academic ability . . . (Baldridge, 1971: 39).*

The expansion of public education in the state through a system of state university campuses and junior colleges, as well as the move of City University to a policy of more open enrollment, severely affected NYU's competitive position. NYU was charging among the highest fees in the nation while attempting to compete with state and city universities which charged almost nothing. In the early 1960s, actual NYU enrollments began to fall far below projections (Baldridge, 1971: 41). Spurred on by a planning grant from the Ford Foundation, NYU's educational role came under intense scrutiny by various committees and by the administration. The selection of a new president, James M. Hester, in 1962 facilitated the process of change and self-examination. As a result of this study and planning, the following changes were proposed in a plan submitted to the Ford Foundation for support:

*First, NYU would significantly upgrade undergraduate ad-
missions policies, thus moving itself out of direct competition
with the public institutions for the bulk of the medium-ability
students. . . . This had a drastic effect on several schools in the
university. Second, most of the key decision-makers thought
that the multischool system of undergraduate education would
have to be abandoned so that duplication of efforts could be
avoided. . . . Third, an "urban university" theme was adopted
as a new institutional character . . . carefully articulated
around service to the New York community, research in urban
problems and preparation of urban specialists. . . . Fourth, the
upgrading of quality involved an attempt to get more full-time
students instead of the part-time group that NYU had long
attracted. . . . Fifth, NYU would concentrate an increasing
proportion of its energies toward graduate and advanced professional training. . . . Finally, the faculty recruitment would
concentrate on obtaining more full-time, advanced-degree
people (Baldridge, 1971: 44–45).*

The changes were fundamental and profound in the university, and
unleashed a large amount of political activity and conflict. In Table 2-1,
the various political actors and their positions on the various changes,
as inferred from the discussion provided in Baldridge (1971: Chapter 4),
are displayed. There are several lessons to be learned from this analysis.

In the first place, it is wrong to assume that disciplinary boundaries
demarcate political struggles either within universities or within other
types of organizations. In the case of New York University, the School
of Commerce and the Graduate School of Business were on opposite
sides in several of the issues. The Graduate School of Business was a
separate unit for graduate and advanced professional degrees, while the
School of Commerce was responsible for the undergraduate program
which included a large part-time, evening school component.

*GSB wanted to establish itself as a major research center and
a nationally reputable business education unit. Its professors
were much more oriented to scholarly research . . . and feared
that the undergraduate School of Commerce was severely
damaging the reputation of business studies at NYU. . . . the
Commerce professors rightly believed they might be out of
their jobs if all the changes were instituted. They feared reduced enrollments, a loss of the night-school program, de-*

TABLE 2-1
Political Interests and Their Positions on
Proposed Changes at New York University

Interests

		University College	Grad. Sch. of Business	Commerce	Engineering	Education	Washington Square College
	Upgrade Admissions Standards	+	+	−	+	0	+
	Urban Theme	0	0	0	0	0	+
Proposed Changes	Abandon Duplication in Undergraduate Education	+	0	−	0	−	+
	More Full-Time Students	+	+	−	0	−	0/−
	More Emphasis on Graduate Education	0	+	−	0	−	+

+ = support
0 = neutral
− = oppose

179

*creases in the size of the faculty, and a general lowering of their
influence in the university (Baldridge, 1971: 53).*

It turns out their fears were justified. "From a high of nearly
300 in the late 1950's the faculty dropped to 61 in 1967–1968 . . .
the full-time student enrollment decreased from a high of 2800 to a
low of 1000" (Baldridge, 1971: 55). The point is that it is important
to consider carefully the extent to which changes are consistently
viewed within a political unit. In this case, there is clear justification
for treating the Graduate School of Business and the School of Commerce as separate political actors.

Second, the analysis helps to highlight why an attempt at coordinating the various undergraduate programs, although unsuccessful in
the past, was now feasible. The basis for the recommendation for consolidation arose from the following conditions:

> *. . . NYU had undergraduate programs in Washington Square
> College, University College, the School of Engineering, the
> School of Commerce, and the School of Education. Many of
> these programs were almost exact duplications, and courses
> often had the same titles. High administrative overhead, ineffi-
> cient use of faculty, and the ineffective utilization of space were
> only a few of the problems that this duplication caused. . . .
> segregation of the courses into schools meant that often stu-
> dents were isolated and lacked the intellectual stimulation
> that comes from diversity in the classroom (Baldridge, 1971:
> 56).*

A previous attempt to consolidate all the undergraduate units,
including the professional schools, which was undertaken in the mid-
1950s, was unsuccessful. The attempt had provoked serious opposition:

> *The faculties of the various schools felt that their distinctive
> programs would be undercut and that individual members of
> the faculty would be hurt by the loss of a favorite course or even
> a job. The deans were opposed to any decrease in programs for
> their college, and the department chairmen saw their areas
> upset by a complete reworking of the course structure. The
> professional schools feared the loss of their undergraduates,
> whereas the liberal arts schools feared an influx of professional
> students who might not be oriented toward liberal arts or who*

might not measure up to their academic standards (Baldridge,
1971: 56).

By the mid-1960s, the hand of the administration was considerably strengthened by the growing fiscal crisis which confronted the university. At this time, the administration cleverly bought off some opposition by designing the Coordinated Liberal Studies Program to involve only the first two years of study for Washington Square College, Education, and Commerce. University College, the School of Engineering, and, of course, the Graduate School of Business were no longer interested in opposing the idea. Furthermore, the Coordinated Liberal studies program "meant that Washington Square College would be greatly expanded by the courses that were drawing on Commerce and Education students" (Baldridge, 1971: 57). This plus the increased emphasis on graduate and professional education, located primarily at the Washington Square campus, were sufficient to ensure the support of that important unit.

Looking at the table indicates that the only substantial opposition to the proposals was likely to come from Commerce and Education, with Engineering being largely neutral. Commerce was full of part-time faculty, and thus could not muster effective opposition. Education was already beginning to lose power because of the growing oversupply of teachers. Moreover, in a contest with interests representing arts, sciences, and graduate education, any of the professional schools were at a disadvantage. Thus, the analysis indicates the fundamental viability of the reform package. It also indicates how the various parts of the package gave important items to the political interests whose support was needed.

It should be clear that what this analytical process provides is a structure for exercising judgment about the political structure of an organization and a set of issues. It scarcely takes the place of such judgment, and is not something that can be applied in a mechanical fashion. At the same time, it provides a disciplined way of beginning to think about the identification of the relevant political units, their positions, and the consequences for understanding organizational politics.

Measuring the Power of Social Actors

Having identified the relevant political actors, or in Freeman's (1978) terms, the units of analysis, it is then necessary to develop estimates of their relative power. This measurement of power is important for predicting what will occur, as well as for developing measures of power that can be used in more complete conceptual schemes for analyzing the determinants and outcomes of power. As with the analysis of political units, the problem is subtle but not intractable.

DISTINGUISHING POWER FROM FORESIGHT

If you hold this book above a table, say "fall, book," and then release the book from your hand, the book will fall back onto the table. Does this mean you have power over the book? Of course it does not. Gravity was responsible for the book's falling, not your persuasiveness, resources, or expertise. Because fundamental to virtually all definitions of power is the idea that some resistance or opposition is overcome, or some action is changed from what it would have been without the intervention of the powerful actor, the assessment of power requires the ability to know what would have happened without the intrusion of the power holder. In the case of our book example, this is an easy task. Gravity is a long-established and well-known physical law of nature. The problem is that in many social situations, understanding of social behavior is much less precise or developed. Such situations pose problems for assessing power.

Consider, for example, the problem of assessing power in some kind of legislative body, such as a senate or representative assembly. A simple but naive approach might be to define power as the proportion of the time a given individual is on the winning side of contested issues. Surely, someone who is on the winning side 80% of the time is more powerful than one who is on the winning side only 20% of the time. Such measurement of power neglects the question, of course, of whether or not the various issues were of equal importance to both persons. Sometimes one does not use power because the issue is not important enough. This point will be developed in more detail in the next chapter. But more fundamentally, it may be true that neither of the two individuals is himself very powerful, in the sense of being able to influence the behavior of others. The first person may be much more adept at forecasting which side is going to win and then lining up accordingly. Similar problems of assessment occur in other contexts also. If a given organizational actor consistently supports the job candidate who is eventually hired, it may mean that the individual is powerful in affecting the choice, or it may be that the individual is a shrewd analyst of others' preferences and is able to forecast how the decision is going to turn out.

Dahl (1957: 212) called this the problem of the chameleon, of which the satellite is a special case. The satellite is a given individual who always follows the lead of someone who is actually powerful in the organization. Since satellites will always come down on the same side as the person with power, it would be impossible to distinguish them in terms of their power by merely counting up the number of times each was on the winning side.

Since power is, in part, an attributed property that can be created merely through such an attribution process, the ability to forecast what is going to occur is an important skill. The exercise of such forecasting skill can provide the social actor with the appearance of power and influence because of his or her consistent identification with the winning side of issues. Nevertheless, as Dahl (1957) argued in discussing the power of individual senators, it is important to be able to distinguish between the ability to influence a situation and the ability to forecast what would have occurred in any event.

Discrimination among chameleons, satellites, and the powerful requires observation of the various social actors prior to the decision making event, as well as a knowledge of their preferences before the political activity began. If one knows the initial preferences, the attempts at influence undertaken, and then the final decision, power can be more reliably diagnosed. Clearly, multiple events make it more feasible to infer power, as March (1966) argued in developing the principle of consistency. On any decision occasion, there is some probability that a given social actor will wind up on the winning side by chance. Such a probability of chance occurrence is reduced as the number of decision contexts increases. The probability is reduced even further when the contest among the various positions is reasonably close. It is clear that merely counting up the number of apparent wins versus the number of apparent losses is not an adequate way of assessing power.

Two examples illustrate the pitfalls involved in diagnosing power in organizations. Each year the Budget and Personnel Committee at the University of California at Berkeley triumphantly reports, in a message to the faculty, the large number of personnel cases for both promotion and merit raises within rank it has considered, and how few times its recommendations have been overturned by the administration. These data are supposed to let the faculty know that faculty power is secure (at least as administered through the budget committee) and that the faculty are, by inference, much more in control with respect to these critical personnel decisions than the administration. The reporting of these data omits two very important facts. First, the budget committee, which acts, in the final analysis, in only an advisory way to the administration, submits a preliminary report, particularly on controversial cases. It is not unknown for the administration to ask for reconsideration of the specific personnel case, nor is it unknown for the committee, in reexamining the case, to discover new facts and new information that lead to a change in its position. The budget committee's statistics, of course, deal only with the administration's overturning final recommendations. How often the budget committee acts as a chameleon or satellite is not reported.

But the problem of inference may be even more severe than was at first supposed. For the budget committee may not only change its tentative decision in the light of feedback from the administration, but the initial decisions may be taken in the context of what the committee expects the administration to want. Friedrich (1937) coined the term "rule by anticipated reactions" to describe this situation. Dahl (1957) has argued that there must be some time lag between the actions of an actor who is said to have power and the responses of those over whom he has such power. "A can hardly be said to have power over a unless A's power attempts precede a's responses" (Dahl, 1957: 204). But clearly, this is not the case. The less powerful social actor may and, in fact, probably will take into account the likely response of the more powerful in framing action in the first place. Thus, an attempt to assess power must try to account for the extent to which initial expressions of preference already reflect the power of others in the organization.

Second, most personnel cases are probably relatively clear-cut in any event. Of the total number considered, only a small proportion actually involve any substantial differences of opinion among the various parties concerning what should be done. The budget committee's power can be assessed only by those cases in which there is some disagreement with the administration over whose views are to prevail. By including those cases in which there is consensus, the amount of apparent committee power is overstated.

This point can be nicely illustrated by considering a situation in which admissions or hiring decisions are to be made by three social actors, which might be individuals or organizational subunits. In Table 2-2, some hypothetical data are presented concerning these decisions. For ease of exposition, assume that the final decision is analyzed from the point of view of A's original decisions. Of 100 candidates or applicants, A initially accepted fifty and rejected fifty. B, with more severe standards, rejected all fifty of those that A had also rejected, but also rejected ten of those that A wanted to accept. C, with somewhat more lenient standards, accepted all fifty of those A had wanted to accept, and also wanted to accept ten that A had wanted to reject. In the final decision, all fifty of A's acceptances were accepted, and eight of A's rejections, which were C's acceptances, were also accepted.

Consider the assessment of the relative power of the three parties. A made 100 decisions and got his way 92% of the time. B made 100 decisions also, and got his way 82% of the time. C made the same 100 decisions, and got his way 98% of the time. C is clearly the most powerful, but A is close behind and B still appears to have some significant amount of power in the system. However, a different picture emerges if only the contested decisions are examined. Of A's fifty acceptances, there were ten contested, the ones that B wanted to reject. Of these ten, A and C got ten decisions and B got zero. Of A's and B's fifty rejections, there were ten that C wanted to accept, of which eight were finally accepted. A and B each won two contests, and C won eight. Now we can consider, using the twenty contested decisions, who won, to assess power in this social system. Of the twenty contested decisions, A got his way twelve times, for 60%, B only two times, for 10%, and C eighteen times, for 90%. The power distribution suddenly doesn't look nearly as equal. By considering only those decisions in which there were disagreements, we discovered that B was almost never able to get his way, and C almost always won. A was more powerful than B, but substantially less powerful than C.

This procedure would estimate the relative power only if the decisions were made independently and reflected the actors' true preferences. If A had been merely trying to follow what he thought C would do, the estimate of relative power would be even more distorted. This simplified example should make the point that in assessing power, one must be careful to consider only those instances in which preferences conflict, for they are the only cases in which relative power can be observed.

TABLE 2-2
Hypothetical Selection Decision Data

Actor A	Actor B	Actor C	Final Decision
Accept 50	Accept 40	Accept 50	Accept 50
	Reject 10	Reject 0	Reject 0
Reject 50	Accept 0	Accept 10	Accept 8
	Reject 50	Reject 40	Reject 42

ASSESSING POWER BY ITS DETERMINANTS

One method for assessing power described by Gamson (1968) and others involves developing an understanding of what causes power in the social system under study. This method then evaluates the various social actors by determining how much of each of these causes of power they possess. Thus, instead of trying to measure power directly, power is assessed by considering how much of each of the determinants of power the various individuals, subunits, or groups possesses.

In order to employ this methodology for diagnosing power distributions, it is essential that one understand the determinants of power in the social system under study, the topic of Chapter 4. It is also necessary to be able to assess how much of each determinant or source of power each of the various social actors in the situation possesses. And finally, since power typically is multiply-determined and there are customarily several sources of power, it is necessary to be able to predict which of the sources is likely to be more important in the situation under investigation.

Of the three steps in the process, the assessment of how much of a given source of power a given social actor possesses may be the most problematic. Consider, for instance, power which is derived from specialized knowledge or expertise. Although one may be able to see that this special knowledge is particularly critical in the social system, it is difficult to determine how much of that particular knowledge or competence various participants possess. Knowledge is not something readily observed, like height, weight, or hair color. If various interests within the organization perceive that some specific competency is an important source of power, they will try to make others believe that they are uniquely expert or knowledgeable in the particular area. If marketing expertise is the critical function, then all actors will behave as if they are competent marketers. If fund raising is a particularly critical skill, then each will attempt to demonstrate contacts and abilities in the fund-raising activity. There is a great likelihood of the occurrence of selective self-presentation to enhance status within the organization. Discerning the amount of various power sources actually possessed by various organizational participants requires some skill.

Another issue involved in evaluating power distributions by assessing the distribution of the determinants of power is that some social actors, who might be potentially powerful, may not recognize the determinants or the fact that they possess them. In this sense, the power is not recognized, and hence will not be used. Even if power positions are recognized, organizational actors may choose not to employ their power. However, in this latter case, the power is potentially there for use. In the case in which power is not recognized, however, it does not even exist as a potential to be employed if favorable conditions occurred.

ASSESSING POWER BY ITS CONSEQUENCES

The distribution of power can also be assessed by examining its consequences as these become manifest in decisions made within the organization. Presumably, power is used to affect choices made within social systems. Then, one way of assessing the distribution of power is to see which social actors benefit, and to what extent in contested decisions within organizations. There are many examples of the consequences of power: budget distributions among subunits, the allocation of positions, the making of strategy and policy choices which are favored by and are favorable to various actors, and so forth.

In order to diagnose the distribution of power by looking at the presumed consequences of the use of such power, several things are necessary. First, it must be possible to recognize those situations in which resources or decisions are likely to be determined on the basis of power in the organization. Second, it must be possible to assess which social actors have gained or lost in the decisions that are made on such critical and contested issues. Thus, one must be able to diagnose both those circumstances in which power has an effect, and who has won or lost in these political contests.

In the next chapter we shall consider in more detail some theories about the conditions under which power is employed in decision making. For the moment, it is important to note that it is often more difficult than one might expect to discern the winners and the losers in the various decisions in which power was used. It is not in the interests of many people within the organization to publicize the winners and losers in contests of power. For the social actors who have fared relatively poorly in the decisions, the announcement of these decisions merely reaffirms their position of relative weakness, and helps to solidify that weakness. Furthermore, to lose a decision is to lose face, and unless the publication of such a loss can be used to mobilize further support, there is little to be gained by making public the extent of the loss. For the winners, there are also some disadvantages in discerning how much was gained in the decision. The winning social actors may be confronted with additional demands if others in the organization are able to see the extent of their benefits. In addition, it is considered unseemly to boast over one's victories. Indeed, the victories, if widely promulgated, may set in motion

187

coalitions against the winners, which will make the winning of future decisions more difficult. Power, as we shall learn in Chapter 5, is often exercised most effectively when it is exercised unobtrusively. This implies that those who have fared relatively well in organizational decisions are not likely to make this fact too widely known.

There is another reason why the outcome of organizational politics may not be too readily visible. As Parsons and Smelser (1956) noted, rationality is more than a description of a decision making process, it is a valued social ideal. March (1976: 69) refers to the theory of rational choice using words such as faith and scripture. Rational decision making is an ideal which, even if not empirically descriptive, is to be kept for both external and internal system maintenance at all costs. Thus, it is in the interests of all who share the belief in the myth of rational choice that decisions appear to be made rationally rather than to be based on power and politics. If this requires making the outcomes of such decisions less visible so that the distribution of rewards are less readily discerned, such activity will be taken. In the absence of hard indicators representing decision outcomes, the belief in rational choice processes will be more easily maintained and the norm of rationality preserved as a socially shared myth.

Thus, winners and losers are often difficult to discern. Winners appear not to have won very much; losers act as if they did better than they had hoped, and quite well all things considered. One can see this posturing in political bodies in which there is a certain grace on both sides after the final vote. Discerning power by observing its consequences, therefore, requires access to decision outcomes that may be problematic except in the case of some public organizations. It requires getting the specific results of policy actions. It is in the interests of few parties to make such information too readily available.

ASSESSING POWER BY ITS SYMBOLS

Ironically, although social actors may attempt to hide the extent to which power has affected decision outcomes, there is often much less reluctance to make the distribution of power within organizations visible through the use of symbols of power. Such symbols include things such as titles, special parking places, special eating facilities, restrooms, automobiles, airplanes, office size, placement, and furnishings, and other perquisites of position and power. Such symbols are particularly likely to be employed to distinguish among vertical levels of power within organizations. Managers at different levels may have different size offices. At one large organization in California, the kind of furnishings in the office, as well as whether or not the floor is carpeted, is determined by hierarchical level. One can go into an office in this corporation and determine quickly by visible inspection what is the relative position of the occupant in the status hierarchy.

Such distinctions may also differentiate among individuals and subunits who are ostensibly on the same hierarchical level. In Barrows Hall on the Berkeley campus, one side of the building has a view of San Francisco and the Golden Gate Bridge. Offices on that side of the building are typically occupied by persons such as the dean, associate dean, and ex-deans of the School of Business Administration, very senior full professors, and on other floors occupied by other departments, the leading social and behavioral scientists from those departments. The offices in a major San Francisco law firm were allocated according to the view and position of the office. This led, on occasion, to the placing of people who had worked together in different parts of the building, because placement was done on the basis of seniority, status, and the desirability of the individual office rather than by the relationship of the office to other law firm members. In a major California utility, the shift in power from engineering to law was visible as lawyers began to get offices on the higher floors of the building, and engineers offices on the lower floors. The Transamerica pyramid is perhaps the clearest physical manifestation of the organizational hierarchy, but the general tendency for both higher ranking executives and higher ranking functions to have higher level offices is quite pervasive.

In Figure 2.1, we have shown a partial map of the campus at Berkeley. One can quickly note that the physical sciences, which have tended to be the more powerful departments at Berkeley, are relatively higher up the hillside. The few exceptions to this general rule can be explained by recognizing that there are also laboratory buildings even higher up on the hill; those departments with some power which are relegated to apparently less favorable locations are actually those that have a large proportion of their faculty in offices located up the hill in these other buildings. An interesting study would involve the assessment of the extent to which departmental power in various organizations is correlated with locational favorability, either in terms of view, office space per departmental member, or centrality in the organization's informal communication network as manifested by physical centrality in organizational space.

Whisler and his colleagues (Whisler, Meyer, Baum, and Sorensen, 1967) have developed a measure of organizational centrality which focuses on the dispersion of salaries within organizations. Another useful

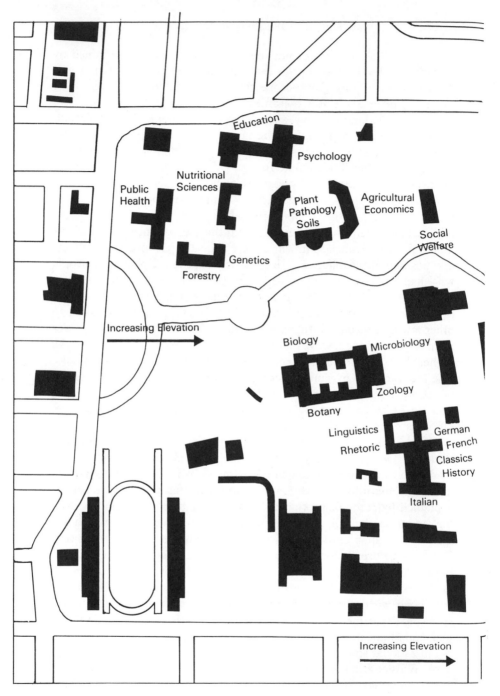

Figure 2-1
Berkeley Campus

190

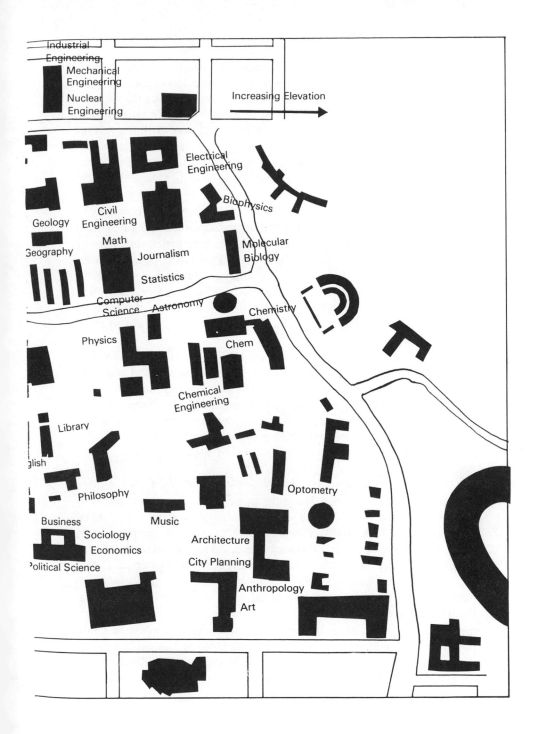

Industrial
Engineering
Mechanical
Engineering
Nuclear
Engineering

Increasing Elevation

Electrical
Engineering

Biophysics

Geology

Civil
Engineering

Math

Molecular
Biology

Geography

Journalism

Statistics

Computer
Science   Astronomy

Chemistry

Physics

Chem

Chemical
Engineering

Library

English

Philosophy

Optometry

Business

Music

Sociology

Economics

Architecture

Political Science

City Planning

Anthropology

Art

indicator of organizational centrality might be the dispersion of office size, characteristics such as furniture and other decoration, and the extent to which offices are private. Our prediction would be that organizations that have more centralization, as measured by Whisler's measure, are also likely to demonstrate more centralization when the various symbols of power and their distribution are considered as well. It would be useful to further relate these indicators of centralization to other measures of the relative dispersion of influence on critical organizational choices.

The provision of social actors with the symbols of power both ratifies their power position within the organization and provides them with power because of the symbols. In a situation in which social power may be difficult to assess, the provision of clear signals of power conveys to others the fact that the social actors who possess these symbols have come to be valued and revered in the organization. This social definition of power becomes, through its physical manifestation in the form of symbols, a shared social reality which serves to convey power to those possessing the symbols.

It is naive to think that such symbols are perfect correlates of power. Offices are not moved wholesale as power waxes and wanes in organizations. Carpets are not taken up and put down as individuals rise and fall in the informal power structure. There are lags and imperfections in the use of such symbols as guides to the power distribution. Nevertheless, these symbols of social influence provide cues which are both visible and positively correlated with distributions of social influence.

REPUTATIONAL INDICATORS OF ORGANIZATIONAL POWER

Another way of finding out where the power lies in organizations is to ask people. Perrow (1970), in a study of twelve industrial firms, asked respondents to rank the four departments of production, marketing, finance and accounting, and research and development in terms of how much power they had within the organizations. Hinings et al. (1974) used a similar though more elaborate questionnaire and interview procedure to assess the relative power of subunits of breweries in Canada. Pfeffer and Salancik (1974), in a study of the power of academic departments at the University of Illinois, asked department heads how much power they thought the various departments possessed. A similar procedure was used by Moore (1979) in his replication of the Illinois study.

Although there has not been much controversy concerning this procedure and its use in studies of power in organizations, there is a great deal of controversy surrounding the reputational measurement of power in community power studies. Hunter (1953) was one of the first to use the practice of asking respondents who had power in his studies of Atlanta, a practice which was followed by other sociologists (e.g., Pellegrini and Coates, 1956; Schulze, 1958). Polsby (1960) has criticized this research procedure by arguing that it presumes an answer to the question of whether or not there is a concentration of power in communities.

> *If anything there seems to be an unspoken notion among pluralist researchers that at bottom* nobody *dominates in a town, so that their first question is not likely to be, "Who runs this community?" but rather, "Does anyone at all run this community?" The first query is somewhat like "Have you stopped beating your wife?" in that virtually any response short of total unwillingness to answer will supply the researchers with a "power elite" along the lines proposed by stratification theory (Polsby, 1960: 476).*

The method applied in studies of organizational power is conceptually similar. Asking department heads to rank or rate the power of other departments presumes that a system of differentiated power exists in the organization. In fact, the asking of the question may produce answers that provide the appearance of a stratified system of power where none really exists. The pluralist solution to this is to study actual community decision making. In the organizational analogue, the parallel would be to study the decision making of organizations to see empirically whether or not an elite set of social actors can be identified. Alternatively, one might see if the reputational indicators of power within the organization correlate with other measures and if power, as assessed by this method, does predict the outcome of organizational decision making. Most of the studies cited did correlate these measures, either with presumed determinants of power or, as in the case of the study of budget decision making at the University of Illinois, with both determinants and decisions reflecting power.

The reputational method for assessing organizational power assumes that: social actors are knowledgeable about power within their organizations; informants are willing to divulge what they know about power distributions; and such a questioning process will not itself create the phenomenon under study, power. The first two concerns are troublesome. Given the normative value of the rational model of choice, many organizational actors may be insensitive to the operation of organizational politics and may be relatively naive about distributions of power within the organization. Those who do know the distribution of influence and are skilled in political strategies have nothing to gain by sharing this knowledge and, in fact, are probably more effective because this knowledge is not widely shared within the organization. Informants may be unwilling to tell you what they know about power within the organization. And, because of the norms concerning politics and rationality in organizations, the very asking of questions is likely to be perceived as illegitimate and upsetting. It is one thing to ask about size, structure, or job attitudes; it is quite another to ask questions about organizational power and politics. Such behavior can get one labeled as a Machiavellian person or someone who has little concern for the normative structure and sensibilities of the organization. Consequently, the reputational method for assessing power can be particularly troublesome when the normative structure of the organization stresses the illegitimacy of power and politics.

This difficulty in assessing power through the use of questionnaires or interviews is illustrated by the following example. In a study of power and resource allocation in two University of California campuses, department heads were interviewed concerning their ratings of the power held by other departments studied, as well as their own. One humanities department chairman, after receiving a copy of the questionnaire in advance of the actual interview, refused to cooperate with the study:

> *. . . if I saw the university enterprise in the terms implied by your questionnaire I would be seeking, frankly, some other way of making a living, instead of practicing the profession I've been engaged in for the last three decades. In fact, my opinion of the premises on which the questionnaire rests is such that I cannot bring myself to devote more than a few moments to this letter . . . (Anonymous, 1978).*

Asking questions about power and decision making clearly violated normative beliefs about the nature and character of universities and academic life. But, such questions may also violate the religion of rationality and profit maximization that pervades business organizations.

When informants can be convinced to reveal what they know about power within organizations, the reputational measure of power does provide some evidence that there are socially shared judgments within organizations concerning influence distributions. In the study of power at the University of Illinois, department chairmen were asked to rate on a seven point scale, the departments in question, as to the amount of power each possessed. As noted previously, only one person asked for clarification of what was meant by power. Although some were not familiar with the power of all the departments, there was enormous consistency in the answers provided. No department which overall was rated in the top third in terms of power was rated by any single chairman as being lower than the top one-third. And no department which averaged in the bottom one-third was rated by any chairman as being higher than the bottom one-third. There was, then, enormous consistency in the ratings, particularly for the most and least powerful departments. This consensus and consistency in power ratings provides some evidence for at least a shared social definition of the distribution of power.

REPRESENTATIONAL INDICATORS

Reputational indicators of power rely both on the knowledge of organizational informants and their willingness to share that knowledge. Such cooperation may not be forthcoming either because of normatively held views of power and politics or for strategic reasons. Furthermore, reputational indicators can be collected only to assess current distributions of influence. If power in organizations is to be studied historically to determine trends in influence, then reputational measures, with their necessarily contemporaneous quality, are insufficient.

Representational indicators of power assess the position of social actors in critical organizational roles such as membership on influential boards and committees or occupancy of key administrative posts. Representational indicators, then, are available as long as position and committee occupants and their affiliations can be identified from organizational records. These data can be collected in a less obtrusive fashion, without violating organizational norms and myths. These indicators are useful supplements to other ways of assessing power in organizations.

Some positions in organizations provide their occupants with power because of the control over information, resources, or other decisions that is inherent in these positions. Some positions in organizations are given to those social actors with the power to signify and ratify their power to others. In most cases, positions which are given to powerful social actors as a consequence of their power also provide those actors with additional power due to the information and decisions that are within the purview of these positions. If these roles can be identified, then by observing the affiliations of the role occupants, one can diagnose the distribution of influence within the organization.

In the study of power of university departments at two University of California campuses, the representational indicator employed was departmental membership on major campus committees. The committees identified had influence over the allocation of a resource, such as faculty positions or research funds, or had influence over an important educational policy or domain. In Table 2-3, the correlations among the average departmental representation on the various committees over a ten-year period are presented. It is clear that there are moderately strong correlations between most of the representational indicators of power. One way of using the information on committee representation is to combine the committees and assess proportional departmental representation on all committees taken together. Committee representation can serve as an indicator of power because the committee positions themselves convey power to their occupants. Powerful departments are also more likely to have larger representation on key committees as a consequence of their power.

TABLE 2-3
Correlations of Department
Representation on Various University Committees

$(n = 40)$

	Committees	Research	Educ. Policy	Educ. Dev.	Grad. Council	Fellowships
Budget	.63[e]	.24[a]	.36[c]	.31[b]	.27[b]	.43[d]
Committees	---	.23[a]	.48[e]	.28[b]	.19	.34[b]
Research	---	---	.12	−.01	.25[a]	.23[a]
Educ. Policy	---	---	---	.43[d]	.29[b]	.26[a]
Educ. Dev.	---	---	---	---	.28[b]	.64[e]
Grad. Council	---	---	---	---	---	.23[a]

[a] $p < .10$ Budget = departmental representation on the budget committee

[b] $p < .05$ Committees = departmental representation on committee on committees which selects other committee members (elected committee)

[c] $p < .01$ Research = departmental representation on committee on research

[d] $p < .005$ Educ. Policy = departmental representation on educational policy committee

[e] $p < .001$ Educ. Dev. = departmental representation on educational development committee

Grad. Council = departmental representation on graduate council, the committee that works with the Dean of the graduate division

Fellowships = departmental representation on the fellowship and scholarships subcommittee of the graduate council

In business firms, a similar procedure can be employed to assess power. Critical executive positions can be identified, and the departmental affiliations of executives who have risen to these positions can be determined, as a way of seeing which subunits are more powerful. Important committees within the firm, such as capital budgeting committees, strategic planning and policy committees, the executive committee, and in some instances, hiring and personnel policy committees can be identified and representation on such committees can be assessed. Departmental, occupational, and individual representation in important roles and on critical committees can provide evidence useful in diagnosing the relative occupational, departmental, and individual power of social actors in the organization.

A SYNTHESIS

It should now be clear that there are a variety of ways of assessing power distributions within organizations, and each has its own strengths and weaknesses. The most reasonable approach in diagnosing power then is to look for a convergence of power indicators within social systems. There should be a correlation between the ranking of the determinants of power, the consequences of power, the symbols of power, and the reputational and representational indicators of power. An index constructed from all of these factors is likely to provide a reasonably good approximation of the distribution of power in the organization at a given time.

Unfortunately, there have been few quantitative, comparative studies of power in organizations conducted up to this time. Indeed, one of the purposes of this book is to synthesize the literature on power in organizations, in the hope of stimulating additional investigation. Two of the more systematic and comprehensive studies were conducted at universities in Illinois and California. Both studies found reasonably good convergence between the reputational and representational power indicators. At Illinois, there was a correlation of .61 ($p < .001$) between the reputational measure of power and total representation on important committees in the university (Pfeffer and Salancik, 1974). In the California study, the correlation was .57 ($p < .001$) between the same two measures (Moore, 1979). In both cases also, there were high correlations between these indicators of power and presumed determinants of power, such as student enrollments and outside grant and contract dollars obtained. There were also high correlations between outcomes or consequences of power such as budget allocations and the allocations of other resources such as research funds and fellowships. Thus, at least in these two studies, there is an indication that some of the various methods of assessing power do converge, providing the ability to diagnose organizational power distributions.

In the past I have asked my organizational behavior class to think of indicators for diagnosing the power distribution of the subject matter groups within the school of business and, on other occasions, to come up with indicators for diagnosing the power distribution in an organization in which they are going to work. In Table 2-4, some illustrative answers are provided. The indicators all represent some manifestation or outcropping of a source or determinant, consequence, or indicator of power in the organization. Each indicator is imperfect, since each may be affected by numerous things other than power, such as history, rules and regulations, and so forth. The point, however, is that the set of indicators taken together can, just as in the case of the two universities, provide some indication of power distributions.

Power distributions may or may not be well defined and stable. One obtains from the process just described some indication of the state of

TABLE 2-4
Sample Indicators of Power in Two Organizational Contexts

Subject Groups Within a School of Business	Functional Departments Within a Business Firm
Number of required courses in the subject	Functional representation among general management positions
Proportion of the faculty at various ranks, controlling for age or length of service	Functional representation among positions on the board of directors
Student/faculty ratio	Salary of executive in charge of each respective function
Amount of fellowship money in the subject field	Number of persons in each function
Group representation on departmental elected policy and planning committee	Level of functional department in organizational structure
Group representation among Dean and Associate Dean positions	Starting salary of new employees in various functional departments
Office locations of group faculty	Physical location of function and its head in the corporate office
National reputation of the subject group	Representation of function on committees such as capital budgeting or executive committees
Proportion of group faculty with joint membership with other subject groups	The relative representation of departments in internal and outside training activities

power within the social organization being examined. If there is little or no convergence among reputational, representational, determinants, and consequences of power indicators, then this probably indicates that the power within the organization is widely dispersed and not organized. Alternatively, it may be that the distribution of influence is in the process of change and the new structure of influence has not yet clearly emerged.

Again, the assessment of power benefits from some analytic discipline. My students and colleagues have often found it useful to explicitly list the various social actors across the top of a piece of paper, and then list all the indicators of power that they can think of down the side of the page. Then, by scoring each actor on each indicator and summarizing the data, an overall picture of the distribution of power in the organization can be obtained. The discipline of writing things down in a structured format helps to ensure that important indicators useful in assessing power are not overlooked; an attempt at some formal weighting system helps to assure that some indicators are not given undue influence in the formation of assessments of social power. Experience indicates that it is feasible, using the various indicators detailed above, to diagnose power systems with reasonable accuracy. At the same time, it is clear that substantial additional research is necessary to further develop these indicators and to examine their interrelationships in a variety of organizational settings.

Case Examples

The preceding discussion about the identification of political actors and the assessment of their power can be illustrated by the use of a few examples. These examples are based on actual data, though the specific organizations will remain anonymous.

DIAGNOSING POWER BY OBSERVING IT IN USE: THE CASE OF ENGINEERING ELECTRONICS

The Engineering Electronics company was located on the San Francisco peninsula. It was a relatively young and fairly small company, with sales of about $10 million. Like many companies in the electronics industry in the area, it was founded and staffed largely by engineers. However, that did not necessarily assist in the diagnosis of power, as some engineers were technology-oriented, others were market-oriented, and still others, particularly those who had been to business school, were financially-oriented.

Engineering Electronics was faced with making a decision concerning into which of two projects they should invest the bulk of their extra

TABLE 2-5
Characteristics of Projects at Engineering Electronics

	Project 1	Project 2
Return on investment	50%	50%
Risk	average	high
Customer Base	millions	12
Competition	scattered	heavy
Amount of downside risk	$200,000	$3,300,000
Size of required investment	$600,000	$3,300,000
Upside potential	good	fair
Amount of know-how to complete project already in company	some	very little
Sponsoring department	marketing	engineering

capital. Both could be pursued, but it was clear that some priorities would have to be set. The two projects' characteristics are detailed in Table 2-5. These characteristics were provided by a student who had worked on the analysis as part of a summer job. When these data were presented in class, with the identification of the backing department omitted, approximately 90%–100% of the class concluded that Project

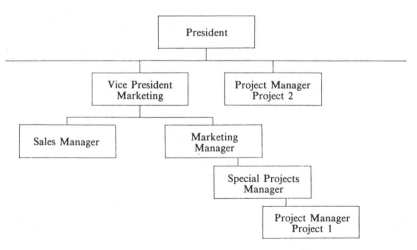

Figure 2.2
Organizational Position of Project 1 and Project 2

1 should be chosen. It has equal investment payoff with substantially reduced financial and market risk.

Interestingly enough, this particular firm chose to put its emphasis on Project 2. Indeed, Project 2's favored position is apparent from the organization that evolved, as shown in Figure 2.2.

Seldom is the use of power and influence so stark and dramatic. The project sponsored by the marketing department lost out almost solely because of their sponsorship. At the same time, the project sponsored by the engineering department won out over financial considerations and over the alternative provided by marketing. The power of engineering, and specifically engineering with a technical emphasis, was clear.

USING REPRESENTATIONAL INDICATORS: THE CASE OF WESTERN ELECTRIC

Access to actual decisions and the kind of detailed information available in the preceding example is often not possible; and, as noted, the use of power is seldom so clear cut. Yet, most organizations have committees, executives, and administrators, and their backgrounds and training are seldom private. Indeed, corporations are required by law to provide information on their highest executives, and sources such as *Dun's* and *Who's Who* also afford a wealth of information. This information can be used to get a picture of the power structure of the organization, using representational indicators.

Consider the case of Western Electric, the manufacturing subsidiary of the Bell System. One might suspect that as a manufacturing subsidiary which sold much of its output to the parent company, the primary power would be held by people with manufacturing and engineering backgrounds. One might also suspect that this power structure is changing, as the Bell System as a whole is forced to compete and as the importance of governmental and other regulatory activity increases.

In Table 2-6, we present some illustrative background information on twenty-five of the top executives of the subsidiary. The domination of the manufacturing function in these data is quite evident. It seems clear that for those with an engineering degree, the road to power in Western Electric has been through manufacturing.

If the shift away from manufacturing and engineering has begun, it is not yet discernible. However, one might expect in about ten or twenty years to see the domination of manufacturing diminished at least in part. This is evidenced by the fact that of those who have been sent to lengthy internal or external training programs, 36.8% are assigned to

TABLE 2-6
Backgrounds of Western Electric Executives

	Degree		Where Career Began		Dominant Work Experience	
	Engineering	Other	Mfg.	Other	Mfg.	Other
Executives	19	6	17	8	20	5
Executive Policy Committee	7	1	7	1	7	1
Corporate Personnel Policy Advisory Committee	4	3	4	3	5	2

manufacturing and 45.3% are assigned currently to either Bell System Sales or other sales operations. Of course, if the employees' backgrounds are primarily in manufacturing, this is just another way of maintaining control over other parts of the operation.

While reading proxy statements and other publications to discern the training and background of corporate officials and members of various organizational committees may not be everyone's idea of a good time, a great deal can be learned about the distribution of power and how it has changed and is still changing.

SEVERAL INDICATORS TOGETHER: A SCHOOL OF BUSINESS

The diagnosis of power distributions is enhanced, of course, when several indicators of power are used together. In Table 2-7, the number of faculty members, administrative positions that are of importance, and the number of chaired full professorships held by various subject fields in a school of business for the years 1969 and 1979 are displayed. A chaired professorship is a specially endowed professorship which always is honorific in nature and in some circumstances, though not the present case, brings extra remuneration or other perquisites. It is clear from the data that the largest groups, Finance and Accounting, which also tended to demonstrate the most growth over the period, ended the period with the most chaired professorships, and were represented in the two associate dean positions. Although the power of some of the other subject groups is less clear from just these data, it seems fair to state that these two fields, finance and accounting, evidence the most power within the school at this time. The fact that the representational indicators of executive positions, the use of resources in acquiring new positions, and the symbolic indicators of power, the chaired professorships, all evidence the same

TABLE 2-7
Indicators of Power in a School of Business

Subject Area	No. of Faculty		No. of Chaired Professorships		Associate Dean
	1979	1969	1979	1969	
Accounting	11	9	4	—	1
Economics and Public Policy	10	7	3	1	—
Finance	14	8	4	1	1
Marketing	8	7	2	1	—
Organizational Behavior	6	7	3	1	—
Management and Decision Sciences	9	7	2	—	—

pattern of results, provides greater confidence in the validity of the analysis.

We have seen in this chapter that although the study of power in organizations is still relatively young, there are some strategies available which facilitate the diagnosis of organizational power distributions and permit the identification of and the measurement of the influence of important organizational political actors. Having begun to understand processes by which social power can be assessed, it is next important to begin to identify the conditions under which such power is likely to play an important role in decision making. This issue is the subject of the next chapter.

Power in University Budgeting: A Replication and Extension

Jeffrey Pfeffer and William L. Moore

This study examines the determinants of power and budget allocations on two campuses of a large, state university system. As in previous studies, faculty positions and budget allocations were a function of student enrollment and departmental power, and departmental power was related to the amount of a department's grant and contract funds as well as enrollment. An additional variable in this study, the level of paradigm development characterizing the department's scientific field, was found to predict the levels of grant and contract funds obtained as well as to help explain budget allocations. In a comparison of resource allocation on the two campuses, it was found that for the campus that faced less scarcity of resources, enrollment was more highly related and departmental power less strongly related to allocations.[•]

Although relatively more budget decisions are now made within organizations using administrative procedures than across organizations using markets (Pondy, 1970), the literature on budgeting within organizations is relatively small. Pondy and Birnberg (1969) studied the budgeting process experimentally, but there has been little additional research using their methodology. Most studies that have examined budgeting within organizations have examined public or quasi-public organizations, undoubtedly because of the easier access to data. The research about budget allocations to federal agencies (Wildavsky and Hammond, 1965; Davis, Dempster, and Wildavsky, 1966; Wildavsky, 1979) is not directly comparable to that in organizations, since such budget allocations are made through legislative processes rather than through administrative decision making.

One of the central issues in budgeting research is the extent to which a political model accounts for observed outcomes in contrast to a rational or bureaucratic model, and the conditions under which the political model is more or less likely to hold. Pfeffer and Salancik (1974) argued that organizational budgeting was a political process. For example, they and others found that power and social-influence processes were more important in decision situations characterized by uncertainty (Pfeffer, Salancik, and Leblebici, 1976; Salancik and Pfeffer, 1978) and scarcity and criticalness (Salancik and Pfeffer, 1974; Hills and Mahoney, 1978), and in decision situations in which information used to make the decisions and the decision outcomes themselves were secret (Salancik and Pfeffer, 1978).

A second issue has been what determines the power of subunits within the organization. Salancik and Pfeffer (1974), in their study of the University of Illinois, found that power accrued to the academic departments that provided grants and contracts for the organization. Pfeffer and Leong (1977) found that in United Funds, the relative dependency of the agency on the Fund and the Fund on the agency helped to explain budget allocations to agencies. Provan, Beyer, and Kruytbosch (1980), also examining United Fund allocations, found that external linkages provided additional influence in the decision-making process. Hills and Mahoney (1978) observed a significant relationship between an academic department's having an outside advisory board and its ability to

© 1980 by Cornell University.
0001-8392/80/2504-0637$00.75

•
The authors gratefully acknowledge the assistance of Jeanne Logsdon with the collection of some of the data and J. Richard Harrison for research assistance with the analysis.

637 Administrative Science Quarterly

obtain incremental budget, providing further evidence for the importance of external linkages. And Freeman and Hannan (Freeman and Hannan, 1975; Freeman, 1979), examining the relative sizes of personnel components in school districts, argued that position in the decision-making process affected power; for example, administrators, at the head of the decision-making and information systems, could protect themselves better from cutbacks under declining enrollments than lower-level groups. Lodahl and Gordon (1973), in a study of 80 departments in four disciplines, found that the level of development of the department's scientific paradigm was associated with the amount of budget support obtained both from outside sources and internally. This raises the possibility that paradigm development may affect power and so budget allocations.

A third issue concerns theory and measurement; that is, how to distinguish power from other related concepts (such as size), how to measure it in a social system, and how to assess the validity of political models versus alternatives. March (1966) argued that power was often incorrectly attributed, and in social-process models of decision making (March and Olsen, 1976), it is maintained that much of what occurs in organizations is accidental rather than the result of interests being consistently pursued by powerful organizational actors.

The present study addresses aspects of all three issues. First, it proposes and tests a more comprehensive model of budgeting in a university, treating both the determinants of power and the effects of power on budget allocations. Second, it addresses the issue of the effect of paradigm development on the budget allocation process. Third, it replicates a procedure for assessing power in social systems that permits the analysis of power historically. Fourth, in the use of both cross-sectional and dynamic analyses, the study addresses the issues of causality and measurement of power. And, finally, by a comparison of the operation of power and other criteria on budgeting on two campuses, the study provides some data on the conditions under which power is more or less important.

BACKGROUND AND HYPOTHESES

The Figure shows the model of power and resource allocation examined in this study. The first link in the model is from the level of paradigm development to the amount of grant and contract dollars received by the department. A

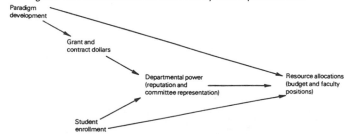

Figure. Model of power in decisions on budget allocations.

638/ASQ

206

higher level of paradigm development makes the results of research expenditures more predictable and more certain, thereby reducing the risk of funding agencies and encouraging the funding of disciplines with more highly developed paradigms. We also argue that paradigm development has a direct effect on resource allocations in a university. Beyer and Lodahl (1976) argued that the higher predictability in academic departments with greater paradigm development would lead to greater consensus over goals and means of goal attainment in such departments, reducing conflict and facilitating coalition formation, and so strengthening the departments in any contest of power. The direct effect of level of paradigm development on budget allocations has not been studied, however. The variable was not incorporated in two studies of budget allocations at universities, Illinois (Pfeffer and Salancik, 1974) and Minnesota (Hills and Mahoney, 1978). And Lodahl and Gordon's (1973) finding of an association between the level of paradigm development and internal levels of budget allocation did not separate the direct effect of paradigm development from the indirect effect of paradigm development influencing grant and contract awards, and so power and budget allocations.

The model also shows the determinants of departmental power. Following the results of Salancik and Pfeffer (1974: 461), we argue that power is a function of the department's ability to provide two important resources — grants and contracts and student enrollment. Grants and contracts are important for the support of graduate education and research, as well as for the overhead generated and the slack (Cyert and March, 1963) that can result from such overhead. Student enrollment is an important resource because budget allocations to this as well as to most state universities are based at least partly on enrollment. In private universities, tuition income is related to the ability to attract students. The importance of student enrollments to departments was shown by Manns and March (1978), who found that curriculum changes, particularly for the less powerful departments, were related to enrollment pressures.

Another possible source of power is national visibility and research reputation. However, Salancik and Pfeffer (1974) found no effect of the national prestige of departments on power, and none is posited in this study. National prestige data were collected so that the finding of no effect on departmental power could be replicated.

Examination of the determinants of departmental power is important because of some inconsistent results from previous studies. Hills and Mahoney (1978: 462) observed no correlation between representation on committees, an indicator of departmental power, and the amount of matching funds obtained. Matching funds are a much more restrictive measure than grant and contract awards. They did not attempt to estimate the predictors of departmental power, nor did they use an interview-based measure of power. Indeed, their two indicators of power were not strongly correlated with each other, with the correlation between having an advisory board and committee representation being only .13. Given the importance of the measurement issues associated with the concept of social power and the fact that the Min-

207

nesota study largely failed to replicate the Illinois results, it is critical to replicate the original Illinois procedure to see if indicators that provided good convergence once could also work in another university.

Studying the determinants of departmental power over time as well as cross-sectionally permits examining some alternative explanations for the results. If the predicted determinants — enrollments and grants and contracts — explain departmental power at a later period even after power is controlled for statistically at the earlier period, we can have more confidence in the direction of causation being as posited in the model.

The evidence for the effect of power on university budget allocations is also not consistent. Pfeffer and Salancik (1974) found that both departmental power and student enrollments were related to budget allocations, but Hills and Mahoney (1978) did not. They did find some evidence for a workload effect on the allocation of discretionary budget increments, particularly during periods of more abundant resources. However, Hills and Mahoney (1978) did not observe a significant positive relationship between committee representation and budget allocations, thus failing to replicate the results of the original Illinois study. Their conclusion, that power operated in times of scarcer resources, was based on the coefficient for the presence of an advisory board variable.[1] However, given the collinearity with the matching funds variable, the interpretation of the coefficient is not completely clear, particularly since including both variables in the regression forced matching funds into the equation with an unexpected and statistically significant negative sign.

Examining budget allocations over time can help to make clear the causality and the dynamics of the process. Once budget allocation at an initial time is statistically controlled, the effects of power, paradigm development, and changes in enrollment on subsequent allocations provide clear evidence for the causal relationship of these variables in the direction specified in the Figure.

One final relationship predicted to account for both budget allocations and changes in allocations not represented in the model is a predicted interaction between paradigm development and enrollment, in which enrollment is a more important predictor of allocations for departments with a more developed paradigm. The underlying argument is similar to that for the direct effect of paradigm development. Enrollment provides a potential argument for the department claiming more resources. Such claims can be met by arguing that class size can be increased, teaching loads altered, or some other accommodation made, but such arguments are more readily countered with the consensus and unanimity characterizing a department having a certain and predictable technology. In the model in the Figure, enrollment is posited to be the only bureaucratic criterion that accounts for budget allocations. Consequently, one would only expect an interaction of paradigm development with this criterion. Grants and contracts are posited to act through departmental power. Research or professional activity, although a valid claim on resources, is not included, first, because it is not as unam-

1

There are numerous problems with the Hills and Mahoney (1978) study, which are beyond the scope of this paper but which make their results less than a direct replication of the original Illinois study. Not only were many of their measures different, but they did not test for the statistical significance of the difference between the regression coefficients estimated for periods of scarce and abundant resources, and the equations themselves probably have problems of autocorrelation, since the authors apparently pooled cross-sectional data over time without attempting to correct for the statistical problems that inevitably result (Hannan and Young, 1977).

biguously or universally measured as enrollment, and, second, because it should be at least partly reflected in the department's national prestige and reputation, which has been found not to predict budget allocations.

METHOD

Data were collected for twenty departments on one campus of a large, prestigious state university system, and the twenty corresponding departments at another campus in the system. The twenty departments were:

Anthropology	Mathematics
Art	Mechanical engineering
Chemical engineering	Philosophy
Chemistry	Physics
Economics	Physiology (Biological
Electrical engineering	sciences at one campus)
English	Political science
French	Psychology
Geology	Sociology
German	Spanish (Spanish and Por-
History	tuguese at one campus)

These departments constituted all those common to the two campuses that offered doctoral degrees and represented most of the letters and science departments. Data were collected for the period 1967–1976, although in some cases, 1968 or 1975 data were the earliest or latest available. These data — on faculty positions, budget allocations, grant and contract funds, and enrollment — were obtained from the university academic planning office.

Measures of Departmental Power

As in an earlier study (Pfeffer and Salancik, 1974) of university budgeting, two types of departmental power measures were used, reputation of the department and its representation on committees. Department chairpersons rated each of the twenty departments on their campus as to the amount of power of the department. A "don't know" response was permitted. The average of all responses excluding "don't know" for each department constituted the department's score for reputational power.

The measure of representation on committees was similar to that used by both Pfeffer and Salancik (1974) and Hills and Mahoney (1978). Important university committees were identified, such as those allocating budget or research funds, selecting members to serve on the various committees, or determining some major educational policy. The committees used in the study were:

Budget and planning	Fellowships and scholarships
Committee on committees	subcommittee of the
Educational development	graduate council
Educational policy	Committee on research
Graduate council	

Documents in the university archives were used to determine departmental representation on the committees. Since in any given year there will be sampling errors, because there are more departments than committee positions, committee representation was averaged over the period to provide a summary measure for each committee individually and for the summated representation on all committees. Such a procedure is, of course, the only feasible way to compare power ratings obtained from reputation and committee representation, since department chairpersons could be reliably interrogated only about current perceptions. For comparability across campuses, the department's proportional representation was used.

Measurement of Paradigm Development

Lodahl and Gordon (1972) measured paradigm development for a sample of seven fields using a questionnaire. Salancik, Staw, and Pondy (1980), in a study of turnover in university department heads, developed indicators of paradigm development based upon language parsimony characterizing the disciplines and the level of integration of knowledge. For parsimony in communication, the indicators were the length of doctoral dissertations (in pages) and abstracts of the dissertations (in words) for a random sample of dissertations from each field. In the present study, a random sample of twenty-five dissertations from each field in 1966 was used to develop estimates of language parsimony by field. The various languages, which are combined in *Dissertation Abstracts,* received the same score. For level of integration of knowledge, Salancik, Staw, and Pondy (1980) used the longest chain of prerequisite courses in a department. In this study, a department's score on this indicator was the longest chain of linked courses (with one being prerequisite to the next) found in the most recent catalogue. Each department's rank score on each of the three indicators was computed and summed to obtain an overall measure of the level of paradigm development. The correlations among the individual indicators of paradigm development were all above .7; moreover, the overall ranking of departments on the paradigm development index correlated highly with Lodahl and Gordon's (1972) ranking for the seven departments common to both studies ($r = .81; p < .01$).

Budget Measures

The dependent variables were the proportion of the budget and full-time equivalent regular faculty positions on each campus that each department obtained for each year during the period. For the cross-sectional analysis, values were averaged for each department over the ten-year period; for the dynamic analyses, initial and final values were used. The budget included just those funds that were allocated by the administration to the departments; it did not include endowment income, specific gifts, or grants and contracts received by the department. In analyzing the operation of power in the budgeting process, it was necessary to restrict the dependent variable to include only those funds that were actually allocated to the departments in competition with other departments.

Hills and Mahoney (1978) noted that budget allocations were incremental and, in large measure, the increments were allocated on a proportional basis. Rather than employing their involved methodology for trying to separate proportional increases from discretionary effects, we transformed enrollments, budgets, and faculty positions into proportions. Then, proportional changes would not appear in the data as changes at all; instead, only changes in the relative share of enrollments, faculty, or so forth, accounted for by a given department, would be registered. This procedure removed the effects of inflation and budget growth, differences in campus size, and other system-wide constants.

RESULTS

The results are presented first by investigating the extent to which the indicators of departmental power converged, and then by examining allocations first cross-sectionally and next over time.

Definition of Variables

In the tables that follow, the notation and definition for the variables are as follows:

Power = interview-based measure of power

Committees = department's proportional representation on total of the university committees studied

Budget Committee = department's proportional representation on the budget committee

Research = department's representation on committee on research

Educational policy = department's representation on educational policy committee

Educational development = department's representation on educational development committee

Graduate Council = department's representation on graduate council committee

Fellowships = department's representation on fellowships and scholarships subcommittee of the graduate council

C-Committee = department's proportional representation on the committee on committees

Paradigm = department's score on index of paradigm development

Enroll = department's share of total student enrollment

Budget = department's proportional share of total budget

Faculty = department's proportional share of total regular faculty positions

Grants = proportion of total grant and contract funds accounted for by the department

En x Par = enrollment by paradigm interaction

Budget-76 = department's share of budget in 1976

Budget-67 = department's share of budget in 1967

Faculty-75 = department's share of regular faculty positions in 1975

Faculty-67 = department's share of regular faculty positions in 1967

Change Enroll = change in proportion of total enrollment accounted for by department over the period

Change Enroll x Paradigm = paradigm by change in enrollment interaction

Comm-E = average proportion of committee positions during the period 1967, 1968, and 1969 accounted for by department

Comm-L = average proportion of committee positions during the period 1974, 1975, and 1976 accounted for by department

211

Table 1

Correlations Among Indicators of Departmental Power (N=40)

	Committees	Budget committee	C-committee	Research	Educational policy	Educational development	Graduate council	Fellowships
Power	.57•••	.45•••	.48•••	.19	.47•••	.35••	.31••	.35••
Committees	—	.78•••	.80•••	.49•••	.63•••	.42•••	.56•••	.50•••
Budget committee	—	—	.63•••	.24•	.36•••	.31••	.27••	.43•••
C-committee	—	—	—	.23•	.48•••	.28••	.19	.34••
Research	—	—	—	—	.12	−.01	.25•	.23•
Educational policy .	—	—	—	—	—	.43•••	.29••	.26•
Educational development	—	—	—	—	—	—	.28••	.64•••
Graduate council	—	—	—	—	—	—	—	.23•

•p≤.10; ••p≤.05; •••p≤.01

Grants-E = average proportion of grants during the period 1967, 1968, 1969 accounted for by department

Enroll-68 = proportion of student enrollment in 1968

Convergence of Power Measures

The correlations among the indicators of departmental power in Table 1 are consistent with those obtained in the study at the University of Illinois (Pfeffer and Salancik, 1974). In particular, the correlation between the department's reputation and average representation on all committees was .61 at Illinois and .57 in the present study.

Determinants of Resource Allocations

Table 2 presents the means, standard deviations, and intercorrelations of the variables used in estimating the model specified in the Figure. The data indicate that paradigm development is essentially independent of representation on committees but is highly correlated with the department chairperson's ratings of the power of other departments. Because the measure of committee representation is the measure available over time, the one that has been used most consistently in studies of budget allocation, and the one less correlated with the other independent variables, it was the one used in subsequent regressions in which power is an independent variable.

Table 3 presents the regression results for the path model implied in the Figure. Both representation on committees and reputation are explained, but only the committee-

Table 2

Means, Standard Deviations, and Correlations Among Variables (N=40)

Variable	Mean	S.D.	Paradigm	Correlation with Enroll	Budget	Faculty	Power	Grants
Committees	.05	.032	.15	.66•••	.17•••	.73•••	.57•••	.39•••
Paradigm	30.54	16.21	—	−.19	.39•••	.15	.65•••	.62•••
Enroll	.05	.03	—	—	.67•••	.84•••	.31••	.12
Budget	.05	.025	—	—	—	.89•••	.60•••	.67•••
Faculty	.05	.025	—	—	—	—	.47•••	.38•••
Power	4.41	1.26	—	—	—	—	—	.46•••
Grants	.05	.077	—	—	—	—	—	—

•p≤.10; ••p≤.05; •••p≤.01

Table 3

Regression Equations Estimating Model of Power and Resource Allocation (N=40)

Grants= −.043+.00311••• Paradigm
(r²=.40)   (.00061)

Power=3.42+12.04• Enroll+7.09••• Grants
(r²=.25)   (6.18)   (2.33)

Committees=.0094+.672••• Enroll+.131••• Grants
(r²=.50)   (.127)   (.048)

Budget= −.0061+.495••• Enroll+.216•• Committees+.000702••• Paradigm+.0100•• ExnPar
(r²=.76)   (.094)   (.087)   (.000131)   (.0040)

Faculty= −.0036+.661••• Enroll+.139• Committees+.000446••• Paradigm
(r²=.81)   (.085)   (.078)   (.000120)

•$p \leq .10$; ••$p \leq .05$; •••$p \leq .01$

representation measure is itself used to explain other outcomes. The results in Table 3 are consistent with the model and with the arguments presented, except there is no significant interaction effect of paradigm development with enrollment in explaining faculty positions. Paradigm development has a strong relationship with the amount of grant and contract funds, and enrollments and grants both are significant in explaining variation in reputation and committee representation. Also, enrollment, departmental power, and the level of paradigm development are significantly related to the allocation of both the budget and faculty positions, there being a significant effect of the interaction of enrollment and paradigm development in explaining budget allocations. Consistent with many of the previous studies of budget allocation, there is evidence for an effect of departmental power; in addition, there is a strong independent effect of paradigm development on allocations.

When prestige in research was measured by a department's national ranking in 1964 (Cartter, 1966), 1969 (Roose and Andersen, 1970), or an average of the two years, it was not statistically significantly correlated with either faculty or budget allocations, even when the two campuses were considered separately. Thus, consistent with the earlier findings of Pfeffer and Salancik (1974), there is no evidence that national prestige significantly affects allocations.

Dynamics of Power and Resource Allocations

The examination of changes in budgets, faculty positions, and power over time enables us to examine the extent to which precedence, as opposed to power, paradigm development, or enrollment, governs the allocation of resources. The analysis and measurement of change remains as controversial as when Bohrnstedt (1969) summarized the literature, but it is generally agreed that (1) the use of gain or change scores is usually inappropriate, as such scores are less reliable than the separate measures from which they are constructed; (2) it is important to control for the initial level of the variable that is changing, because the direction and amount of change may be a function of the initial level from which the change is measured (for instance, as in regression toward the mean); (3) if one controls for the

Table 4

Regression Equations Predicting Faculty, Total Budget, and Power Over Time (N=40)

Budget−76=.00046+.721••• Budget−67+.194••• Change Enroll+.165••• Committees+.000147• Paradigm+.0112••
(r^2=.95)   (.051)   (.055)   (.039)   (.000077)   (.0044)
     Change Enroll×Paradigm

Faculty−75=.0018+.688••• Faculty−67+.230••• Change Enroll+.224••• Committees+.0150••• Change
(r^2=.94)   (.058)   (.048)   (.045)   (.0048)
     Enroll×Paradigm

Comm-L=.020+.124 Comm-E+.163•• Grants-E+.310• Enroll−68
(r^2=.24)   (.127)   (.069)   (.172)

•$p \leq$.10; ••$p \leq$.05; •••$p \leq$.01

initial level of the variable but still uses change scores, definitional dependence is introduced; and (4) therefore the most commonly found dynamic models today, particularly in the sociological literature, are those that predict the value of a variable at a given time with the values of that variable at some earlier time, plus the other variables that are of theoretical interest (Freeman and Hannan, 1975; Hannan and Freeman, 1978).

Another issue in the present study is that for two of the variables, grants and committee representation, the value assigned to a department in any single year is unlikely to be a very reliable indicator of the department's real position at that time period. Grants can fluctuate markedly from year to year, depending on the funding of proposals; committee representation is also unstable because the number of departments exceeds the number of positions on committees. To provide more stable and reliable estimates, three-year averages were computed at the beginning and end of the ten-year period.

The results of the dynamic analyses are shown in Table 4. The models predicting both budget and faculty are similar, except that there is no main effect of paradigm development on faculty positions. In both instances, change in enrollment over the period is significantly associated with later resource allocations after initial allocations were statistically controlled, indicating that this bureaucratic criterion had an effect on allocations over time as well as cross-sectionally. In addition, power and enrollment change interacting with paradigm development also affected allocations. The sign on the interaction term means that changes in enrollment have more effect on later resource allocations, the higher the level of paradigm development. The equations for faculty and budget are virtually unchanged whether or not power is averaged over the period or the initial estimate of power is used in the analysis; in both cases, power is statistically significant. The initial level of enrollment in the department is not statistically significant, and its inclusion in the estimated equations does not change the coefficients.

The prediction of power over time is also shown in Table 4. When grants and enrollment at the initial period are included in the regression, there is no effect of power at the earlier

646/ASQ

214

time on power subsequently. This is due, in large part, to grants and enrollment being associated with power at both the earlier and later times. There is no effect of change in enrollment or change in grants on power at the end of the period. These results, though not as strong as the results for budgets and faculty, are still consistent with the argument. As in the case of power analyzed cross-sectionally, grants and enrollment predict power, and the fact that grants and enrollment at the earlier period predict power at the end of the period, even when initial power is statistically controlled, provides evidence consistent with the direction of causality indicated by the model.

Finally, it is useful to compare the results presented in Table 4 with a naive model that includes only the same variable at an earlier point in time. In the literature of economics, forecasting models are often compared not to random chance but rather to a direct extrapolation of the past. Similarly, there is some interest in assessing the extent to which variables such as power, paradigm development, and enrollment change improve the prediction of later budgets over forecasting a later budget from an earlier budget. Budget allocations in 1967 accounted for 88 percent of the variance in budget allocations in 1976, indicating that the addition of the variables of enrollment change, power, paradigm development, and the interaction of enrollment change with paradigm development together accounted for an additional 7 percent of the variance. Faculty allocations in 1967 accounted for some 85 percent of the variation in faculty positions in 1975, leaving some 9 percent of the variation explained by the other variables. Of course, all of the theoretically important variables, including power, were statistically significant, providing support for the model as outlined. Power at the earlier time accounted for 16 percent of the variation in power at the end of the period, meaning that enrollments and grants accounted for an additional 8 percent of the variance over what could be explained by a naive model.

As frequently demonstrated in studies of governmental budgeting, these data on resource allocations indicate the great importance of precedence; however, paradigm development, power, and changes in enrollment are all significant in explaining the residual variance in allocations not accounted for by precedence.

Size and Departmental Power

The concept of social power remains controversial both theoretically and empirically. In the present case, then, it is important to demonstrate not only that the power measures converge and that they are related to allocations both cross-sectionally and over time, but also that the measures of power are distinct from other concepts, such as departmental size. In particular, one can argue that (1) number of faculty leads to the amount of funding from grants, since the larger the faculty, the larger the number of potential grant applicants; (2) enrollment is a measure of departmental size; (3) the number of faculty in the department is another indicator of size, along with enrollment; (4) the number of faculty leads to departmental representation on committees

215

— the larger the department, the larger the number of committee positions that can be filled; (5) faculty size is related to the number of courses in the longest prerequisite chain, an indicator of the size of the curriculum; and therefore, (6) all of the variables in the model are either indicators of or correlates of size.[2] This line of reasoning argues that the results presented here are not theoretically useful because of the conceptual and empirical dependencies built in to the operationalization of the model.

A close inspection of the argument reveals that although it may be plausible, it does not conform to the patterns observed in the data. In the first place, inspection of Table 2 reveals that the measure of paradigm development is empirically distinct from either size as measured by enrollment $(r = -.19)$ or size as indexed by the average number of faculty $(r = .15)$. Second, we can compute a multiple regression predicting grants and including both paradigm and faculty size as predictors:

$$\text{Grants} = -.082 + .00276 \text{ Paradigm} + .927 \text{ Faculty} \quad r^2 = .44$$
$$\qquad\qquad\quad (.00059) \qquad\qquad\quad (.377)$$

Although both coefficients are statistically significant at less than the .05 level of probability, the coefficient for the paradigm development variable is almost twice as large compared to its standard error as the coefficient for faculty size. Moreover, comparing this regression with the one reported in Table 3 indicates that adding faculty size increases the amount of explained variance by only 4 percent and leaves the significance of paradigm development unchanged.

Furthermore, if enrollment is an indicator of department size, as is representation on committees, then it would be unlikely that both variables would be statistically significant in both the cross-sectional and the dynamic regression analyses. Indeed, if all the variables were measuring the same concept, then there should be only one significant independent variable, particularly since the presumed multicollinearity would increase the size of the standard errors and lead to a conservative test for statistical significance. Moreover, the alternative of size being represented in all the variables fails to account for the model's explanatory power when initial and final allocation values are used in an analysis of changes in allocations over time.

Our findings about the validity of size as a plausible alternative are similar to those reported previously by Pfeffer and Salancik (1974: 146), who concluded that there was substantial evidence that the results obtained are not due to the fact that the variables are all measuring the same thing or that the variables are all surrogate measures for subunit size.

COMPARISONS OF CAMPUSES

Table 5 shows a comparison of the twenty departments on the two campuses. Campus A has lost more faculty positions and had a less rapid rise in budget than campus B. The departments on campus A lost 11.9 percent of their faculty positions from 1967 to 1975, while those on campus B were growing by .4 percent. And, the total budget for the departments on campus A increased 51.6 percent over the

2
This alternative argument was suggested by a reviewer of the article.

Table 5

Values for Selected Variables for 20 Corresponding Departments on Campus A and Campus B, Average for 1967–1976

Variable	Campus A	Campus B
Graduate majors	3,503	1,444
Undergraduate majors	6,322	7,413
Faculty, 1967	771	469
Faculty, 1975	679	471
Grants received	301	104
Funding from grants per year	$10,777,400	$ 4,359,072
Funding from grants per regular faculty	$ 16,305	$ 9,294
Budget, 1967	$18,200,000	$ 9,089,962
Budget, 1976	$27,600,000	$16,330,000
Enrollment, 1968	14,751	10,121
Enrollment, 1975	14,645	10,497

period 1967 to 1976, while it increased 79.6 percent for campus B. Thus, it appears that the departments on campus A faced a more scarce resource environment than the corresponding departments on campus B.

As Salancik and Pfeffer (1974) and Hills and Mahoney (1978) argued, scarcity of resources is likely to lead to an increase in the effect of power on budget allocations because scarcity intensifies the contest for resources. Power, a resource itself, is less likely to be used when resources are adequate to meet most of the demands of the departments. Following this line of argument, we would expect that power would be more strongly related to budget allocations on campus A. By extension, one could also argue that the enrollment criterion would be used relatively more in budget allocation decisions on campus B.

If campus A were indeed more political, in part because of the greater scarcity of resources, then one can further argue that power is more likely to vary more across departments and to be more predictable from the hypothesized determinants of power on campus A. Campus B, with less emphasis on power, provides the opportunity for greater use of simple bureaucratic criteria for resource allocation.

The results of regressions computed separately for the two campuses (Table 6) are generally consistent with the arguments presented. The regressions estimating grants as a function of paradigm development indicate no differences in the magnitude of the coefficients between the two campuses. This result provides some additional confidence in the earlier conclusion that paradigm development affected grants received as a general, environmental factor, so that one would not have expected to observe differences between the two campuses.

As expected, there is some evidence that power at campus A is more differentiated and is more predictable from the two determinants of departmental power, grants and enrollment. The reputation measure of power has approximately the same value averaged over the twenty departments on the two campuses (campus A = 4.48; campus B = 4.33), but the variance in responses is somewhat greater on campus A than on campus B, though the difference is not

217

Table 6

Regressions Estimating Model for Each Campus Separately (N=20)

Grants
A: Grants = −.035 + .00278••• Paradigm
(r^2 = .47)   (.00066)

B: Grants = −.044 + .00309••• Paradigm
(r^2 = .29)   (.00105)

Reputational measure of power
A: Power = 2.95 + 19.40•• Enroll + 10.88•• Grants
(r^2 = .45)   (8.12)   (3.79)

B: Power = 4.04 + 1.028 Enroll + 4.74 Grants
(r^2 = .04)   (8.62)   (2.86)

Representational measure of power
A: Committees = .0029 + .713••• Enroll + .2133•• Grants
(r^2 = .54)   (.193)   (.0898)

B: Committees = .016 + .590••• Enroll + .0861 Grants
(r^2 = .44)   (.160)   (.053)

Budget

A: Budget = −.0055 + .360•• Enroll + .303•• Committees + .000723••• Paradigm + .0087 Enroll × Paradigm
(r^2 = .80)   (.137)   (.121)   (.000196)   (.0057)

B: Budget = −.0072 + .662••• Enroll + .083 Committees + .000738••• Paradigm + .0150•• Enroll × Paradigm
(r^2 = .70)   (.140)   (.139)   (.000191)   (.0064)

Faculty

A: Faculty = −.0011 + .534••• Enroll + .271•• Committees + .000342• Paradigm + .00216 Enroll × Paradigm
(r^2 = .81)   (.135)   (.119)   (.000193)   (.0056)

B: Faculty = −.0043 + .839••• Enroll − .019 Committees + .000493••• Paradigm + .0105•• Enroll × Paradigm
(r^2 = .84)   (.107)   (.106)   (.000146)   (.0049)

Change in budget

A: Budget−76 = .0022 + .708••• Budget−67 + .288••• Change Enroll + .220••• Committees + .0147•• Change
(r^2 = .96)   (.082)   (.076)   (.058)   (.0068)
      Enroll × Paradigm

B: Budget−76 = .0058 + .753••• Budget−67 + .253••• Change Enroll + .064••• Committees + .0146•• Change
(r^2 = .94)   (.064)   (.055)   (.058)   (.0061)
      Enroll × Paradigm

Change in faculty

A: Faculty−75 = .00055 + .717••• Faculty−67 + .170•• Change Enroll + .238••• Committees + .0142• Change
(r^2 = .96)   (.085)   (.076)   (.062)   (.0068)
      Enroll × Paradigm

B: Faculty−75 = .0038 + .654••• Faculty−67 + .260••• Change Enroll + .185•• Committees + .0188•• Change
(r^2 = .91)   (.086)   (.068)   (.072)   (.0075)
      Enroll × Paradigm

Change in power

A: Comm−L = 1.42 + .00314• Enroll−68 + .00000419••• Grants−E
(r^2 = .49)   (.00156)   (.0000108)

B: Comm−L = 1.909 + .208• Comm−E
(r^2 = .07)   (.133)

•$p \leq$ .10; ••$p \leq$ .05; •••$p \leq$ .10

statistically significant (variance A = 2.00; variance B = 1.27; F = 1.57, n.s.). Of course, the means of proportional representation on committees are equal, being .05 for the two campuses. Again, however, the variation is somewhat higher on campus A than on campus B, although the difference is not statistically significant (variance A = .00133; variance B = .000745; F = 1.78, n.s.). Both the coefficients for the variables predicting committee representation are

650/ASQ

218

somewhat larger on campus A, and the variables predicting the reputation measure are statistically significantly larger for campus A than for campus B ($p < .10$ in both cases). To test for the statistical significance of the differences between the coefficients for the same variable in the regressions for campus A and campus B, the t-test for differences among regression coefficients was used. The estimated coefficients for the same explanatory variable in the campus A and campus B equations were b_a and b_b, and σ_a and σ_b were their respective estimated standard errors; then the t-statistic was computed as $t = (b_a - b_b) / \sqrt{\sigma^2_a + \sigma^2_b}$.

In the equations predicting budget, the coefficient for the total enrollment variable is significantly larger for campus B ($p < .05$), and the coefficient for the committee-representation measure is significantly larger for campus A ($p < .05$). The results from the regressions examining change in resource allocations are not as strong. There are no significant differences in the coefficients predicting number of regular faculty positions on the two campuses. However, the coefficient for the committee-representation measure of power is significantly larger for campus A ($p < .05$) in the regression predicting budget in 1976. Furthermore, the relative magnitudes of the coefficients tend to be consistent with the arguments, even when the differences between coefficients do not reach statistical significance.

The results of examining differences in the operation of the model diagrammed in the Figure on the two different campuses support the argument that greater resource scarcity leads to stronger effects of power and more variance in the distribution of power. Of course, there were other differences between the two campuses besides the relative scarcity of resources, so that other explanations of the results cannot be ruled out. Unfortunately, the start of the period covered by the study coincided almost perfectly with the start of a period of unremitting scarcity for the university system as a whole, and the availability of data precluded expanding the data base backward in time. This means that it is not possible to use different time periods to test for the effects of scarcity as Hills and Mahoney (1978) did. However, the results of the two-campus analysis on the effects of scarcity are consistent with the basic findings of the previous studies of resource allocations in universities.

DISCUSSION AND SUMMARY

The data reported in this study help to resolve some of the ambiguities that have developed from earlier research examining budget allocations in universities. Using essentially similar methodology and measures, this study replicated the findings of the University of Illinois study (Pfeffer and Salancik, 1974) about the determinants of power and the effects of power on budget and faculty position allocations. In contrast to the study of budget allocation at the University of Minnesota (Hills and Mahoney, 1978), the present study found a positive relationship between representation on committees and grant and contract funds, as well as budget allocations. This suggests that the failure of the Hills-and-Mahoney study to replicate the earlier work may derive more from differences in measures and procedures than

219

from differences in the budget allocation process in the different research sites.

The data also help to resolve the issue of the role of the concept of paradigm development in understanding allocations. Paradigm development had a direct effect on grants and contracts, and, even when departmental power and enrollment were statistically controlled, on budget allocations. This finding is consistent with the position that departments that are in scientific fields with more highly developed paradigms develop the coalitions and consensus necessary to advocate their case for resources.

The comparison of the two campuses that varied in scarcity of resources provided further support for the scarcity arguments advanced by both Salancik and Pfeffer (1974) and Hills and Mahoney (1978). At the same time, the statistical significance of many of the coefficients for both campuses, even though their magnitudes varied, provided further evidence for the generality of the model and of the procedures used to operationalize and test it.

Finally, the use of dynamic as well as cross-sectional analyses furnished additional evidence on the question of the direction of causality. Controlling for initial allocation levels, power, paradigm development, and changes in enrollment had effects on subsequent levels of resource allocations consistent with the model represented in the Figure.

In understanding power and political processes within organizations, it seems clear that it is time to proceed to comparative studies in which the extent to which power is used is stable, and the determinants of power vary. As Hannan and Freeman (1978) argued, organizations vary in the extent to which they are political. Although there is some evidence about what accounts for political activity, such as resource scarcity, substantial research is required to begin to understand comparative organizational power. The evidence from this and other studies of budget allocation indicates the importance of including specific operationalizations of social power as well as variables assessing technological uncertainty and the operation of bureaucratically rational decision criteria.

Research on organizations has barely begun to use budget and other forms of resource allocations to test various organizational theories and issues. For example, it is possible to examine the magnitude of leadership effects by examining allocation changes when leaders change and to explore the conditions under which such effects vary. It is feasible to examine the effects of information systems on decision making by noting how changes in what is measured or how it is reported affect the apparent criteria that predict allocations. And, it is possible to examine the effects of changes in organizational structure, environmental constraints, and resource scarcity by exploring how the coefficients in a model of budget allocation vary both over time and in different contexts.

220

REFERENCES

Beyer, Janice M., and Thomas M. Lodahl
1976 "A comparative study of patterns of influence in the United States and English universities." Administrative Science Quarterly, 21: 104–129.

Bohrnstedt, George W.
1969 "Observations on the measurement of change." In Edgar F. Borgatta (ed.), Sociological Methodology, 1969: 113–133. San Francisco: Jossey-Bass.

Cartter, Alan M.
1966 An Assessment of Quality in Graduate Education. Washington: American Council on Education.

Cyert, Richard M., and James G. March
1963 A Behavioral Theory of the Firm. Englewood Cliffs, NJ: Prentice-Hall.

Davis, Otto A., M. A. H. Dempster, and Aaron Wildavsky
1966 "A theory of the budgetary process." American Political Science Review, 60: 529–547.

Freeman, John
1979 "Going to the well: School district administrative intensity and environmental constraint." Administrative Science Quarterly, 24: 119–133.

Freeman, John, and Michael T. Hannan
1975 "Growth and decline processes in organizations." American Sociological Review, 40: 215–228.

Hannan, Michael T., and John H. Freeman
1978 "Internal politics of growth and decline." In M. W. Meyer and Associates (eds.), Environments and Organizations: 177–199. San Francisco: Jossey-Bass.

Hannan, Michael T., and Alice A. Young
1977 "Estimation in panel models: Results on pooling cross-sections and time series." In David R. Heise (ed.), Sociological Methodology, 1977: 52–83. San Francisco: Jossey-Bass.

Hills, Frederick S., and Thomas A. Mahoney
1978 "University budgets and organizational decision making." Administrative Science Quarterly, 23: 454–465.

Lodahl, Janice Beyer, and Gerald Gordon
1972 "The structure of scientific fields and the functioning of university graduate departments." American Sociological Review, 37: 57–72.
1973 "Funding the sciences in university departments." Educational Record, 54: 74–82.

Manns, Curtis L., and James G. March
1978 "Financial adversity, internal competition, and curriculum change in a university." Administrative Science Quarterly, 23: 541–552.

March, James G.
1966 "The power of power." In David Easton (ed.), Varieties of Political Theory: 167–185. Englewood Cliffs, NJ: Prentice-Hall.

March, James G., and Johan P. Olsen
1976 Ambiguity and Choice in Organizations. Bergen, Norway: Universitetsforlaget (Columbia University Press, distributor).

Pfeffer, Jeffrey, and Anthony Leong
1977 "Resource allocation in United Funds: An examination of power and dependence." Social Forces, 55: 775–790.

Pfeffer, Jeffrey, and Gerald R. Salancik
1974 "Organizational decision making as a political process: The case of a university budget." Administrative Science Quarterly, 19: 135–151.

Pfeffer, Jeffrey, Gerald R. Salancik, and Huseyin Leblebici
1976 "The effect of uncertainty on the use of social influence in organizational decision making." Administrative Science Quarterly, 21: 227–245.

Pondy, Louis R.
1970 "Toward a theory of internal resource-allocation." In Mayer N. Zald (ed.), Power in Organizations: 270–311. Nashville: Vanderbilt University Press.

Pondy, Louis R., and Jacob G. Birnberg
1969 "An experimental study in the allocation of financial resources within small hierarchical task groups." Administrative Science Quarterly, 14: 192–201.

Provan, Keith G., Janice M. Beyer, and Carlos Kruytbosch
1980 "Environmental linkages and power in resource-dependence relations between organizations." Administrative Science Quarterly, 25: 200–225.

Roose, K. D., and C. J. Andersen
1970 A Rating of Graduate Programs. Washington: American Council on Education.

Salancik, Gerald R., and Jeffrey Pfeffer
1974 "The bases and use of power in organizational decision making: The case of a university." Administrative Science Quarterly, 19: 453–473.
1978 "Uncertainty, secrecy, and the choice of similar others." Social Psychology, 41: 246–255.

Salancik, Gerald R., Barry M. Staw, and Louis R. Pondy
1980 "Administrative turnover as a response to unmanaged organizational interdependence." Academy of Management Journal, forthcoming.

Wildavsky, Aaron
1979 The Politics of the Budgetary Process, 3rd. ed. Boston: Little, Brown.

Wildavsky, Aaron, and Arthur Hammond
1965 "Comprehensive versus incremental budgeting in the Department of Agriculture." Administrative Science Quarterly, 10: 321–346.

Leadership and Decision Making in Organizations

9. Decisions, Presidents, and Status

MICHAEL D. COHEN
University of Michigan

JAMES G. MARCH
Stanford University

9.0 Introduction

Elsewhere (Cohen, March, and Olsen, 1972) we have examined in some detail the character of a garbage can decision process. That general perspective is basic to many of the studies reported in this book. Essentially, we have argued that any decision process can be viewed as a channeled confluence of four streams: problems, choice opportunities, solutions, and participants. The garbage can model calls attention to six main attributes of a decision system affecting decisions:

(1) The load on the system. As the load increases, so also does the number of decisions that are made by flight or oversight.
(2) The timing of problems, choices, solutions, and participation. Which problems and solutions are attended to in the context of which choices depends on when they appear and who is available to participate.
(3) The distribution of time. Those problems, solutions, and attitudes that are persistently present are attended to more consistently than are those that are sporadic.
(4) Structural channels limiting the flows. Rules limiting the flow of problems to choices (the access structure) or the flow of participants to choices (the decision structure) change the process and the outcomes.
(5) The garbage can context. The movement of problems to particular choices affects not only the choices to which they move but also the choices they leave alone. Decisions are made by "flight" and "oversights".
(6) The pleasures of the process. Problems and solutions are debated (at least in part) for the positive rewards associated with the debate rather than for the decision outcomes.

Taken collectively, these attributes of decision making in organizations suggest a heavily time-dependent decision process. The process

174

is one in which major changes can occur for what seem to be rather fortuitous reasons of timing; it is a process in which much of the behavior seems to be directed toward exercising problems in the context of choices rather than solving them; but it is also a process in which many outcomes are dominated by stable structural and time distribution factors. The three properties appear to be inconsistent insofar as they suggest a simultaneous consequence of unpredictability and stability. They are, in fact, interrelated and joint consequences of the system.

Some of the discussions in this book focus particularly on the impact of time sequencing on events; others focus on the overt process of argumentation that characterizes garbage can situations; others examine the sources of stability in garbage can processes. The present chapter continues the later treatment. We attempt to identify the stable underlying logic of some major classes of decisions within American higher education. Against the background of that explication of the sources of stability in decisions and the role of presidential leadership in them, we examine the question of executive power in organized anarchies and the status certification consequences of formal decision procedures.

9.1 The Logic of Choice in American Colleges

American colleges and universities are organizations with unclear goals and technologies and fluid participation. Opportunities for choice in higher education can easily become complex "garbage cans" into which a striking variety of problems, solutions, and participants may be dumped. Debate over the hiring of a footbal coach can become connected to concerns about the essence of a liberal education, the relations of the school to ethnic minorities, or the philosophy of talent. At the same time, there are conspicuous sources of decision stability within the college structure. Some people consistently spend more time than others. Some problems are always there. There are important structural and normative constraints on the access and decision structures. The culture is one that rewards the performances of participation. Relatively light loads on the system produce relatively frequent decisions by "flight" or "oversight". In order to understand university decision making adequately we need to supplement an awareness of the opportunities for time-dependent complexity with a look at the occasions and ways in which choices are driven in a relatively consistent, relatively stable way. We require a look at what we will call the logic of decision in universities.

Any such examination is, of course, subject to gross overgeneralization. It is quite unlikely that New York University or the University

175

of Illinois will operate in the same way as Ripon College or California Lutheran College. Size and wealth make substantial differences. Such an examination is also subject to simple error. The search for the "real" decision logic is a difficult and often dubious activity, typically contaminated with ideological mythology. Without denying these problems, we want to try to describe our impressions of the ways in which decision outcomes are produced in some key areas of university internal governance, and particularly our impressions of the role of major administrators in them.

The analysis is essentially an interpretation of data available to us from the literature and a series of interviews with presidents, chief academic officers (i.e., academic vice-presidents, deans of the college, etc.), chief business and financial officers (i.e., business and financial vice-presidents, treasurers, business managers), and assistants to the president. These interviews were made in a 42-school sample and included 41 presidents, 39 chief academic officers, 36 chief business and financial officers, and 28 assistants to the president.[2]

We consider four domains of decision that are important within a modern American college:

1. *The operating budget.* The distribution of financial resources among the departments.
2. *Educational policy decisions.* The establishment of curricula and academic organization.
3. *Academic tenure decisions.* The granting of indefinite tenure to individual academic personnel.
4. *Planning.* The development of long-run plans for capital expenditures, academic development, and institutional growth.

We asked presidents to nominate another president whom they viewed as successful, and we then asked for the criteria on which the nomination was based. The results in Table 9.0 indicate that presidents consider fiscal matters, educational policy, and the quality of academic personnel to be important aspects of their success (along with growth, quiet on campus, and the respect of their constituencies). Planning is traditionally an important function of executive leadership. These four domains do not include all of the decisions made within the university or college that might concern a president or other active participants. Indeed, some presidents probably devote at least as much time to landscaping and parking. But the four domains are easily recognized by students of colleges as some of the more important activities of educational governance. They form the justification for a significant number of meetings, a substantial amount of paper, and a perceptible level of political and bureaucratic energy.

176

Table 9.0. Evidence of success cited by 35 choosing presidents**

Criteria	Total mentions	% of 83 mentions	% of 35 respondents who mentioned each criterion	Estimated % of total mentions among all presidents
Fiscal	6	7.2	17.1	6.6
Educational program	8	9.6	22.8	10.0
Growth	9	10.8	25.7	13.7
Quiet	11	13.2	31.5	10.3
Quality of faculty	8	9.6	22.8	11.6
Quality of students	2	2.4	5.7	3.1
Respect of faculty	8	9.6	25.7	8.7
Respect of students	6	7.2	17.1	4.9
Respect of community	7	8.4	20.0	7.9
Other	18	21.7	–	23.2
Totals	83	99.7	*	100.0

*Does not total 100 because respondents could mention more than one. "Other" percentage was not calculated as it could be mentioned more than once by a single respondent.

**This estimate is made by applying weights which correct for the bias introduced into the sample by stratification.

We asked our respondents to describe briefly the processes involved in making operating budgets, academic policy, and academic personnel decisions. We asked them to characterize the long-run plan in the college, what it covered, and how it was developed. We asked them to focus particularly on the role of the president in these activities. The summary descriptions that follow are based primarily on the responses we received.[3]

9.1.0 *The Operating Budget*

The operating budget in American colleges and universities can be described in terms of three fundamental accounting flows.

I. The *enrollment cycle* flow. The rate and pattern of enrollment in the college and in the departments depend on the educational program in the school, its reputation, its competitors, and the level of demand for education relative to the supply. Resources come to the university because of the student enrollment. In private universities, the main flow is normally through direct tuition charges to the students and their families. Secondary flows from families (donations) and sometimes legislatures (subsidies) depend largely on maintaining or increasing student enrollment. In public colleges and universities, the main flow

177

is from legislatures reacting to the number of students enrolled, with secondary flows from tuition and federal subsidies. Resources coming to the university from the student enrollment flow are then distributed by the university to the departments in the operating budget.

II. The *institutional reputation* flow. Presidents and others seek support for the institution from outside agencies. They claim certain properties for the institution (e.g., age, prestige, innovativeness, poverty, uniqueness) as justification for support; or they offer to provide such properties if given the support. Resources come to the school as a function of the cogency of its appeal and the availability of outside resources. The outside agencies include foundations, legislatures, and major donors. Through endowment, current administrations reap the benefits of past reputations. These resources are then distributed to the departments in the operating budget.

III. The *research reputation* flow. Departments, laboratories, institutes, and individual research workers solicit funds from research support institutions. These are primarily institutions of the federal government (e.g., National Institutes of Health, National Science Foundation, National Aeronautics and Space Administration, the several cabinet-level departments). To a lesser extent they are private foundations (e.g., Ford Foundation, Carnegie Corporation, Sloan Foundation, Rockefeller Foundation). The size of the flow depends on the availability of resources within the particular domain of the department and on the nationally recognized research strength of the department or individual research worker. The resources come directly to the research group, with a fraction flowing to the university generally as overhead.

These three major flows are shown in Figure 9.0. We have emphasized them as accounting flows because we think the administrator's role in operating budget decision making is strongly conditioned by the mundane relationship between income and expenditure. (See Simon, 1967.) That fact has been somewhat obscured by the traditions of governmental budgeting with respect to public institutions of higher education. Within those traditions it sometimes appears that income is an "act of God" – or at least of legislatures. But the administrators with whom we talked were quite aware that legislators were de facto parents and that perhaps 90 percent of the public operating budget is determined by the student enrollment and by some standard formulas, that is to say, by implicit tuition charges.

The dynamics of the flows are such as substantially to restrict

178

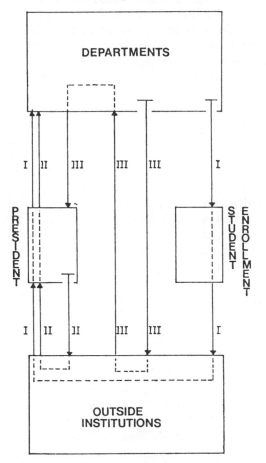

Figure 9.0. Major accounting flows determning operating budgets in American colleges and universities

presidential influence over the main thrust of the operating budget. Consider first the *enrollment cycle*. We observed two major styles of dealing with income received from student enrollment: (1) Direct payment of the tuition or some major fraction of it to the department or school involved. (2) Payment to the college and then reallocation on some basis to the departments. Since the departments control enrollments (through the classic departmental control over academic "pricing" – curriculum requirements, grading, and teaching formats), it is hard to see how there can be any really significant differences between the two alternatives in the longrun. Control over departmental enrollments gives the departments enormous leverage in the internal bargaining.

179

The bargaining leverage is attenuated, however, under certain conditions. For example, if the demand for education within the college is strong, and if the amount of teaching delivered per unit of resources is fixed, the flow of resources can be used to influence the flow of enrollment. *If* an academic administrator can increase the number of faculty in a department, and *if* that increase does not change the average teaching productivity in the department, he can produce a redistribution of enrollment within the college without changing the overall enrollment. The internal reallocation of resources modifies the implicit prices (e.g., the teacher/student ratio or degree requirements) charged by the various departments in the direction of lowering the prices in the favored departments. If a strong demand for educating in the college assures that "outside" competition will not be able to take advantage of the new internal prices, some students will shift from one department to another. Thus, the enrollment flow is brought into equilibrium at a new position determined by the arbitrary reallocation of resources.

The restrictions are rather severe, however. On the one hand, most colleges cannot presume the unconditional student enthusiasm that makes external competition with respect to programs largely irrelevant. On the other hand, among those colleges with strong student demand, only a handful can assume that an increase in resources for a given department will lead that department to increase its attractiveness to students (rather than the obvious alternative of increasing its attractiveness to faculty by reducing teaching load).

A second attenuation of the bargaining leverage of departments on enrollment occurs in choices between departments that are largely interchangeable from the point of view of student demand. One might suspect that the total student demand for courses in sociology and social psychology is more stable than the demand for either one of them, that the total student demand for courses in English and comparative literature is more stable than the demand for either one of them. Waves of students shift fairly easily from one to another as the number of courses offered, the size of classes, and the popularity of teachers change. As a result, it is easier to use a short-run arbitrary flow of resources to increase English enrollment at the expense of comparative literature (and thus to make a stable shift in relative emphasis) than it is to induce a stable shift from physics to English. In this respect, an organization with a large number of departments works in favor of administrative influence.

A third attenuation of departmental leverage is the frequent inability of academic departments to act strategically – particularly during periods of relatively strong outside demand for faculty. In order to use the enrollment cycle as a bargaining device the department must be

180

prepared to endure some short-run dislocations. It must be prepared to increase enrollment systematically to produce future resources, a procedure which requires coordination within the department and a willingness to incur current costs in anticipation of future benefits. Heavy turnover in faculty, or rules of faculty equality, make such a strategy difficult to adopt since the benefits are unlikely to be realized by the faculty bearing the costs.

In general, the student enrollment flow provides an administrator with little flexibility. He must, for the most part, ratify the market and approve the allocation of resources in the way dictated by enrollment. He may make marginal variations in that pattern. He may occasionally help to get a new department started. He may, under some conditions, be able to intervene in such a way as to affect demand, for example, by encouraging reduction of requirements so that (under "free trade") a new distribution of enrollment might emerge. He may be able to exploit the difficulties departments have in looking more than one year ahead. With some understanding of the system, in fact he can probably do more than most academic administrators do. But he acts within a rather tight set of constraints.

The *institutional reputation* flow is in direct contrast with the enrollment cycle. First, it is minor for most institutions. Second, it is the flow most subject to top administrator influence. Third, it has a much less dynamic character.

Operating budget resources from the institutional reputation flow (along with their close cousin, the endowment) are minor factors in the budget of most American colleges and universities. However, even at schools at which such resources are quite minor, presidents tend to view them as very important. They are the resources that give the president the greatest sense of control over expenditure. Along with endowment income, they tend to be "his" resources.[4] As the obvious spokesman for the whole institution, the president receives them. Although they are frequently received with commitments on their use, some fraction of them are "free", and some fraction of the committed resources go into already budgeted activities and thereby free other funds.

The relative stability of the institutional reputation flow stems from a long lag in the process. The pattern of expenditures undoubtedly affects the magnitude of the flow, but rarely within the tenure of one president. Changes in the institutional reputation of a college and university attributable to one president normally affect the flow of resources to a subsequent one. In the normal tenure of a president, the major opportunity for increasing the flow is through merchandising the college, through persuading outside institutions that the college is better than is currently believed or that it might become better.

181

Presidents do that and some have their successes; but it is hard to look at the statistics on endowment over time without concluding that the institutional reputations of American colleges and universities change a good deal more slowly than do their presidents.

Internally, of course, the smallness of the short-run effects of presidential action on presidential resources through the institutional reputation flow increases presidential independence. Within rather wide boundaries the institutional reputation operating funds can be distributed arbitrarily whitout affecting the flow of those funds in the succeeding few years. Such a result stems, in large part, from the basic ambiguity within a college of objectives and technology, which can make almost any course of action plausible.

This does not mean that presidents can be capricious. There are other influences on their behavior, and more claims on the money than there is money. In fact, with ambiguous criteria and slow feedback, we might reasonably predict that presidents and other administrators would turn heavily to *social* validation of their resource allocation decisions. A pattern of expenditures becomes legitimate because a large group of people believe it is legitimate. Despite the fact that the intrinsic constraints are weak – indeed because of that fact – presidential behavior is remarkably uniform.

The *research reputation* flow has been the subject of considerable investigation and grief over the past few years. Like the institutional reputation flow, the research reputation flow is a small one for most colleges. Where it does exist, the administrator is characteristically a minor figure. He does not initiate proposals. He rarely intervenes in them, indeed, rarely sees them. College presidents with whom we talked did not view themselves as having any significant year-to-year control over that part of the operating budget. Some wished they might have such control but did not view it as a serious possibility except through the "bloc grant" proposal that were gaining some popularity in granting agencies and Congress prior to 1969. The enthusiasm of presidents for institutional grant funding is well documented in the recommendations of such bodies as the Association of Land Grant Colleges, which are technically associations of colleges but actually associations of college presidents.

Not only is the flow outside the control of the president, it is also a leverage on funds under his control. Outstanding faculty at major institutions control substantial resources directly through research grants; they can and do use that control and the threat of departure (with consequent loss of funds and reputation) as a device for influencing the allocation of other resources. In recent years at major universities the teaching load in physics has very rarely been as great as the teaching load in French.

182

This research reputation flow is of critical importance to the president of any large, well-known American university. It represents a substantial part of his annual operating budget. It is a basis for attracting and retaining high-quality faculty. It is a primary sign of success as a president. In many terms that the president recognizes as valid, major research grant recipients have higher status than do presidents within the academic community.

The annual operating budget is largely determined by these three flows. But the impact is not the same in all colleges. In fact, we think we can characterize most American colleges and universities rather simply in terms of the extent to which their operating budget depends on the three flows. We will identify four basic budgeting types.

Type A is the university for which the enrollment cycle is relatively unimportant. For most purposes these universities draw upon the institutional reputation and research reputation flows in order to develop their budgets. Income from students is significant, but the colleges are largely shielded from the consequences of enrollment demand by the strong general demand for attendance. Basically, these are the prestigious private universities of the United States, representing about 1 percent of the four year colleges and universities in the country. In terms of numbers this is clearly an insignificant group. In terms of reputation it includes the giants of American private education.

Type B is the university which relies heavily on both the enrollment flow and the research reputation flow with little (or substantially less) coming from the institutional reputation. These are the major public universities and some private universities in the United States. They represent a major locus of growth in American higher education in the period from 1950 to 1965.

Type C is the college for which research reputation is relatively unimportant. These are the prestigious, small colleges in the United States. Their budgets rely heavily on income from the enrollment cycle and on institutional support and endowment. In terms of numbers of schools and numbers of students, this type is not very common, but it includes the best-known private, liberal-arts colleges in the country.

Type D is the college or university for which the enrollment cycle accounts for virtually all the income and operating budget allocations. This is the mean, mode, and median of American higher education. It includes most of the schools and most of the students. In these schools the enrollment market dominates budgeting. Sometimes, for some of them, the demand for education has served to blunt the obviousness of the "customer"; but for most of them most of the time, the budgeting problem is one of finding a set of allocations that produces an

183

educational program that attracts enough enrollment to provide the allocations.

Table 9.1 shows our estimates of where these types of schools are found in a sixfold division of colleges and universities by size and wealth. What this and our earlier remarks may suggest is the awkwardness of talking about governance at all. Insofar as large parts of the

Table 9.1. Types of mixes of accounting flows in operating budgets, by type of schools

Type of school	Relatively rich	Relatively poor
Large	Type A	Type B
	Type B	Type D
Medium	Type A	Type D
	Type B	
	Type C	
	Type D	
Small	Type C	Type D
	Type D	

budget, for example, research budgetary items, are not so much decisions as collections of independent agreements assembled for the convenience of the accountants into a common document, we need to reconsider the meaning of decision in a university context. Insofar as other large parts of the budget are embedded in the long-run complications of the enrollment cycle, we need to describe a process that is heavily constrained by "market" factors.

We are also left with some possible interpretations of the problems of budgetary control confronting American college presidents. In particular, we should note:

1. Strong research reputation in the faculty makes weak budget presidents. On the whole, that means that most of the better known academic institutions will have "weaker" presidents than the less known institutions, and presidents who transfer "up" into such schools will find themselves "weaker" than they were before.

2. Prestige in the institution makes weak students. Where the demand for entrance is strong, the policy-making force of the enrollment cycle is blunted.[5]

3. Public universities make weak budget presidents. The president of a public university must simultaneously negotiate the appropriations for his operating budget from the legislature or some intervening body and negotiate the allocation of that budget among his departments. The simultaneity and public character of those two negotiations restrict him seriously.

184

In general, the operating budget of an American university is heavily constrained by accounting procedures, particularly the very elementary requirements of the enrollment cycle. As a result, there are many things that an administrator cannot do. The administrators with whom we talked were aware of this, particularly within Type D schools. At the same time, administrators seemed to be somewhat less aware of, or somewhat less interested in, the flexibility the system did offer them. So long as the constraints are met, there is the potential for rather substantial discretionary action. For example, we suspect that many presidents fail or are not willing to distinguish sharply shifts in the operating budget that will disturb the *total* enrollment from shifts that will disturb only the internal allocation of that total enrollment. The former are problems; the latter are opportunities.

9.1.1 *Academic Policy Decisions*

By training, background, and basic commitment, college presidents are academic in orientation. Studies by Ferrari (1971) and Bolman (1965) indicate that over 80 percent of all presidents have been faculty members. It is natural, therefore, that presidents should have a special concern with academic policy decisions. Most presidents take pride in the academic program of their school and see themselves as performing an important supportive role with respect to that program. They accept credit for new programs and recent changes which they have initiated or supported.

For the most part, however, and particularly in the larger schools, college presidents do not appear to have much to say about academic policy. Indeed, the term policy is probably somewhat misleading if it conveys a notion of systematic collective decision-making. The set of activities that are subsumed under the general term academic policy are the organization of academic departments, the organization of the educational program, degree requirements and alternatives, courses and course assignments, patterns of student education. To describe these as resulting from anything approximating high-level decision based on policy would be wrong. Presidents and their chief academic subordinates concede that much of the structure of academic policy is determined in the individual departments – realistically, often in the individual classroom.

Formally, academic policy is almost always portrayed as the responsibility of the faculty. By the standard academic constitution, the faculty is granted control over degrees and educational programs. The traditions of faculty control are embedded deeply in the culture of academe. Except in some minor ways, college administrators show little desire to question that tradition. They accept the mythology of "the faculty" even when the size and diversity of the institution clearly makes talking about "the faculty" no more sensible than talking about "the students".

At the same time, the presidents recognize that even in a small, liberal arts college the collective decisions of the faculty rarely do more than condition slightly and ratify the actions of the departments and individual teachers. Academic "policy" is the accretion of hundreds of largely autonomous actions taken for different reasons, at different times, under different conditions, by different people in the college. This collection of actions is periodically codified into what is presented as an educational program by the college catalog or a student or faculty handbook.

Consider as a first example of academic policy the academic expectations of faculty and students. What are legitimate programs? What is a legitimate workload? What are legitimate quality and quantity expectations?

These simple working conditions of education are viewed as being primarily the concern of faculty and students. Their importance to parents, or to employers or governmental licensing agencies (particularly in the case of professional education) is, for the most part, secondary. As a result, most colleges leave the conditions of education to informal bilateral negotiations between students and faculty. These negotiations take place daily in the classroom, each term in the enrollment and grade lists, and continuously in student-faculty interaction. The results of the negotiation may be formally ratified by the appropriate faculty body, but they often exist simply as a shared understanding within the community. Teachers who enjoy teaching and students who enjoy being taught form enclaves. Teachers who do not enjoy teaching and students who do not enjoy being taught form other enclaves.

The latter coalition is a frequent one. Suppose that a group of faculty views teaching as a job. That is, as something one does in order to be able to do something else (e.g., play golf, sit in the sun, do research). And suppose a group of students views studying as a job; that is, as something one does in order to be able to do something else (e.g., earn a living, sit in the sun, do research). Under such conditions one would expect the bilaterally negotiated educational program to include:

(a) A joint agreement to assert that both teachers and students are working very hard.
(b) A joint agreement to restrict work.

Such agreements are common in American higher education, as they

186

are throughout noneducational work situations. Given the basic organizational situation, the surprise is not that work restriction is practiced, but that work is. If faculty and students had the purely and narrowly selfinterested goals of which they are sometimes accused, educational programs would consist in the minimally acceptable external facades.

Negotiated work levels are not responsive to conventional bureaucratic interventions. Presidents and others have criticized the resistance of informal agreements to change. The criticism sometimes misses the point. The outcomes of bilateral negotiation between faculty and students are little affected by policy proclamations by presidents or academic councils, although they may be ratified, somewhat inhibited, or modestly stimulated by such machinery. Significant changes appear to result (as for example at Berkeley and San Francisco State College) from widespread shifts in faculty and student attitudes. These shifts lead to direct renegotiations at the classroom and department levels that collectively modify the nature of the academic program.

For example, the bilateral bargains between faculty and students appear in recent years to have been renegotiated at some schools in the direction of reducing the traditional scholarship demands on students and faculty and increasing the political demands. Politically acceptable faculty are allowed by students to substitute new criteria and styles of scholarship for those conventional within their disciplines. Politically acceptable students are allowed to substitute ideological development, political activity, or unusual terms of scholarship. These renegotiations of the educational program involve a small minority of students at American colleges and universities, but at a few institutions the number has apparently been large enough to result in appreciable change in the overall educational program.

Whether such changes are viewed as attractive or unattractive, they illustrate the process by which academic policy is actually affected. American college administrators have generally been unwilling or unable to participate significantly in the broad attitudinal changes that underlie such shifts. For the most part, college presidents have not felt they had either the mandate or the platform for producing shifts in the demands that students and faculty make on each other, and have been more inclined to try to make modest bureaucratic limitations on the process than to participate in it.

Consider a second example of academic policy: the structure of general educational requirements (commonly called breadth requirements) imposed on students. This set of rules, by which the claims of liberal education are satisfied, is a persistent source of minor conflict within a college or university and occasionally erupts into a major dispute. Our impression is that faculties struggle with such questions,

187

trying to capture some idea of what a good education is. But since that question is one which few reasonable men can answer with confidence, the outcomes are dominated by three somewhat more mundane considerations:

(1) The willingness of students to be coerced into taking courses they would not choose to take independent of the requirement. Students place limits on the proportion of their total studies that can be directed in this way, on the difficulty of the courses that are required, and on the subject matter that may be included. These limits become increasingly compelling as the overall demand for education declines.

(2) The enrollment needs of various departments. As we have noted above, the enrollment cycle is a major factor in resource allocation. Normally, one cannot have a large French department without large enrollment in French. One cannot support many graduate students as teaching assistants in political science without large enrollments in introductory political science courses. One cannot justify many science laboratories without substantial enrollments in introductory laboratory science courses. An awareness of the virtue of French, political science, and chemistry as elements of a liberal education is facilitated by an awareness of the benefits of enrollments.

(3) The desire to have small classes. To have many small classes, the college or university must ordinarily have some large classes that can be taught using modest faculty resources. Two devices of educational policy are used together to accomplish this – required courses and a structure of prerequisites that force enrollments in a few introductory courses. Both are justified – appropriately – in terms of educational considerations. There are reasons why one might require that an educated man have exposure to subjects outside his major field and why one might expect a student to study elementary material before he studies advanced material. However, practical considerations of university life almost certainly amplify such beliefs, so that some prerequisites and some breadth requirements are less educationally relevant than they are argued to be.

We do not mean to suggest that these considerations are illegitimate. The point is simply that though educational policy discussions are couched in terms of the educational needs of students, they tend to be substantially influenced by the necessities of organizational life in a university. When the chairman of the department of history argues for a required course for all university students in the history of some

188

nonwestern society, he need not examine the relative importance of the education (which he believes in) and the implied growth of the history department (which he also believes in). What is good for history is good for the university.

The result is that educational policy, insofar as it is a matter for the general faculty, tends to be a fairly straightforward "log-roll" among the major faculty groups. The price of a requirement in humanities is a requirement in natural sciences. The major participants will not ordinarily see it that way, of course. Policy is negotiated without clear distinctions between nobility and necessity.

We observed little inclination among administrators to participate in this log-rolling. For the most part, they did not see their interests as being heavily involved; nor did they often have a clear program that was much differentiated from the natural outcome of the log-roll. Thus, the two most conspicuous recent trends – the overall reduction in breadth requirements and foreign language requirements – have not been affected significantly by administrative action (although through the enrollment cycle such changes have substantial effects within a college or university).

The "major" decisions of academic policy that produce administrative activity are rarely heroic. Presidents sometimes involve themselves moderately in questions of instructional calendars (e.g., quarter versus semester) or in questions of new academic departments or schools (e.g., Black Studies) or in questions of schoolwide curriculum requirements. In general, the president's role has been relatively unimportant in recent years except in a few cases where he has entered the educational policy arena with limited objectives. Typically this has been because educational policy has produced an effect on those things that a president considers immediately important – most notably quiet on the campus, the financial position of the school, and the reputation of the president among his constituents.

Although presidents are educators by experience and by identification, they are not educators by behavior. They notice the anomaly. One of the most reliable complaints of an American college president is the degree to which he is removed from educational matters. He is committed to success in his job. He does not consider academic policy achievements as a major factor in the evaluation of his success. He does not feel he has any serious leverage. He is a nostalgic realist.

9.1.2 *Academic Tenure Decisions*

Academic tenure, as it has existed for the past 30 years, is a major organizational commitment. Assuming that a faculty member ordinarily receives tenure sometime during his thirties, a tenure decision is

189

essentially a 30 year contract. At present prices the face value of the contract, quite aside from other commitments, is somewhere from $ 400,000 to $ 1 million in salary alone. As college administrators have discovered under conditions of budget restrictions, academic salaries are both the largest part of the college budget and one of the parts least susceptible to short-run downward modification.

In addition, tenure is an important symbolic act. Actions on tenure and beliefs about those actions form a major basis for the faculty reward structure within a college. The widespread belief that tenure depends on research productivity has conditioned not only a whole generation of academic workers but also a large number of contemporary theories of academe and its ills. It has been used as an excuse and explanation for bad teaching, bad manners, and bad research.

Whether the excuses, explanations, and beliefs are correct may perhaps be questioned, but it is impossible to question their ubiquity. Moreover, the ritual of the decision process is carefully designed to maintain the beliefs. Each year thousands of department chairmen solicit tens of thousands of letters supporting the claims to tenure made by members of their staff. These letters and other supporting documents are processed through a typically complex series of assessments by faculty committees, departments, deans, executive committees, and provosts until they arrive at the president's desk. At each stage, the process is made to appear more powerful than it is in at least two senses: (1) The rate of moving to tenure is almost certainly higher than believed. (2) The "failures" are rarely real failures. They succeed later (often at a different school) and often become at least as distinguished in research as those who "succeeded" originally.

In the past quarter century college presidents have operated under conditions that have made the substance of tenure decisions relatively less important to them than the associated ritual. There are at least seven clear reasons for this:

First, most of the costs of the long-term contract in a tenure decision are borne by subsequent administrations. Although presidents concern themselves with long-term consequences for the institution – often more than others within the organization – it is natural for those costs to be somewhat less pressing than some others.

Second, with a high turnover of faculty, the contract is really not an 30 year one. This is particularly true for a school where faculty members are likely to have options for movement.

Third, with continued inflation and flexible salary schedule the contract is not as expensive a commitment as it appears nor as absolute.

Fourth, with rapid growth, tenure decisions of the past represent

190

a smaller part of the institution's total commitment than would be true under stable conditions. So long as growth is maintained, tenure commitments are balanced by expansion of the nontenured staff, and do not preclude further tenure commitments.

Fifth, in some cases the costs have seemed to be largely borne by the federal government through research grants. A senior research star is a good financial investment, not a net cost. Not only can substantial elements of his salary be funded extramurally, he brings additional funds to support others. Although this situation has directly affected only a small minority of the tenure decisions within American colleges and universities, it probably has contributed to a belief that tenure decisions are not, in fact, as costly as they appear to be.

Sixth, with a shortage of qualified faculty and an active market for faculty, there appears to be no way of maintaining a faculty without granting tenure rather liberally. The alternative, in principle, is higher salary. In many cases, the institutional structure of salary schemes make such a tradeoff difficult. Even where it does not, few presidents are likely to want to save future dollars by paying present dollars.

Seventh, the president has no basis for believing that his judgment is better than the process. Moreover, even if he believes he knows better, he knows that he has no good way to demonstrate the superiority of his judgment in any reasonable length of time.

We would expect presidents of some schools to be more concerned with the substance of tenure decisions than presidents of others. Presidents of schools where turnover of faculty is low and where growth is modest or nonexistent would involve themselves more directly in tenure decisions than would presidents of high turnover and rapidly growing schools. Although our data from interviews are not adequate to a firm text of such ideas, we believe that they are generally consistent with such conclusions. Relatively active presidents tended to be in the very small handful of prestigious institutions of stable size and the larger group of stable-sized, low-prestige colleges off the major academic market place.

Most of the presidents we interviewed had never rejected a tenure recommendation that came to them through the internal faculty and administrative reviewing process. The overall rejection rate – at the final approval point – appears to be no more than 5 percent and probably closer to 1 percent. Some presidents, though by no means all, tried to involve themselves earlier in the process in order to develop a consensus before the time for their formal action arrived. This was much more characteristic of presidents in small schools than of those in large ones. In larger schools, presidents typically viewed their role in tenure decisions as ratifying the actions recommended by chief academic officer and the appropriate faculty-administrative committees. This would break down seriously only in the occasional case in which some major part of the president's constituency became activated. Recently this has almost exclusively involved student protest against the refusal of tenure to a popular teacher and community-trusted protest against the granting of tenure to a politically unpopular professor. Spectacular as such cases sometimes are and as difficult as they may become for a president, they have been and still are infrequent.

We have argued, however, that this situation is based on the seven key reasons listed above. The last 25 years have been a special era in the history of American higher education that appears to be ending or to have ended. Growth rates have slowed considerably. As a result, market demand for faculty and faculty turnover appear destined to be reduced.[6] The rate of growth of research support has declined. All of these factors are likely to increase presidential activity in tenure decisions. Through him, both symbolically and perhaps directly, local and internal factors seem likely to become somewhat more important than they have been (e.g., teaching, university service, good collegue-ship) and cosmopolitan, national, and professional factors somewhat less important. We are likely to have an increase in the number of complaints about "cronyism" or "personal favoritism" and a decrease in the number of complaints about a professor's primary allegiance lying with his outside professional groups.

Although it is hard to imagine that academic tenure decisions will become a major source of attention for most presidents, the ritual consider actions associated with tenure will continue to be important. The reputed quality of the faculty and the research standing of the school (two important dimensions to many presidents) can be influenced by creating a climate of belief in the importance of research. This climate has been constructed by emphasizing the research basis through a system of reports, market offers, research "stars", and the like. For most purposes, the accuracy of a "publish or perish" characterization of the concrete tenure rules is less critical than a wide acceptance of research productivity as a norm of the system.

We would expect to find presidents concerned that the dogma of research be reinforced by the litany of promotion procedures. As the pressures upon presidents have changed (e.g., from students and from sources of funds), we can expect the dogma and the litany to be revised, and the perceived reasons for tenure decisions to shift. With research, teaching, and service standards vague and uncertain, it is particularly important that the president announce that they are being

192

used. And this is not simply a strategy of deception. It is also a recognition that if one is going to influence such diffuse things as the research identity of an institution, the influence will come about in large part by changing the pictures of people within the institution of what they are good at and what those who are rewarded are good at. A general acceptance of teaching dogmas will probably produce more teaching, even though the changes in peoples' beliefs are almost certain to be greater than the changes in their behavior.

9.1.3 *Planning*

Planning is a primary responsibility of executive leadership and is so certified by traditional administrative theory and by innumerable modern treatments. In our interviews, we never heard an administrator deny the importance and virtue of planning within the college. In many cases they observed that this had not been a function that was well performed within the college previously. In some cases they observed that it was not a function that was easy to perform. But the fundamental value of planning was asserted by all, and in approximately the same terms by all.

Most administrators accepted two basic organizational axioms with respect to planning:

1. A primary responsibility of leadership is that of providing, broad, general direction to the organization.
2. Orderly direction requires a clear specification of objectives, an identification of alternative routes to those objectives, and a choice among those alternatives.

In short, one must have a plan.

Moreover, it was generally accepted that the plan should be comprehensive. It should involve academic planning, fiscal planning, physical planning, personnel planning, research planning, and organizational planning in an integrated and consistent master plan. The frequently recited stories of physical planning that proceeds without attention to the academic plan of the university are seen as horror stories.

Despite this unanimous acceptance of the importance of planning, we saw little evidence of planning in American colleges and universities – at least planning in the terms indicated above. At each of the colleges in our sample we asked presidents and their chief subordinates whether their college had a "plan". We also asked what role the plan played in current decisions. The answers varied somewhat across four main alternatives:

193

1. Yes, we have a plan. It is used in capital project and physical location decisions.
2. Yes, we have a plan. Here it is. It was made during the administration of our last president. We are working on a new one.
3. No, we do not have a plan. We should. We are working on one.
4. I think there's a plan around here someplace. Miss Jones, do we have a copy of our comprehensive 10-year plan?

Most schools had a capital-physical plan of some sort, and most of these were subject to relatively continuous review and revisions. Few people were completely satisfied with such planning. Nearly everyone agreed that it rarely took adequate account of "academic" considerations. It was often felt that actual decisions were essentially independent of the plan. There were persistent problems in identifying a rational basis for a particular plan. Nevertheless, such plans were reasonably well-accepted and reasonably institutionalized.

In a similar way, many schools had fiscal plans of one sort or another. It was not uncommon to find plans for future operating budgets. Plans for fiscal problems associated with income uncertanties (e.g., endowment earnings, grant income, tuition/enrollment) were common, particularly among nonpublic institutions. In public institutions legislative-administrative tactics seemed to make it impossible to develop serious contingent plans for alternative levels of public appropriations. Plans to deal with cash flow difficulties (particularly associated with heavy dependence in tuition income) or with the short-term investment of temporary sources of cash were common. Long- and medium-range budget planning, however, seemed to be very modest and hyper-routine. Other fiscal planning was, for the most part, "technical" in the sense that it did not ordinarily involve considerations beyond the maintenance of the best financial position possible for the institution.

Some schools have academic plans. Some of these are voluminous – the natural consequence of asking each department to prepare a plan and then binding all the documents together without editing. Few administrators thought the academic plans were useful in decision making. On the whole academic plans seem to suffer from two conspicuous administrative problems: (1) They often had no connection to any decisions that anyone might be called upon to make. (2) They rejected the idea of scarcity. At best they were lists of what the various academic departments wished Santa Claus would bring them. At worst, they were fantasies, neither believed in nor intended to be believable.

Presidents believe in comprehensive planning, but do virtually

194

none of it. How do we understand such an inconsistency and what are its consequences?

We believe that the phenomena of planning – and the corresponding administrative attitudes – are the striking consequences of the inconsistencies between universities as organizations and the models of organizations with which administrators are familiar. Plans, in their usual form, particularly long-run comprehensive plans, presume substantial clarity about goals, substantial understanding of the basic technology of the organization, and substantial continuity in leadership. Universities have none of these, except – possible – in the capital-physical-fiscal-planning area. Presidents frequently come to the presidency from outside the organization and are frequently succeeded by someone from outside the organization. Their terms are short relative to the length of time involved in a "plan". Except for their chief officers in business-finance, their main subordinates will remain in office for an even shorter period. Boards of trustees are rarely organized to maintain continuity in anything more than general fiscal policies. Presidents emphasize the importance of making a mark on the institution. They have little stake in continuity with the past. They may hope for continuity with the future, but they would have to be extraordinarily naive to expect their successor to spend much time "implementing" someone else's plan. Despite the obeisance paid it, comprehensive planning has little reality for presidents in the form in which we usually conceive it.

Long-run planning in universities is something other than long-run planning. In particular, we would identify four major things that plans become:

1. Plans become *symbols*. Academic organizations provide few "real" pieces of feedback data. They have nothing closely analogous to profit or sales figures. How are we doing? Where are we going? An organization that is failing can announce a plan to succeed. An institution that does not have a reactor can announce a plan for one, and is probably valued higher than a university without such a plan.

2. Plans become *advertisements*. What is frequently called a "plan" by a university is really an investment brochure. It is an attempt to persuade private and public donors of the attractiveness of the institution. Such plans are characterized by pictures, by ex cathedra pronouncements of excellence, and by the absence of most relevant information.

3. Plans become *games*. In an organization in which goals and technology are unclear, plans and the insistence on plans become an administrative test of will. If a department wants a new

195

program badly enough, it will spend a substantial amount of effort in "justifying" the expenditure by fitting it into a "plan". If an administrator wished to avoid saying "yes" to everything, but has no basis for saying "no" to anything, he tests the commitment of the department by asking for a plan.

4. Plans become *excuses for interaction*. As several students of planning have noted, the results of the process of planning are usually more important than the plan. The development of a plan forces some discussion and may induce some interest in and commitment to relatively low-priority activities in the departments/schools. Occasionally that interaction yields results of positive value. But only rarely does it yield anything that would accurately describe the activities of a school or department beyond one or two years into the future. As people engage in discussions of the future they may modify each other's ideas about what should be done today, but their conclusions about what should be done next year are likely to be altered in the interim by changes in personnel, political climate, foundation policy, or student demand.

The side benefits of plans seem enough to sustain talk of planning and a modest level of activity, but not enough to motivate either intense administrative involvement or a community-wide commitment to execute what has been written. As long as education is a process particularly sensitive to the character and individual interests of those who teach and those who study, the direct rewards of planning activity both for presidents and for others can be expected to remain relatively low.

9.2 Presidential Power

The examination we have made of the logic of decision in four areas of college decision making suggests some complications in the idea of executive power. The American college president plays a far from dominant role in these four conspicuous areas of college decision making. He is important. He has power. The processes, however, have logics that he cannot alter, and normally does not want to alter.

It is unlikely that we can determine how much power the American college president has or should have. Such questions require a specification of a model of executive/administrative power that has proven impossible to make. (See March, 1966.) However, we can consider some possible reasons why the president's power is an issue and a problem, and we can examine some implications of those reasons. To

196

do this, we will assert that the following propositions are plausible without detailed argumentation or evidence:

1. Most people believe in a simple force model of organizational choice. That is, they believe that power (force) is distributed among participants and that decisions are approximated by the weighted average of individual wishes (where the weights are the power indices of the individuals).
2. The simple force model of organizational choice accounts for a good deal less of the variation in outcomes than is believed. There are other factors that are relevant in important ways.
3. The president is both perceived to have and, in fact, does have more power than most (perhaps all) other participants in college or university decision making.
4. Power, the interpretation of power, and the assessment of individual leadership behavior are considered against the background of an egalitarian ideology within the United States.

Notice that the second point is not a direct argument that "power" is distributed more "equally" than is commonly believed. The argument is that a simple force model is incorrect, that there are substantial "nonpower" factors in decisions. Since these are somewhat independent of "power" as reflected in the standard model, they are as less likely to help the "strong" in direct proportion to their strength. Thus, in effect they equalize apparent power.

The decision processes we have described are not easily characterized in simple "force" terms. Decisions are typically not made by a confrontation of well-organized factions, with victory to the strongest. The factions are not well-organized. They are rarely all activated at one time. They rarely have any significant staying power. As a result of egalitarian norms the American college president is faced with a set of beliefs about the amount of power he should have and the amount of power he does have that assure some resentment toward him. In addition, given perceptions of power and the force-independent features of the processes, he is faced with a disparity between his potential power and beliefs about his power that assure his disappointment and the disappointment of others. He is resented because he is more powerful than he should be. He is scorned and frustrated because he is weaker than he is believed capable of being. If he acts as a "strong" president, he exposes his weakness. If he acts as a "democratic" president, people consider him timid. For the most part, his behavior has only modest impact on beliefs about presidential legitimacy or power.

We can illustrate the situation very simply. In Figure 9.1 we plot

197

perceptions of power against hierarchical position within the organization. We have simplified considerably by assuming that there is a linear relationship between power and hierarchical position and that the "total power" perceived within the system is fixed, but neither of those simplifications is critical to the argument.

The horizontal line represents the *evaluative* norm within the university. We have portrayed the simple case of a pure egalitarian ideology. The steep line represents the *cognitive* norm within the university. It reflects the attribution of power within the organization. The intermediate line is the *behavioral* situation (the exerciseable power) within the university. It is more steep than the evaluative norm (assertions 3 and 4) and less steep than the cognitive norm (assertions 1 and 2).

Since he is at the top of the hierarchy, the president is represented by the three endpoint values in Figure 9.1: his *legitimate* power (point *c*), his *actual* power (point *b*), and his *perceived* power (point *a*).

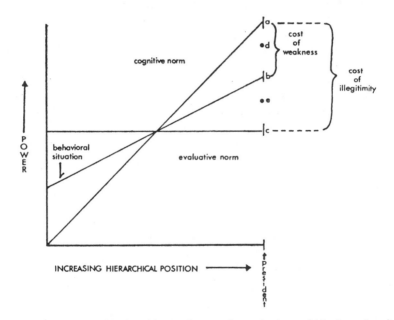

Figure 9.1. Hierarchical position and perceptions of power within the university

From this it is easy to see that the president is subject to two major costs with respect to power: The first costs are the costs of illegitimacy – the difference between the perceived power of the president and his legitimate power (a–c). According to our assertions, these costs will always exist. The second costs are the costs of weakness – the

The costs of illegitimacy are realized in resentment toward the

198

office and the person holding it, in pressure to reduce the power of the president, in motivational assumptions about the behavior of presidents (e.g., "power-hunger"). The magnitude of the costs of illegitimacy depends on the extent to which the power model of the university is accepted and the extent to which norms of equality apply.

In general, we would expect to find the degree of acceptance of the power model to increase with the degree of conflict in the organization, the size of the organization, the average pleasure derived from politics by participants in the organization. We would expect the acceptance of norms of equality to increase with the degree of differentiation between hierarchical status orders and other (e.g., professional) status orders, with the opportunities for exit from the organization provided within the environment, with the degree of public control of the institution, and with the recency of presidential accession to the office.

The costs of weakness, on the other hand, are paid in criticism for timidity, in disappointment among supporters, and in reduced self-esteem. The magnitude of these costs depends on the extent to which the power model is accepted and the actual power of the president (or, in effect, the number and scope of other factors in decisions). We would expect the actual power in these terms to increase with the slack in the system. Slack serves as a buffer from exogenous forces. We would expect the actual power to increase when other participants become more dependent on the organization, for example, when exit opportunities decline. We would expect power to increase as the social significance of universities decreases.

This kind of analysis provides an interpretation of one familiar sequence of university events. If slack declines at the same time as the social importance of universities and conflict in them increases, complaints about presidential timidity will increase at a more rapid rate than complaints about presidential illegitimacy (which may in fact decline). Objections to presidential weakness will be particularly notable in large, public institutions. If subsequently the opportunities for exit by other administrators, students, and faculty decline, complaints of both kinds decline; but the decline is most notable with respect to perceptions of weakness of presidents. Presidents become both stronger and more legitimate, particularly the former.

We can add to the analysis in Figure 9.1 by considering the president's own perception of the ditribution of power. In general, we would expect presidents to see their power as somewhat more than that presumed by the egalitarian norm and as somewhat less than that believed by non-presidents. What difference does this make?

In our discussion we have assumed that the president's perception of his power has no direct effect on either legitimate power or perceived power. However, it could affect actual power. If the presi-

199

dent sees his own power as greater than it actually is (say at point d), the cost of weakness will still be (a–b) (since his perception cannot change the facts in a positive direction). If, on the other hand, he perceives his power as less than it actually is (point e), he will generally not realize all of his actual potential power. The costs of weakness are, in fact either (a–b) or (a–e), which ever is larger. Presidents who underestimate their power and act in terms of that underestimate will not affect their costs of legitimacy (unless the perceptions of power are actually a function of events as well as models) but will affect the costs of weakness.

If the president overestimates his power, he will think he can do something that, in fact, he cannot. If the president underestimates his power, he will think he cannot do something that, in fact, he can. Generally, the former errors are more conspicuous, both to the president and to his audiences, than are the latter. As a result, we would expect ordinary learning to lead the president to reduce his estimate of his own power (though he may easily still overestimate it).

Combining these observations, we obtain the following kind of progression: A president is more likely to overestimate his power in early years of the presidency than in the later years. This occurs because he is coming to the presidency from the universe of non-presidential beliefs about presidential power (which tend to be high), because he has high hopes, and because a honeymoon with his audiences makes the costs of illegitimacy less conspicuous. The result is a large power-expectation gap for the president and a large number of errors of attempting to do things he cannot. Over time, the president reduces his estimate of his power as he learns from the errors. His learning reduces the power-expectation gap, decreases the frequency of those errors, increases the (less conspicuous) errors of timidity, and increases the cost of weakness. At the same time, familiarity with the president as president raises the legitimacy of his position among his constituencies, with a resulting decline in the costs of legitimacy. According to this analysis, presidents should ordinarily experience systematic increases in the complaints about their timidity over time and systematic decreases in the complaints about their illegitimacy.

Presidents are not the only actors in the college scene who experience the phenomena we have indicated. In particular, student leaders, faculty leaders, and trustees can be located on Figure 9.1 in a similar way. If we are substantially correct, the costs of weakness and the costs of legitimacy are less for them, but some of the same phenomena obtain. They will generally find themselves less powerful than they expected and less powerful than their constituents expect them to be.

200

9.3 The Certification of Status

We have argued that several key domains of academic decision are subject to a logic that makes the official procedures for decision only marginally relevant to decision outcomes. Choices are made, but much of the activity in formal choice situations does not directly affect them. As a result, beliefs about the power of major participants are predictably confounded. We need to add a final note on the decision procedures themselves.

A system of university governance is a system for simultaneously making and validating decisions, exercising problems, and certifying status. The first of these functions dominates most discussions. We identify the system of governance as the procedure by which major decisions are made: Who is allowed access to the university – as student, faculty member, trustee, donor, employee? How are the scarce financial resources of the university allocated? How do the participants in the university use their time? What are the formats and rules of the teaching function? What research is done?

Governance as problem exercising is also familiar to readers of this volume. Several of our discussions have considered the conditions under which formal decision procedures become opportunities for exercising problems, rather than solving them. Where access and decision structures are relatively open in an organized anarchy, many decisions will be made; but if there is a moderate load, most of the decision energy will be spent attending unsuccessfully to problems collected in attractive garbage cans.

The status certification function of governance is less commonly discussed. For many participants, the process and structure of university governance are more important than the outcome – at least within wide ranges of possible outcomes. Participation is not a means but an end. Academic institutions easily become *process*-rather than *output*-oriented. Goals provide scant evidence on whether the output of the decision process within academe is desirable, but participation in the process is a conspicuous certification of status. Individuals establish themselves as important by virtue of their rights of participation in the governance of the institution.

To illustrate the phenomenon, consider the implications of the following simply hypothesis: Most people in a college are most of the time less concerned with the content of a decision than they are with eliciting an acknowledgment of their importance within the community. We believe that some substantial elements of the governance of universities can be better understood in terms of such a hypothesis than in terms of an assumption that governance is primarily concerned with the outcomes of decisions. Presidents are more insistent on their

201

right to make a decision than on the content of the decision. Faculty members are more insistent on their right to participate in faculty deliberations than they are on exercising that right. Students are more insistent on their right to representation on key decision bodies than they are on attending meetings. Boards of trustees are more insistent of defining the scope of their authority than they are on using it.

Much of the argument is over the symbols of governance. Who has the right to claim power? Since the main symbols of power and status are participation and victory, the university decision-making system is crowded with instruments of participation and platforms for claims of victories: select committees, faculty senates, ad hoc groups, reviews, memoranda, votes, meetings, rallies, conferences. The system is typically not crowded with actual participation except where validation of status positions is involved. Unless some highly symbolic conflict can be arranged, it is often hard to sustain student and faculty interest in the activities of a committee whose existence they apparently consider a matter of some importance. The situation has been illustrated well in recent years by instances of distinguished faculty, who rarely before had attended a general faculty meeting, coming to a meeting to discuss whether students should be allowed to attend.

As a system for making decisions, the standard college governance system is open to a number of vital challenges. It is not clear that it has a major role in the outcomes of decisions; that anyone seriously wants it to have such a role; that it is constituted in such a way as to make such a role feasible. The formal structure of governance does, however, provide some gradations of deference and a forum for debating the rights to participation. Not everyone receives as much deference as he might like. Arguments over scarce deference can be just as ferocious and just as serious as arguments over "real" resources. Universities, like countries, may struggle for a long time to decide the participation rights of member groups. But by providing numerous parallel decision system with numerous levels of overlapping committees, titles, and responsibilities, universities are relatively efficient in reducing conflict over status resources.

By calling attention to the importance of status, we do not intend to demean it. That academic man cares more for his self-respect than for his material well-being (if he does) may not be entirely a vice. And if he does, he may perhaps be excused the luxury of fighting more for the former than for the latter. Moreover, the right to participate is a necessary prerequisite to making the threat to participate; and the threat to participate is, at least in principle, a prime device for exerting influence over the course of events without being present (see Chapter 3). Although we do not believe that claims for status are generally

202

explicable as conscious efforts to construct a basis for subsequent threat, they have that potential whether intended or not.

Least of all should persons concerned about the substance of university decisions scorn a concern by others in the allocation of status. Such variations in concern form the basis for one of the most common of organizational exchanges – the exchange of status for substance. As Dale Carnegie (1936) has observed, the most natural coalition in the world is between someone who wants to sell pots and pans and someone who wants to be admired. In a world in which most people care more about their self-esteem than they do about what pots and pans are bought, anyone who has the opposite scale of values is in strong trading position. In important ways, universities are such a world. A person who is interested in changing a university may have some chance of doing so if he is willing to accord status to others within the community and is able to prevent the decisions in which he is interested from becoming garbage cans for collectively insatiable status concerns.

For the same reasons, concerns about participation status probably contribute to general stability of decision outcomes. Status concerns can become a problem to be discussed in the context of almost any choice. In classic garbage can terms, they may effectively prevent almost any specific choice from being made; but they leave most things untouched. They force the commitment of large shares of decision energy to the problems of constitutional rights. Much of the machinery and many of the participants are constrained to discuss those problems. This leaves little time or energy to overcome what we have called the logic of choice.

9.4 Conclusion

By examining the reports from college administrators on decision making in American colleges and universities, we have tried to elaborate the garbage can view of decision making in an organized anarchy. In particular, we have tried to suggest how the logic of decision in four key areas of university action provides a stability that is significantly independent of the detailed timing in flows of problems, solutions, choices, and participants. The flows are channeled by the terrain.

The results lend support, though in less elegant form, to Stava's (Chapter 10) discussion of the way in which an elaborately political and explicitly complex process in Norway led to a series of decisions rather closely approximated by a simple normative rule; to March and Romelaer's (Chapter 12) discussion of the impact of consistent participation in decision making in a university; and to Kreiner's (Chapter

203

8) and Christensen's (Chapter 16) discussions of the interplay between curriculum decision making and curriculum in a Danish free school.

Such a view, however, poses some problems of interpretation of executive power and of the functions of governance. We have argued that a serious view of the decision process in universities is inconsistent with a simple force model of power. This supports Enderud's (Chapter 17) contention that a focus on beliefs about power is necessary in order to interpret individual reports on a power distribution. Inconsistencies between the model of power in organizations held by many participants and the model we have outlined yield predictions about the development of beliefs about college administrators that seem to us to have some face validity. For example, standard descriptions of the presidential role tend to be heroic in their view of presidential importance. The portrait of reality we have sketched implies a more limited presidential role. A president probably has more power than other single individuals but he faces a poorly understood and rather tightly constrained managerial world. His ability to control decision outcomes is often less than expected by those around him and by himself. This leads to a predictable set of beliefs about presidential power and the exercise of it.

Finally, we are led to draw some implications of our interpretation for understanding the events that take place within formal decision arenas. Kreiner (Chapter 8), Christensen (Chapter 16), Olsen (Chapter 13), Weiner (Chapter 11), and Enderud (Chapter 17) have all observed ways in which the right to participate in decisions appears to be more important than actual participation and ways in which formal decision procedures are ritual confirmation of those rights. Such observations are consistent with at least some interpretations of a long stream of literature on organizational participation and alienation and recent examinations of the symbolic elements in political life.

In contemporary American colleges, a widely-shared egalitarian ideology contributes to making status a prime scarce resource and thus to making the certification of status a major concern. This, in turn, lends stability to many streams of decision outcomes by creating a heavy problem load on a system with modest decision energy.

NOTES:

1 This chapter borrows extensively from a longer discussion of some of the issues of leadership in organized anarchies (Cohen and March, 1974).
2 The sample is stratified into six categories. "Relatively wealthy" schools are defined as those in the top fifth of the distribution of 4-year colleges by income per full time student. All others are designated "relatively poor". Schools are classed as "large" if they have 9,000 or more students, "medium" if they have between 1,500 and 8,999 full time students, and "small" when the student body is 1,499 or less. Seven schools were drawn randomly into

204

each of the 3 x 2 = 6 sample cells. Further information on sampling and estimating procedures can be found in Cohen and March (1973).

3 We are indebted particularly to Nancy Block and Jackie Fry for their work in listening to the tapes, responses, and providing summaries and transcripts of those responses to control our faulty memories.

4 At some of the best-endowed universities, endowments flow directly to the subunits in the university rather than to the president. Although those presidents tend to be enthusiastic about the "each ship on its own bottom" ideology, they are also aware of their substantial irrelevance to the expenditures stemming from such independent sources.

5 There are many interpretations of the strong positive correlation between prestige of an institution and student unrest. Most of them, correctly in our view, stress factors that have rather little to do with conditions on the campus except as a pretext. We wish simply to add the observation that a school that has 10 outstanding applicants for every place in the freshman class is unlikely to feel enrollment cycle pressure to be attentive to student needs or desires.

6 For a discussion of some of the faculty personnel consequences of the end of growth see McNeil and Thompson (1971).

Environments and Strategic Choice in Organizations

╫E Kim S. Cameron

Organizational Adaptation and Higher Education

The recent report of the National Commission on Excellence in Education [46] concluded that "the educational foundations of our society are presently being eroded by a rising tide of mediocrity that threatens our very future as a nation and a people. What was unimaginable a generation ago has begun to occur — others are matching and surpassing our educational attainments." The explicit objective of the commission's report was "to generate reform of our educational system in fundamental ways and to renew the nation's commitment to schools and colleges of high quality throughout the length and breadth of our land."

A variety of recommendations were made in the report, which called for innovation and adaptation on the part of educational institutions. These recommendations focused both on elementary and secondary schools and on colleges and universities. However, before educational institutions can implement these recommendations, they must become both knowledgeable and adept at instituting organizational change. They will need to become effective at implementing innovation, reform, and adaptation. One purpose of this special issue of the *Journal of Higher Education* is to point out ways in which reforms, innovations, and adaptations can and have occurred successfully. Hopefully, these articles will contribute to the renewal of America's educational institutions in general and of liberal arts colleges in particular.

Our focus in this issue is mainly on liberal arts colleges, for reasons pointed out in the *Introduction,* and on the concept of adaptation, as opposed to innovation or reform, for reasons that will become clear

Kim S. Cameron is director, Organizational Studies Program, National Center for Higher Education Management Systems.

Journal of Higher Education, Vol. 55, No. 2 (March/April 1984)
Copyright © 1984 by the Ohio State University Press

later. This article reviews what is known about organizational adaptation and points out types of adaptation that will be needed in institutions of higher education in the future. The focus is a conceptual one, and specific adaptive actions taken by institutions are not reviewed. Rather, the purpose is to give the reader a framework within which to comprehend adaptation in educational organizations.

In the first section, major conceptual approaches to organizational adaptation are reviewed. The second section discusses the probable environment that institutions of higher education are likely to face in the future that will require adaptation. The third section discusses some adaptive strategies and institutional characteristics that will be needed by colleges and universities if they are to remain effective.

Section 1: Approaches to Organizational Adaptation

"Organizational adaptation" refers to modifications and alterations in the organization or its components in order to adjust to changes in the external environment. Its purpose is to restore equilibrium to an imbalanced condition. Adaptation generally refers to a process, not an event, whereby changes are instituted in organizations. Adaptation does not necessarily imply reactivity on the part of an organization (i.e., adaptation is not just waiting for the environment to change and then reacting to it) because proactive or anticipatory adaptation is possible as well. But the emphasis is definitely on responding to some discontinuity or lack of fit that arises between the organization and its environment.

This kind of organizational change is not the same as "planned change," or what is often called Organization Development (OD). Adaptation focuses on changes motivated by the external environment; OD focuses on changes motivated from within the organization. OD is generally oriented toward changes in individual attitudes and behaviors and in the organization's culture; adaptation is more concerned with organization-level change (see, e.g., [12]). Goodman and Kurke [23] differentiated adaptation and planned change in the following ways:

> Planned organizational change deals with the basis of change; adaptation deals with the conditions or sources of change. Planned organizational change focuses primarily on change within the organization, but the adaptation literature focuses primarily on populations of organizations, and on organization-environment interfaces, and on changes within an organization that are environmentally dictated. The planned organization literature emphasizes the process of actually creating change rather than writ-

ing about the processes of change (adaptation literature). The planned organizational change literature is devoted to methods and techniques, but the adaptation literature is devoted to theorizing about the change processes or outcomes. [23, p. 4]

This article, and this issue in general, focuses on the process of adaptation because of the pervasive influence of the external environment on liberal arts colleges. Several articles in this issue (e.g., Zammuto, Pfnister, Martin) point out the threats that face liberal arts colleges because of changing environments. Most observers agree that environmental turbulence and complexity have greatly accelerated in recent years (see [58, 59, 41, 52]) and that the ability of organizations to cope with those changes is being stretched. As Toffler noted:

> I gradually came to be appalled by how little is actually known about adaptivity, either by those who call for and create vast changes in our society, or by those who supposedly prepare us to cope with those changes. Earnest intellectuals talk bravely about "educating for change," or "preparing people for the future." But we know virtually nothing about how to do it. In the most rapidly changing environment to which man has ever been exposed, we remain pitifully ignorant of how the human animal copes. [58, p. 2]

Toffler's observation, that little is known about adaptation, is beginning to be rectified somewhat on the organization level. The body of literature on organizational adaptation is relatively new (most of it has appeared since 1970), but it has nevertheless become quite extensive. In fact, it is so extensive that a summary of it must, of necessity, be selective and abridged. Therefore, in this first section, general themes are discussed and examples are used, but a comprehensive survey is not attempted.

One way to organize the conceptual approaches to organizational adaptation is to use a continuum anchored on one end by the assumption that managers have *no* power to influence the adaptability and long-term survival of their organizations. On the other end of the continuum is the assumption that managers have *complete* power to create adaptability and to ensure long-term survival. Figure 1 summarizes the major approaches to organizational adaptation on the basis of this continuum. These approaches to adaptation are briefly explained below.

Approaches Assuming Little or No Managerial Influences

Aldrich [2], Aldrich and Pfeffer [3], Hannan and Freeman [24], Birnbaum [8], McKelvey [39], and others have proposed and elaborated

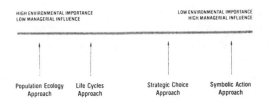

FIG. 1. Categories of Approaches to Organizational Adaptation

a "population ecology" or "natural selection" view of organizational adaptation. The population ecology approach to adaptation focuses on changes in environmental "niches" (i.e., subunits of the environment that support organizations). Two types of "niche" change can occur that lead to organizational adaptation. One is a change in the size of the niche, or the amount of resources available to organizations. The other is a change in the shape of the niche, or the type of organizational activities supported. Zammuto and Cameron [68] pointed out what adaptations are required of populations of organizations when faced with these different types of changes in environmental niches. For example, when a population of organizations encounters a change in niche shape (e.g., certain organizational activities are no longer supported), generalist organizations—those involved in a wide range of activities—are most adaptative. Successful adaptation requires becoming more diversified. On the other hand, when populations of organizations encounter changes in niche size (e.g., fewer resources are available), specialist organizations—those that are especially good at a narrow range of activities—are most adaptative. Successful adaptation requires organizations to specialize.

The population ecology approach suggests that adaptation is meaningful only if viewed from the population level of analysis (i.e., single organization changes are largely irrelevant). According to advocates, this level of analysis is important because of the many constraints and inertias inhibiting managerial action in organizations (i.e., formal structure, past history, norms, policies, and so on). The only meaningful change occurs as major shifts among entire populations of organizations, not as minor adjustments in existing organizational forms. The environment is viewed as such a powerful and pervasive force that it selects those organizational forms (or adaptations) that are to persist and other organizational forms die out. (For example, Hannan and Freeman [24] suggest that unstable environments select generalist organizations and stable environments select specialist organizations.) The process is considered to be much like biological selection theories. The fittest species — those that evolve characteristics that are compatible with the environment — survive while other species become extinct. Most organizations adapt, therefore, not because of intelligent or creative managerial action but by the random or evolutionary development of characteristics that are compatible with the environment. Managerial discretion and influence is neither present nor relevant.

Another approach to adaptation that emphasizes evolutionary change and the powerful role of the environment but that allows for more managerial discretion is the "life cycles" approach to adaptation (see [13, 14, 51] for reviews). Single organizations are the preferred units of analysis, and they are assumed to progress through at least four sequential stages of development. At each stage, unique organizational features develop in order to overcome certain general problems encountered by all organizations. Without direct managerial intervention to alter this natural evolution, organizational adaptations tend to follow a predictable sequence. Cameron and Whetten summarized the sequence as follows:

> Organizations begin in a stage, labelled "creativity and entrepreneurship," in which marshalling resources, creating an ideology, and forming an ecological niche are emphasized. [The problem faced by the organization in this stage is to build legitimacy and acquire the resources needed to survive.] The second stage, the "collectivity" stage, includes high commitment and cohesion among members, face-to-face communication and informal structures, long hours of dedicated service to the organization, and an emerging sense of collectivity and mission. The organizational emphasis is on internal processes and practices, rather than on external contingencies. [The problem faced by the organization is mobilizing the work force and building interdependence.] In the third stage, "formalization and control," where procedures and policies become institutionalized, goals are formalized, conservatism predominates, and flexibility is reduced. The emphasis is on efficiency of production. [The organizational problem in this stage is coordinating and stabilizing the work force and improving efficiency.] The fourth stage emphasizes "elaboration of structure" where decentralization, domain expansion, and renewed adaptability occur, and new multipurpose subsystems are established. [The organizational problem is overcoming rigidity and conservatism and expanding to meet new constituency demands.] [13, p. 527]

In each new stage of development, certain problems are encountered that are overcome by progressing on to the next life-cycle stage. That is, organizations encounter similar issues as they develop over time, and adaptation occurs by acquiring characteristics of the next life-cycle stage. This new stage solves the issues encountered in the previous stage but also generates issues that motivate further life-cycle development. Therefore, this approach to adaptation assumes that there is a natural tendency in organizations to follow a life-cycle pattern of development.

Two assumptions modify this approach and make it less deterministic than the population ecology view. The first assumption is that managers can speed up, slow down, or even abort this sequential development by their actions. That is, they can cause an organization to stay in an early stage for a long time, to move through the sequence very rapidly, or to go out of business before ever reaching subsequent stages. Second, these stages are most typical of the early history of organizations. After the fourth stage is reached, organizations may recycle through the sequence again as a result of unusual environmental events, leadership turnover, organizational membership changes, and so on. Managerial action can help determine which stage is returned to after stage 4 (see [14]).

Approaches Assuming Substantial Managerial Influence

On the other end of the continuum are approaches to adaptation that consider the decisions and actions of managers, not the external environment, to be the most important causes of organizational adaptation. They emphasize that managers can choose which environment the organization operates in, they can control and manipulate the environment, they can scan and thereby predict in advance environmental events, and so on. In short, organizations are not assumed to be at the mercy of an immutable environment; rather, they can act and influence their environment. The diverse literature on adaptation resulting from managerial action is organized into two major categories for the purpose of review. Several different models of adaptation are subsumed under each category.

One major category of adaptation models is the "strategic choice" approach [17, 3, 5]. A sampling of the different models summarized by this approach includes the "resource dependence" model [49], the "political economy" model [61], the "strategy-structure" model [16], and models by Miles and Snow [40], Miles and Cameron [42], March [35], and Miller and Friesen [43]. Whereas these authors recognize the importance of external environmental influences and the need for a fit between environment and an organization's structure and process [31], a variety of strategies are available to managers that can modify the environment and determine the success or failure of adaptation. As Chamberlain stated:

> Organizations are obviously not pushed and pulled and hauled by market forces which overwhelm them; rather, they demonstrably choose to follow a certain course of action which differs from other courses which they might have chosen and which, indeed, some of their number do elect to follow. Discretion is present. How important it is in the end result is still a moot point, but at least there is no basis for pretending that it has no effect. [15, p. 47]

The strategic choice approach is illustrated by Miles and Cameron [42], who found that organizations adapted very successfully to an extremely turbulent and hostile environment by implementing three types of strategies in sequence: "domain defense" strategies (designed to enhance the legitimacy of the organization and buffer it from environmental encroachment), "domain offense" strategies (designed to expand in current areas of expertise and exploit weaknesses in the environment), and "domain creation" strategies (designed to minimize risk by diversifying into safer or less turbulent areas of the environment). (See Cameron [11] for a discussion of these strategies in higher education organizations.)

Miles and Snow [40] suggested that organizations develop a particular orientation—a "strategic competence"—that leads them to implement these various types of strategies at different times and in different ways. For example, "prospector" organizations are inclined to be "first in," to implement strategies early and innovatively. "Analyzer" organizations are inclined to wait for evidence that the strategy will be successful before implementing new adaptations. "Defenders" seek for stability and are slow to adapt. "Reactors" implement strategies sporadically and are often unable to follow through with a consistent adaptive response. Miles and Snow [40] and Snow and Hrebiniak [57] have found empirical evidence linking these strategic orientations to effective adaptation under varying environmental conditions.

Miller and Friesen [43] studied thirty-six organizations and 135 different organizational adaptations in order to identify how organizations adapted over time. They used historical case studies so a longitudinal time-frame could be observed. Evidence for the strategic choice approach was found as they identified several major "archetypes of organizational transition." The most prominent archetypes among successful organizations were entrepreneurial revitalization, scanning and troubleshooting, consolidation, centralization and boldness, and decentralization and professionalization. These authors concluded that "there do not appear to be a very great number of common transition types" [43, p. 288]. That is, only a few major adaptation strategies implemented by managers are typical of a large variety of organizations.

One major issue that permeates the strategic choice approach is whether adaptations are implemented incrementally (i.e., small, piecemeal changes are put into place by managers) or in a revolutionary way (i.e., major shifts occur affecting many organizational elements). On the one hand, some writers suggest that organizations adapt by "muddling through" or by implementing "a succession of incremental changes" [32]. Change occurs without requiring major aberrations from the routine. As March put it:

> Managers and leaders propose changes, including foolish ones; they try to cope with the environment and to control it; they respond to other members of the organization; they issue orders and manipulate incentives. Since they play conventional roles, organizational leaders are not likely to behave in strikingly unusual ways. And if a leader tries to march toward strange destinations, an organization is likely to deflect the effort. Simply to describe leadership as conventional and constrained by organizational realities, however, is to risk misunderstanding its importance. Neither success nor change requires dramatic action. The conventional, routine activities that produce most organizational change require ordinary people to do ordinary things in a competent way. [35, p. 575]

On the other hand, Miller and Friesen [44] represent those who argue that adaptation occurs in a revolutionary way. They point out that organizations possess a great deal of momentum, or inertia, that serves to inhibit alterations or reforms. Past strategies, structures, goals, political coalitions, myths and ideologies, and so on contribute to that momentum, so that major adjustments in a substantial part of the organization have to be made in order for adaptation to occur.

> Organizational adaptation is likely to be characterized by periods of dramatic revolution in which there are reversals in the direction of change across a significantly large number of variables of strategy and structure.
> Revolutions that display reversals for a high proportion of variables occur with very significantly high frequency. These major reorientations seem to take place because many excesses or deficiencies have developed during periods of pervasive momentum or because a new strategy requires realignments among many variables. Thus there follows a myriad of structural and strategic reversals. [44, pp. 593, 612]

The second category of adaptation models on this end of the continuum is called the "symbolic action" approach [48, 47, 18, 7]. It differs from the strategic choice approach by focusing on change in symbols, interpretations, and stories as opposed to change in structure and technology. The logic of this approach is that organizations are glued together mainly by the presence of common interpretations of events, common symbols, common stories or legends, and so on or by a "social construction of reality" [7]. Social construction of reality means that the interpretation of reality in an organization is a product of social definition. Shared meanings are much more important than are events themselves. Part of the socialization process in organizations is giving members access to these common meanings. The role of the manager, in turn, is to create, manipulate, or perpetuate these meanings so that they are accepted in the organization and thereby influence organizational behavior. Pfeffer summarized this perspective in the following way:

> The activity of management is viewed as making what is going on in the organization meaningful and sensible to the organizational participants, and furthermore developing a social consensus and social definition around the activities being undertaken. Management involves more than labeling or sense making — it involves the development of a social consensus around those labels and the definition of activity. [48, p. 21]

Organizational adaptation comes about through the use of a variety of strategies involving language, ritual, and symbolic behavior designed to modify organization members' shared meanings. Weick [65] referred to this as "enacting" the external environment. Several of the more prominent methods of adaptation in this approach are as follows:

1. *Interpreting history and current events.* "The effectiveness of a leader lies in his ability to make activity meaningful for those in his role set — not to change behavior but to give others a sense of understanding what they are doing and especially to articulate it so they can communicate about the meaning of their behavior. . . . If in addition the leader can put it into words, then the meaning of what the group is doing becomes a social fact. . . . This dual capacity . . . to make sense of things and to put them into language meaningful to large numbers of people gives the person who has it enormous leverage" [50, pp. 94–95].
2. *Using rituals or ceremonies.* Gameson and Scotch [22] noted the ritualistic function of firing managers and coaches of professional sports teams whose win-loss records were bad. The firings did not so much represent a substantive change as they did a symbolic one designed to give the impression that things would get better. Inaugurations, ceremonies, and commencements are sym-

bolic functions used frequently to manage meanings and interpretations in order to influence organizational adaptation.
3. *Using time and measurement.* Time spent is one measure of the
   importance of organizational activities [47]. Therefore, spend-
   ing more time at one activity than another helps managers convey
   messages of priority to other organization members. Similarly,
   what is measured almost always receives more attention in organizations than what is not measured. Adaptation is facilitated by
   managers, therefore, through their use of time and quantitative
   measurement.
4. *Redesigning physical space.* Providing a new physical setting
   often conveys the message that something new is going on or
   that a different direction is being pursued. Similarly, attributes
   of physical settings often are interpreted as manifestations of
   power in offices and buildings (e.g., larger space, higher space,
   more central space, and so on). Pfeffer noted that "skilled
   managers understand well the importance of physical settings
   for their symbolic value. The size, location, and configuration
   of physical space provide the backdrop against which other managerial activity takes place, and thereby influence the interpretation and meaning of that other activity" [48, p. 41].
5. *Introducing doubt.* "The introduction of doubt into a loosely
   coupled system is a much more severe change intervention than
   most people realize. Core beliefs, such as the presumption of
   logic and the logic of confidence, are crucial underpinnings that
   hold loose events together. If these beliefs are questioned, action
   stops, uncertainty is substantial, and receptiveness to change is
   high" [66, p. 392].

Each of these strategies of adaptation under the symbolic action
approach assumes substantial power on the part of managers to change
the definition of the external environment and to change organizational behavior in response to those definitions. The environment is
not assumed to be immutable (as with the population ecology approach); on the contrary, it is assumed to be almost entirely a product
of social definition. Adaptation occurs by changing definitions.

Review

By way of review, aproaches to organizational adaptation can be
organized into at least four categories based on the importance of the
rolcs played by the external environment and by management in influ-

encing organizational survival. The population ecology approach assumes a prominent role for the environment and virtually no role for management action. The life cycles approach assumes a prominent role for the environment and evolutionary forces, but some discretion is assumed for management in altering those naturalistic forces. The strategic choice approach assumes a prominent role for both environment and management, but the balance is shifted toward management. The strategies implemented by managers can change the external environment as well as the organization. The symbolic action approach assumes a prominent role for management, through the ability to manipulate symbols and social definitions, and a less prominent role for the external environment.

Having reviewed the major approaches to adaptation, the question remains: What does this mean for institutions of higher education? Is one approach to adaptation better than another? What should managers and administrators in institutions do to make their organizations more adaptable?

To answer these questions, it is necessary to review the environmental conditions that are likely to face institutions of higher education in the future. That is, to understand how colleges should adapt, it is first necessary to understand what conditions will be characteristic of the external environment that perpetuate imbalances and require adaptation. The next section speculates on what future environments will be like for educational organizations.

Section 2. The Nature of Postindustrial Environments

It is generally acknowledged that factors in the external environment are increasing in their influence on organizations. Organizations are more frequently being required to be good at adaptation in order to survive. Roeber noted, for example:

> The characteristic mode of change in Western industrialized countries has been integrative, and the key characteristic is loss of slack. Partial equilibrium solutions are becoming less satisfactory, particularly where interaction between organizations and their social environment is involved. Consequently, the environment is becoming more of a factor inside organizations and requires more explicit attention. [52, p. 154]

Roeber's point, that the environment is becoming more dominant at the same time that organizations are faced with less slack, suggests that adaptive strategies should constitute a critical concern of future managers.

Several authors have discussed the changes that are occurring in the external environment that make attention to it more crucial than ever before. These changes are leading to what some call postindustrial society [56, 6], the technetronic era [9], the information society [38], the telematic society [37], and the third wave [59]. These authors all point out that environments in the future will be radically different for institutions than are the current environments of industrialized society. In a recent provocative article, for example, Huber [28] pointed out several ways in which postindustrial environments will be different from present or past environments. He stated that "postindustrial society will be characterized by more and increasing knowledge, more and increasing complexity, and more and increasing turbulence. These, in combination, will pose an organizational environment qualitatively more demanding than those in our experience" [28, p. 4].

Taking "increasing knowledge" as an example, environments of the future will contain a great deal more knowledge than is currently available. Because knowledge feeds on itself, the current knowledge explosion is likely to continue at exponential rates. The availability of computers that are more "friendly" (i.e., little, if any, training needed), more "intelligent" (i.e., able to coach the user), and more up-to-date (i.e., have access to more cutting-edge data) will contribute to both the availability of existing knowledge to institutions and the generation of new knowledge. Because knowledge will be able to be distributed rapidly, managers and administrators in institutions will have more information upon which to base decisions and less need to interact in face-to-face meetings to obtain it. Knowledge will become more continuous in its availability, more wide-ranging in the subjects it covers, and more direct in its sources.

This increase in knowledge and its availability through computer technology is also likely to produce increased complexity in the environment. Complexity is generally defined by three dimensions: numerosity, specialization or diversity, and interdependence. Miller explained the relationship between these three factors: "As a system's components become more numerous, they become specialized, with resulting increased interdependence" [45, p. 5]. That is, managers and administrators in institutions in a postindustrial environment will be exposed to a greater number of environmental elements (i.e., time and distance buffers will be greatly reduced by communication and transportation technologies, and more elements in the environment will become directly relevant). This abundance of environmental elements will force a greater degree of specialization of managers and administrators since overload could quickly occur otherwise. Increased specialization will, in turn, lead to the requirement of even greater interdependence among managers and institutions. Although institutions will have to be more loosely coupled in structure to cope with this environmental complexity [31], they will also need to become more tightly coupled in their information exchange.

The knowledge explosion and the increased complexity of the environment also contribute to a greater degree of turbulence. That is, increased access to information will require more rapid decision making and action implementation. Events in this kind of an environment will, as a result, occur more rapidly, and the timeliness required of managers will produce a tendency toward short time-frame strategies. More decisions in less time, along with a tendency toward shorter and more numerous events, will lead to a major increase in the turbulence of organizational environments (see [28] for an elaboration).

Increases in knowledge, complexity, and turbulence in postindustrial environments will place enormous strains on managers of educational organizations. In particular, although the necessity of designing and implementing adaptive strategies will dramatically increase, the "bounded rationality" [36] of managers will act as a constraint on their ability to do so. That is, the cognitive capacity of managers can be exceeded easily by the necessity to consider all the information and events present in a postindustrial environment. It is simply impossible for managers to initiate adaptive strategies in the same ways in postindustrial environments as they do now. The institutions themselves will have to be designed so as to enhance their ability to adapt, aside from the manager's specific strategies. Simon explained this requirement in the following way:

> Organizational decision making in the organizations of the postindustrial world shows every sign of becoming a great deal more complex than the decision making of the past. As a consequence of this fact, the decision-making process, rather than the processes contributing immediately and directly to the production of the organization's final output, will bulk larger and larger as the central activity in which the organization is engaged. In the postindustrial society, the central problem is not how to organize to produce efficiently (although this will always remain an important consideration), but how to organize to make decisions—that is, to process information. [56, pp. 269-70]

In view of these turbulent conditions, it becomes clear that all four approaches to organizational adaptation will be required as managers and administrators encounter the postindustrial environment. Institutional forms will have to emerge that are compatible with a diversity of environmental elements (the population ecology approach). Transitions to new stages of development will have to be closely monitored and planned for since they will occur more rapidly and sporadically in a postindustrial environment (the life cycles approach). Strategic choices by managers will be required that enhance the adaptability of the institution by expanding information search capacities while constraining information-processing requirements in order to make the choices more reasonable (the strategic choice approach). Interpreting the environment for the institution will become an even more critical task for managers due to its complexity and turbulence (the symbolic action approach).

Although none of these activities (i.e., designing diversity into institutions, managing rapid organizational transitions, implementing strategic choices, and interpreting the environment) are unknown to managers and administrators, the nature of the postindustrial environment and the phenomenon of bounded rationality will require that they be implemented in the kinds of institutions that have not been common in the past. That is, the nature of the institutions themselves will need to be different if they are to be adaptive to this new environment. The third section of this article proposes some characteristics that will be required by institutions of higher education and by managers in order to remain adaptable in future environments.

Section 3. Adaptability and the Janusian Institution

In discussing the challenges of managing organizations during turbulent times, Drucker observed some characteristics that managers must assure if organizations are to survive. "The one certainty about the times ahead, the times in which managers will have to work and to perform, is that they will be turbulent times. And in turbulent times, the first task of management is to make sure of the institution's capacity for survival, to make sure of its structural strength and soundness, of its capacity to survive a blow, to adapt to sudden change, and to avail itself of new opportunities" [19, p. 1]. For managers and administrators in higher education to assure capacity for survival, strength and soundness, adaptability to sudden change, and the ability to take advantage of new opportunities in a postindustrial environment with turbulence, information overload, rapid-fire events, and complexity all increasing at exponential rates, they will need to become Janusian thinkers and develop Janusian institutions.

Janusian Thinking

Rothenburg [53] introduced the concept of "Janusian thinking" while investigating the creative achievements of individuals such as Einstein, Mozart, Picasso, and O'Neill, as well as fifty-four highly creative artists and scientists in the United States and Great Britain. Janusian thinking is named after the Roman god Janus, who was pictured as having at least two faces looking in different directions at the same time. Janusian thinking occurs when two contradictory thoughts are held to be true simultaneously. The explanation or resolution of the apparent contradiction is what leads to major breakthroughs in insight.

> In Janusian thinking, two or more opposites or antitheses are conceived simultaneously, either as existing side by side, or as equally operative, valid, or true. In an apparent defiance of logic or of physical possibility, the creative person consciously formulates the simultaneous operation of antithetical elements and develops those into integrated entities and creations. It is a leap that transcends ordinary logic. What emerges is no mere combination or blending of elements: the conception does not only contain different entities, it contains opposing and antagonistic elements, which are understood as coexistent. As a self-contradictory structure, the Janusian formulation is surprising when seriously posited in naked form. [54, p. 55]

The surprising nature of Janusian formulations results from the preconception that two opposites cannot both be valid at the same time. However, holding such thoughts engenders the flexibility of thought that is a prerequisite for individual creativity. Such flexibility is also the key to effective problem solving. As pointed out by Interaction Associates:

> Flexibility in thinking is critical to good problem solving. A problem solver should be able to conceptually dance around the problem like a good boxer, jabbing and poking, without getting caught in one place or "fixated." At any given moment, a good problem solver should be able to apply a large number of strategies. Moreover, a good problem solver is a person who has developed, through his understanding of strategies and experiences in problem solving, a sense of appropriateness of what is likely to be the most useful strategy at any particular time. [30, p. 15]

Similarly, perpetuating Janusian characteristics in institutions also has the effect of producing flexibility and adaptability, and it enables organizations to cope better with unpredictable environmental events. A large variety of sometimes contradictory characteristics must be present in order to make adaptation effective on the institution level. For example, Weick pointed out some of these contradictory characteristics by asserting:

The problem of organizational effectiveness has traditionally been punctuated into conclusions such as those that the effective organization is flexible and productive, satisfies its members, is profitable, acquires resources, minimizes strain, controls the environment, develops, is efficient, retains employees, grows, is integrated, communicates openly, and survives. I would like to propose a different set of punctuations. Specifically, I would suggest that the effective organization is (1) garrulous, (2) clumsy, (3) superstitious, (4) hypocritical, (5) monstrous, (6) octopoid, (7) wandering, and (8) grouchy. [64, p. 193]

Several Janusian characteristics are discussed below that are proposed as necessary in effective higher education institutions in postindustrial environments.

Janusian Institutions

In addition to being aware of and implementing all four of the approaches to adaptation discussed previously, managers and administrators will need to perpetuate the following characteristics in their postindustrial institutions. Both loose coupling and tight coupling will be required. A loosely coupled system is one where connections among elements are weak, indirect, occasional, negligible, or discontinuous (see [62, 66]). Diffusion from one part of the organization to another occurs unevenly, sporadically, and unpredictably, if it occurs at all. Loose coupling refers to process looseness, not necessarily structural looseness. Tightly coupled systems, on the other hand, are controlled and coordinated so as to achieve specified goals. Centralization and hierarchy are prevalent so that all organizational action is directed toward similar purposes. Structure and process are interdependent (see [55]).

Lutz [33, 34] recently pointed out that the main responsibility of managers in higher education is to reinforce and perpetuate the tightly coupled elements in their institutions. Weick's statement is used as support for this point of view: "The chief responsibility of the administrator in a loosely coupled system is to reaffirm and solidify those ties that do exist" [67, p. 276]. Lutz responded: "That is exactly the point I was trying to make in my article, hence its title. To reaffirm and strengthen organizational ties or couplings is the administrator's chief responsibility. As university administrators fail in that responsibility, higher education is going to be in trouble" [34, p. 297].

The point of view advocated in this article is contrary to that of Lutz. In order for institutions to be adaptive in postindustrial environments, both tight and loose couplings will need to be reinforced and reaffirmed by administrators. Neither can predominate permanently over the other. One reason for this is that initiating innovations requires loose coupling, but implementing innovation requires tight coupling. "During the initiation (discovery) stage, the organization needs to be as flexible and as open as possible to new sources of information and alternative courses of action. . . . During the implementation stage, however, . . . a singleness of purpose is required . . . in order to bring the innovation into practice" [20, p. 175].

Postindustrial institutions of higher education will be required to remain loose enough to develop multiple, innovative adaptations. At the same time, they must be tight enough to implement them quickly and to change major components of the organization as needed. The self-design characteristics called for by Hedberg, Nystrom, and Starbuck [26], Weick [63], and Galbraith [21] — where high levels of experimentation and temporariness exist — will need to be matched with the ability to communicate and act quickly and efficiently through tight coupling. To do this, new arrangements such as ad hoc structures, collateral or parallel processes, or matrix arrangements may have to become much more common.

Actions designed both to achieve stability and to achieve flexibility will be required. Adaptation, in a technical sense, is designed to reestablish equilibrium between the organization and its environment. As mentioned earlier, adaptation is motivated by an imbalance or discontinuity between the requirements of the environment and the organization. Adapting to meet these requirements, therefore, makes the organization more stable but also less flexible. Adaptation establishes a certain organizational history that provides continuity, but it makes less likely radical departures from current functioning.

Adaptability, on the other hand, generally refers to the ability to cope with novel changes in the environment by maintaining a repertoire of unique, unconnected responses. It is synonymous with flexibility. Maintaining adaptability requires that organizational histories be at least partially forgotten so that improvisations can occur as required. Too much flexibility inhibits a sense of continuity and identity, and too much stability inhibits the ability to respond to completely new environmental features [66].

In postindustrial environments, institutions will need to be both stable (i.e., maintain a strong identity and a common interpretation of the environment) and at the same time be flexible (i.e., have a high degree of experimentation, trial-and-error learning, detours, randomness, and improvisation) as they encounter environmental elements that they have never before experienced. Because pressures will be present to fragment institutions, a strong identity and sense of institutional history is needed, but that identity and history must be systematically ignored in some circumstances. Mechanisms designed to erase organizational memory and to kill previous frameworks will be as important as mechanisms designed to operationalize current frameworks and reinforce the institution's culture. Short-term stability and long-term adaptability will both be prerequisites of effectiveness.

A wider search for informatoin as well as mechanisms to inhibit information overload will be required. Postindustrial environments will require that institutions increase their sensing and receptor capabilities because of the tremendous amount of knowledge that will be available. Not being aware of critical elements in the environment could lead to an institution's demise. With increasing turbulence and complexity coupled with an exponential growth in the amount of knowledge available, managers and administrators will have to increase markedly their abilities to acquire that knowledge (see [25]).

On the other hand, these same environmental characteristics can quickly lead to information overload. There will simply be too many fragmented elements to consider at one time. Because of the constraints of bounded rationality [36], mechanisms will have to be present to filter knowledge and reduce the amount that must be attended to [1].

To satisfy these two contradictory requirements, institutions may need to develop specialized scanning units, ad hoc probing and sensing groups, formalized interpretation systems, boundary spanning units, and so on [28]. The purpose of such units would be to both gather more information and to reduce, synthesize, or select out information required for adaptation decisions.

More consensus in decision making while also having more heterogeneity will be needed. In institutions where a high level of consensus exists, change and adaptation can occur both rapidly and efficiently. Time is not required to consider multiple, conflicting points of view or coalitional interests. The institution can be mobilized much more quickly when faced with disruptive environmental events than when the multiple stake holders do not agree on a common action.

Ashby's [4] "law of requisite variety" indicates, however, that complexity in one element must always be matched by equal complexity in another element. Contingency theorists (e.g., [10, 31]) have found that this principle applies to the relationship between organizations and their environments. Complexity in the environment must be met with complexity (i.e., heterogeneity) in the organization for equilibrium to occur. There will be a requirement in postindustrial environments, therefore, for intraorganizational heterogeneity (i.e., multiple viewpoints, specialization, diversity) to exist in order for institutions to maintain adaptability. Too much homogeneity, on the one hand, can lead to "groupthink" phenomena [29] and to narrowness of strategic alternatives. Too much heterogeneity can lead to revolution and anarchy in adaptation. Both consensus and homogeneity as well as diversity and heterogeneity, therefore, are needed simultaneously as prerequisites of adaptability.

To achieve these two contradictory states simultaneously, institutions will need to rely on new kinds of computer decision support systems that allow preferences and interests to be instantaneously aggregated and compared [28], new varieties of consensus-building group decision processes [60], formalized diffusion mechanisms that gather preferences and build commitment among institutional members when adaptation is required, redundant structures and process mechanisms that function independently, and so on.

Other characteristics of Janusian institutions also will be important to cope with postindustrial environments, such as high specialization as well as high generality of roles, proactivity and reactivity in strategic decisions, continuity of leadership and the infusion of new leaders with new ideas, deviation amplifying and deviation reducing processes, and so on. These characteristics are not elaborated here because of the constraint of space. However, the important point to be made is that the adaptability needed by institutions in postindustrial environments will require that Janusian characteristics be present. The deliberate redesign and restructuring of institutions will be a necessary prerequisite for these new environments.

The presence of Janusian thinking in individuals and Janusian characteristics in organizations often appears to be frightening (because of unpredictability) or even silly (because of inconsistency). However, it is precisely because of this attribute that both individuals and organizations operate successfully in turbulent and unknown environments. Initiating both continuity and change in leadership, specialization and generalization, proactivity and reactivity, and other seemingly contradictory characteristics will produce the adaptability necessary for effective institutions of higher education in the future.

Summary

The first section of this article reviewed different approaches to organizational adaptation. These approaches were categorized according to the amount of discretion they assumed for managers and the importance of the external environment. It was argued in the second section that each of these approaches will be required to operate simultaneously in institutions of higher education in a postindustrial environment. That environment was described as being characterized by more and increasing knowledge, complexity, and turbulence.

In addition to relying on these four common approaches to adaptation, however, it was proposed that managers and administrators will also be required to help design and perpetuate characteristics and processes in their institutions that have been somewhat uncommon in the past. That is, self-contradictory attributes will need to be developed and reinforced both in individual administrators and in their institutions in order to maintain adaptability in a postindustrial environment. Educational institutions with these characteristics and processes were labelled "Janusian" institutions because of the presence of contradictory phenomena that operate simultaneously within them.

The intent of this article, then, has been not only to review and provide a framework for the organizational adaptation literature but to propose how adaptation might be best facilitated in institutions of higher education. Liberal arts colleges, like other types of colleges and universities, will survive and prosper as they become adept at implementing adaptive strategies in the required ways and as they develop characteristics that match with the demands of the postindustrial environment.

References

1. Ackoff, R. L. "Management Misinformation Systems." *Management Science,* 14 (1967), 147–56.
2. Aldrich, H. *Organizations and Environments.* Englewood Cliffs, N.J.: Prentice-Hall, 1979.
3. Aldrich, H., and J. Pfeffer. "Environments of Organizations." *Annual Review of Sociology,* 2 (1976), 79–105.
4. Ashby, W. R. "Principles of the Self-Organizing Dynamics System." *Journal of General Psychology,* 37 (1947), 13–25.
5. Barnard, C. I. *The Functions of the Executive.* Cambridge, Mass.: Harvard University Press, 1938.
6. Bell, D. *The Coming of Postindustrial Society.* New York: Basic Books, 1973.
7. Berger, P., and T. Luckmann. *The Social Construction of Reality.* New York: Doubleday, 1967.
8. Birnbaum, R. *Maintaining Diversity in American Higher Education.* San Francisco: Jossey-Bass, 1983.
9. Brezezinski, Z. *Between Two Ages: America's Role in the Technetronic Era.* New York: Viking Press, 1970.

10. Burns, T., and G. M. Stalker. *The Management of Innovation.* London: Tavistock, 1961.

11. Cameron, K. S. "Strategic Responses to Conditions of Decline: Higher Education and the Private Sector." *Journal of Higher Education,* 54 (July/August 1983), 359–80.

12. Cameron, K. S., and R. E. Quinn. "The Field of Organizational Development." In *Classics in Organization Development,* edited by R. E. Quinn and K. S. Cameron. Oak Park, Ill.: Moore Publishing, 1983.

13. Cameron, K. S., and D. A. Whetten. "Perceptions of Organizational Effectiveness Over Organizational Life Cycles." *Administrative Science Quarterly,* 26 (1981), 525–44.

14. ———. "Models of the Organization Life Cycle: Applications to Higher Education." *Review of Higher Education,* in press.

15. Chamberlain, N. W. *Enterprise and Environment: The Firm in Time and Place.* New York: McGraw-Hill, 1968.

16. Chandler, A. D. *Strategy and Structure: Chapters in the History of the American Enterprise.* Cambridge, Mass.: M.I.T. Press, 1962.

17. Child, J. "Organizational Structure, Environment, and Performance: The Role of Strategic Choice." *Sociology,* 6 (1972), 1–22.

18. Cohen, M. D., and J. G. March. *Leadership and Ambiguity: The American College President.* New York: McGraw-Hill, 1974.

19. Drucker, P. F. *Managing in Turbulent Times.* New York: Harper and Row, 1980.

20. Duncan, R. B. "The Ambidextrous Organization: Designing Dual Structures for Innovation." In *The Management of Organization Design: Strategies and Implementation,* edited by R. H. Kilmann, L. R. Pondy, and D. P. Slevin, pp. 167–88. New York: Elsevier North Holland, 1976.

21. Galbraith, J. R. "Designing the Innovating Organization." *Organizational Dynamics,* 11 (1982), 5–25.

22. Gameson, W. A., and N. R. Scotch. "Scapegoating in Baseball." *American Journal of Sociology,* 70 (1964), 69–76.

23. Goodman, P. S. and L. B. Kurke. "Studies of Change in Organizations: A Status Report." In *Change in Organizations,* edited by P. S. Goodman, pp. 1–46. San Francisco: Jossey-Bass, 1982.

24. Hannan, M. T., and J. Freeman. "The Population Ecology of Organizations." *American Journal of Sociology,* 82 (1977), 929–64.

25. Hedberg, B. L. T. "How Organizations Learn and Unlearn." In *Handbook of Organizational Design,* Vol. 1, edited by P. C. Nystrom and W. H. Starbuck, pp. 3–27. New York: Oxford University Press, 1981.

26. Hedberg, B. L. T., P. C. Nystrom, and W. H. Starbuck. "Camping on Seesaws: Prescriptions for a Self-Designing Organization." *Administrative Science Quarterly,* 21 (1976), 41–65.

27. Huber, G. P. "Decision Support Systems: Their Present Nature and Future Applications." In *Decision Making: An Interdisciplinary Inquiry,* edited by G. R. Ungson and D. N. Braunstein. Boston: Kent, 1982.

28. ———. "The Nature and Design of Postindustrial Organizations." *Management Science,* in press.

29. Janis, I. *Victims of Groupthink*. Boston: Houghton-Mifflin, 1972.

30. Interaction Associates. *Tools for Change*. San Francisco: Interaction Associates, 1971.

31. Lawrence, P., and J. W. Lorsch. *Organization and Environment*. Homewood, Ill.: Irwin, 1967.

32. Lindblom, C. E. "The Science of Muddling Through." *Public Administration Review*, 20 (1959), 79–88.

33. Lutz, F. W. "Tightening Up Loose Couplings in Organizations of Higher Education." *Administrative Science Quarterly*, 27 (1982), 653–69.

34. ———. "Reply to More on Loose Coupling." *Administrative Science Quarterly*, 28 (1983), 296–98.

35. March, J. G. "Footnotes to Organizational Change." *Administrative Science Quarterly*, 26 (1981), 563–77.

36. March, J. G., and H. A. Simon. *Organizations*. New York: Wiley, 1958.

37. Martin, J. *Telematic Society: The Challenge for Tomorrow*. Englewood Cliffs, N.J.: Prentice-Hall, 1981.

38. Masuda, Y. *The Information Society*. Bethesda, Md.: World Future Society, 1980.

39. McKelvey, W. *Organizational Systematics: Taxonomy, Evolution, and Classification*. Berkeley: University of California Press, 1982.

40. Miles, R. E. and C. C. Snow. *Organizational Strategy, Structure, and Process*. New York: McGraw-Hill, 1978.

41. Miles, R. H. *Macro Organizational Behavior*. Glenview, Ill.: Scott Foresman, 1980.

42. Miles, R. H., and K. S. Cameron. *Coffin Nails and Corporate Strategies*. Englewood Cliffs, N.J.: Prentice-Hall, 1982.

43. Miller, D., and P. H. Friesen. "Archetypes of Organizational Transition." *Administrative Science Quarterly*, 25 (1980), 268–99.

44. ———. "Momentum and Revolution in Organizational Adaptation." *Academy of Management Journal*, 23 (1980), 591–614.

45. Miller, J. G. "Living Systems: The Organization." *Behavioral Science*, 17 (1972), 1–182.

46. National Commission on Excellence in Education. *A Nation at Risk: The Imperative for Educational Reform*. Report to the Secretary of the U.S. Department of Education, Washington, D.C., 1983.

47. Peters, T. J. "Symbols, Patterns, and Settings: An Optimistic Case for Getting Things Done." *Organizational Dynamics*, 7 (1978), 3–23.

48. Pfeffer, J. "Management as Symbolic Action: The Creation and Maintenance of Organizational Paradigms." In *Research in Organizational Behavior*, Vol. 3, edited by L. L. Cummings and B. M. Staw, pp. 1–52. Greenwich, Conn.: JAI Press, 1981.

49. Pfeffer, J., and G. R. Salancik. *The External Control of Organizations*. New York: Harper and Row, 1978.

50. Pondy, L. R. "Leadership Is a Language Game." In *Leadership: Where Else Can We Go?*, edited by M. W. McCall and M. M. Lombardo, pp. 87–99. Durham, N.C.: Duke University Press, 1978.

51. Quinn, R. E., and K. S. Cameron. "Organizational Life Cycles and Shifting Criteria of Effectiveness: Some Preliminary Evidence." *Management Science,* 29 (1983), 33–51.

52. Roeber, R. J. C. *The Organization in a Changing Environment.* Reading, Mass.: Addison-Wesley, 1973.

53. Rothenburg, A. *The Emerging Goddess.* Chicago: University of Chicago Press, 1979.

54. ———. "Creative Contradictions." *Psychology Today* (June 1979), 55–62.

55. Scott, W. R. *Organizations: Rational, Natural, and Open Systems.* Englewood Cliffs, N.J.: Prentice-Hall, 1981.

56. Simon, H. A. "Applying Information Technology to Organization Design." *Public Administration Review,* 34 (1973), 268–78.

57. Snow, C. C., and L. G. Hrebiniak. "Strategy, Distinctive Competence, and Organizational Performance." *Administrative Science Quarterly,* 25 (1980), 317–35.

58. Toffler, A. *Future Shock.* New York: Random House, 1970.

59. ———. *The Third Wave.* New York: Morrow, 1980.

60. Van Gundy, A. B. *Techniques of Structured Problem Solving.* New York: Van Nostrand Reinhold, 1981.

61. Wamsley, G., and M. N. Zald. *The Political Economy of Public Organizations.* Lexington, Mass.: D. C. Heath, 1973.

62. Weick, K. E. "Educational Organizations as Loosely Coupled Systems." *Administrative Science Quarterly,* 21 (1976), 1–19.

63. ———. "Organizational Design: Organizations as Self-Designing Systems." *Organizational Dynamics,* 6 (1977), 30–46.

64. ———. "Re-punctuating the Problem" In *New Perspectives on Organizational Effectiveness,* edited by P. S. Goodman and J. M. Pennings, pp. 146–84. San Francisco: Jossey-Bass, 1977.

65. ———. *The Social Psychology of Organizing.* Reading, Mass.: Addison-Wesley, 1979.

66. ———. "Managing Change Among Loosely Coupled Elements." In *Change in Organizations,* edited by P. S. Goodman, pp. 375–408. San Francisco: Jossey-Bass, 1982.

67. ———. "Administering Education in Loosely Coupled Schools." *Phi Delta Kappan,* 63 (1982), 673–76.

68. Zammuto, R. F., and K. S. Cameron. "Environmental Decline and Organizational Response." Discussion paper. National Center for Higher Education Management Systems, Boulder, Colorado, 1983.

Institutional Environments and Resource Dependence: Sources of Administrative Structure in Institutions of Higher Education

Pamela S. Tolbert

Two theoretical perspectives are combined to explain the pattern of administrative offices in public and private institutions of higher education. The first perspective, resource dependence, is used to show that the need to ensure a stable flow of resources from external sources of support partially determines administrative differentiation. The second perspective, institutionalization, emphasizes the common understandings and social definitions of organizational behavior and structure considered appropriate and nonproblematic and suggests conditions under which dependency will and will not predict the number of administrative offices that manage funding relations. The results of the analyses indicate that dependence on nontraditional sources of support is a strong predictor of administrative differentiation and demonstrate the validity of integrating these two theoretical perspectives.[*]

In explaining the formal structure of organizations, classic organization theory emphasizes problems of coordination and control of work activities (e.g., Taylor, 1911; Weber, 1946; Simon, 1956). Reflecting this tradition, research on sources of growth in the administrative component of organizations has typically focused on factors such as size and complexity that are assumed to impede the efficient supervision of tasks (Terrien and Mills, 1955; Bendix, 1956; Anderson and Warkov, 1961; Pondy, 1969; Blau, 1970; Hsu, Marsh, and Mannari, 1983).

Recent work on this problem, however, places greater emphasis on environmental relations and influences than on internal relationships as determinants of administrative structure (Freeman, 1973; Meyer and Brown, 1977). A number of different perspectives on organizational environments and the way in which environments affect organizational behavior and structure have emerged. In one, the environment is conceptualized in terms of other organizations with which the focal organization engages in direct exchange relations (Levine and White, 1961; Thompson, 1967; Pfeffer and Salancik, 1978). Administrative structure, from this perspective, reflects efforts to ensure a stable flow of resources and to manage problems and uncertainties associated with exchange transactions. Increasing dependence on exchange relationships produces administrative differentiation as organizations create offices and positions to manage these relationships.

In a second approach, the environment is conceptualized in terms of understandings and expectations of appropriate organizational form and behavior that are shared by members of society (Zucker, 1977, 1983). Such normative understandings constitute the institutional environment of organizations. Organizations experience pressure to adapt their structure and behavior to be consistent with the institutional environment in order to ensure their legitimacy and, hence, their chances of survival (Meyer and Rowan, 1977; DiMaggio and Powell, 1983).

This research integrates these two perspectives to explain administrative differentiation in colleges and universities. A central premise of this approach is that dependency relationships can, over time, become socially defined as appropriate and legitimate. It is hypothesized that when relations are

[*]
Helpful comments by Paul DiMaggio, John Meyer, Jeffrey Pfeffer, Robert Stern, William Stevenson, Ray Zammuto, Lynne Zucker, and the ASQ reviewers are gratefully acknowledged. Special thanks are owed to George Jakubson for his extraordinarily generous assistance with the computer program and analytic procedures.

281

institutionalized in this way, variations among organizations in actual level of dependency will be unrelated to the number of administrative offices associated with the management of the relations. When an organization enters into an exchange relationship that runs counter to institutionalized patterns, however, the maintenance of this relationship will generally require intensive administrative effort. It is hypothesized that when relations are not institutionalized, increasing dependence will be directly associated with the proliferation of administrative offices to manage the relationship. Thus, the institutional environment defines the conditions under which increased dependency leads to administrative differentiation. This research investigates these hypotheses, focusing on patterns of dependence among higher education institutions and the number of administrative offices that manage these dependencies.

THE INSTITUTIONAL ENVIRONMENT AND RESOURCE DEPENDENCE

In modern, rational-legal societies, organizations are typified as systems of rationally ordered rules and activities (Weber, 1946). Because of this shared typification, behavior that occurs in an organizational setting is particularly apt to be perceived as rational and "fact-like," not reflecting the random error of personal idiosyncracies. In this context, organizational practices and policies readily become institutionalized, that is, they become widely accepted as legitimate, rational means to attain organizational goals (Zucker, 1977; Meyer and Rowan, 1977; Scott and Meyer, 1983). Such widespread social conceptions of appropriate organizational form and behavior constitute the institutional environment of organizations. Organizations experience pressure to conform to these common understandings of rational and efficient structure, since violating them may call into question the legitimacy of the organization and thus affect its ability to obtain resources and social support (Rowan, 1982; Tolbert and Zucker, 1983; DiMaggio and Powell, 1983).

Using this framework, two additional propositions are advanced here. The first is that the institutional environment of organizations is differentiated. It is not that some organizations are constrained by the institutional environment while others are not; rather, there are different expectations for different types of organizations. Many of the commonplace distinctions that are drawn between public and private organizations reflect such differentiated expectations. Second, patterns of interorganizational exchange relations, as well as elements of structure, are presumed to be subject to the process of institutionalization. In other words, in the institutional environment there are normative understandings of appropriate and inappropriate organizational dependency patterns.[1]

Structural arrangements associated with institutionalized dependencies often become institutionalized as well. Thus, organizations characterized by a common, socially defined dependency pattern will exhibit similar structural features — common administrative offices, formal policies, and so forth. Since these elements of structure are part of the organizations' institutional environment, their presence in organizations will not be directly related to actual increases or decreases in the level of dependency.

[1]
The intense debate over the bail-out of the Chrysler Corporation by the federal government is a highly visible example of the institutionalized nature of dependencies. Criticisms of the government's actions clearly reflected not only long-run cost concerns, but common conceptions of the appropriateness and legitimacy of public support of a private organization (see Chapman, 1979; Friedman, 1979; Samuelson, 1979).

Dependency relations that are not institutionalized are generally less predictable, more uncertain. As these relations become an increasingly important source of support for the organization, the number of administrative offices and positions associated with the management of the relations is likely to grow. In this case, the magnitude of dependency will predict administrative differentiation. Formal offices are created to serve a directly functional role in negotiating and managing the demands and problems accompanying the relationship. They serve a symbolic role as well, since their presence can act as an indicator, or signal, of the organization's commitment to the exchange relationship (Spence, 1973, 1974; Meyer, 1979). Thus, the institutionalization of dependency relations determines whether or not increasing dependence will directly affect the proliferation of formal administrative offices within organizations.

ADMINISTRATIVE DIFFERENTIATION AND PATTERNS OF DEPENDENCE

In applying these ideas to an examination of administrative differentiation in colleges and universities, distinctions must be made between public and private institutions. The two types of institutions have a long-standing tradition of drawing on different sources of financial support. Public institutions have typically relied heavily on governmental sources of support, especially support from state legislatures, while private institutions have received their income primarily from tuition, endowments, and gifts and grants from private donors.

These patterns derive historically from a major legal decision addressing the issue of state control over institutions of higher education. During the colonial period, state governments provided substantial subsidies to private institutions within their jurisdictions. In 1819, however, a Supreme Court ruling established the autonomy of private higher education institutions from government supervision and control. Following this decision, states rapidly withdrew support from these institutions (Rudolph, 1962; Brubacher and Rudy, 1965). While private institutions became increasingly reliant on tuition and privately sponsored endowment funds as primary sources of revenues, an ideology developed to accompany this independence, promoted largely by the institutions themselves. As Rudolph (1962: 189) noted, "Before long, college presidents would be talking like President Eliot [of Harvard University] as spokesmen for rugged individualism, for the virtues of independence and freedom from state support."

Over time, differences in dependency relations for public and private colleges and universities have become institutionalized; dependence on different sources of support is viewed as an appropriate difference between the two types of organizations. Patterns of support for public and private colleges and universities provide evidence of the institutionalization of these dependencies, as shown in Table 1.

Private institutions have regularly derived approximately 10 percent of their income from private gifts and donations, whereas public institutions have typically received only about 2 percent of their income from this source. Public institutions, on the other hand, have been able to depend heavily on state and

Table 1

Percentage of Revenues of Public and Private Colleges and Universities from Major Sources of Support, 1939–1974*

	Public				Private			
	State	Federal	Tuition	Gifts	State	Federal	Tuition	Gifts
1939–49	61.9	13.5	20.3	1.9	3.1	.1	57.0	13.8
1953–54	65.6	16.0	13.3	3.1	2.6	19.1	47.0	16.6
1959–60	59.4	21.6	13.2	3.4	2.1	25.9	43.8	15.6
1961–62	44.0	18.6	10.4	2.4	1.7	23.2	32.4	10.6
1963–64	42.9	19.1	11.2	2.2	3.0	26.5	30.4	10.6
1967–68	44.5	17.8	11.6	.6	1.3	28.2	33.6	7.6
1970–71	47.5	11.7	13.1	1.9	2.2	12.1	35.8	9.5
1971–72	46.3	11.8	13.7	1.9	2.2	11.8	35.8	9.7
1972–73	47.1	12.1	13.4	2.0	2.3	11.5	35.6	9.4
1973–74	47.9	11.1	12.9	2.0	2.7	11.0	35.8	9.5

*Data for the years 1939–1960 are from O'Neill (1973); data for the remaining years are from U.S. Department of Health, Education and Welfare, National Center for Education Statistics, *Financial Statistics of Higher Education.*

local legislatures for support. This is clearly not the case for their private counterparts. Moreover, the proportion of revenues derived from each of these major sources shows remarkably little variation within each set of institutions over the 20-year period. Only revenues from the federal government show any substantial change, reflecting waxing and waning support for academic research. This overall stability suggests strongly institutionalized patterns of dependency relations. Private donors and alumni target private colleges and universities as appropriate beneficiaries of their largesse, while government agencies favor those in the public sector as appropriate recipients.

Consequently, public institutions typically find it more difficult to obtain significant financial support from private funding agencies and alumni than do private institutions. The latter, in turn, often find governmental bodies, particularly state and local legislatures, extremely reluctant to offer financial support. A small but noteworthy indication of this is the move by many private institutions to relabel themselves as "independents." This accompanies efforts by these institutions to attract public sources of funding (Breneman and Finn, 1982).

It has been argued that it is only when dependency relations are not institutionalized that the degree of dependency will predict administrative differentiation. Thus, it is hypothesized:

Hypothesis 1: Dependence on public sources of support will strongly predict the number of administrative offices that manage public-funding relations among private institutions.

Hypothesis 1a: Dependence on public sources of support will not predict the number of public-funding offices among public institutions.

Hypothesis 2: Dependence on private sources of support will strongly predict the number of administrative offices that manage private-funding relations among public institutions.

Hypothesis 2a: Dependence on private sources of support will not predict the number of private-funding offices among private institutions.

If differentiation is linked simply to the management of particular types of dependency relations, there should be no interaction effects of control and dependency as predictors of differentiation. If administrative differentiation is affected by the institutionalization of the relationship, dependence on particular sources of support should show an interactive relationship with control in predicting differentiation.

METHOD

Data

Data used in the analyses are from the Higher Education General Information Survey (National Center for Education Statistics, 1980) and other secondary data sources for 1975–1976. The survey is conducted annually among two- and four-year institutions of higher education in the United States and gathers a variety of information on these institutions, including enrollment, sources of revenues, and expenditure patterns. In addition, the survey asks respondents to list key administrative officers and their positions; each position is then assigned a common job code, based on the description of the associated administrative responsibilities. These data have two advantages. First, they are the only publicly available data on college and university administration at the national level. Second, because common job codes are assigned, there is no problem with functionally equivalent offices having different job titles.

Sample

The sample was drawn from the set of higher education institutions classified by the Carnegie Commission as either doctorate-granting or as "comprehensive." This included all major research institutions, universities granting at least 20 Ph.D.'s yearly, and institutions offering professional programs in addition to a basic liberal arts curriculum. These institutions were stratified by public and private control, and a random sample was drawn within each stratum. The resulting sample contained 281 institutions, of which 167 were public and 114 were private.

Measuring Administrative Differentiation

From the list of coded administrative positions, six were selected as having major responsibility for managing relations with external sources of financial support. These were used to measure the dependent variables, the number of offices with primary responsibility for the management of private-funding sources and the number responsible for dealing with public-funding sources.

Administrative positions with responsibility for managing private funding include those of chief development officer, director of alumni relations, and director of admissions. The job description of the duties of the chief development officer includes obtaining financial support from alumni and other organizations, coordinating volunteer fund-raising activities, and managing general public relations activities (Jones, 1977). The duties of the director of alumni relations are very similar, though obviously targeted specifically at alumni groups. The director of admissions is responsible for the recruitment, selection, and admission of students. Since tuition fees are often a significant source of private-sector support, how the recruitment and selection processes are managed can have an important impact on the institution's support base.

285

Responsibility for dealing with sources of public funding is assigned to the director of the information office, the chief planning officer, and the director of institutional research. The duties of the director of the information office center on providing information about the institution to students, faculty, and the general public. This includes preparing and reviewing news releases and information bulletins, and managing relations with the news media. The director of institutional research carries out research on the institution itself and disseminates this information to appropriate sources (e.g., legislative or governmental agencies). The responsibilities of the chief planning officer include monitoring and managing state and federal relations, as well as long-range planning to allocate institutional resources. It should be noted that the office of each serves a variety of functions, not all directly involving funding relations.

Table 2 shows the percentage of public and private institutions that report having each of these administrative positions. The percentage of private institutions reporting the presence of a

Table 2

Percentage of Public and Private Institutions Reporting Selected Administrative Positions for Funding Relations

Administrative positions	Public	Private
Chief Development Officer	47.9	83.3
Director of Admissions	66.5	86.8
Director of Alumni Relations	50.3	61.4
Chief Planning Officer	43.7	28.9
Director of Information	43.1	25.4
Director of Institutional Research	45.5	24.6

chief development officer and a director of admissions is significantly higher than that of public institutions. A noticeably higher proportion of private institutions also reports having a director of alumni relations, although the difference does not reach significance. Public institutions, on the other hand, report significantly more often having the positions that manage relations associated with sources of public funding.

These results accord with expectations derived from both the institutionalization and resource dependence perspectives. In the first perspective, structural patterns are expected to be associated with institutionalized dependencies. Thus, the greater frequency of private-funding offices among private institutions and public-funding offices among public institutions is predicted. Likewise, from a resource dependence perspective, private-funding offices would be expected to occur more frequently among private institutions that presumably depend more heavily on private sources of support, while the reverse would be expected for public-funding offices.

However, the resource dependence perspective suggests that increasing dependence should predict an increase in such offices, regardless of the type of organizational control. If, in contrast, the creation of these offices is affected by the institutionalization of dependency relations, increased dependence on public funding should be a better predictor of the occurrence of the three public-funding offices in private institutions than in public ones. Similarly, the creation of the three private-funding offices should be more strongly predicted by dependence on private funds in public universities.

Measuring Dependence

Dependence was measured by the proportion of the institution's total revenues derived from four primary sources of support: government appropriations, government grants and contracts, gifts and grants from private sources, and "self-generated" funds — tuition, fees, and endowment income. The first category, government appropriations, is a source of support traditionally viewed as a mainstay of public institutions, while the last two categories are support that is conventionally associated with private status. Although public and private institutions have both received government grants and contracts for research since World War II (Nelson, 1978), government grants will be treated here as technically a public source of support.

Control Variables

In addition to the measures of dependency, the analyses included two other independent variables as controls: size and a measure of research orientation. Size, measured here by total student enrollment, has often been linked to administrative differentiation (Terrien and Mills, 1955; Blau, 1970; Hsu, Marsh, and Mannari, 1983). This measure was logged to correct for skewedness. The complexity of administration in institutions with a strong research orientation, measured by the percentage of total expenditures allocated for research activities, might also be expected to produce administrative differentiation. Thus, these variables were included to ensure that the observed relationships were not merely reflections of differences in size or between research and nonresearch institutions.

ANALYSIS

To test the effects of resource dependence on administrative differentiation, two dependent variables were created, one based on the number of public-funding offices reported and one based on the number of private-funding offices reported. Table 3 shows the means and standard deviations of the variables by type of institution.

Table 3

Means and Standard Deviations of Resource-Dependence Variables by Type of Institution

Variable	Public (N = 167)		Private (N = 114)	
	Mean	S.D.	Mean	S.D.
Size (in 1000's)	16.511	11.214	8.722	6.556
% Expenditures for research	9.133	8.691	8.344	8.822
% Revenues				
Government appropriations	48.044	13.659	2.345	4.920
Government grants	11.708	7.506	13.642	10.217
Private gifts	2.462	2.242	7.837	5.275
Self-generated	15.496	8.322	51.034	19.289
Number of public-funding offices	1.396	.876	.876	.877
Number of private-funding offices	1.718	.938	2.389	.760

In each case, the dependent variable can assume one of only four possible values (0–3). Because multivariate linear analyses are based on assumptions requring an interval level of measurement for the dependent variable (Maddala, 1983), the use of ordinary-least-squares techniques is inappropriate.[2] Instead, an ordered probit model was employed. This is an extension of a dichotomous probit model that is applicable to analyses involving ordinal dependent variables (McKelvey and Zavoina, 1975; Winship and Mare, 1984). With this analytic procedure, a distinction is drawn between an underlying theoretical dependent variable, which has an interval scale of measurement, and the observed dependent variable, which is ordinal. In the present case, the latent theoretical variable may be thought of as the amount of pressure for administrative differentiation; the observed variable is the presence of zero, one, two, or three offices.

More formally, if Y^* is the underlying theoretical variable, and Y is the observed variable, then it is assumed:

$$Y^* = \beta X + u, \tag{1}$$

where $u \sim N(0, \sigma^2)$. To set the scale of measurement, $\sigma^2 \equiv 1$ (see Jöreskog and Sörbom, 1981).

Then:

$$Y = \begin{cases} 0 \text{ if } Y^* \leq \alpha_0 \\ 1 \text{ if } \alpha_0 < Y^* \leq \alpha_1 \\ 2 \text{ if } \alpha_1 < Y^* \leq \alpha_2 \\ 3 \text{ if } \alpha_2 < Y^* \end{cases} \tag{2}$$

The alphas in this equation represent the threshhold points in the distribution of Y^* at which the observed Y takes on a different value. The relationship between the latent variable, Y^*, and the observed Y is depicted in Figure 1.

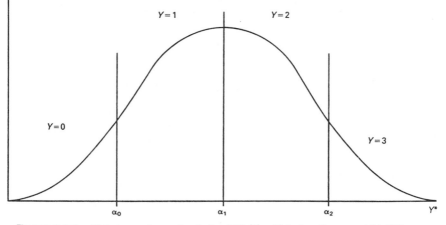

$f(Y^*)$

$Y=1$ | $Y=2$

$Y=0$

$Y=3$

α_0 α_1 α_2 Y^*

Figure 1: Relationship between observed ordinal variable (Y) and latent continuous variable (Y^*).

2

Linear regression models are based on the assumption that the distribution of data points around the regression line yields a set of error terms with a mean of zero and a constant variance. When dealing with an ordinal dependent variable, these assumptions are generally not valid (McKelvey and Zavoina, 1975).

Combining the first two equations implies that:

$$\begin{aligned} P(Y = 0|X) &= \\ P(Y^* \leq \alpha_0|X) &= \\ P(\beta X + u \leq \alpha_0) &= \\ P(u \leq \alpha_0 - \beta X) &= \\ F(\alpha_0 - \beta X), \end{aligned} \tag{3}$$

288

where $F(\alpha_0 - \beta X)$ signifies a standard normal cumulative density function (see Figure 1). This can readily be extended to the other values of Y. Because ordered probit models take into account ceiling and floor restrictions on probabilities, they are highly preferable to linear models when the observed Y is markedly skewed (Winship and Mare, 1984).

Maximum likelihood methods (Berndt et al., 1974; McKelvey and Zavoina, 1975; Chow, 1983) were used to obtain estimates of the parameters of the model. Separate analyses were carried out for each dependent variable, using the full sample of institutions. These analyses were then repeated, using the subsamples of public and private institutions.

RESULTS

Table 4 presents the results of the ordered probit analysis of the number of public-funding offices, using the full sample of institutions. The beta coefficients represent the slope coefficients in the latent regression, or the increment in Y^* brought about by a unit change in the independent variable. The first alpha coefficient is automatically set to zero for normalization. The other two alphas represent the remaining cutpoints in the distribution of Y^*. The λ is a test of the overall significance of the model, based on a comparison of the presented model with one in which the betas are constrained to be zero.

Table 4

Ordered Probit Analysis of Public-Funding Offices in Total Sample

Independent variables	B	S.E.	t-value
Constant	−.231	.200	−1.16
Size	$.267^{-4}$	$.774^{-5}$	3.45•••
% Research expenditures	−.006	.012	−.50
Control (public)	.653	.363	1.70•
% Government appropriations	.038	.033	1.12
% Government grants	.016	.013	1.17
Control x appropriations	−.032	.016	−1.95••
Control x grants	−.028	.016	−1.77•
α_1	1.137	.095	12.00•••
α_2	2.183	.135	16.17•••
Log L	−333.07		
λ	44.44•••		

•$p<.10$; ••$p<.05$; •••$p<.01$.

There are clear interactive effects of control and dependence on government grants and appropriations. Apart from size, the strongest and only significant predictors of the number of public-funding offices are public control and the interaction terms.

In Table 5 the analysis is repeated, using the number of private-funding offices as the dependent variable.

Dependence on private gifts and self-generated sources of funding are not, by themselves, strong predictors of the number of offices. The interaction term for control and dependence on private gifts does emerge as significant, however, along with the terms for control and for size.

Table 5

Ordered Probit Analysis of Private-Funding Offices in Total Sample

Independent variables	B	S.E.	t-value
Constant	1.678	.499	3.36•••
Size	$.171^{-4}$	$.763^{-5}$	2.25•••
% Research expenditures	.008	.009	.85
Control (public)	−1.210	.492	−2.46•••
% Private gifts	−.003	.022	−.14
% Self-generated	.013	.013	.57
Control x gifts	.061	.034	1.87•
Control x self-generated	.013	.013	.98
α_1	1.996	.113	8.79•••
α_2	2.050	.133	15.41•••
Log L	−333.65		
λ	53.18•••		

•$p<.10$; ••$p<.05$; •••$p<.01$.

Both analyses suggest, then, that the effect of dependency on administrative differentiation varies for public and private institutions. To examine this more closely, the analyses were repeated, using the subsamples of each type of institution.

The ordered probit analyses for public-funding offices by public and private institutions are shown in Table 6.

Table 6

Ordered Probit Analysis of Public-Funding Offices in Public and Private Institutions

Independent variables	Public			Private		
	B	S.E.	t-value	B	S.E.	t-value
Constant	.521	.343	1.52	−.469	.240	−1.96••
Size	$.187^{-4}$	$.895^{-5}$	2.08••	$.680^{-4}$	$.241^{-4}$	2.83•••
% Research expenditures	−.005	.013	−.34	−.020	.030	−.68
% Government appropriations	.005	.005	.97	.037	.018	1.94••
% Government grants	−.009	.015	−.64	.018	.023	.78
α_1	1.156	.122	9.47•••	1.001	.253	6.78•••
α_2	2.207	.167	13.23•••	2.223	.177	11.38•••
Log L	−209.49			−120.46		
λ	6.30			18.62•••		

•$p<.10$; ••$p<.05$; •••$p<.01$.

Among public institutions, only size emerges as a strong predictor. Increasing dependence on public sources of support has no substantial effect on the number of public-funding offices. Overall, the low value of λ indicates that these variables add little to the prediction of administrative differentiation. Among private institutions, on the other hand, dependence on governmental appropriations is significantly related to differentiation. The test statistic for the overall model is also significant in this case. These results, then, are consistent with the first hypothesis and its corollary.

Table 7 presents the analyses for private-funding offices by type of institution. As hypothesized, increasing dependence on private sources of support, particularly private gifts, is a much stronger predictor of differentiation in public than in private

Table 7

Ordered Probit Analysis of Private-Funding Offices in Public and Private Institutions

Independent variables	Public B	Public S.E.	t-value	Private B	Private S.E.	t-value
Constant	.475	.250	1.90**	1.567	.695	2.54***
Size	$.100^{-4}$	$.834^{-5}$	1.20	$.686^{-4}$	$.297^{-4}$	2.31**
% Research expenditures	.016	.012	1.33	−.021	.020	−1.06
% Private gifts	.059	.030	1.92**	.006	.025	.24
% Self-generated	.018	.012	1.51	.001	.008	.06
α_1	.957	.112	7.81***	1.166	.292	3.99***
α_2	2.060	.153	13.47***	2.179	.307	7.09***
Log L	−212.87			−117.20		
λ	13.92**			9.00		

$*p<.10$; $**p<.05$; $***p<.01$.

institutions. In the latter case, the measures of dependence on each source have virtually no relationship to the number of private-funding offices. Thus, these results provide support for the second set of hypotheses as well.

As expected, dependence on public or private sources of funding predicts the proliferation of administrative offices only when the dependencies are not aligned with traditional patterns. In other words, dependence on a given exchange relationship may or may not lead to the creation of offices and positions to manage those relationships. Since institutionalized dependencies are often accompanied by the institutionalization of structural components, organizations characterized by such relations adopt those components ceremonially, independent of actual levels of support. Thus, increasing dependence does not necessarily produce administrative differentiation. It is only when dependency relations are not institutionalized that increasing dependence is strongly associated with the development of separate administrative offices to manage them.

DISCUSSION

These analyses suggest that an institutionalization perspective defines conditions under which hypotheses generated by a resource dependence perspective will hold. There are, however, alternative explanations and modifications of this argument to be considered. First, it could be argued that the results of the analysis simply reflect the limited variance of the independent variables when dependencies follow traditional patterns. Examination of the means and standard deviations of the variables, shown in Table 3, substantially weakens the plausibility of this argument. None of the measures of traditional dependencies (e.g., government appropriations among public institutions, gifts and donations among private institutions) has a markedly restricted variance. The range for the measure of dependence on government appropriations among public institutions is from 10 to 84 percent of total revenues; the range for dependence on private gifts is from 1 to 33 percent among private institutions. Thus, this alternative is not supported by the data.

It might also be argued that the relationship between dependence and administrative differentiation should be reciprocal.

While a plausible case may be made for this, the central concern of the present analysis is to demonstrate the link between two general theoretical perspectives that focus primarily on the sources of administrative differentiation rather than on the consequences. The latter, however, remains an interesting problem for further research.

CONCLUSIONS

Contemporary research on organizations has produced a variety of theoretical perspectives, each pointing to different explanatory factors. Although the complementarity of different perspectives is sometimes acknowledged (Aldrich and Pfeffer, 1976; Ulrich and Barney, 1984), empirical research typically draws on a single theoretical approach in explaining particular cases of organizational behavior and structure. Positive outcomes are interpreted as evidence of the validity of that perspective.

It is clear, however, that most of the perspectives that currently guide research are not truly competitive, such that support for one undermines another. Instead, they are more likely simply to be applicable under different conditions, as was the case in this study. By combining resource dependence and institutionalization perspectives, a much fuller explanation of the process of administrative differentiation was provided than could have been provided by either perspective independently.

Organizational phenomena are much too complex to be described adequately by any single theoretical approach. Current research on organizations could benefit greatly if researchers were to pay closer attention to specifying the points of intersection of different theoretical perspectives and to combining these perspectives to provide more complete explanations of the behaviors they study.

REFERENCES

Aldrich, Howard, and Jeffrey Pfeffer
1976 "Environments of organizations." In A. Inkeles (ed.), Annual Review of Sociology, 2: 79–105. Palo Alto, CA: Annual Reviews.

Anderson, Theodore, and Seymour Warkov
1961 "Organizational size and functional complexity: A study of administration in hospitals." American Sociological Review, 26: 23–38.

Bendix, Reinhard
1956 Work and Authority in Industry. New York: Wiley.

Berndt, E. K., B. H. Hall, R. E. Hall, and J. A. Hausman
1974 "Estimation and inference in non-linear structural models." Annals of Economic and Social Measurement, 3: 653–666.

Blau, Peter
1970 "A formal theory of differentiation in organizations." American Sociological Review, 35: 201–218.

Breneman, David, and Chester Finn, Jr.
1982 "An uncertain future." In D. Breneman and C. Finn (eds.), Public Policy and Private Higher Education: 1–62. Washington, DC: Brookings.

Brubacher, John, and Willis Rudy
1965 Higher Education in Transition. New York: Harper & Row.

Chapman, Stephen
1979 "No-fault capitalism." New Republic, 181 (November 17): 11–14.

Chow, Gregory
1983 Econometrics. New York: McGraw-Hill.

DiMaggio, Paul, and Walter Powell
1983 "The iron cage revisited: Institutional isomorphism and collective rationality in organizational fields." American Sociological Review, 48: 147–160.

Freeman, John
1973 "Environment, technology and the administrative intensity of manufacturing organizations." American Sociological Review, 38: 750–763.

Friedman, Milton
1979 "Are jobs the issue?" Newsweek, 94 (September 10): 66.

Hsu, Cheng-Kuang, Robert Marsh, and Hiroshi Mannari
1983 "An examination of the determinants of organizational structure." American Journal of Sociology, 88: 975–996.

Jones, Dennis
1977 A Manual for Budgeting and Accounting for Manpower Resources in Postsecondary Education. Washington, DC: National Center for Education Statistics.

Jöreskog, Karl, and Dag Sörbom
1981 Analysis of Linear Structural Relationships by Maximum Likelihood and Least Squares Methods. Uppsala: University of Uppsala.

Levine, Sol, and Paul White
1961 "Exchange as a conceptual framework for the study of interorganizational relationships." Administrative Science Quarterly, 5: 583–601.

Maddala, G. S.
1983 Limited Dependent and Qualitative Variables in Econometrics. Cambridge: Cambridge University Press.

McKelvey, Richard, and William Zavoina
1975 "A statistical model for the analysis of ordinal level dependent variables." Journal of Mathematical Sociology, 4: 103–120.

Meyer, John, and Brian Rowan
1977 "Institutionalized organizations: Formal structure as myth and ceremony." American Journal of Sociology, 83: 340–363.

Meyer, Marshall
1979 "Organizational structure as signaling." Pacific Sociological Review, 22: 481–500.

Meyer, Marshall, and M. Craig Brown
1977 "The process of bureaucratization." American Journal of Sociology, 83: 364–385.

National Center for Education Statistics
1980 Longitudinal File of Financial, Enrollment and Faculty Statistics for Institutions of Higher Education: 1974–75 to 1977–78. Washington, DC: NCES.

Nelson, Susan
1978 "Financial trends and issues." In D. Breneman and C. Finn (eds.), Public Policy and Private Higher Education: 69–142. Washington, DC: Brookings.

O'Neill, June
1973 Sources of Funds to Colleges and Universities. Washington, DC: Carnegie Foundation.

Pfeffer, Jeffrey, and Gerald Salancik
1978 The External Control of Organizations. New York: Harper & Row.

Pondy, Louis
1969 "The effects of size, complexity and ownership on administrative intensity." Administrative Science Quarterly, 14: 47–61.

Rowan, Brian
1982 "Organizational structure and the institutional environment: The case of public schools." Administrative Science Quarterly, 27: 259–279.

Rudolph, Fredrick
1962 The American College and University. New York: Knopf.

Samuelson, Paul
1979 "Judging corporate handouts." Newsweek, 94 (August 13): 58–61.

Scott, Richard, and John Meyer
1983 Organizational Environments. Beverly Hills, CA: Sage.

Simon, Herbert
1956 Administrative Behavior. New York: Macmillan.

Spence, Michael
1973 "Job market signaling." Quarterly Journal of Economics, 83: 355–374.
1974 Market Signaling. Cambridge, MA: MIT Press.

Taylor, Fredrick
1911 Principles of Scientific Management. New York: Harper & Row.

Terrien, Fredric, and Donald Mills
1955 "The effects of changing size on the internal structure of organizations." American Sociological Review, 20: 11–13.

Thompson, James
1967 Organizations in Action. New York: McGraw-Hill.

Tolbert, Pamela, and Lynne Zucker
1983 "Institutional sources of change in organizational structure: The diffusion of civil service reform, 1880–1930." Administrative Science Quarterly, 23: 22–39.

Ulrich, David, and Jay Barney
1984 "Perspectives in organizations: Resource dependence, efficiency and population." Academy of Management Review, 9: 471–481.

Weber, Max
1946 Essays in Sociology. New York: Oxford University Press.

Winship, Christopher, and Robert Mare
1984 "Regression models with ordinal variables." American Sociological Review, 49: 512–525.

Zucker, Lynne
1977 "The role of institutionalization in cultural persistence." American Sociological Review, 42: 725–743.
1983 "Organizations as institutions." In S. Bacharach (ed.), Research in the Sociology of Organizations, 2: 1–47. Greenwich, CT: JAI Press.

Institutional History and Ideology:
The Evolution of Two Women's Colleges

TED I.K. YOUN

Boston College

KARYN A. LOSCOCCO

State University of New York at Albany

IN THE LATE 1980s, WHEATON COLLEGE in Massachusetts and Russell Sage College in New York faced what had become an inescapable decision for women's colleges: whether to remain single-sex or to become coeducational. Wheaton officials rejected the college's historic mission in favor of coeducation. Russell Sage reaffirmed its identity as an educational institution for women. The similarities between two organizations that made different choices when faced with similar environmental forces, present a unique opportunity to examine the forces that predict continuity or change.

At first glance, each college appears to have calculated rationally in arriving at its decision. Wheaton effected a major transformation during relatively favorable economic conditions. The college had just successfully completed a $26 million capital campaign, and had balanced its budget for the 22nd year in a row. The chair of the board of trustees reflected: "We are in a position of strength; we should make a major strategic move now."[1] Russell Sage College, though less prestigious and financially far more vulnerable, clung stubbornly to the concept of single-sex education for women, but only after careful search and deliberation. After a period of tumultuous debates, Russell Sage's leaders concluded that the college could carve out a unique niche by continuing to fill a crucial gap in educational choices for women.

On closer examination, however, these outcomes represent more than institutional responses to financial considerations—indeed, the more vulnerable institution stood by its historic mission. Nor is increased competition for enrollments—the rationale offered by the leaders of the two colleges—a sufficient explanation of their responses. The historical and organizational context, we believe, is an independent dimension that affected the gathering, use, and interpretation of information needed to make the decisions.

Our account of the two decisions begins with a history of each college, emphasizing explanations of decision making that focus on the institutional

1991   21

aspects of organization-environment relations. The exclusion of women from higher education during the nineteenth century led Emma Willard, Catharine Beecher, Mary Lyon, and Eliza Baylies Wheaton to establish seminaries for women. When these seminaries, beset with constant financial difficulties, were criticized for a lack of rigor, some educators implemented reforms; others transformed their institutions into colleges that imitated the higher education typically offered to men. In both cases, environmental pressures led to conformity among organizations in a particular field. This push to *isomorphism* is powerful; organizations make choices that lead them to resemble one another even if this push is neither rational nor efficient. Dominant organizations compel weaker and vulnerable organizations in the field to imitate their seemingly successful and legitimate institutional form. The more vulnerable organization selects the most appropriate routine from the apparently successful organization.[2]

Recent literature on decision making questions the assumptions of earlier "rational choice" models that deem organizational decision making necessarily purposive, involving the systematic maximizing of utility.[3] Our historical evidence shows that choices in organizations often are made without regard to goal-related preferences. Decision makers ignore their own stated preferences especially as environmental uncertainty increases. Intentions and actions are connected loosely in making decisions; rituals and symbols often matter more than the outcome of the decision.[4] Indeed, symbols often construct realities that ameliorate post-decision disappointments since the consequences of the choice are unknown in advance.[5]

Our inductive analysis of the choices made by these two colleges draws on interviews with key organizational decision makers and their consultants, newspaper accounts, internal memos, proceedings, and newsletters, and published histories.[6] Placing these case studies in their historical context illuminates the relationship between decision making and organizational change, and identifies the linkages.

WHEATON: FROM FEMINISM TO A NEW PARTNERSHIP

In January 1987, the Wheaton College trustees considered a coeducation proposal, largely based on a subcommittee report showing that fewer women were willing to enter an all-female college.[7] The trustees appeared to arrive at their decision quickly, but postponed final action until the May meeting to "allow for wider consultation with members of the Wheaton family, including sharing our findings and convictions and soliciting their views."[8] Campus constituencies responded negatively to the announcement. Shock, anger, and sadness were evident at the class meetings held later the same day and at the next faculty meeting. Stunned students and alumnae characterized the action as "rubber stamping" and questioned the swiftness of the decision.[9] Lawsuits ensued—a predictable reaction at a college that once renamed its bachelor of arts degree the "bachelor of sisterhood."[10]

The trustees, backed by the president of the college, stood firm. On May 24, the board chair sent a letter to the members of the Wheaton College community, stating that "the trustees have reached their decision and the trustees expect the implementation of coeducation at Wheaton College to proceed as quickly as possible."[11] The president expressed sympathy for the concern of students and alumnae, but argued that "we are vulnerable to forces beyond our control....The College we all love cannot remain indefinitely as it is."[12] Asked to respond to criticisms of the decision, the president added, "Can you imagine a corporation letting its shareholders decide on long-range planning issues? Colleges aren't just like corporations, but it is not a bad parallel."[13]

Our interviewees used the language of rational and willful choice to interpret the decision. A concern for the declining rate of female applicants in recent years, the trustees and president insisted, outweighed student and alumni opposition. "It was a matter of making several value choices in facing applicant market problems," the outgoing chair of the trustees explained:

> Do we shrink to a smaller institution? Do we lower our quality? Do we go for a more aggressive recruitment plan? Or is the coeducation plan a viable option?

> We cannot possibly reduce our college size and maintain a quality liberal arts program....not much you can do to lower the standards. Our recruiting staff have been pouring in 150 percent energy. One can only do so much for the recruitment....That leaves only one possible option.[14]

The trustees, the chair noted, demonstrated that "someone was running the place." The faculty, he added, had its chance.

> Our faculty were asked to think about the future of our college several years ago. The faculty members were the principal actors to examine our future. But they were unable to reach a concrete agreement regarding the future plan. We were seeing a growing crisis of applicants but we were drifting. In 1986, it became clear that the next principal actors were trustees. The trustees met and started to work on a long-range plan.[15]

The trustees and president unabashedly emphasized the departure from former institutional routine by promulgating a new mission for Wheaton. "An examination of massive shifts in work and family patterns," the president said, "...calls for the creation of a new kind of partnership between men and women. We need a new model, neither male nor female oriented."[16] Coeducation, decision makers argued, would solve the problem of uncertain enrollments, though this specific solution actually presupposed the problem. Wheaton's leaders, invoking an interpretive language of "a new partnership between men and women," thereby matched the solution to the problem.

RUSSELL SAGE: "THE FUTURE IS FEMALE!"

Some Russell Sage faculty members began to discuss the future of the college in 1985. A trustee-established enrollment options committee then examined the Sage applicant pool and enrollment patterns, as well as reports from other single-sex colleges that recently become coeducational. Russell Sage, a less prestigious private college than Wheaton, might have successfully competed for students with public four-year colleges that charged lower tuition by offering more comprehensive undergraduate professional programs. But, transforming Russell Sage into a coeducational college would have entailed many difficulties, especially generating major capital for athletic facilities, sports teams, and residence halls.

Still these rational dimensions were not of primary importance to the enrollment options committee when it ratified Sage's single-sex status. "For more than 70 years, the college has been a place where women excel," concluded the committee chair, "We believe they will continue to excel. We have confidence that the environment provided by Russell Sage College will make that difference."[17] "It is obvious the trend has been the other way. I think we have accepted the difficult challenge," a committee member added, "So if we can keep our high standards, we will be unique. That is our niche."[18] The president of the college, acknowledging that he had once favored admitting males, now said that the trustees' 19-to-1 vote for remaining single-sex "was what we had hoped for." The decision, he added, would have pleased Emma Willard, the founder of Troy Seminary, which eventually became Russell Sage College.[19] It certainly elated most members of the Russell Sage family. Two faculty members led a procession to a statue of Emma Willard, where they hung a banner that read, "The Future Is Female!" Student marchers then floated 1,100 balloons, one for each female undergraduate. Each balloon said: "It's a girl!"

Why did the same problem—maintaining future enrollments in the face of a steadily declining applicant pool and looming financial uncertainty—produce two different responses? The record suggests that differing environmental conditions affected these institutions.

Almost all private colleges faced the problem of enrollments during the 1980s, but small single sex colleges were especially affected by declining numbers of applicants. Figure 1 shows that Russell Sage experienced a 48 percent decline in applicants from 1978 to 1987—a dramatic change.

Wheaton, in contrast, kept roughly the same level of applicants throughout this period.

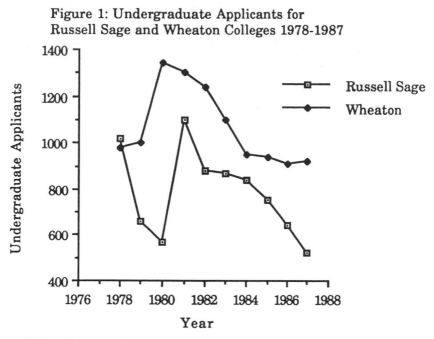

Figure 1: Undergraduate Applicants for
Russell Sage and Wheaton Colleges 1978-1987

Source: College Entrance Examination Board

How selective was the institution—how many applicants were admitted and how many enrolled? Was Russell Sage in a better position than Wheaton? There were signs of hard times at Russell Sage. Figure 2 shows that Sage annually admitted almost nine out of ten applicants to meet its enrollment goals throughout the 1980s. Wheaton had a more comfortable margin than Sage, though most applicants to the Seven Sisters colleges considered Wheaton a less-prestigious, safer third or fourth choice. The ratio of admitted students to applicants in the same period at Wheaton was four to ten, although the picture was becoming increasingly competitive in 1986-87.

Which college was more secure financially? Wheaton had just completed a successful sesquicentennial capital drive by raising $26 million in 1987. By 1987 the total voluntary contributions to Wheaton rose to eight times larger than its 1970 level. Russell Sage, on the other hand, struggled with a smaller than $4 million endowment and raised less than $2 million annually. The college substantially relied on tuition revenues to meet operating expenditures. (See Figure 3)

1991   25

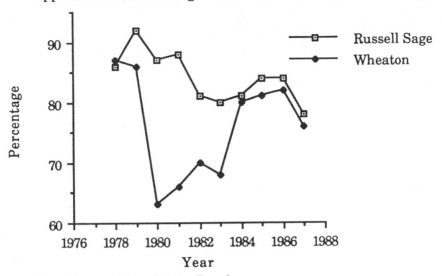

Figure 2: Proportion of Accepted Students from Applicants at Russell Sage and Wheaton 1978-1987

Source: College Entrance Examination Board

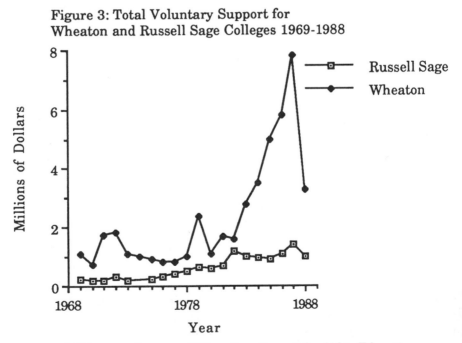

Figure 3: Total Voluntary Support for Wheaton and Russell Sage Colleges 1969-1988

Source: Annual Voluntary Support of Education, Council for Aid to Education

How could the weaker, more vulnerable institution remain a single-sex college, while the more selective, wealthier college adopt coeducation? What explains these puzzling outcomes?

ISOMORPHISM IN HISTORY

Examining the evolution of *classes* of organizations—in particular, the emergence of an "organizational field"—helps to explain institutional transformation.[20] Paul J. DiMaggio and Walter W. Powell define an organizational field as the "structuring" of a particular institutional form into a set of similar organizations that "constitute a recognized area of institutional life." and form patterns of coalition.[21] The organizational field assures the development of mutual awareness among similar colleges that are involved in a common enterprise. A college's organizational field includes colleges that share applicant pools, types of curricula, and specific educational goals. The concept, though, is neither rigidly defined nor static. A college that shares applicant pools but not curricula, for example, may be part of a focal college's organizational field. The concept helps to explain decision making because disparate organizations exhibit strong *isomorphic propensities*, or mimetic tendencies, as they form an organizational field.[22]

Wheaton and Russell Sage were "structured into" two distinct organizational fields, partly as a result of differences in their institutional histories and their clientele. These adaptations help to explain the different environments that Wheaton and Sage faced, and the different responses offered. To demonstrate the power of isomorphism among organizations in the same field, we examine the histories of Wheaton and Russell Sage during two key periods in the history of women's higher education: the shift from the seminary era to the women's college era, and the subsequent move from women's colleges toward coeducation.

The early nineteenth century movement for the education of girls, who would be "the rearers of children and the moral companions of men," met little opposition.[23] Before the 1850s, however, such education did not extend to the colleges. Instead, women's collegiate level education was carried out largely in seminaries denoted by high standards and stern discipline.[24] The women who led these seminaries—including Emma Willard and Eliza Wheaton—believed strongly in the educational emancipation of women and in preparing women to earn a living.[25] Emma Willard founded Troy Seminary (which eventually became Russell Sage College) in 1821.[26] Eliza Wheaton was instrumental in founding Wheaton Seminary in 1834, which began with a sizable endowment from her father-in-law in memory of his deceased daughter.[27] Graduates of the early seminaries established more than 90 additional seminaries, enrolling over

11,000 students before 1872.[28] Figure 4 shows the pattern of seminary and college foundation.

Seminaries never enjoyed a stronghold in higher education. Representatives of male colleges constantly criticized the seminaries for their lack of substantial endowments, their limited programs, and the tendency for a proprietor-principal to control seminary life and curriculum.

After the Civil War, three developments challenged the continued existence of the seminaries. During the 1850s, Mary Sharp and Elmira College introduced an alternate, collegiate education for women—deemed more progressive by leading educators. The period of women's college founding is bracketed by Vassar College, which opened in 1865, and Sarah Lawrence which opened in 1910. In between came Smith (1875), Wellesley (1875), Bryn Mawr (1880), and Mills (1885). Second, by the late 1860s, most states mandated the availability of public secondary education for women. The opening of Oberlin (1837) and Antioch (1852) as coeducational colleges also challenged the seminaries.[29] Leaders of the early women's rights movement were convinced that coeducation was essential for women's emancipation from their "separate sphere" and for gender equality in higher education.[30]

Rhetoric about domesticity remained important after the Civil War, but many American families increasingly recognized college education as "a good investment" for women.[31] The female seminaries felt these environmental pressures keenly. "You are aware of the problem which confronts a school of this grade," the newly appointed president of Wheaton Seminary told the trustees in 1897, "The rise of high schools on the one side and the rise of colleges on the other have squeezed us thin. What shall we do to be saved?"[32] As colleges became the socially recognized institution for women, most seminaries, Table 1 shows, adopted a collegiate form of organization—either single-sex or coeducational.[33] Remaining seminaries were viewed as outmoded particularly after the 1880s. Dense ties among seminaries meant that changes in one institution almost necessitated changes in closely-linked organizations. Such institutional changes gained added legitimacy by conforming to the evolving rules of external organizations, including standards set by professional associations and accrediting institutions.[34]

Wheaton Seminary maintained its enrollments until the 1890s when it experienced serious financial problems as matriculations declined. The *coup de grace* occurred in 1893, when Mount Holyoke, a seminary that resembled Wheaton but with a stronger reputation and prestige, became a college, thereby undermining Wheaton's legitimacy.[35] Similarly, the successful establishment of Vassar College and especially of Simmons College (1899) may have prompted the eventual transformation of Emma Willard's seminary into Russell Sage College. Simmons College was an important guide for Eliza Kellas, the first president of Russell Sage, in the early years of her administration.[36]

Table 1: Institutions Offering Degrees to Women

Type of Institution	Year				
	1834	1880	1920	1960	1988
Female Seminaries (Diplomas)	96*	62*	22	13 (Est.)	4 (Est.)
Women's Colleges, Private (Bachelor's or First Professional Degrees)	—	29*	191 (Est.)	288**	96**
Coeducational Colleges, Private (Bachelor's or First Professional Degrees)	—	78	291 (Est.)	570	762

Sources: National Center for Educational Statistics, U.S. Department of Education, Washington, DC.
Annual Report of U.S. Commissioner of Education, 1870-1917, U.S. Office of Education, Washington, DC.
Biannual Survey of Education in the United States, 1918-1958. U.S. Office of Education, Washington, DC.
Education Directory, U.S. Office of Education, Washington, DC.
Colleges and Universities, U.S. Office of Education, Washington, DC.
Directory of Postsecondary Educational Institutions, U.S. Office of Education, Washington, DC.
American Colleges and Universities, 1904-1985, American Council on Education, Washington, DC.

Note: Institutions offering degrees beyond bachelor's degrees or first professional degrees are not included.
*Cited in Thomas Woody, *A History of Women's Education in the U.S.*, two vols. (1929).
**From the estimates made by the Coalition for Women's Colleges, Washington, DC.

Figure 4 shows waves of events in the history of women's colleges that demonstrate streams of change in organizational form. Major seminaries were instituted between 1821 and 1834; leading women's colleges were founded between 1870 and 1880. Seminaries that became colleges between 1910 and 1920 became coeducational colleges in 1986 and 1987, whereas women's colleges that were founded between 1850 and 1927 became coeducational in 1968 and 1969. Particular events within a period may thus trigger the emergence and diffusion of new forms within clusters of closely connected organizations.[37]

Organizations habitually seek solutions to analogous problems from the sources that provided satisfactory solutions in the past.[38] Colleges, for ex-

Figure 4: Evolution of Women's Educational Institutions

Seminary Era, 1820-1835	Women's Collegiate Era, 1850-1927	CoEducational Era, 1969-1987
Troy Sem. (1821)	Russell Sage Coll. (1916)*	
Mount Holyoke Sem. (1836)	Mount Holyoke Coll. (1893)*	
Hartford Sem. for Women (1828)**		
Ipswich Sem. (1826)**		
Wheaton Sem. (1834)	Wheaton Coll. (1911)	Wheaton Coll., Coed (1986)
	Simmons Female Coll. (1899) Simmons Coll. (1910)*	
	Women's Coll. of Baltimore (1885) Goucher Coll. (1910)	Goucher Coll., Coed (1986)
	Women's Coll. of Frederick (1895) Hood Coll. (1913)*	
	Elmira Female Coll. (1855) Elmira Coll. (1890)	Elmira Coll., Coed (1969)
	Connecticut Coll. (1910)	Connecticut Coll., Coed (1969)
	Vassar Coll.	Vassar Coll., Coed (1969)
	Skidmore Coll. (1911)	Skidmore Coll., Coed (1969)
	Sarah Lawrence (1926)	Sarah Lawrence, Coed (1968)
	Wellesley Coll. (1875)*	
	Smith Coll. (1875)*	
	Bryn Mawr (1880)*	
	Mills Coll. (1885)*	
	Barnard Coll. (1899)*	

Note: The year in parenthesis indicates the year of the founding of the college
*Colleges remained as single-sex institutions
**Hartford closed in 1836, and Ipswich closed in 1834.

ample, often look for new employees where they have found satisfactory employees in the past. Senior level managers, we've already noted, move within the same institutional circle. Colleges tend to adopt successful curricular models from similar organizations, and to look for applicants from similar pools.

Isomorphic change helps to explain historical patterns of transformation among women's colleges as well as the recent outcomes at Wheaton and at Russell Sage. In the history of women's higher education, pressures to conform to forms of "legitimate" organization forced weaker, vulnerable seminaries to model themselves after the collegiate form.[39] Then, structurally equivalent, but separate, institutional fields emerged within the "college" rubric. These fields became sources of "mutual awareness among participant organizations" and legitimacy.[40]

Wheaton and Russell Sage both evolved from female seminaries into selective private institutions dedicated to the higher education of women, but when important differences emerged, they identified with colleges having similar student demography, size, wealth, types of curricula, and prestige—not with each other. Wheaton's history, for example, included other examples of swift decision making at the expense of caution. Wheaton's president, contemplating a rapid change from seminary to college in 1910, was unsympathetic to the anger and frustration of opponents who "deplored the changing nature of education for women, as many still did when they surveyed the drive towards collegiate education and the concept of adopting 'men's ways.'"[41] Emma Willard, in contrast, opposed a college education for women, while emphasizing curricular reforms among seminaries.[42] Willard's stance became institutionalized into a pattern of deliberation and caution when the seminary and the college contemplated change. Troy Seminary, for example, did not acquire a collegiate charter until the Russell Sage family provided a substantial sum of endowment in 1916.

The Russell Sage "family" demonstrated greater loyalty and commitment, measured, for example, by comparing the annual giving patterns of alumnae. Figure 5 shows that between 1975 and 1988, a crucial period of declining enrollments for both colleges, Russell Sage increased the percentage of alumnae participation from 30 percent to 48 percent, and the amount of donations from $150,000 to $420,000. During the same period, Wheaton lost a sizeable number of alumnae contributors, though the total amount of voluntary support increased.[43]

Wheaton used more elaborate admissions criteria that yielded students from fairly homogeneous and socially privileged backgrounds. Russell Sage's selection processes and greater emphasis on vocational education led to the recruitment of heterogeneous students with diverse career aspirations.[44] From the outset, Emma Willard and her pupils stressed the importance of preparing women for work as well as for family roles.[45]

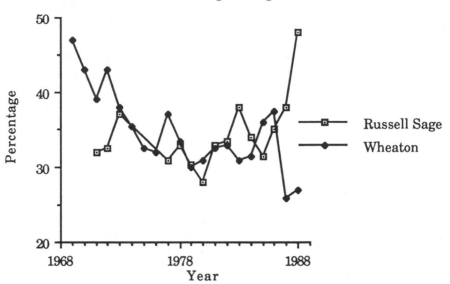

Figure 5: Alumni Donors as % of Alumni of Record for Wheaton and Russell Sage Colleges 1969-1988

Russell Sage and Wheaton, having entered into different organizational fields after becoming colleges, looked to different institutions for solutions to the enrollment problem. The enrollment options committee at Russell Sage College initially gathered data from many sources, but focused on a small group of closely related, similar institutions. A committee member reported:

> We were no longer paying attention to tons of data collected by our committee staff. We agreed only to read reports prepared by two colleges which recently became coeducational institutions: Skidmore College and Vassar College....Vassar College's report was different...partly because Vassar used the coeducational curriculum as a device to improve its academic programs, namely its fine arts program.Vassar was interested in male students who might be fine arts or performing arts majors. Finally, we studied the situation at Skidmore and Simmons....any items from [Skidmore and] Simmons caught our eyes.[46]

The targets of information were thus narrowed to Skidmore College, which had recently become a coeducational institution and Simmons College, a single-sex institution since its founding.[47] A Skidmore dean had collected anecdotal evidence that women were hurt by coeducation, and concluded that "at Skidmore, women are increasingly discouraged from participating in campus leadership positions."[48] The report, despite its limited scope, profoundly influenced Russell Sage's decision-makers. "That really did it!" the president exclaimed, "even though we were suspicious of this before."[49] Information about single-sex education at Simmons College strengthened the case. Longstanding ties between Russell Sage and Simmons College were strengthened by personnel exchanges. Several faculty members moved from Simmons to Sage, and the Russell Sage president was previously the Simmons provost.[50] Leaders at Russell Sage noted that Simmons admitted women of diverse ages, while enhancing career-oriented programs such as nursing, business, and public service. A career education alternative for maintaining enrollments was particularly suited to Russell Sage, with its diverse curriculum that emphasized vocational and public service. Prior financial crises led Russell Sage to create graduate, evening and adult, and junior college divisions that enhanced tuition revenues. Therefore, leaders at Russell Sage focused on information from Simmons, a single-sex institution with a student market similar to its own and with considerable emphasis on vocational education for women. Having reaffirmed its commitment to single-sex education, the Russell Sage institutional network continued to include Simmons and Hood.

Though never a strong competitor to the Seven Sisters in the enrollment market, Wheaton's continued emphasis on selectivity and a strong liberal arts curriculum led its officials to be more attentive to Wellesley, Smith, and Mount Holyoke than to less selective colleges, despite other dissimilarities.[51] But during the coeducation controversy, Wheaton chose to align itself with leading New England coeducational colleges—Williams, Bowdoin, Trinity, and Connecticut. Wheaton trustees assumed responsibility for long-range planning after the faculty reported its inability "to reach a concrete agreement regarding the future plan." A perceived "growing crisis of female applicants," instilled a sense of urgency in the trustees.[52] The trustees appeared to rely on an impressive number of information sources, but accorded special weight to the experiences of Vassar, Goucher, Connecticut College, and Skidmore—similar colleges that recently and successfully adopted coeducation.[53] At least two Wheaton trustees, and some faculty representatives, visited Connecticut College to learn about that college's transition to coeducation.[54] The president of Wheaton stated that the Twelve-College Exchange, coeducational schools that formerly had been single-sex, would provide a strong reference group: "Wheaton can learn much from their experience as we make our transition from single sex to coeducation."[55] Institutional mimicry was not conducted in a predatory or coercive fashion; the successful institutions in a field were willing to assist followers.[56]

Why, then, didn't Wheaton reaffirm its single-sex mission, thereby following Wellesley, Smith, Bryn Mawr, and Mount Holyoke? Such a reaffirmation would have further weakened Wheaton's declining standing in the prestige hierarchy among women's colleges. Wheaton could now distance itself from the hegemony of the Seven Sisters. After a year of coeducation, one senior administrator at Wheaton stated, "We no longer have to sit in the backyard of Wellesley, Smith, and Mount Holyoke and be regarded as a rather distant cousin. We are now looking at leading coeducational college markets."[57] Wheaton drew closer to similar former women's colleges that opted for coeducation, such as Connecticut College and Skidmore College, and to formerly male colleges, such as Bowdoin and Trinity.

Table 2 displays patterns of student choice of colleges among groups of institutions that include Russell Sage and Wheaton. This table shows a fair degree of stability in the list of Sage competitors between 1985 and 1988— years that straddled the decision to remain single-sex. Wheaton, in contrast, moved into a different institutional field—including Williams, Bowdoin, Trinity, and Boston College—after becoming coeducational.

Table 2: Approximate Ranking of College Choices among Applicants to Russell Sage and to Wheaton College

Russell Sage		Wheaton	
1985	1988	1985	1988*
Simmons	Simmons	Mount Holyoke	Connecticut
Ithaca	Ithaca	Connecticut	Mount Holyoke
Siena	Skidmore	Skidmore	Boston College
Skidmore	Siena	Smith	Vassar
Vassar	Hartwick	Wellesley	Bowdoin
	Hood College	Vassar	Skidmore
			Williams
			Trinity

Note: This table was constructed from the College Entrance Examination Board's annual survey of college applicants. Rank ordering is based on requests made by applicants to send their SAT scores to respective institutions. Such a request is not necessarily an indicator of seriousness since the student still is at a tentative stage of the application process. Therefore, this table is no more than an approximation.
*In 1988, Wheaton admitted males for the first time.

Isomorphism thus helps to explain the development and transformation of our focal colleges. To understand the dynamics of isomorphism, we examined how rules and actors drove these organizational actions. Theories of organizational decision making have recently undergone substantial change. The classical form of decision making assumes that organizations base choices upon well-defined preferences. Our interpretation is not based on the self-evident assumptions of the classical theory of choice. Rather, the logic of choice making at these organizations was more contextual and interpretative, conditions within which institutional isomorphism had an effect. Recent research suggests that ambiguity beleaguers organizational life.[58] Ambiguous preferences, for example, challenge the conventional logic that preferences precede action in decision making. Preferences, instead, are discovered through action. Thus, it is more important to interpret and understand the meaning of a decision retrospectively than to judge the outcome.[59]

Initially the Wheaton and Russell Sage decision makers conducted systematic inquiries with an eye to the consequences of their decisions, as the rational model would predict. Wheaton trustees, claimed the board chair, seriously considered coeducation because of "economic necessity and survival of the college in the long run."[60] Yet the decision makers disregarded much information that might be used in choice making as each college faced increased ambiguity. Leaders focused on key institutions in the field perceived to be central to their choice. Wheaton trustees emphasized reasonably successful transformations from single-sex to coeducation at Connecticut, Vassar, and Skidmore. Wheaton, the trustees concluded, would fare better if it moved out of the organizational field encompassing Wellesley, Smith, and Mount Holyoke since the college lacked their endowments, prestige, and applicant markets.

Wheaton trustees, lacking foreknowledge of the consequences of their decisions, made their decision according to historical and organizational appropriateness, rather than on the basis of a systematic search for the optimal alternative.[61] The record included no discussion of "the new partnership between men and women" before the decision, but the president emphasized a redefined coeducation in subsequent speeches aimed at assuring constituencies about the wisdom of the move. Wheaton leaders moved to a "construction of intention" after the fact.[62]

Historically based rules for defining action also guided the decision at less prestigious and financially more strained Russell Sage, where the choice to remain single-sex might have caused more short term damage. The enrollment options committee, after making a choice consistent with these norms, tried to match their intention to the action. Russell Sage's multidivisional structure appeared to provide an buffer that accorded rationality to the decision to remain single-sex. But the buffer was clearly inadequate, since the college experienced a substantial decline in applicants between 1978 and 1987. More likely, decision makers harnessed this logic after the fact to bolster their decision. In any event, Russell Sage officials did not compile the information that might justify further expansion of an applicant pool that already included aspirants to many different programs.

Indeed, the information collection process at both colleges involved surveillance, not a systematic search.[63] Wheaton and Russell Sage gathered massive amounts of information. But Wheaton and Russell Sage officials, respectively, emphasized anecdotal evidence from Vassar, Connecticut, and Goucher, and from Simmons and Skidmore. This evidence was not an ingredient for action but a source of reaffirmation of "appropriate" organizational choices.[64] As ambiguity about the probable success of the chosen alternative increased, decision makers created symbols that acknowledged the organization's shared interpretation of reality and minimized or deterred post-decision disappointments.[65]

Faced with potential enrollment declines, the president of Wheaton took pains to show how the college's problems matched the solution with the symbolic "new partnership" in coeducation.[66] Such an explanation or interpretation was found by linking Wheaton to traditional single sex colleges that recently became successful coeducational colleges—Connecticut, Skidmore, and Vassar.[67] The search for an institutional model and mimetic actions were critical to Wheaton's actions.

Russell Sage officials, paying more attention to the symbolism of the decision than to the possible consequences, had less need to invoke shared values.[68] Still, these officials offered mixing "education and the world of work" in vocational programs, such as nursing and business, as a symbol for those who might need it—a symbol in keeping with the philosophy of Emma Willard.[69] The association with Simmons College—a successful single sex institution with similar organizational goals—reinforced the choice made at Russell Sage. Decision makers at each college, nevertheless, constantly reassured their respective communities that they had made legitimate and responsible choices after careful planning, analysis, and systematic use of information.

Most conventional studies of decision making treat choice in terms of a decision process that defines constraints and opportunities placed on participants, but some recent studies emphasize that the allocation of attention among decision actors explains outcomes. James March introduced the idea of "choice opportunity."[70] Decision making in an organization may be dependent on who is available to attend to which problems at a given state and who is attentive to which solutions. The idea is that individuals and groups are involved at different points of decision processes; not all individuals and groups in an organization exercise their influence simultaneously. Complexities associated with the allocation of attention often result in unexpected outcomes in decision processes.

At Wheaton, the president asked the faculty planning group, which he established in 1985, to examine the problem of declining applicants. The president and the trustees hoped to have a plan of action from the faculty group, but the year went by without taking any concrete action. The vagaries of demands placed on faculty members and the divergent attention spans and interests of faculty actors led to an emphasis on curricular issues, especially women's studies, at the expense of coeducation. The faculty effort to tackle long range planning, including coeducation, a senior faculty member lamented, led to the establishment of two dozen ad hoc commit-tees and many hopelessly divided debates.[71]

The trustees grew impatient as they observed a stalemate largely caused by weak faculty leadership. Wheaton's 1986 applicant market condition, they concluded, demanded a decisive move. The trustees held retreats in which the problem—the relatively smaller number of female applicants and the implications for future enrollments—and the solution—coeduca-tion—became clear at the same time.[72] This confluence presented a "choice opportunity" for the trustees. "In a position of strength," the chair argued, "we should make a major strategic move now."[73] The lack of sustained attention among the faculty leaders presented an opportunity for the trustees, led by a decisive chair, to claim the coeducation issue.

Russell Sage trustees confronted many important issues in early 1987, and coeducation received less trustee attention than decisions involving the physical plant and curriculum.[74] The trustees drifted from a mild interest in coeducation to inattention and indecisiveness. The faculty planning group, in contrast, extensively studied the issues related to coeducation. Vocal leaders from the social sciences and women's studies discussed de-tailed analyses of how coeducation might or might not work at Sage. An ac-tive group of alumnae, which held at least a dozen planning meetings over two years, supported this faculty activity.[75] By the time the trustees studied the situation, the issue rode on a larger wave of support from faculty, stu-dents, and alumnae. A majority of the trustees had little to add to the pre-vailing opinion, while anecdotes from Skidmore College that suggested a damaging effect of coeducation swayed the undecided board members. The connection between the problem and the solution then seemed at hand. Actors, problems, and solutions in organizations, in these two cases, were loosely linked. The logic of choice making, therefore, may be explained partly by the allocation of attention among diverse actors. The point at which particular groups gained access to the decision processes in these or-ganizations seems to have affected the type of information deemed useful.

SUMMARY AND CONCLUSION

During the nineteenth century, observed Carl N. Degler, the movement for female education spread swiftly and successfully, but higher education was viewed as a male prerogative because it prepared students for vocations restricted to men.[76] Seminaries were the alternative institutional form of women's education; they were later replaced by women's colleges. Seminaries and early women's colleges, plagued by financial difficulties and criticized for their less rigorous curricula and unqualified faculties, soon modelled themselves after what appeared to be more legitimate and more successful forms.[77]

We have examined the role of isomorphism in explaining contrasting key decisions that represent further steps in the evolution of two single-sex colleges. The history of women's educational institutions suggests the importance of organizational networks for understanding the decisions at Wheaton and at Russell Sage. Each college was part of a defined structure, or organizational field, in which changes in one organization led to changes in others.[78] Wheaton may have modeled itself after Connecticut College, while Russell Sage turned to Simmons College to reaffirm its single-sex structure.

A historical dimension may often be critical for understanding decisions in organizations. Wheaton was at risk in a declining market of women students who desired single-sex education. Such students were more likely to turn to the prestigious Seven Sisters, with whom Wheaton could not compete. Steeped in a long history of upper middle class education, it was easier for Wheaton to forsake femaleness than to adopt a more broad-based class approach, such as vocational education. Russell Sage's tradition of preparing women for work roles made it more natural to extrapolate vocational curricula than to admit men.

As organizations face increased ambiguity in turbulent environments, decision makers experience difficulty in matching organizational performance to goals. At Wheaton, maintaining the long-standing single-sex mission became increasingly difficult as the prospect of keeping up with the applicant pool began to dwindle in the 1980s. Wheaton trustees, convinced that the chances were poor for finding a desirable solution to this problem as a single-sex institution, solved their uncertainty by introducing coeducation. In attempting to match this solution to a problem, Wheaton invoked the need for a new partnership between men and women.

Russell Sage faced similar environmental uncertainty resulting from the general decline in demand for single-sex education, but its officials perceived a stronger possibility for solving the problem without altering the institutional mission. An apparently flexible and differentiated structure, and strong student and alumnae sentiment, encouraged Russell Sage officials to reaffirm the principle of single sex college education for women despite an ever-narrowing niche. Wheaton offered symbols of change, while Russell Sage emphasized the symbolism of refusing to change. The leaders of both colleges successfully harnessed symbols to interpret their chosen actions. In fact, symbols minimized post-decision disappointments, and were important expressions of the leaders' competence and authority.

This analysis confirms the importance of institutional explanations of decision making. The relationship of organizations to their environments appears to have played a major role in these decisions, but so did internal processes and the attention of key decision makers. Wheaton College and Russell Sage College are two important representatives of higher educational institutions for women.

Perhaps the major shortcoming of our study is its reliance on retrospective interviews and the reconstruction of events surrounding the decisions made. Unfortunately, it would have been even more difficult to gain access to the key decision makers during the process. Further research should assess the relative effects of beliefs on decision making, given environmental constraints—especially the role of rationality in the face of uncertainty. This study may guide such research by demonstrating the importance of the institutional environment, organizational leaders, and the rational and symbolic aspects of decision making. Russell Sage and Wheaton made seemingly rational decisions; yet they adopted different institutional forms. Attention to the complex forces that enter into organizational decision making clarifies this paradox.

NOTES

This research was supported by a faculty summer research grant from the State University of New York Research Foundation to the first author and by a Drescher Award, conferred by the N.Y.S/UUP Affirmative Action Committee, to the second author. We gratefully acknowledge the comments of Elaine Backman, J. Richard Harrison, Glenn Carroll, and Paul DiMaggio, and are especially thankful to the people from Wheaton and Russell Sage who permitted us to interview them. The interpretations of events presented here are those of the authors alone, and do not necessarily reflect the position or endorsement of those interviewed.

1. Interview with the outgoing chair of the board of trustees of Wheaton College, April 1, 1988, Cambridge, Mass.

2. See J. Pfeffer, and G. Salancik, *The External Control of Organizations* (New York: Harper and Row, 1978), Paul J. DiMaggio, and Walter W. Powell, "The Iron Cage Revisited: Institutional Isomorphism and Collective Rationality in Organizational Fields," *American Sociological Review*, 48 (1983), 147-160, L.G. Zucker, and P.S. Tolbert, "Institutional Sources of Change in the Formal Structure of Organizations: The Diffusion of Work Service Reform, 1880-1935," paper presented at the annual meeting of American Sociological Association (Toronto, Canada, 1981), and R.R. Nelson, and S.G. Winter, *An Evolutionary Theory of Economic Change* (Boston, Mass.: Belknap Press, 1982).

3. See Michael D. Cohen, and James G. March, *Leadership and Ambiguity* (New York: McGraw-Hill, 1974), Charles E. Lindblom, "The Science of Muddling Through," *Public Administration Review*, 19 (1959), 79-99, P. Slovic, B. Fischhoff, and S. Lichtenstein, "Behavioral Decision Theory," *Annual Review of Psychology*, 28 (1977), 1-39, and Amos Tversky, and Daniel Kahneman, "Judgment Under Uncertainty: Heuristics and Biases," *Science*, 185 (1974), 1124-1131.

4. See J.M. Beyer, "Ideologies, Values, and Decision-making in Organizations," in Paul C. Nystrom and William H. Starbuck, eds., *Handbook of Organizational Design*. (Oxford, U.K.: Oxford University Press, 1981), S. Christensen, "Decision-making and Socialization," in James G. March and J.P. Olsen, eds., *Ambiguity and Choice in Organizations* (Bergen, Norway: University of Norway, 1976), M.S. Feldman, and James G. March, "Information in Organizations as Signal and Symbol," *Administrative Science Quarterly*, 26 (1981), 171-186, and W.A. Gamson, *Power and Discontent* (Homewood, Ill: Dorsey, 1968).

1991   39

5. See M. Edelman, *The Symbolic Uses of Politics* (Urbana, Ill.: University of Illinois Press, 1960), J. Richard Harrison, and James G. March, "Decision-making and Post-decision Surprises," *Administrative Science Quarterly*, 29 (1984), 26-42, and L. Sproul, S.S. Weiner, and D. Wolf, *Organizing an Anarchy* (Chicago, Ill.: University of Chicago Press, 1978). See also See J. Hirschleifer, and J.G. Riley, "The Analytics of Uncertainty and Information—An Expository Survey," *Journal of Economic Literature*, 17 (1979), 1375-1421.

6. In the course of our fieldwork, we interviewed 18 individuals. They include two presidents (one from each institution) six trustee members (three from each college including chairs of the boards and chairs of key subcommittees involved with planning), two institutional historians (one from each institution), two additional faculty members (one from each), four administrators (two from each), and two alumni leaders. We were limited in our attempts to gain first-hand information from key meetings at Wheaton College. Legal disputes between alumnae and the college made college representatives wary of our attendance at trustee meetings. We therefore relied much more on documents and on a limited number of interviews in our analysis of the events at Wheaton.

7. A long retreat preceded this annual meeting and not all trustees participated in this retreat.

8. Interview with a recent Wheaton graduate, February 16, 1988. A similar remark was expressed by a graduate. See "Wheaton Case Gets Court Date," the *Providence Journal Bulletin*, March 8, 1988.

9. *Newsweek*, April 27, 1987.

10. The Bristol County Probate Court issued a final court order granting Wheaton's request to use it's assets for coeducation, but the suits filed by nine individuals concerning the use of the Campaign funds led to setting legal limits on the future uses of the funds. On the baccalaureate, see Frederick Rudolph, *Curriculum: A History of the American Undergraduate Course of Study Since 1636* (San Francisco, Calif.: Jossey-Bass, 1983).

11. Memorandum from the trustee chairman, May 24, 1987.

12. From an interview by Sarah Lyall of the *New York Times*, April 26, 1987.

13. *Chronicle of Higher Education*, May 20, 1987, 30-31.

14. Interview with the outgoing chairman of the Wheaton trustees, April 1, 1988, Cambridge, Mass.

15. Interview with the outgoing chairman, April 1, 1988, Cambridge, Mass.

16. Memorandum from the president of Wheaton College, January 28, 1987.

17. From an interview by Shawn Gazin of the *Knickerbocker News*, May 16, 1987.

18. *Times-Union*, Albany, N.Y., July, 1987.

19. Interview with the president of Russell Sage College, February 26, 1988, Troy, N.Y.

20. See G.R. Carroll, and J. Delacroix, "Organizational Foundings: An Ecological Study of the Newspaper Industries of Argentina and Ireland," *Administrative Science Quarterly*, 28 (1982), 274-291, G.R. Carroll, "Organizational Ecology," *Annual Review of Sociology*, 10 (1984), 71-93, M.T. Hannan, and J.H. Freeman, "The Population Ecology of Organizations," in M.W. Meyer et al., eds., *Environments and Organizations* (San Francisco, Calif.: Jossey-Bass, 1978), 177-199, and Arthur L. Stinchcombe, "Social Structure and Organizations," in James G. March, ed., *Handbook of Organizations*, (Chicago, Ill.: Rand-McNally, 1965), 142-193.

21. See G.L. Cafferata, "The Building of Democratic Organizations: An Embryological Metaphor," *Administrative Science Quarterly*, 27 (1982), 280-303, and M. Meyer, "Persistence and Change in Bureaucratic Structures," paper presented at the annual meeting of American Sociological Association (Toronto, Ontario, 1981).

22. Paul J. DiMaggio and Walter W. Powell, "The Iron Cage Revisited," 143, 148.

23. Carl.N. Degler, *At Odds: Women and Family in America from the Revolution to the Present* (New York: Oxford University Press, 1980), 309.

24. See Lynn D. Gordon, *Gender and Higher Education in the Progressive Era, 1890-1920* (New Haven, Conn.: Yale University Press, 1990).

25. For more extensive evidence see Thomas Woody, *A History of Women's Education in the United States*, 2 vols., (New York: Octagon Books, 1979 [1929]).

26. See J. Patton, *Russell Sage College: The First Twenty-five years, 1916-1941* (Troy, N.Y.: Walter Snyder, 1941).

27. See H.E. Paine, *The Life of Eliza Baylies Wheaton: A Chapter in the History of the Higher Education of Woman* (Cambridge, Mass.: Riverside Press, 1907).

28. Thomas Woody, *A History of Women's Education in the United States*, 441.

29. See Barbara M. Solomon, *In the Company of Educated Women: A History of Women and Higher Education in America* (New Haven, Conn.: Yale University Press, 1985).

30. See Patricia A. Graham, "Expansion and Exclusion: A History of Women in American Higher Education," *Signs*, 3 (1978), 759-773, and Rosalind Rosenberg, "The Limits of Access: The History of Coeducation in America," in John M. Faragher and Florence Howe, eds., *Women and Higher Education in American History*, (New York: Norton, 1988),107-129.

31. See Lynn D. Gordon, *Gender and Higher Education*, 19.

32. President of Wheaton Seminary in his speech to the trustees, 1897, quoted in P.C. Helmreich, *Wheaton College, 1834-1912: The Seminary Years* (Norton, Mass: Wheaton College, 1985), 72.

33. See Helen L. Horowitz, *Alma Mater*. (New York: Knopf, 1984) and Thomas Woody, *A History of Women's Education in the United States*, passim.

34. L. Zucker, "Organizations as Institutions," in S. Bacharach, ed., *Research in the Sociology of Organizations* vol. 2. (Greenwich, Conn: JAI, 1983).

35. P.C. Helmreich, *Wheaton College*, 62, and G.H. Hubbard, "Wheaton Seminary, Norton, Mass," *New England Magazine*, 18 (1) (1898), 102-115.

36. J. Patton, *Russell Sage College*, 26.

37. L.G. Zucker, and P.S. Tolbert, "Institutional Sources of Change," passim.

38. See Richard M. Cyert, and James G. March, *A Behavioral Theory of the Firm* (Englewood Cliffs, N.J.: Prentice-Hall, 1973).

39. See A.C. Cole, *A Hundred Years of Mount Holyoke College: The Evolution of Educational Idea* (New Haven, Conn.: Yale University Press, 1940), P.C. Helmreich, *Wheaton College*, passim, Rosalind Rosenberg, *Beyond Separate Spheres: Intellectual Roots of Modern Feminism* (New Haven: Yale University Press, 1982), and Thomas Woody, *A History of Women's Education, passim*.

40. Paul J. DiMaggio, and Walter W. Powell, "The Iron Cage Revisited," passim.

41. P.C. Helmreich, *Wheaton College*, 86.

42. Thomas Woody, *A History of Women's Education*, 138, and J. Patton, *Russell Sage College*, 9.

43. After 1987, the percentage of alumni support to the total amount of financial support declined at Wheaton. This sudden drop in voluntary support may be explained by the fact that Wheaton completed its Sesquicentennial campaign in 1987. The level of alumni support after it became a coeducational college in 1988. In addition, Wheaton reportedly returned $127,000 to 56 donors who asked for their donation back in 1988. It was done under an out-of-count settlement. Many of 56 donors are alumni (see *New York Times*, March 8, 1989). This form of repayment might have contributed to the total amount in 1988.

44. See G.F. Shepard, "Female Education at Wheaton College," *New England Quarterly*, 1 (4) (1933), 804-824, and J. Patton, *Russell Sage College*, passim.

45. A. Lutz, *Emma Willard, Daughter of Democracy* (Washington, D.C.: Zenger Publishing, 1929), and Ann Frior Scott, "The Ever Widening Circle: The Diffusion of Feminist Values from the Troy Female Seminary, 1822-1872," *History of Education Quarterly*, 19 (1979), 3-25.

46. Interview with a senior member of the board of trustees of Russell Sage College, March 30, 1988, Troy, N.Y.

47. R.R. Nelson, and S.G. Winter, *An Evolutionary Theory of Economic Change*, passim.

48. From "A Decade of Coeducation: A Report and Some Recommendations, Skidmore College, 1971-1981," by Francine Hoffman, Dean of Students, Skidmore College.

49. Interview with the president of Russell Sage College, February 26, 1988, Troy, N.Y.

50. J. Patton, *Russell Sage College*, passim.

51. See Elaine Kendall, *Peculiar Institutions. An Informal History of the Seven Sister Colleges* (New York: Putnam, 1976), and James M. Taylor, *Vassar* (New York: Info Press, 1915).

52. Interview with the outgoing chairman of the board of trustees of Wheaton College, April 1, 1988, Cambridge, Mass.

53. Interview with a senior member of the board of trustees of Wheaton College, May 14, 1988, Boston.

54. Interview with a member of the board of trustees of Wheaton College, May 14, 1988, Boston.

55. Interview with the president of Wheaton College, August 16, 1988, Norton, Mass.

56. M. Levi, "The Predatory Theory of Rule," *Politics and Society*, 10 (1981), 431-463.

57. Deirdre Carmody, "Wheaton Assesses First Co-ed Year," *New York Times*, March 8, 1989.

58. See A.O. Hirschman, *Development Projects Observed* (Washington, D.C.: The Brookings Institution, 1967), James G. March, "Decision Making Perspective: Decisions in Organizations and Theories of Choice," in A.H. Van de Ven and W.F. Joyce, eds., *Perspectives in Organization Design and Behavior* (New York: Wiley, 1981), and W.H. Starbuck, "Acting First and Thinking Later: Theory Versus Reality in Strategic Change," in J.M. Penning, et. al., eds., *Organizational Strategy and Change* (San Francisco, Calif.: Jossey-Bass, 1985).

59. See Richard E. Neustadt, and E.R. May, *Thinking in Time: The Use of History for Decision-makers* (New York: Free Press, 1986).

60. Interview with a member of the board of trustees of Wheaton College, May 14, 1989. See also "Twenty Tough Questions about Co-Education," *Wheaton Alumni Magazine*, Spring 1987.

61. Jon Elster, *Sour Grapes: Studies in the Subversion of Rationality* (New York: Cambridge University Press, 1983).

62. See, for example, James G. March, and J.P. Olsen, *Ambiguity and Choice in Organizations* (Bergen, Norway: University of Norway, 1976), and K.E. Weick, "Educational Organizations as Loosely Coupled Systems," *Administrative Science Quarterly*, 21 (1976), 1-19.

63. See Harold L. Wilensky, *Organizational Intelligence: Knowledge and Policy in Government and Industry* (New York: Basic Books, 1969), and Martha S. Feldman, and James G. March, "Information in Organizations as Signal and Symbol."

64. Martha S. Feldman, and James G. March, "Information in Organizations as Signal and Symbol."

65. See Burton R. Clark, "Organizational Saga in Higher Education," *Administrative Science Quarterly*, 17 (2) (1972), 178-186, and M. Edelman, *The Symbolic Uses of Politics*, passim; Richard Harrison, and James G. March, "Decision-making and Post-decision Surprises," and L. Sproul, S.S. Weiner, and D. Wolf, *Organizing an Anarchy*.

66. Memorandum from the president of Wheaton College to the Wheaton community, January 28, 1987.

67. Interview with the president of Wheaton College, August 16, 1988, Norton, Mass.

68. Robert Nisbet, and L. Ross, *Human Inference: Strategies and Shortcomings of Social Judgment* (Englewood Cliffs, N.J.: Prentice-Hall, 1980).

69. Memorandum from the president of Russell Sage College, January 28, 1987.

70. See James G. March, and J.P. Olsen, *Rediscovering Institutions: The Organizational Basis of Politics* (New York: Free Press, 1989), J.W. Kingdon, *Agendas, Alternatives, and Public Policies* (Boston, Mass.; Little Brown, 1984), and James G. March, "Footnotes to Organizational Change," *Administrative Science Quarterly*, 26 (1981), 563-577.

71. Interview with member of Wheaton faculty, August 16, 1988, Norton, Mass.

72. Interview with the outgoing chair of Wheaton's Trustees, April 1, 1988, Cambridge, Mass.

73. Interview with the chair of the Russell Sage Trustees, May 2, 1988, Troy, N.Y.

74. Interview with the outgoing chair of Wheaton's Trustees, April 1, 1988, Cambridge, Mass.

75. Interview with Russell Sage College faculty member, May 2, 1988, Troy, N.Y.; interview with Director of Alumni Affairs, Russell Sage, April 22, 1988.

76. Carl N. Degler, *At Odds*, passim.

77. Thomas Woody, *A History of Women's Education*, passim.

78. See Paul J. DiMaggio, and Walter W. Powell, "The Iron Cage Revisited," passim.

Organizational Change

INTRODUCTION TO THE
TRANSACTION EDITION

REISSUING THIS BOOK as it appeared originally, nearly a quarter century earlier, does not mean I believe it can not be improved upon. Not only can it be; I myself shall shortly point out parts of it that I would change if I were rewriting it. I simply could not summon up the energy to start over from scratch.

Moreover, I think the book has substantial merits, and I was reluctant to see it disappear while it still could be of use and interest to students of organization and to managers. Of the four chapters, the first three are mainly descriptions of organizational processes that seem to me to be as valid now as when they were written. To be sure, I was not the first to make many of the observations in those chapters; a great deal had been written about organizational change long before my excursion into this field. What I tried to do, however, was to provide a comprehensive, concise, simple overview of the subject, based on the literature and my experience. In my judgment, the three descriptive chapters succeed in pulling together a good many diverse strands of knowledge.

They are also still timely. The obstacles to organizational change have not altered much in number, character, or difficulty over the years, notwithstanding a steady stream of books on the subject offering all manner of formulae for reducing or surmounting them. My discussion was not rendered obsolete by the passage of time.

Another reason for my reluctance to let the book go out of print is that its substantive chapters are foundation stones for some of my subsequent work.[1] I included capsule summaries of these chapters whenever I relied on them in later writings, but anyone who wanted a more complete statement was referred to the original. I feel obliged, therefore, to try to keep this volume readily available to those readers of the later books who might be skeptical enough and interested enough to examine the underpinnings of my arguments.

Even those who accept these grounds for keeping the original form of the three substantive chapters, however, may have their doubts about my preserving the fourth chapter, which consists of efforts to draw theoretical lessons from the other three. For I myself came to question a number of those inferences. Some need elaboration; some need rephrasing; one should be reversed. Why reproduce all those?

The answer is that I believe republishing the initial presentation along with a discussion of its deficiencies in this introduction conveys my message more trenchantly than would a mere substitution of corrected text. Ventilating the ambivalences, the hesitations, the modifications of judgment, and the reversals of field seems to me to be more instructive than concealing these vacillations behind a facade of newfound verities. Let me illustrate.

ON THE IMPORTANCE OF *NOT* CHANGING

I should, for example, have taken greater pains to ensure that my stark depiction of change-inhibiting factors in organizations is not construed as a denunciation of those factors. I can understand how one might conclude from my presentation that they are detrimental and ought to be condemned and suppressed. After all, most of us assume that organizational survival in a challenging world requires a high level of adaptability. Consequently, anything that reduces flexibility must be a threat to survival. Constraints on change, by definition, diminish flexibility. Hence, it would seem, they are harmful and should be done away with.

This apparent truism is an oversimplification of organizational realities. For one thing, organizational flexibility is not unequivocally beneficial; it, too, entails risks to survival.[2] For another, survival *means* the maintenance of many established behavioral and structural patterns; organized entities *are* essentially lasting patterns of these kinds. If many prevailing patterns in a given organization are disrupted, the organization loses its form and character, its identity, its very existence as an ongoing entity. A high degree of continuity is therefore as indispensable to the durability of an organization as the capacity to change is. I took this premise so much for granted that I failed to mention it, let alone emphasize it. I certainly should have.

As a matter of fact, this defining property of organizations is the main reason why so many of the formulae for overcoming resistance to change are unsuccessful. Because change inhibitors are not pathologies, but are built-in qualities intrinsic to organizations, they persist in the face of the most determined efforts to weaken and overcome them. Organizations by their very nature are homeostatic, which is what makes each of them recognizable from day to day, year to year, decade to decade.[3]

ON POWER IN ORGANIZATIONS

Another point I stated elliptically is the proposition that power

323

in organizations tends to diffuse gradually during periods of tranquility and security and to concentrate abruptly by means of upheavals in periods of stress and uncertainty (pp. 108-10). The connection between this assertion and the limits of change certainly does not leap out at the reader. I should have made it more explicit.

The logical link between the limits of change and the putatively incessant leveling ("gradational") tendencies of power in organizations can be found in the sections of the book describing the multiplication of constraints on organizational discretion (e.g., pp. 31-39, 72-75) and the ever-increasing specialization of knowledge and skills in organizations (e.g., pp. 15-23).[4] The proliferating constraints and specialties are usually established piecemeal, each to further a particular goal or value. The guardians of those goals and values then serve as interest groups to defend them—that is, as new power centers—thereby increasing the negotiations required before any action can be taken. Thus, much scattering of power takes place not as a deliberate strategy, but as an incidental, unnoticed by-product of other innate organizational tendencies.

This process is intensified because organizations contained within other organizations are driven by the same dynamics as their more inclusive counterparts (pp. 79-86). Striving for greater autonomy—within the system if possible, by secession if not—is a common way of seeking to reduce some forms of organizational uncertainty. Such self-assertion by suborganizations further complicates and prolongs negotiations over decisions, adding to the gradational thrust of organizational power.

The widely recognized costs of concentrated power reinforce this thrust. When all key decisions in an organization are made by a single group, or by a mere handful of groups, bottlenecks that impede both action and the flow of essential information eventually develop. Such conditions breed difficulties, stir resentment, arouse resistance, and ultimately generate efforts by adversely affected interests to broaden participation in the making of decisions. In this fashion, the concentration of power itself generates pressures toward decentralization.

With gradational tendencies driven by so potent a combination of forces, one might be forgiven for inferring that they must be constantly grinding down differences in power in the long run. While this reasoning was justifiable as far as it went, however, it did not go far enough. The gradational tendencies I described are self-limiting most of the time. Long before they reach the end toward which a straightline extrapolation seems to be carrying them, contrary forces are set in motion that arrest or reverse them. The diffusion of power frequently engenders movements toward centralization because diffusion commonly exacerbates delay, deadlock, and disorder. Leaders confronted by *this* type of uncertainty usually attempt to control or suppress other power centers and to accumulate power in their own hands so as to hasten action and establish order. At the same time, these conditions predispose the rank and file to support such leadership measures. Dispersal of power begets pressures and opportunities to concentrate power.

Moreover, I would later decide that from an evolutionary standpoint, the scattering of power among large numbers of smaller organizations vacates the environmental niche occupied by larger ones, thereby creating fresh openings in that habitat for overarching new giants to form.[5] And in that habitat, facing few challenges from organizations of comparable dimensions, the new giants flourish, at least for a while. Eventually, additional overarching organizations form and join them, encouraged by the success of the initial entrants into the unpopulated habitat or by the perception on the part of smaller organizations that they need to unite to secure themselves in the changing world. Confronted by the uncertainties of this volatile environment, even some giants coalesce, bringing about the emergence of supergiants. Power tends to migrate upward in this fashion.

I therefore shifted to the view that the drift of power toward concentration is as innate and as continuous as the tendency toward dispersal, and may possibly be dominant.

Today, that view, too, seems to me to overstate the case. I now believe I should not have suggested *either* direction of drift is the dominant one, or that one is necessarily more sudden or convulsive than the other. Both impulses exert their thrust simultaneously. Depending on circumstances at particular times and places, now one and now the other prevails for an interval. Though it is occasionally convenient to treat the impulses separately for analytical purposes, doing so poses a danger of neglecting the balance between them, or of taking a cyclical trend for a secular one.[6]

I was aware of this danger and should have avoided it. Unfortunately, when you immerse yourself in a problem, your perspectives and priorities are easily distorted. Conventional wisdom going back at least as far as Aristotle holds that power in human collectivities oscillates between concentration and dispersal over time. Different theorists posit different dynamics to explain *why* the oscillations occur, but their perceptions of *what* goes on are remarkably convergent. The swings are apparently "natural" to organizations; the opposing tendencies are rarely in perfect equipoise, and each actually foments the other. We need to keep both in mind at once in order to understand either. I was remiss in failing to do so.

ORGANIZATIONAL AGE AND FLEXIBILITY

I was still wider of the mark in what I said here (p. 99) about the connection between the age of organizations and their ability to change. Eventually, I felt obliged to repudiate it publicly.[7]

Originally, I suggested that old organizations must have conquered the factors limiting flexibility; otherwise, they would not have survived to old age. To be sure, I left myself an escape hatch when I noted that an inflexible organization could also reach old age if it occupied an unchanging ecological niche. But I implied that few long-lived organizations would be in this condition. Most, I thought, would owe their longevity to their ability to change readily despite the passage of time. They might even become *more* flexible as they aged because, having survived for so long, they would learn how to dodge environmental bullets that would carry off younger, less experienced counterparts. It was all quite logical.

Yet even at the time, I was troubled. Many of the factors inhibiting change obviously gain strength over time. Through accumulation, the number of constraints increases. That's why older organizations commonly seem to have difficulty adjusting to new circumstances. The major thrust of the first three chapters of this book was consistently in this direction. It was only the need to account for the long life of old organizations in a challenging environment that led me to fly in the face of my own logic.

Ultimately, I came to the view that the length of life of organizations is largely a matter of chance.[8] Survival, it seems to me, is not determined by any individual attribute, but by the luck of having a combination of traits—some deliberately designed, many acquired accidentally and even unwittingly—

327

that happen to work successfully in a particular set of environmental circumstances. According to this theory, even if all organizations in a given set were equally flexible or inflexible, some, because of *other* differences, would weather environmental changes that extinguish others. And conversely, in a set of organizations displaying different degrees of flexibility, the more flexible ones would not always fare better; environmental conditions might sometimes favor more *rigid* ones because they are unburdened by the aforementioned costs (p. xi) of preserving their flexibility. In this view, then, older organizations are not necessarily exceptionally and enduringly flexible; they may only be the beneficiaries of good fortune to whom we *impute* great flexibility as an explanation of their long life.

One might object that there is only a minuscule likelihood of a rigid organization being lucky enough to survive the large numbers of environmental challenges it would have to overcome to reach old age. But a minim of low-probability phenomena should be *expected* in any large group of chance events arrayed in a frequency distribution; they form a tail on the curve. Probability theory alone could account for the tiny percentage of organizations that attain great age, even if they are subject to the same change inhibitors as other organizations. We do not have to postulate that they are magically exempt from forces evidently inherent in the processes of organizing and aging. So I eventually abandoned the position put forth in this book.

In addition, I am now less disposed than I was to accept the notion that the life expectancy of organizations is positively associated with their age—in other words, that older organizations have prospectively longer futures than younger ones (pp. 99-100). Intuitively, it seemed right; old familiar organizations create an impression of perdurability, inevitability, invulnerability. Also, as we have just seen, since I assumed flexibility was essential to survival, and that older organizations must therefore have developed great flexibility to have lasted so long, it followed logically that they are sufficiently clever and adroit to go on indefinitely. But if, as I have explained, age and flexibility are *not* correlated, then the future lengths of life of an old and a young organization picked at random may not be so different after all. Here again, my later thinking cast doubt on a proposition that earlier looked self-evidently true. The best one can say about it is that the final returns are not yet in.

FLEXIBILITY AND THE SIZE OF ORGANIZATIONS

I have also come to doubt my inference in this book (pp. 101-06) that large organizations must be more flexible than smaller ones. Since large organizations are usually more complex than small ones, we should anticipate that they would generate more conflicts and more problems of internal negotiation and coordination, and would consequently be more prone to rigidity. Furthermore, some studies indicate that much innovation occurs not in old established systems, but in new, small operations. So there are good grounds for presuming that large organizations are more cumbersome and ponderous than their smaller neighbors.

But, I reasoned, they also have more resources and internal diversity, which could both stimulate and allow them to do more research, perform more experiments, and assume more risks than their smaller fellows. Impressionistically, I decided these factors outweighed the others.

In retrospect, I believe the question is still open. To those interested in this question, I recommend suspension of judgment until more evidence comes in.

I am also less confident than I was about my assertion that organization size and the prospects of survival are positively correlated (p. 107). The absolute number of small organizations that die in any period is doubtless much greater than the absolute number of deaths of large organizations in the same interval. But if the deaths are related to the total population of each class, then, just as in the relationship between age and survival, the *relative* death *rates* may not be so dissimilar. That would be consistent with my hypothesis that chance rather than inflexibility provides the better explanation of organizational death. Since the date of my first statement, a great deal of research in the "population ecology" of organizations has been done, some of which I must admit tends to confirm my *initial* impression. But I think the results are not yet definitive. It is too early to say.

A ZIGZAG ROUTE

The organizational world does not yield up its secrets easily. Even when those who study it agree on facts, their explanations often differ. Indeed, as I have demonstrated, the explanations offered by an individual student may change over time. We advance slowly, and not in straight lines. I hope readers who have come this far with me will not be put off by the prospect of traveling some paths tried once and later renounced.

Herbert Kaufman
New Haven, Connecticut
January, 1994

Notes

1. *Administrative Feedback: Monitoring Subordinates' Behavior* (Brookings Institution, 1973); *Are Government Organizations Immortal?* (Brookings institution, 1976); *Red Tape: Its Origins, Uses, and Abuses* (Brookings Institution, 1977); *The Administrative Behavior of Federal Bureau Chiefs* (Brookings Institution, 1981); *Time, Chance, and Organizations* (Chatham House, 1985, 1991)
2. *Time, Chance, and Organizations*, pp. 72-76.
3. On this principle rests the hypothesis about organizational evolution sketched out in this book (pp. 110-13) and elaborated in *Time, Chance, and Organizations*, chaps. 1-6.
4. These trends are spelled out more fully in *Are Government Organizations Immortal?*, pp. 67-68, and *Red Tape*, chap. II.
5. *Time, Chance, and Organizations*, pp. 131-35.
6. According to some theorists, there *is* a secular trend toward a different kind of world; *Time, Chance, and Organizations*, pp. 119-23.
7. *Ibid., pp.*. 82-83, *n*. 18
8. *Ibid.*, chap. 4, and (1991 ed.) pp. 167-77.

BUT ORGANIZATIONS DO CHANGE

CHANGE DOES OCCUR IN ORGANIZATIONS in spite of the barriers impeding it. For one thing, some forces automatically conduce to change, so that any organization managing to survive for more than a very brief period inevitably adjusts to new conditions whether its members and leaders want to or not, and, in fact, whether they know it or not. For another, the inhibitors of change, powerful as they are, can be neutralized, and often are, by strategies devised for this very purpose.

INVOLUNTARY CHANGE

Theoretically, as I have said, an organization could sustain itself forever once it gets started; it has no fixed life span. Just as a biological organism remains the same organism though every cell in its body be replaced in the course of its lifetime, so an organization can remain the same organization even though every member in it be replaced in the course of time (see Appendix). But the parallel ends here. The replacement cells in organisms are usually indistinguishable from their predecessors; the replacement personnel in organizations are all a little bit different from their predecessors (and from each other), particularly if they are of different generations. Inevitably, therefore, they produce changes in their organizations. The process may be very gradual and consequently almost imperceptible to all but the most careful observer. Nevertheless, it goes on relentlessly.

Personnel turnover is characteristic of large organizations that endure for longer than very short intervals. For myriad reasons, people leave or are expelled, and organizations that persist for several human generations obviously will turn over their total membership through the years. (Indeed, the organizational potential for survival beyond the lifetimes of people is one of the major reasons for forming organizations. They are instruments for the preservation of knowledge and wealth to be passed along and accumulated by later generations, and they may also serve as lasting monuments to those who found them.) New blood comes in, no matter what anyone may prefer.

Newcomers to organizations, no matter how carefully screened, bring with them values and perceptions at least a little divergent from those prevailing among members and leaders of long standing. Society harbors a great many subcultures, technologies, and specialties, and this diversity prevents homogenization of the population. Hence, new viewpoints will creep into every organization regardless of efforts to keep them out (notwithstanding a few cases that have been remarkably successful in insulating themselves). In addition, organizations often hire personnel away from their competitors when they can, in order to get people with both training and strategic information, and such recruits bring with them some of the norms of the organizations they left. Furthermore, people looking for jobs learn what the criteria of selection are, and many applicants learn to appear to conform to those standards even though they do not fully .accept them. Thus, the methods of screening never exclude all potential deviants from the organizational norms.

Above all, however, the memories that guide and drive older members of organizations lose their hold on younger members. Old fears and old aspirations take on archaic qualities for new generations. The scars of a deep economic depression, for example, may make its victims cautious, insecure; the resulting lack of daring and the eager embracement of boring but safe routines may suffer rejection and even scorn from a subsequent generation reared in comparative affluence. The enjoyment of material possessions by fathers who had few of them in their own early years does not similarly inspire sons reared in, and psychologically unsatisfied by, material abundance. Rapid economic growth can be an all-absorbing goal for people who have known the miseries of a marginal, subsistence standard of living; other goals—racial justice, ecological balance, social amenities, to mention a few— become much more salient later on, as the relative increments of benefit begin to decline and the costs rise. What seems like recent experience to one group in an organization is remote history to another. As the inexorable succession of generations proceeds, therefore, the structure and behavior of organizations also change. Oldtimers may be willing to rest on their laurels, but newcomers are impatient to win theirs.

In many organizations, the gradual changing of the guard is accompanied by tensions and conflict. The participants perceive what is happening and fight openly. Often, however, the departures of newcomers from familiar patterns are so modest as to be tolerable to older members. The small departures accumulate over time, so that the organizations change without anyone being fully aware of what is happening and without anyone even consciously willing it.

In sum, organizations accommodate to their changing environments in spite of the barriers to change because they cannot always avoid adjusting and frequently do not even know they are doing so.

VOLUNTARY CHANGE

MOTIVATIONS TO PROMOTE CHANGE

Organizations also change, however, because people deliberately change them. The motives of people who want change are very much like the motives of other people who are moved to resist change; whether an individual is inspired by these motives to agitate for reform or to stand fast on the status quo is determined by his position in, and perceptions of, the system. Many people on both sides are animated by self-interest, but it is in the self-interest of those who feel deprived to try to reconstitute things and in the self-interest of those who are advantaged to hang on to what they have. In like fashion, many who put the survival of the organization above all else will construe this value as requiring the organization to stay exactly as it is; others with the same concern will be more anxious about the jeopardy in which inflexibility allegedly places the organization, and will interpret their commitment as obliging them to foster receptivity to change. People concerned chiefly with a particular organizational feature—some aspect of output or method, for example—

will oppose all changes threatening that feature, but will vigorously promote or support changes favoring it. Even advocates of the same ends may divide over means, some perceiving prevailing arrangements as serving those ends (e.g., perceiving large, centrally-directed school systems as producing better education) while others see extensive modifications (e.g., decentralization of school administration) as the only way to accomplish the agreed-on goals.

In short, every organization is under pressure from innovators and reformers as well as from defenders of things as they are, and the motivations of the former may be of much the same character and intensity as those of the latter. The forces for change, like the forces against it, are numerous and varied. But the barriers to change described in Chapter I present formidable obstructions to the proponents of change. Whether they enjoy any success at all depends on their ability to surmount the systemic obstacles, to remove the mental blinders, and to neutralize or reverse the opposition blocking their way.

Offsetting Systemic Obstacles

Importing resources. When the prime cause of inability to change is the lack of resources to effect the measures widely recognized and agreed upon, obtaining resources from other organizations that have them in abundance is the usual way out of the dilemma. It is not an easy task. People with plentiful resources seldom have great confidence in organizations with meager assets, and they worry about pouring their own substance into futile ventures that drain the benefactors without really helping the beneficiaries. They also fear that they may be supporting their own competition. In any event, they are understandably reluctant to deprive themselves in order to assist others.

Organizations nevertheless do acquire resources from other organizations. They may have to pay exorbitant prices, it is true, in interest or shares in the returns or other concessions to the suppliers or lenders. They may resort to a kind of extortion, playing on the fears and the guilt of the richer organizations. They may be able to mobilize sufficient political support to persuade governments to assist them. Resource-poor organizations have had to become adept at every mode of persuasion.

The benefactors tend to perceive their resource-transferring programs as evidence of their own altruism and bountiful generosity. The beneficiaries are apt to describe it as self-interested and exploitative, and niggardly to boot—a bid for valuable strategic advantages at cut rates, and a largely symbolic response to urgent human needs. Nevertheless, transfers of resources continue. Rich countries send and lend funds, equipment, and supplies to underdeveloped countries. They give them technical advice and train their people in modern trades and professions so as to overcome deficiencies in skills. In the United States, corresponding programs are conducted on a growing scale to benefit our own disadvantaged groups and areas.

The dream of succeeding by nothing more than the sweat of one's own brow has not altogether vanished. The vision of owing nothing to anyone, materially or morally, for the vigor of one's organization—of being one's own boss in every sense—still has a strong appeal. Nonetheless, in today's world most people and most organizations have to seek resources from outside their own reserves in order to break the bonds of resource limitations.

Concentrating resources. An even more difficult technique of coping with resource limitations is to set priorities for the application of resources to problems and to stand by those priorities. As we have seen, in the public sector, the dynamics of the system run the other way; the thrust of the incentives is toward spreading resources over as broad a front as possible, which often allows so little for each program as to prevent the mobilization required to set out boldly in any new direction. This reality wars with the need for choice.

Furthermore, experts disagree on which activities should receive prompt attention and which should be deferred if an organization is to lift itself out of the pit of resource limitations and adjust to changing conditions. When it comes to modernizing national economies, for example some specialists will argue for concentrating on heavy industry, others give first priority to agricultural modernization, and still others believe in building consumer demand and letting the market take care of the rest. Some experts defend sequential development of selected economic sectors, holding that an economy advances itself like an amoeba, sending out salients behind which the rest of the system then flows; others urge balanced growth on a wide front. There is no consensus yet.

Moreover, the interests affected by the ordering of priorities are at odds with each other. Which ones will benefit immediately, and which ones will be deprived until some distant future? How long will consumers wait before they rebel against the allocation of resources to heavy industry in disproportionate amounts? Why modernize armies when the civilian populace is in dire need, or why capitulate to short-range, private, civilian clamor for more consumer goods when the whole system is in jeopardy from external enemies? Why improve telephones when infant mortality is still high? Even if theorists should agree on the proper choices in such situations, the people who stand to gain or lose by the decisions will not.

In authoritarian systems, policy decisions of this kind are made relatively quickly, once the leaders have committed themselves to change. In democratic systems, in which power is diffused, it is much more difficult to arrive at such decisions and to stick with them. Extraordinary feats of leadership are needed, and even extraordinary leaders may require the leverage of dangers to the whole system that are so clear and imminent as to cause contesting groups to set their differences aside temporarily, or at least to reduce the intensity of their combat.

Nevertheless, for all the difficulties and problems involved, choices are made. Despite uncertainties about the proper course of action and divisive passions set loose by priority-setting, most organizations and nations manage to chart their courses when they need to. And they succeed in mobilizing even severely limited resources to adjust to the changing environment.

Avoiding sunk costs. Limitations on resources often stem from sunk costs. Investments of any kind tie up resources that might be used in other ways, reducing degrees of freedom. If they lose their utility before their anticipated lives are over, they are especially burdensome. Therefore, when change demands an influx of resources, an organization with enormous assets in the form of massive investments may find itself in as tight a bind as one with few assets. For this reason, all organizations tend to look for ways of holding down their sunk costs.

Minimizing such costs is not easy in an industrial society, for obvious reasons. Yet three tendencies, all in early stages and small in scale, suggest that the impulse to do so is there and that the means to do so will perhaps be found someday. The first of these tendencies is the use of disposable commodities in place of durables. The second is the use of modular units that can be easily moved and recombined. The third is leasing equipment instead of buying it. All three hold down sunk costs to some extent.

Disposable, short-lived items are attractive because production of commodities is increasingly on a mass, automated basis while repair and maintenance are still essentially handicraft operations. The cost of the latter over the life of a long-lived product may exceed the cost of acquiring the product. We may thus be approaching the point where it is more economical to build cheaply and replace frequently than to keep up a well-made and long-lasting but obsolescent, expensive-to-service, and costly item. To the extent that manufactured items bind organizations to the status quo, such a shift would constitute a profoundly liberating measure. Admittedly, building cheaply and for short product lives may merely guarantee continuing markets and raise profits while lowering quality, in which event buyers will be worse rather than better off. But obsolescence may be a result of new developments, not merely of age; product durability does not necessarily stave it off. Service costs are now almost prohibitive and will continue to rise. Building in durability adds to production costs and lengthens the period of commitment to current practices. Easily replaceable apparatus is a release from these encumbrances. In spite of the risks of abuse, therefore, we will probably see more of cheap and short-lived products, and in a wider variety of hitherto unimaginable applications, as time goes on.

The possibilities of modular design are indicated by the growing practice of putting movable walls in the interiors of office and public buildings. These permit rearrangement of the interiors as needed, at a comparatively modest cost. Extending the logic of such construction, we may envision whole buildings made up of prefabricated components that can be reconfigured when conditions warrant, and eventually replaced more inexpensively than is possible with present construction techniques. For the same reasons, we may also expect the popularity of mobile homes, classrooms, libraries, exhibits, and similar institutions to rise rapidly and the use of inflatable and collapsible furniture to increase. To be sure, the savings achieved by such practices in the present day are far from revolutionary. If the pace of societal and technological change continues at its recent levels, however, it probably is not visionary to anticipate more widespread use of such products as a means of escaping the bondage of sunk costs.

Leasing equipment instead of buying it releases organizations that do not need a particular item on a full-time basis from the necessity of tying up capital in it. The lessor, on the other hand, by leasing it to many customers and thereby keeping it in operation more of the time than any single lessee could, can afford to replace it more quickly than a single lessee could. The customers thus get better equipment than they could otherwise afford, and at the same time are able to reduce sunk costs.

Sunk costs constitute only a fraction of the barriers to organizational change, and the strategies summarized here impinge on only some of the sunk costs. In themselves, therefore, these strategies are not major liberating factors. Yet they deserve notice because they do offer some clues to future patterns of organizational behavior, as organizations search for ways to surmount barriers to change.

Lifting official constraints. In the day-to-day problems of most organizations it is probably not limited resources that seem the most inhibiting but constraints imposed by accumulations of laws, rules, and regulations. Disabling as resource shortages are to members and leaders who want to introduce change, I have the impression that most of them would be prepared to cope with these shortages if only they were emancipated from the web of requirements and surveillance in which they feel entrapped. No one ever has all the money he would like to have in order to do his job properly, but being denied discretion makes the money problems seem all the worse. Indeed, to have adequate resources but circumscribed discretion might be even more frustrating. That is why the universal plea of those who seek change is for a lifting of official constraints on their actions.

Their battle cry is, "authority commensurate with responsibility." As I understand it, the meaning is, "Turn my friends and me loose!" Or more accurately, perhaps, "Give us more independent power!" To interpret their request solely in terms of a hunger for power or a desire to escape supervision in order to improve their chances for personal gain would be unduly cynical, notwithstanding occasional corroborating instances of such motivations. Generally, a sincere eagerness to get on with the job also plays a role. At least, it is an equally plausible explanation.

For customers and clients are not the only people infuriated by the delays, the facelessness, the evasions, the timidity, and the arrogance of bureaucracies. The members of organizations who find themselves enmeshed in intricate procedures and restrictions, watched and reviewed and inspected and investigated and called to account every step of the way, are even more outraged by their inability to act with expedition and justice and common sense according to their own lights, and to adjust policies as individual situations seem to them to warrant. For them, power means more than self-aggrandizement; it means deliverance from their bureaucratic bondage, a chance to display their prowess, the possibility of changing things they believe need changing.

To put it another way, spokesmen for change ask to be trusted—trusted to attain a satisfactory balance among all the values the network of official constraints is intended to ensure, trusted not to embarrass their superiors and colleagues by actions that reflect detrimentally on them and on the organization, trusted to take advantage of the specialized knowledge and skills in the organization that can improve their performance. Procedures premised on the view that subordinates will do wrong in all these ways unless kept in check do indeed reduce the chance of error or misfeasance, but they also increase the inequities, mistakes, and sometimes disasters resulting from inaction. Errors of omission made by individuals who are immobilized by prohibitions and directives may be worse than any errors of commission they might make on occasion. Freedom to act, to exercise discretion, and therefore to alter policies, programs, and procedures implies leadership confidence in the liberated agents.

At a high level of abstraction, almost every informed commentator will sympathize with this position. In practice, however, the specific decisions about who is to be liberated are less consensual. Top management thinks the battle mottoes mean that the upper levels will be unleashed, but field personnel and interest groups with influence at local levels visualize sweeping decentralization. Every administrative echelon wants authority delegated to itself but is reluctant to delegate authority to the levels lower down. Territorial officers construe decentralization as ordaining power for them, but functional specialists read it as a Magna Charta for their offices.

Determining which participants in the life of an organization are to be released from official constraints in order to encourage organizational change depends on what changes—what policies and procedures and goals— one wants to advance. When an advocate of change knows what he wants to achieve, he will promptly agitate against the constraints that stand in the way and for broader discretion to those who will help him to realize his ends. Much of the energy allocated to lifting official constraints is therefore concentrated on particular provisions of the existing corpus of law and regulation. As a general principle, however, all contestants subscribe to the idea of broader discretion, and conceivably to the concept that more discretion for everyone, not just themselves, might be salutary. The strictures of accumulated weight lie heavy on all.

Efforts to throw off this weight are partly responsible for the rapid increase in the number of public corporations, or mixed public-private corporations, in American government in recent years. Both new and old public functions have been turned over to them (as exemplified by both Comsat and the venerable old Post Office), including housing, transportation, urban renewal, and hospitals. Neighborhood development corporations are burgeoning. In the more distant future, education, health, and natural-resource management may go the same route. Corporations have appeared and flourished at the local, state, federal, and even international levels. Including the profusion of "special districts," many of which are public corporations, the number of these agencies is impressive and growing fast.

The advantages of the public corporation over the traditional bureau reside in the former's exemption from the restraints that envelop the latter. Hemmed in by jurisdictional limitations, by elaborate procedural requirements with regard to finances, personnel, purchasing, and other housekeeping chores, and by the hazards and detailed controls of the appropriations process, bureaus often cannot accomplish the missions given them. The corporate form generally excepts a government agency from many of these obligations, while leaving it with the powers and the public-interest perspective that motivate governmental assumption of the function. For this reason, it is becoming an increasingly popular instrument; the layers of safeguards and commands that contain the discretion of bureaus have unfitted them for the tasks that now confront them, forcing the designers of governments to employ a relatively new device to get out from under.

Reorganizing. Yet another way of upsetting systemic obstacles to change is reorganizing. This is commonly defended in terms of rationalizing disorderly administrative arrangements, improving efficiency, "streamlining," coordinating, and promoting similarly favored engineering concepts and images of symmetry. More realistically, Simon, Smithburg, and Thompson have explained the practice in terms of redistributing influence and emphasizing different values.[1] As a weapon in the arsenal of change seekers, it works by disrupting established lines of access and other regularities that keep people doing the old things in the old ways. In the interval of uncertainty about relationships and practices that follows any reorganization, those who want to break away from old norms may be able to introduce new behavior patterns that could never take root without a prior disturbance of the habitual arrangements. Reorganization is frequently nothing more than a "shake-up" intended to loosen the system a little.

In particular, reorganizations unsettle those unofficial and unplanned constraints on behavior that constitute the "informal organization" and cannot be readily reached by other means. These inertial forces are hard to identify and are hard to counteract even when they are identified. Occasionally, when the advocates of change discern that an informal group or liaison stands in their way, they may try to neutralize it by coopting its most active members into their own camp. By and large, though, the informal system is shadowy and elusive, and reorganization is an appealing way of dealing with it because a reorganization can upset the informal system without explicitly identifying it.

Reorganization is not without its risks to the changes sought by those who employ it. While the temporary disarray and confusion may create opportunities to advance favored plans as against ongoing practices, they also afford opportunities to competing innovators. And even in the absence of competition, reorganizations often produce wholly unanticipated effects; that is why the results of so many reorganizations are so at variance with the aims of their sponsors. Creating a better *climate* for change does not always produce only the change one wants.

Nevertheless, reorganizing is a popular strategy with proponents of organizational change who run up against the deep-rooted, customary modes of behavior. Apparently, they prefer the possibility of undesirable change to the certain objectionable consequences of staying put.

TAKING OFF MENTAL BLINDERS

The assaults on the systemic obstacles to change are directed at factors "external" to the individuals who make up organizations. In contrast, strategies for taking off mental blinders seek to overcome sources of resistance that are primarily "inside" each individual.

Recruiting unorthodoxy. Some organizations, uneasy about the dangers of inadaptiveness, try to assure themselves of innovative pressures by deliberately scouting for recruits with unorthodox viewpoints and ways of thinking. For all the reasons noted in the previous chapter, heterodoxy is not and cannot be characteristic of the great majority of new members and leaders; most of them must be fitted into the ongoing system. Even so, executives and personnel managers concerned for the future as well as with the present typically search for minds untrammeled by the conventions of their organizations. They may isolate these people in planning units or confine them to advisory capacities rather than put them in positions of formal authority, but they do not deprive themselves of the options to which the unconventional people may alert them.

Recruiting unorthodoxy does not consist in hiring individuals whose behavior or dress is bizarre, though it does imply some tolerance for the exotic. Creative minds seldom signal themselves in such fashion. Neither is there any test or battery of tests that reliably identifies the creative person; the elements of creativity elude description and measurement. Opinions of referees who know a candidate well, understand what is wanted of him, and have some objectivity are usually a better guide. Still better is a record of his past performance. At best, however, finding and engaging imaginative, original thinkers is a difficult, uncertain undertaking.

A simpler way to add members and leaders not locked into an organization's entrenched patterns is to recruit at least some members from trades and professions other than the ones predominant in the organization. Not that the other trades and professions are any freer of mental blinders; far from it. But they have different blinders, which produce some different perceptions, assumptions, and values. Occupational variations in an organization may thus provoke diverse ideas and constructive tensions. Similarly, representation of various geographical areas, social classes, ethnic groups, and educational backgrounds benefits an organization above and beyond the satisfaction of democratic ideological objectives; it engenders an atmosphere in which multiple viewpoints and interests can counterbalance the impulses toward a rigid and deadening consensus.

Recruiting unorthodoxy also implies some degree of "lateral entry" into the upper ranks of the organization (as opposed to promotion from within almost exclusively). If the upper ranks are filled entirely by members who have served in the lower ranks, they will be populated by individuals who have internalized the organization's norms and thus lost some of their freshness of viewpoint and unconventionality. "New blood" must be

349

brought in at all levels if a strategy of cultivating heterodoxy is to be effective.

And, finally, it implies the wisdom of assembling at least several unorthodox people in each distinctive grouping or specialty. The lone deviant, with no one to reinforce him, will feel too powerless to impress his views on the system and too insecure to cleave to those views. Experimental evidence indicates that social pressures induce outward conformity with group consensus, even when the consensus is clearly wrong, and suggests that the conformity may even be inward as well as outward; the isolate is apparently likely to become more conventional than anyone else.[2] Thus, if representatives of varied backgrounds are brought into organizations in order to encourage nonconforming contributions to decision-making processes, the purpose will be defeated unless the number of nonconformists attains some "critical mass." To be sure, they may be most conventional in their own small circles, but in the larger context they are not, and they will not retain their unconventionality long if they must hold out alone against the larger context.

Training and retraining. Recruiting heterodoxy is not really a way of taking the mental blinders off an organization's leaders and members in general; rather, it is a way of adding to the organization's roster some people on whom the systemic blinders were never imposed. However, no organization can depend exclusively on recruitment to keep the doors open to the winds of change. Therefore many organizations, and especially large ones, maintain training programs that encourage and assist originality on the part of conventional members who show some promise in that direction. If this wording sounds a bit skeptical, it is because the exigencies of day-to-day operations tax the capacity of organizations to train people to perform even the normal routines; as I observed in Chapter I, most training is intended to fit people into ongoing systems. It would therefore be surprising if time, money, and inclination to make nonconformists of members who already meet some systemic needs were provided abundantly and enthusiastically in most organizations. Yet there is no doubt that it has become established practice in some organizations to try to broaden horizons, at least at the leadership levels. In conferences, seminars, and discussion groups, formally constituted or gathering informally, exchanges of views have become ways of challenging received wisdom and stimulating imagination.

Ultimately, however, when insiders educate each other they soon lapse into confirming traditional lore. Organizations that want to broaden horizons therefore rely much more heavily on outside stimuli. They deliberately expose their up and coming leaders to extraorganizational ideas.

Exposure to extraorganizational ideas. The usual way of exposing leaders in organizations to extrinsic intellectual influences is to bring them into contact with academics working in the same or related areas. The university, after all, is supposed to be not only the custodian of past knowledge but also the generator of new knowledge. Professors are accustomed to addressing groups brought together for pedagogic purposes. Under the pressures and incentives of their occupational standards, they write the treatises that embody and summarize the most recent findings in their fields and therefore presumably are qualified to instruct and inspire groups too preoccupied with day-to-day operations to keep abreast of recent developments in appropriate disciplines. The professors' schedules are flexible, so they tend to be more available for appearances than most people who ply other trades. For these reasons, organizations intent on avoiding narrow parochialism, stodginess, and obsolescent information in their leadership groups have adopted all sorts of measures to expose them to the wisdom of academics.

The old-fashioned method is to recognize advanced training with higher job classifications and salaries; the organization supplies only the incentive, leaving the initiative and the expense to the employee. More recently, organizations have assumed more and more of the burdens of arranging, or at least paying for, the exposure. They set up seminars, bringing in academics to lecture to, and lead discussions among, the organizations' members. Or they send their personnel to training institutes, where the trainees, housed together for weeks at a time, are offered concentrated diets of seminars and lectures; the advantage of such institutes is that they can operate on a larger scale because they draw their students from many different organizations, so that the net cost to each participating organization is lower, and the quality of the syllabus and the faculty is presumably higher, than those which any individual organization could achieve if it ran its own program. Some organizations have even adopted the principle of the "sabbatical"—or extended period of leave with pay—so that selected members can attend a university or sojourn with a research institution, refreshing mind and spirit away from the deadening routines and pressures of the job.

These practices are increasingly expensive, but they seem to be spreading despite rising costs. Do they really work? Do they actually lift the blinders from personnel who would otherwise lose their edge? Appraising the results of any form of higher education is always a troublesome task. We know that these expensive activities, which deprive organizations of some of their key people for extended periods of time, win the acquiescence, if not the enthusiastic approval, of hardheaded executives, legislators, and businessmen. Perhaps that is the best answer we can give. At any rate, in order to keep themselves adaptive and au courant, organizations do employ these means, effective or not. For these purposes, evidently, uncertain instruments are judged better than none.

They are not the only instruments, however. Even organizations of only modest size maintain working libraries, circulate periodicals, call attention to relevant new publications. They commission studies by consultants. They encourage and fund attendance by their members at meetings of professional societies. They maintain their own research units. Wherever there is a stream of ideas that impinges on their activities, they try to dip into it. And thus they try to fight against the closing of minds that helps render organizations incapable of change.

REDUCING INCENTIVES TO OPPOSE CHANGE

Strategies aimed at increasing the ability of people in an organization to change its structure or behavior deal with factors that would inhibit change even if everyone in the organization wanted to change. Many of them, of course, do not want change—not necessarily because they are afflicted with mental blinders or because they cannot make headway against the systemic obstacles but because change imposes on them costs they would not otherwise have to bear. The status quo rewards them; the new situation would penalize them. Quite sensibly, under these conditions, they resist change even when it is possible.

Simon, Smithburg, and Thompson, analyzing the methods of obtaining compliance with organizational policy on the part of an organization's clientele, set out an inventory of procedures equally applicable in principle to *all* sources of calculated resistance.[3] They describe the kinds of costs that often arouse resistance and the steps by which these costs can be reduced. They suggest, for example, ways to make compliance easy, so that the costs of modifying longstanding habits are lowered; ways to identify proposed innovations with widely accepted values so as to minimize the moral costs of obedience to changes about which many people may have ethical misgivings; ways to cut self-interest costs by minimizing disturbance of prevailing practices and relations; to diminish "rationality costs" by carefully developing and communicating acceptable justifications of the innovations; and ways to reduce "subordination costs" by consultations with affected parties so that they do not feel as though they are being pushed around. Simon and his colleagues also review the techniques by which acceptance of change can be made more rewarding than opposition, such as conferring legitimacy on the new way of acting, deliberately developing informal as well as formal penalties for violations of the new norms, and broadening the range of inducements to comply with new requirements.

I shall not rehearse their analysis in detail. I will pause, however, to elaborate a little on one of their points especially relevant to what I have said about calculated opposition to change. They observe that often the victims of change can be compensated for their losses and thus induced to abandon their opposition. This is as true within an organization as it is in the organization's dealings with its clientele. Pension systems or high-paying sinecures, for example, may motivate people to make room for new blood in key positions. Union welfare funds financed out of increased profits from technological innovations may be used to maintain the incomes of workers laid off as a result of technological improvements, thereby eliminating one reason for the workers to oppose the improvements. (Since many work incentives are not financial, this strategy seldom eliminates all opposition, however. Nor does it alter the incentives of union leaders, whose power at bargaining tables, in the councils of union national and international headquarters, and in politics is associated directly with the size of their memberships. The interests of the leadership are by no means identical with the interests of the rank and file.) To reduce resistance to personnel reclassification plans, it is standard operating procedure to guarantee that no one's pay will be diminished if the plans are adopted, and sometimes, indeed, everyone is offered a pay increase to sweeten a potentially bitter pill. In some situations, needless positions may be added to a reorganization plan in order to provide titles and status for influential leaders who would otherwise oppose the plan.

Appealing to self-interest in these ways is likely to be less successful when the chief reason for opposition is concern about the future quality of the organization's service or product, or about the future security and character of the organization itself. Reassuring such opponents that neither the well-being and character of the organization nor the excellence of its output will be adversely affected by the recommended change is the only way to quiet their opposition. Writing special provisions to safe-guard those values, granting veto rights to members of the opposition, assigning operation of the revised system to people trusted by the opposition, and limiting the pe-riod in which the changes are valid (thereby requiring the proponents to obtain extensions if they want the changes to continue, and automatically giving the opposi-tion new chances to block adoption) are among the tactics by which such reassurance is provided. The Constitution of the United States, for example, probably would have failed of adoption had it not been for the addition of the Bill of Rights. Osteopaths responded to opposition to their methods on the part of medical doctors by including substantial amounts of standard medical training in their professional schools, and by agreeing to high standards of licensure. The legislation giving the President authority to reorganize the executive branch of the government would have been defeated had its statute not originally had only a two-year life and provided for a congressional veto of any reorganization plans proposed by the Presi-dent. From the point of view of proponents of change, such steps to reassure opponents weaken the reforms they urge. But people who resist changes on grounds of principle are usually the most determined of all adver-saries, and meeting their objections so as to remove or reduce their incentives to fight is therefore of exceptional strategic importance. Some observers will regard the prin-cipled resisters of specific proposed changes as stubborn, narrow-minded, self-righteous diehards; others will see them as heroic defenders of the faith; but in either case, the fate of innovations frequently hinges on the elimi-nation of their opposition's incentives to prevent adoption.

Of course, organizational loyalty can sometimes be invoked to shame opponents into silence, if not to obtain their support of change; appeal to "principle" is not a single-edged instrument. But the argument that you are demonstrating loyalty to a system by laboring to change it is subtler and more complicated than the steadfast defense of the system as it stands. Therefore, innovators usually have to make their case in other terms.

Reducing the incentives to oppose change is ordinarily a different order of strategy than offsetting systemic obstacles and removing mental blinders. The last two methods may be urged by advocates of organizational flexibility to create a more favorable atmosphere for *any* kind of change rather than particular, specified changes; employing these methods may facilitate changes which the spokesmen for flexibility might themselves oppose. Thus, for instance, procedures for amendment were included in the Constitution even though they entailed the risk that the Constitution would be changed in ways the framers never intended; ensuring the capacity to change the document in *some* way was clearly considered a lesser danger than preventing unwise change by prohibiting *all* change.

The methods of removing incentives to resist change, by contrast, are usually directed against specific targets. The sponsors of change, knowing why particular individuals line up against them, contrive to render those reasons nugatory. Only those individuals and those reasons are affected (except incidentally); the general climate is made no more hospitable to other kinds of change than it ever was. Chances are, however, the more limited strategy is the most commonly employed and perhaps the most successful one.

"THE EVER-WHIRLING WHEEL OF CHANGE"

Taken all together, the factors making for change in organizations turn out to be strong enough to overcome the powerful forces against it. Some of these factors are generated by circumstances over which human beings individually and collectively have no control; willy-nilly, circumstances bring change about. Others are the planned efforts of people, some designed to prevent generally the kind of ossification that can hurt an organization, some calculated to attain a more limited end. Plans of the first kind lessen the obstacles to changes of all kinds, plans of the second kind reduce only those obstacles to specific proposals for reform. Collectively, they make it possible for organizations to survive even in environments in flux.

This assessment of forces brings us back to the questions with which we started. If organizations can and do change, why should any of them ever die because they fail to do so? If the blinders are taken off at least partially, if systemic obstructions are surmounted, if incentives to resist are neutralized, if some adjustment takes place automatically, and if there are individuals and groups in virtually every organization who, for reasons of their own, perceive the need for change and labor to accomplish it, it is surprising that all organizations do not manage to avoid the unpleasant and even lethal consequences of rigid adherence to their old forms and ways.

Obviously, the thrust toward change and the checks on it are fairly evenly matched. It is tempting to fall back on a physical metaphor and declare that every action produces an opposite reaction that is sometimes equal (in which case nothing changes) and sometimes slightly weaker (in which case some changes occur). In fact, how-

ever, organizational realities appear to be more complicated than that. Proposed changes not only encounter the
conservative tendencies surveyed in the first chapter; they
also bring into play another group of factors. To these
I turn in the next chapter.

SOME THEORETICAL IMPLICATIONS
OF THE ARGUMENT

IN THE PRECEDING CHAPTERS, I tried to offer a personal, impressionistic synthesis of what has been observed, said, written, and demonstrated about organizational change, and I have suggested some explanations of the organizational behavior described. If the descriptions are faithful and the explanations valid, then a number of conclusions about the world of organizations may be drawn from them.

Ideally, the conclusions would be empirical statements deduced in strictly logical fashion from the preceding premises, and the accuracy or inaccuracy of the inferences would bolster confidence in or refute the argument. Unfortunately, not many of the inferences are sufficiently precise to permit the kind of measurement implicit in this scientific paradigm. And even the few that are this precise have not yet actually been subjected to careful and exact analysis. In that regard, I cannot even pretend to approach the scientific ideal.

What follows, therefore, is largely a logical exercise. I think it is a useful one, for if most of the assertions made in the previous pages are true, and if my reasoning in this chapter is not grossly in error, they compel some conclusions that are at least interesting and a few that I find surprising. Perhaps going off the deep end in this way will inspire (or provoke!) the sort of rigorous investigation that may improve the formulation offered here or, in the course of proving it false, contribute to the improvement of some other.

LITTLE BY LITTLE

There are people who apparently believe that the only way to accomplish systemic change is by totally destroying an existing system and constructing a new one. They are answered by defenders of gradual change, who see the dangers and costs of uprooting ongoing institutions as excessive. The rejoinder of the advocates of massive change is that doing things little by little is too slow and, anyway, merely refurbishes the old instead of building something new. The two views are almost never reconciled.

In point of fact, the differences are as much rhetorical as substantive. No one really believes that *everything* about a system can be changed all at once or even over a short time. Nor does anyone really believe that irritations, discontents, and injustices must be quietly endured indefinitely by the disadvantaged victims of systemic defects. Therefore, advocates of drastic and sweeping changes ordinarily tolerate continuation of many established practices, focusing only on selected ones which they consider to be especially important. Correspondingly, the guardians of tradition can accept all kinds of modifications if these do not threaten the particular continuities having special importance for them. For this reason, each group can make some concessions to the other without yielding on any matters of fundamental principle, and thus they manage to live with each other (though not without tension and turbulence) in spite of the issues that divide them.

Because the definitions of revolution as against evolution are so largely matters of perspective, it is difficult to sort out the issues. Most people would probably agree on the relevant *dimensions* of change: the number of organizational attributes altered, the importance of those attributes, the extent of the alterations, and the period of time in which the alterations are completed probably describe the common distinctions between the terms. Fewer would agree on how to count attributes, on the measurement of the importance or the extent of change, or on the appropriate unit of time in individual cases. Consequently, what is massive and sudden to one observer will be called infinitesimal and glacial by another. Changes in race relations in the United States illustrate the point.

If we take a generation—twenty-five or thirty years, say—as a time frame, however, the factors reviewed in the preceding chapters almost ensure that any large organization will at the end of the interval be considered in all important respects more like what it was at the beginning than different from what it was at the beginning. There will be exceptions, of course, and many ambiguities. But in most cases, the continuities will be dominant and will include most of the distinguishing characteristics of each organization.

This stability is not a result of conscious choice or preference, although many people do like it. Rather, like biological change, it is an outcome of the way the world is ordered. The built-in tendencies of organizations not to change, and the dampers that come into play when change is nevertheless introduced, keep the number, magnitude, and importance of changes within rather narrow limits over any comparatively short period, such as a human generation. Perhaps it will be possible some day to redesign the whole dynamics of the biological and organizational worlds. Short of that (and we are still far short of it), we may learn to offset some of the damping factors but we apparently cannot eliminate them.

That is why, within this time horizon, organizational change takes place and will continue to take place by the accretion of small modifications of existing, ongoing systems. The process is not a result of a deliberately selected policy but, if the foregoing argument is correct, a characteristic of the organizational world just as it is of the biological world.

Controversy over changes will not always be proportionate to their magnitude or number or speed. People may attach great importance to modifications of modest scope compared to the scale of the whole enterprise on which they are worked; they may develop passionate loyalties to symbols, including purely arbitrary symbols like the names of telephone exchanges. And they may fight fiercely over these changes, small as the changes are by any objective index of extent. Thus, to say that organizational change normally occurs little by little is not to say it is accomplished harmoniously and easily.

It is not my intention to ridicule such concern for apparently limited changes. On the contrary, if the accumulation of limited changes is the way most large changes are accomplished, then concern for small ones, and a willingness to fight for them, can be essential for organizational adaptation. Anyway, it would be most presumptuous for any person to deride the values of others because they are attached to relatively small things—especially since each of us has his own values of this kind.

Rather, my purpose is to indicate the bearing of these inferences on the revolution-evolution discussion as it applies to organizational change. Try as we will, declaim as we may, most change in large organizations will be decidedly limited over the span of any human generation, and it is only by a steady accumulation of changes over longer periods that truly extensive transformations will take place.

ORGANIZATIONAL TURNOVER

Because organizations change only little by little, their survival rate should be closely associated with the rate of change in their environment. That is, if the environment also changes slowly, they should have no trouble adapting in spite of their own gradual pace of change. If the environment changes swiftly or unexpectedly, one would anticipate a fearful slaughter of organizations.

We are all prone to say that the world changes with blinding speed, even in the course of a single human lifetime. Obviously, the assertion is full of ambiguities, but it makes intuitive sense. Therefore, we may expect a very high death rate among organizations solely from failure to adapt. As we have seen, the fragmentary evidence at our disposal indicates that the organizational death rate is indeed great, and that failure to adapt is one of the plausible putative causes. The pieces seem to fit together, empirically as well as logically.

Yet if we examine the survival rate, we have a hard

time explaining why so many organizations presumably afflicted with rigidity manage to continue as *long* as they do in such a fluid environment. Without more reliable information about the organizational population and about environmental change, we can engage only in guesswork. But it is conceivable that large numbers of organizations live on for long periods in spite of the restraints on their ability to change themselves and their ways because the envirnoment is far *less* shifting and hostile than prevailing belief holds. That is, in the course of a human generation, the environment may make only modest demands on organizations, to which only the weakest ones are incapable of adjusting.

Deductive reasoning from the premises of the earlier chapters can thus lead in either of two diametrically opposed directions, and the choice must be regarded as an open one until we have better data than we have now. Only one thing is clear: whether the environment is stable or changing, benign or hostile, turnover among organizations will go on.

The death of any organization is usually accompanied by pain for at least some of the people associated with it. The compassionate desire to minimize such suffering induces some students to seek to reduce organizational mortality. Others consider organizational death and birth inefficient and wasteful ways of effecting innovations. So they seek ways to reduce mortality by increasing innovativeness.[1]

Not only is it unlikely, for reasons we have seen, that organizational mortality will ever be eliminated; it is also distinctly possible that the costs of overcoming the obstacles to change in ongoing organizations are higher than the costs of organizational death and replacement by new and different organizations. It may be more economical to introduce some innovations by replacing organizations than by reforming them. In fact, the death of intransigent or rigid but influential organizations may facilitate social change more readily than marginal adjustments that keep the old organizations alive but resistant to innovation. Turnover is thus not only unavoidable but possibly salutary.

ORGANIZATIONAL AGE

Whether turnover is high or low, whether the environment is benign or menacing, and no matter what the distribution of turnover by organizational age classes, we can expect to find a range of ages in any large organizational population, including some organizations that survive for extremely long periods (compared to human life spans) in spite of all the presumed obstacles to such longevity. These long-lived cases lend some credence to the hypothesis that organizations do not have species-limited life spans like most organisms.

Nevertheless, we are so accustomed to projecting onto organizations the properties of organisms (indeed, of people) that we ascribe to them attributes they may not have. I dare say, for example, that most of us would agree intuitively with the proposition that organizations grow more rigid as they grow older, just as most organisms do; and with the statement that as organizations grow older, their remaining life expectancy declines. Yet if we proceed from the argument in the preceding chapters, we come to just the opposite conclusion. By and large, the argument implies that the longer an organization survives, the more flexible it ought to be. And the longer it has already lived, the longer it is likely to persist into the future.

AGE AND FLEXIBILITY

Even if the environment of an organization changes gradually (in the time frame of a human generation), a very old organization must have overcome many change inhibitors to have lasted so long. The only exception would be an organization that has found an ecological niche in which the environment is almost invariant, making the total triumph of change inhibitors an asset rather than a liability. In all other cases, to have a long existence, with identity uninterrupted over generations, is proof of flexibility *cum* continuity. There is no *guarantee* that the secrets of success will be passed along from generation to generation in the organization, but one of the advantages of organizations over solitary individuals is that they do provide institutional memories longer than a human lifetime. Consequently, the chances are good that at least some of the advantages of experience will be passed along. Hence, older organizations ought logically to have acquired a broader repertory of adaptive skills than their younger counterparts.

I am not saying, "Older means wiser." Rather, I am denying that, when we speak of organizations, greater age automatically means more rigidity and less ability to change. On the contrary, if we could measure flexibility in some way, it might well turn out to be *positively* correlated with age. In this respect, the logic of the preceding chapters challenges common belief and organismic metaphors.

AGE AND LIFE EXPECTANCY

In like fashion, the logic of the preceding chapters suggests that the expectancy of life remaining to any organization ought to be positively correlated with the organization's age.[2] After all, if an organization is sufficiently traditional to maintain its continuing identity through generation after generation, yet sufficiently flexible to get past all the dangers from environmental changes along the way, it must either have been created with a very successful adaptive mechanism or have acquired one. If the mechanism served so well through so many environmental vicissitudes in the past, there is no self-evident reason why that honing and refining should not permit it to work well in response to the hazards and demands of the future. There is no *assurance* that it will; ancient organizations, like ancient biological species, can and doubtless do disappear. Logically, however, from the foregoing premises, the odds appear to run with age. This deduced hypothesis recognizes the organizational capacity for learning even if that capacity yields a good deal less flexibility (as a result of change inhibitors) than the word *learning* ordinarily connotes.

We are so accustomed to thinking of life in organismic terms, as a more or less fixed quantity irretrievably and irreplaceably depleted as it is consumed, that the idea of life as a growing balance instead of a declining one in the future of aging organizations contradicts one of our firm reference points. (Not even a breeder nuclear reactor, which produces fuel as it consumes fuel, is in the same category, superficially tempting as that analogy is.) Indeed, it appears that older biological species, let alone individual organisms, enjoy no such advantage over younger ones; previous and future longevity seem unrelated for them. In the world of living things, human organizations would thus be highly unusual if they do in fact exhibit this trait. Yet that is exactly what is implied by what precedes in this volume.

ORGANIZATIONAL SIZE

The logic of the argument offered here also raises questions about another popular belief, the assumption that organizations grow less capable of change as they increase in size. This belief finds support not only in common intuitions about large-scale bureaucracies and in common experience but even in the premises of my own argument: many of the barriers to change surveyed earlier seem more prominent in large organizations than in small ones. The deliberate programming of behavior, the division of work into minute tasks promoting tunnel vision, the accumulations of official and unofficial constraints on behavior, and the multiplication of interorganizational agreements all appear to be of greater intensity in larger organizations. It would seem to follow, therefore, that the larger an organization grows, at least when it comes to exceed some optimum size, the more rigid it becomes.

But if we take account of *all* the premises of my argument, they seem on balance to point in precisely the other direction—that is, to indicate that flexibility (defined as the capacity to conceive of changes and as receptivity to innovations) is related directly to organizational size. In other words, as a general rule, the larger an organization is, the more flexible it is likely to be.

THE THRUST TOWARD BIGNESS

This is not to say that organizations deliberately seek to increase their size in order to augment their flexibility. Rather, bigness is often an outgrowth of the aversion to uncertainty, and the accompanying flexibility (to be discussed below) both attends and reinforces this type of adjustment.

Size here refers to the number of people within an organization's boundaries. I postulated in Chapter III a tendency on the part of organizations to move from accommodation toward control, and to continue moving in this direction on that continuum until stopped by other forces. Since much of the unpredictability stimulating this response originates in adjacent organizations,[3] the impulse to bring them under control (when obliteration is infeasible) leads to efforts ranging from an extreme of complete absorption to some kind of federal arrangement all the way to confederation or loose association. All of these entail extending organization boundaries so as to bring the source of uncertainty under the control of some kind of acceptable leadership. Absorption brings it under the existing leadership of one of the organizations involved. Federation, confederation, and loose association bring all the organizations involved under the control of a common leadership established for the purpose, the differences among the forms turning on how much manipulative authority is conferred on the common leadership (or is acquired by it) as compared to the power retained by the component organizations. In all cases, however, the end of the process is a more inclusive organization embracing the combined membership of all the participating organizations.

Thus, reducing unpredictability by such means gives rise to larger and larger organizations, often by adding a more inclusive organization to the existing population.[4] In the economic sphere, not even public policies designed to prevent such inclusive organizations (trusts and cartels, for example) from forming have succeeded in suppressing this drive. In one way or another, undeterred by hostile laws and by political boundaries, firms manage to find ways to act in concert as though they were parts of more inclusive organizations, whether or not the containing organization is visible. In the political sphere, every grouping of people under governing bodies has given rise to efforts to group their governments, from leagues of city-states to empires, from nation-states to regional associations of governments and to the United Nations. The irrepressible push in this direction has led some observers to remark on the universal pressure to raise the level of integration in organizations.[5] The underlying cause, it seems to me, is the organizational aversion to unpredictability.

Hence organizations tend to get bigger and bigger. But, contrary to popular belief, not necessarily at the cost of their flexibility.

BIGNESS AND FLEXIBILITY

Size and experimentation. Big organizations, because they usually have more resources at their disposal, are better able than small ones to support experiments that open up new possibilities for them, and they are better able to take advantage of opportunities afforded them by the discoveries of others. Admittedly, as I noted in the first chapter, organizations can be big and rich and still have resource problems because of sunk costs. And organizations can be big without necessarily being rich. All in all, however, other things being equal, large organizations usually are in a better position to experiment than small ones, and chances are good that even big ones with resource problems experiment more than small, rich ones. To be sure, small organizations appear on the scene doing things that big ones have not thought of; a good deal of social experimentation apparently takes this form. But when it comes to a deliberate search for new ways of doing things and new things to do, there is reason to suspect the big ones are out in front.

In the first place, in large organizations resources that would otherwise go to long-standing participants can be diverted with impunity to experimentation because deprivations shared by many members reduce the burdens on each to tolerable proportions. Small organizations usually lack this means of gathering the wherewithal for experimentation because each participant bears such a heavy part of the load that he resists.

In the second place, large organizations can duplicate internally the kind of probing and testing represented by the birth and death of small organizations in the broader social context. That is, using various subsystems for the purpose, they can try several different ways of doing the same thing in order to see which ones succeed, then proceed with the most promising systems and methods and abandon the others. They can create a kind of interior marketplace or competitive arena for ideas in which a "natural" selection takes place, thus preparing themselves for all kinds of possible environmental shifts without knowing ahead of time which shifts are likely to occur or what response is likely to be most effective.

In the third place, although the complexity of large organizations increases the number and force of change inhibitors, it also exposes many different kinds of specialists to each other's ideas and perspectives and interests. This exposure virtually ensures a flow of fresh ways of formulating and attacking problems—more, certainly, than will occur in a small organization encompassing a narrower range of specialties and tasks. Both small and large organizations are beset by tendencies that freeze them into their ongoing patterns, but large organizations probably stand a better chance of being jarred out of their ruts by their own internal diversity.

In the fourth place, large organizations are normally better able to assemble a "critical mass" of specialists in vital areas who can spark each other to develop new approaches to familiar problems. Small organizations are seldom in a position to gather such a "faculty" of experts, so they have more trouble recruiting them. Their isolated experts lack the stimulus and challenge and support of a face-to-face group of fellow professionals.

For these reasons, if for no others, large organizations can develop more repertories of behavior than their small counterparts, and these repertories come in handy as environmental conditions alter. This is one way in which bigness and flexibility go together.

Bigness and individual options. Big organizations also tend to allow freer play for individual preferences and idiosyncrasies than small ones do. As we have seen, they hold out many more role images for members to aspire to, and they generally offer a wider range of real role choices to choose among. Their composition is more heterogeneous, which in the long run broadens their tolerance of, and receptivity to, the unconventional. All organized life, as we have seen, requires conformity, but the degree of conformity that large organizations can impose and the range of behavior over which they can exert influence are often more limited than the corresponding capacities of small organizations; variety is built into the large ones. Finally, the impersonality of large organizations, whatever its vexations, constitutes a triumph of what Talcott Parsons has called achievement norms as against ascriptive norms (that is, recognition for accomplishment and competence rather than status) and universalistic rather than particularistic norms.[6] The result is that accidents of birth are less imprisoning; doors are opened to many who would otherwise be prevented from impressing themselves upon the system and registering their interests on its decisions; the system is loosened a little. In all these ways, large organizations willy-nilly generate and consider many more alternative ways of organizing and acting than do small ones.

These differences do not spring from qualitative differences in the people who inhabit organizations of different size, although it is conceivable that some self-selective membership factor is at work. Rather, the dynamics of systems of different size produce these effects. In smaller organizations, for example, the fortitude and determination required to stand up against the consensus of a face-to-face group are exceptional; the hostility of close comrades is usually much harder to endure than the disapprobation of the majority in large, impersonal surroundings. Moreover, the deviant is more visible in the smaller setting; social pressures on him to conform are more continuous and intense. What is more, a single nonconformist might upset the whole routine of a small system, while a large system may be less concerned about his oddities because it is not similarly threatened; the importance of conformity in the former leads to greater efforts to keep people in line or weed them out.

Taken all together, these elements explain why the tyranny of the village is often more oppressive than the coldness of the metropolis. They also explain why large organizations are often more able and willing to change than small ones.

SIZE AND SURVIVAL

If flexibility contributes to survival, and big organizations enjoy flexibility, then the survival rate of large organizations ought to be higher than that of small ones.[7] If large organizations have a good survival rate, then most very old organizations ought to be large ones. These inferences dovetail with those on age, flexibility, and life expectancy. Whether or not they are empirically valid is hard to say on the basis of the data now available on the age, size, and population of organizations. Logically, the inferences are consistent.

The expectation that big organizations would have a more favorable survival rate derives not only from the foregoing assumptions about flexibility but also from the theoretical capacity of large systems to absorb shocks and come through. They can contract and retrench in times of environmental pressure because they can excise troublesome subsystems and still continue, a course of action that is seldom feasible for small systems. By temporarily transferring slack resources from one part of the system to ailing parts, they can sustain the ailing parts until conditions are more hospitable to them. By drawing a little on all parts of the system in good times, they can build substantial reserves to be used in emergencies without draining any of the parts of their strength. In all, as we have already observed, they are better cushioned against variation in the environment. Where small organizations succumb, large ones often find the means to survive.

Large ones do go under, of course. In fact, it is quite possible that there is a size beyond which flexibility and survival rates begin to decline—a point of diminishing returns. Many economists comment on diseconomies of scale and other afflictions of firms that have become too big. No one can deny the possibility. But there is no such logical implication in the premises of this study. From a strictly deductive point of view, bigness and a comparatively high probability of survival seem to go together most of the time.

GRADATIONAL TENDENCIES OF POWER IN ORGANIZATIONS

My argument also compels me to conclude that power in organizations tends to diffuse slowly—gradually to distribute itself more and more evenly among the components and, eventually, among the members—in the course of time. It never reaches completely equal distribution—that state of harmonious reciprocity envisioned by philosophical anarchists and to a lesser extent by economic models of perfect competition—because long before it approaches such an ideal, other forces redistribute it unevenly again. But the continuing, the unremitting, force (as opposed to discontinuous, discrete counterforces) engenders slow movement toward greater uniformity of power.

At the risk of being taken too literally, I suggest that the appropriate analogy is to the geological gradational forces on the land portions of the earth. Wind and water and other erosive factors tend to level out the surface, abrading mountains and filling in depressions, constantly smoothing out the land. From time to time, a cataclysmic event will heave up a chain of peaks or a volcanic cone, or leave a vast scar across the surface. The gradational forces go on grinding things smooth. They have never fully polished the surface (although it is said to be smoother than a bowling ball in relative terms), and will never do so unless the periods between uphcavals lengthen enormously. If it were not for the upheavals, however, they would eventually succeed.

In roughly comparable fashion, many organizational change inhibitors owe their effect to the gradational tendencies of power. They consist in a capacity to block unwanted action—a capacity acquired, as we have seen, by more and more components of a system the longer the system exists without change. That is why innovation in such an organization demands great investments of energy. It is also why so many organizational upheavals transfer power to a central leadership; the need for action sometimes wins more support than the desire for participation.

The metaphor should not be pressed too far. Geological upheavals do not seem to occur in reaction to gradational forces, nor do the forces of gradation owe their existence to upheavals. In contrast, upheavals that concentrate power in organizations are triggered to a large extent by the effects of previous power diffusion, and demands to share power in turn are caused partly by reaction to upheavals. The geological and organizational processes are not at all the same. As a figure of speech, to clarify one element of the analysis, the analogy is useful only to illuminate the proposition that in the absence of occasional episodes of centralization, power in organizations gravitates downward. Or to put it another way, if you see an organization that has not undergone an upheaval in many years, the likelihood is that the power is more widely shared than it was originally. And the longer the organization goes without an upheaval, the more it is likely to continue to drift in the same direction. It does not follow that every organizational upheaval centralizes power, or that every period of relative tranquility diffuses it. But if my interpretation is valid, then these will be the tendencies in most such instances.

ORGANIZATIONAL EVOLUTION

Is there, in all this, a secular trend toward some dominant organizational form? Are the lines of development proceeding step by step toward an all-inclusive, immortal, global form of organization? Do the lines of evolution converge on a single ultimate outcome?

Some observers have seemed to think so. Marx, for instance, presented a unilinear theory of historical development that would presumably end in a world-wide state of unchanging equilibrium and harmony once the warfare between classes was terminated by the triumph of the proletariat. More recently, a group of biologists and anthropologists foresaw the emergence of a universal "epiorganism" as the final stage in the rise of the level of integration that began its ascent when life moved from the single-celled through the multicellular form of biological organization to the development of social forms.[8] Still more recently, Roderick Seidenberg predicted the appearance of "post-historic man,"[9] who would be a prisoner of his unchanging organizations as prehistoric man was a prisoner of his unchanging "instincts."

Others see social evolution, like biological evolution, as multilinear,[10] fanning out in many directions at once, with the process of mutation and natural selection going on for as long as mankind and other forms of life endure. Continuing differentiation and diversification offset the disappearance of species selected out. The birth of new types at least balances out the death of the old.

From the premises presented in this volume, I must conclude that both forecasts are right. The views are not mutually exclusive, but complementary. Both unilinear and multilinear evolution take place simultaneously, and neither nullifies the other.

The analysis of organizational age and size, and the thrust toward more inclusive organizations, do indeed suggest development of huge systems encompassing more and more of the people in the world (though as members of subsystems rather than of the parent systems directly) and exercising influence over more and more functions. Each such creation will be a kind of upheaval, though not necessarily violent, increasing centralization in human affairs. The initial attempts will be hesitating and circumscribed, so even at their start these institutions will be weak; the gradational tendencies of power will weaken them further and some may even fall apart. But the forces that gave rise to them in the first place will generate new efforts, and as the leaders of the new system deal with the internal and external sources of uncertainty confronting them, they will produce additional centralizations of power from time to time. There is a secular trend toward global leadership institutions, and there is no reason to think, on the basis of any of the evidence now at hand, that it will be halted. Perhaps it will eventually reach an impasse, as George Orwell predicted in *1984*, with the process coming to an end as three massive systems achieve a state of perfect equilibrium among themselves. It seems to me more likely that the unpredictable elements in such a condition and the delicacy of the equipoise will lead inevitably to the final step, a global directorate of some sort. Indeed, it may be said that the growth and outward thrust of organizations have already established a single world-wide system, so that the next step is merely the development of a leadership group with world-wide perspectives and interests different from those of any of the current participants, and with resources for registering those viewpoints and concerns on the behavior of the system.

Such a comprehensive system will not mean uniformity or stasis. Within it, new forms will appear and old ones will give way; turnover will persist. Some of the new forms will be better suited to the conditions of their times and places than others, and will therefore multiply, in turn giving rise to new variants. In short, organizational evolution will continue for a long time, proceeding along many lines, just as it always has.

These tendencies do not portend a restful, carefree, harmonious world in the foreseeable future. Organizations will continue to change slowly, and the difference between their rate of change and the speed of changes in human aspirations and expectations will generate familiar tensions for many generations to come. Organizations will still be born in hope and optimism and go down in sadness and disappointment. Perhaps the rising level of integration will curtail some of the most egregious human follies; it is not unreasonable to hope so. But the main features of organizational behavior today will be recognizable to people in the near future, whatever happens.

Recognizing the factors that shape events has in the past been the prelude to mastering them. The Tolstoyan view of history, which portrays even the greatest of leaders as mere chips on the crest of historic tides they do not control, may prove too pessimistic; mankind may yet emerge as master of its own destiny. The deciphering of the genetic code and the astonishing development of computers in the last half of this century may constitute a threshold to a future that the ordinary mind cannot even imagine. Evolutionary processes that now function blindly, through chance, may be steered and directed.

If so, understanding the forces that now govern us will be more urgent than ever, for tinkering with the processes could have disastrous consequences. In any event, however, knowing the natural history of organizations will be increasingly important because large-scale organizations are here to stay as long as human culture survives; there will be no return to a world of simpler, smaller units. To preserve the values of a free society and of democratic life within these systems is a challenge of vast proportions. Perhaps it can never be met, but only if we broaden and deepen our insights into organizations will there be any chance at all that it can.

Footnotes to Organizational Change

James G. March

Five footnotes to change in organizations are suggested. They emphasize the relation between change and adaptive behavior more generally, the prosaic nature of change, the way in which ordinary processes combine with a confusing world to produce some surprises, and the implicit altruism of organizational foolishness.•

INTRODUCTION

Organizations change. Although they often appear resistant to change, they are frequently transformed into forms remarkably different from the original. This paper explores five footnotes to research on organizational change, possible comments on what we know. The intention is not to review the research results but to identify a few speculations stimulated by previous work.

Footnote 1: Organizations are continually changing, routinely, easily, and responsively, but change within them cannot ordinarily be arbitrarily controlled. Organizations rarely do exactly what they are told to do.

Footnote 2: Changes in organizations depend on a few stable processes. Theories of change emphasize either the stability of the processes or the changes they produce, but a serious understanding of organizations requires attention to both.

Footnote 3: Theories of change in organizations are primarily different ways of describing theories of action in organizations, not different theories. Most changes in organizations reflect simple responses to demographic, economic, social, and political forces.

Footnote 4: Although organizational response to environmental events is broadly adaptive and mostly routine, the response takes place in a confusing world. As a result, prosaic processes sometimes have surprising outcomes.

Footnote 5: Adaptation to a changing environment involves an interplay of rationality and foolishness. Organizational foolishness is not maintained as a conscious strategy, but is embedded in such familiar organizational anomalies as slack, managerial incentives, symbolic action, ambiguity, and loose coupling.

STABLE PROCESSES OF CHANGE

A common theme in recent literature, particularly in studies of the implementation of public policy, is that of attempts at change frustrated by organizational resistance. There are well-documented occasions on which organizations have failed to respond to change initiatives or have changed in ways that were, in the view of some, inappropriate (Gross, Giaquinta, and Bernstein, 1971; Nelson and Yates, 1978).

What most reports on implementation indicate, however, is not that organizations are rigid and inflexible, but that they are impressively imaginative (Pressman and Wildavsky, 1973; Bardach, 1977). Organizations change in response to their environments, but they rarely change in a way that fulfills the intentions of a particular group of actors (Attewell and Gerstein, 1979; Crozier, 1979). Sometimes organizations ignore clear instructions; sometimes they pursue them more forcefully than was intended; sometimes they protect policymakers from

•
I am grateful for the assistance of Julia Ball; for the comments and collaboration of David Anderson, Vicki Eaton, Martha Feldman, Daniel Levinthal, Anne Miner, J. Rounds, Philip Salin and Jo Zettler; and for support by the Spencer Foundation, the National Institute of Education, the Hoover Institution, and the National Center for Higher Education Management Systems. References to some 129 items from the text have been eliminated from the text at the request of the editor. Persons interested in a more complete set of references can obtain one from the author.

383

folly; sometimes they do not. The ability to frustrate arbitrary intention, however, should not be confused with rigidity; nor should flexibility be confused with organizational effectiveness. Most organizational failures occur early in life when organizations are small and flexible, not later (Aldrich, 1979). There is considerable stability in organizations, but the changes we observe are substantial enough to suggest that organizations are remarkably adaptive, enduring institutions, responding to volatile environments routinely and easily, though not always optimally.

Because of the magnitude of some changes in organizations, we are inclined to look for comparably dramatic explanations for change, but the search for drama may often be a mistake. Most change in organizations results neither from extraordinary organizational processes or forces, nor from uncommon imagination, persistence or skill, but from relatively stable, routine processes that relate organizations to their environments. Change takes place because most of the time most people in an organization do about what they are supposed to do; that is, they are intelligently attentive to their environments and their jobs. Bureaucratic organizations can be exceptionally ineffective, but most of the organizations we study are characterized by ordinary competence and minor initiative (Hedberg, Nystrom, and Starbuck, 1976). Many of the most stable procedures in an organization are procedures for responding to economic, social, and political contexts. What we call organizational change is an ecology of concurrent responses in various parts of an organization to various interconnected parts of the environment. If the environment changes rapidly, so will the responses of stable organizations; change driven by such shifts will be dramatic if shifts in the environment are large.

The routine processes of organizational adaptation are subject to some complications, and a theory of change must take into account how those processes can produce unusual patterns of action. Yet, in its fundamental structure a theory of organizational change should not be remarkably different from a theory of ordinary action. Recent research on organizations as routine adaptive systems emphasizes six basic perspectives for interpreting organizational action:

1. **Rule following.** Action can be seen as the application of standard operating procedures or other rules to appropriate situations. The underlying process is one of matching a set of rules to a situation by criteria of appropriateness. Duties, obligations, roles, rules, and criteria evolve through competition and survival, and those followed by organizations that survive, grow, and multiply come to dominate the pool of procedures. The model is essentially a model of selection (Nelson and Winter, 1974).

2. **Problem solving.** Action can be seen as problem solving. The underlying process involves choosing among alternatives by using some decision rule that compares alternatives in terms of their expected consequences for antecedent goals. The model is one of intendedly rational choice under conditions of risk and is familiar in statistical decision theory, as well as microeconomic and behavioral theories of choice (Lindblom, 1958; Cyert and March, 1963).

384

3. **Learning.** Action can be seen as stemming from past learning. The underlying process is one in which an organization is conditioned through trial and error to repeat behavior that has been successful in the past and to avoid behavior that has been unsuccessful. The model is one of experiential learning (Day and Groves, 1975).

4. **Conflict.** Action can be seen as resulting from conflict among individuals or groups representing diverse interests. The underlying process is one of confrontation, bargaining, and coalition, in which outcomes depend on the initial preferences of actors weighted by their power. Changes result from shifts in the mobilization of participants or in the resources they control. The model is one of politics (March, 1962; Gamson, 1968; Pfeffer, 1981).

5. **Contagion.** Action can be seen as spreading from one organization to another. The underlying process is one in which variations in contact among organizations and in the attractiveness of the behaviors or beliefs being imitated affect the rate and pattern of spread. The model is one of contagion and borrows from studies of epidemiology (Rogers, 1962; Walker, 1969; Rogers and Shoemaker, 1971).

6. **Regeneration.** Action can be seen as resulting from the intentions and competencies of organizational actors. Turnover in organizations introduces new members with different attitudes, abilities, and goals. The underlying process is one in which conditions in the organization (e.g., growth, decline, changing requirements for skills) or deliberate strategies (e.g., cooptation, raiding of competitors) affect organizational action by changing the mix of participants. The model is one of regeneration (Stinchcombe, McDill, and Walker, 1968; White, 1970; McNeil and Thompson, 1971).

These six perspectives are neither esoteric, complicated, nor mutually exclusive. Although we may sometimes try to assess the extent to which one perspective or another fits a particular situation, it is quite possible for all six to be pertinent or for any particular history to involve them all. An organization uses rules, problem solving, learning, conflict, contagion, and regeneration to cope with its environment, actively adapt to it, avoid it, seek to understand, change, and contain it. The processes are conservative. That is, they tend to maintain stable relations, sustain existing rules, and reduce differences among organizations. The fundamental logic, however, is not one of stability in behavior; it is one of responsiveness. The processes are stable; the resulting actions are not.

SOME COMPLEXITIES OF CHANGE

Organizations change in mundane ways, but elementary processes sometimes produce surprises in a complex world. As illustrations of such complexities, consider five examples: the unanticipated consequences of ordinary action, solution-driven problems, the tendency for innovations and organizations to be transformed during the process of innovation, the endogenous nature of created environments, and the interactions among the system requirements of individuals, organizations, and environments.

Unanticipated Consequences of Ordinary Action

Each of the six perspectives on action described above portrays organizations as changing sensibly; that is, solving problems, learning from experience, imitating others, and regenerating their capabilities through turnover of personnel. These processes, however, may be applied under conditions which, though difficult to distinguish from usual conditions, are sufficiently different to lead to unanticipated outcomes. In particular, we can identify three such conditions:

First, the rate of adaptation may be inconsistent with the rate of change of the environment to which the organization is adapting. Unless an environment is perfectly stable, of course, there will always be some error arising from a history-dependent process (e.g., learning, selection); but where an environment changes quickly relative to the rate at which an organization adapts, a process can easily lose its claim to being sensible. It is also possible for an anticipatory process (e.g., problem solving) to result in changes that outrun the environment and thereby become unintelligent. Second, the causal structure may be different from that implicit in the process. If causal links are ignored, either because they are new, or because their effects in the past have been benign, or because the world is inherently too complex, then changes that seem locally adaptive may produce unanticipated or confusing consequences. Such outcomes are particularly likely in situations in which belief in a false or incomplete model of causality can be reinforced by confounded experience. Third, concurrent, parallel processes of *prima facie* sensibility may combine to produce joint outcomes that are not intended by anyone and are directly counter to the interests motivating the individual actions (Schelling, 1978).

Most of the time, these unanticipated outcomes are avoided, but they are common. Consider the following illustrations:

Learning from the response of clients. Clients and customers send signals to organizations, the most conspicuous one being the withdrawal of their patronage. We expect organizations to respond to such signals. For example, although customer withdrawal is a major device used by market organizations to maintain product quality, it is not always effective. As Hirschman (1970) observed, it is likely that the first customers to abandon a product of declining quality will be those customers with the highest quality standards. If it is assumed that new customers are a random sample from the market, a firm is left with customers whose standards are, on the average, lower and who complain less about the reduced quality. This leads to further decay of quality, and the cycle continues until the quality consciousness of new customers equals that of lost customers; i.e., until the firm's most quality-conscious customers are no more concerned about quality than the average customers in the market. This cycle of regeneration can lead to a fairly rapid degradation in product or service.

Rewarding friends and coopting enemies. Employees of governmental regulatory agencies sometimes subsequently become employees of the organizations they regulate. The flow of people presumably affects the relations between the organizations. In particular, the usual presumption is that expectations of future employment will lead current governmental

386

officials to treat the organizations involved more favorably than they would otherwise. However, if the regulated organizations provide possible employment as an incentive for favorable treatment, they risk producing a pattern of turnover in the regulatory agency in which friends leave the agency, and only those unfriendly to the organization remain. Alternatively, some organizations attempt to coopt difficult people (e.g., rebels), on the assumption that cooptation leads to controlled change, since opponents are socialized and provided with modest success. However, insofar as the basic strategy of cooptation is to strip leadership from opposition groups by inducing opposition leaders to accept more legitimate roles, a conspicuous complication is the extent to which cooptation provides an incentive for being difficult, and thereby increases, rather than reduces opposition. .

Competency multipliers. Organizations frequently have procedures to involve potentially relevant people in decision making, planning, budgeting, or the like. The individuals vary in status, knowledge about a problem, and interest in it. Initial participation rates reflect these variations; however, individuals who participate slightly more than others become slightly more competent at discussing the problems of the group than others. This induces them to participate even more, which makes them even more competent. Before long, the de facto composition of the group can change dramatically (Weiner, 1976). More generally organizations learn from experience, repeating actions that are successful. As a result, they gain greater experience in areas of success than in areas of failure. This increases their capabilities in successful areas, thus increasing their chances of being successful there. The sensibleness of such specialization depends on the relation between the learning rates and the rate of change in the environment. The process can easily lead to misplaced specialization if there are infrequent, major shifts in the environment.

Satisficing. It has been suggested that organizations satisfice, that is, that they seek alternatives that will satisfy a target goal rather than look for the alternative with the highest possible expected value (March and Simon, 1958; Cyert and March, 1963). Satisficing organizations can be viewed as organizations that maximize the probability of achieving their targets, but it is not necessary to assume quite such a precise formulation to suggest that organizations that satisfice will follow decision rules that are risk avoiding in good times, when the best alternatives have expected values greater than the target, and risk seeking in bad times, when the best alternatives have expected values less than the target (Tversky and Kahneman, 1974). As is noted below, the association of risk-seeking behavior with adversity requires some qualification; but insofar as such a pattern is common, it has at least two important consequences. First, organizations that are facing bad times will follow riskier and riskier strategies, thus simultaneously increasing their chances of survival through the present crisis and reducing their life expectancy. Choices that seek to reverse a decline, for example, may not maximize expected value. As a result, for those organizations that do not survive, efforts to survive will have speeded the process of failure (Hermann, 1963; Mayhew, 1979). Second, if organizational goals vary with organizational performance and the performance of other com-

387

parable organizations, most organizations will face situations that are reasonably good most of the time. Consequently, the pool of organizations existing at any time will generally include a disproportionate number that are risk-avoiding.

Performance criteria. Organizations measure the performance of participants For example, business firms reward managers on the basis of calculations of profits earned by different parts of the organization. The importance of making such links precise and visible is a familiar theme of discussions of organizational control, as is the problem of providing similar performance measures in non-business organizations. However, in an organization with a typical mobility pattern among managers, these practices probably lead to a relative lack of concern about long-term consequences of present action. Performance measurement also leads to exaggerated concern with accounts, relative to product and technology. Measured performance can be improved either by changing performance or by changing the accounts of performance. Since it is often more efficient, in the short run, to devote effort to the accounts rather than to performance (March, 1978a), a bottom-line ideology may overstimulate the cleverness of organizational participants in manipulating accounts.

Superstitious learning. Organizations learn from their experience, repeating actions that have been associated with good outcomes, avoiding actions that have been associated with bad ones. If the world makes simple sense, and is stable, then repeating actions associated with good outcomes is intelligent. Yet relative to the rate of our experience in it, the world is sometimes neither stable enough nor simple enough to make experience a good teacher (March and Olsen, 1976). The use of associational, experiential learning in complex worlds can result in superstitious learning (Lave and March, 1975). Consider, for example, the report by Tversky and Kahneman (1974) of the lessons learned by pilot trainers who experimented with rewarding pilots who make good landings and punishing pilots who make bad ones. They observe that pilots who are punished generally improve on subsequent landings, while pilots who are praised generally do worse. Thus, they learn that negative reinforcement works; positive reinforcement does not. The learning is natural, but the experience, like all experience, is confounded, in this case by ordinary regression to the mean.

These six examples of unanticipated consequences are illustrative of the variation in behavior that can be generated by elementary adaptive processes functioning under special conditions. They suggest some ways in which undramatic features of organizational life can lead to surprising organizational change.

Solution-Driven Problems

There seems to be ample evidence that when performance fails to meet aspirations, organizations search for new solutions (Cyert and March, 1963), that is, for new people, new ways of doing things, new alliances. However, changes often seem to be driven less by problems than by solutions. Daft and Becker (1978) have argued the case for educational organizations and Kay (1979) for industrial organizations; but the idea is an established one, typical of diffusion theories of change.

We can identify at least three different explanations for solution (or opportunity) driven change. In the first, organizations face a large number of problems of about equal importance, but only a few solutions. Thus, the chance of finding a solution to a particular problem is small; if one begins with a solution, however, there is a good chance that the solution will match some problem facing the organization. Consequently, an organization scans for solutions rather than problems, and matches any solution found with some relevant problem. A second explanation is that the linkage between individual solutions and individual problems is often difficult to make unambiguously. Then, almost any solution can be linked to almost any problem, provided they arise at approximately the same time (Cohen, March, and Olsen, 1972; March and Olsen, 1975). When causality and technology are ambiguous, the motivation to have particular solutions adopted is likely to be as powerful as the motivation to have particular problems solved, and many of the changes we observe will be better predicted by a knowledge of solutions than by a knowledge of problems. A third interpretation is that change is stimulated not by adversity but by success, less by a sense of problems than by a sense of competence and a belief that change is possible, natural, and appropriate (Daft and Becker, 1978). Professionals change their procedures and introduce new technologies because that is what professionals do and know how to do. An organization that is modern adopts new things because that is what being modern means. When a major stimulus for change comes from a sense of competence, problems are created in order to solve them, and solutions and opportunities stimulate awareness of previously unsalient or unnoticed problems or preferences.

Transformation of Innovations and Organizations

Students of innovation in organizations have persistently observed that both innovations and organizations tend to be transformed during the process of innovation (Browning, 1968; Brewer, 1973; Hyman, 1973). This is sometimes treated as a measurement problem. In that guise, the problem is to decide whether a change in one organization is equivalent to a change in another, or to determine when a change has been implemented sufficiently to be considered a change, or to disentangle the labeling of a change from the change itself. To treat such problems as measurement problems, however, is probably misleading. Seeing innovations as spreading unchanged through organizations helps link studies of innovation to models drawn from epidemiology; but where a fundamental feature of a change is the way it is transformed as it moves from invention to adoption to implementation to contagion, such a linkage is not helpful.

Organizational change develops meaning through the process by which it occurs. Some parts of that process tend to standardize the multiple meanings of a change, but standardization can be very slow, in some cases so slow as to be almost undetectable. When a business firm adopts a new policy (Cyert, Dill, and March, 1958), or a university a new program (March and Romelaer, 1976), specifying what the change means can be difficult, not because of poor information or inadequate analysis, but because of the fundamental ways in which changes are transformed by the processes of change. The developing character of change makes it difficult to use stan-

389

dard ideas of decision, problem solving, diffusion, and the like, because it is difficult to describe a decision, problem solution, or innovation with precision, to say when it was adopted, and to treat the process as having an ending.

Organizations are also transformed in the process. Organizations develop and redefine goals while making decisions and adapting to environmental pressures; minor changes can lead to larger ones, and initial intent can be entirely lost. For example, an organization of evangelists becomes a gym with services attached (Zald and Denton, 1963); a social movement becomes a commercial establishment (Messinger, 1955; Sills, 1957); a radical rock radio station becomes an almost respectable part of a large corporation (Krieger, 1979); and a new governmental agency becomes an old one (Selznick, 1949; Sproull, Weiner, and Wolf, 1978).

These transformations seem often to reflect occasions on which actions taken by an organization (for whatever reasons) become the source of a new definition of objectives. The possibility that preferences and goals may change in response to behavior is a serious complication for rational theories of choice (March, 1972, 1978a). Organizations' goals, as well as the goals of individuals in them, change in the course of introducing deliberate innovations, or in the course of normal organizational drift. As a result, actions affect the preferences in the name of which they are taken; and the discovery of new intentions is a common consequence of intentional behavior.

Created Environments

In simple models of organizational change, it is usually assumed that action is taken in response to the environment but that the environment is not affected by organizational action. The assumptions are convenient, but organizations create their environments in part, and the resulting complications are significant. For example, organizations are frequently combined into an ecology of competition, in which the actions of one competitor become the environment of another. Each competitor, therefore, partly determines its own environment as the competitors react to each other, a situation familiar to studies of prey-predator relations and markets (Mayr, 1963; Kamien and Schwartz, 1975). Also, if we think of adaptation as learning about a fixed environment, the model is somewhat different from one in which the environment is simultaneously adapting to the organization. The situation is a common one. Parents adapt to children at the same time that children adapt to parents, and customers and suppliers adapt to each other. The outcomes are different from those observed in the case of adaptation to a stable environment, with equilibria that depend on whether the process is one of hunting or mating and on the relative rates of adaptation of the organization and the environment (Lave and March, 1975). Finally, organizations create their own environments by the way they interpret and act in a confusing world. It is not just that the world is incompletely or inaccurately perceived (Slovic, Fischoff, and Lichtenstein, 1977; Nisbet and Ross, 1980), but also that actions taken as a result of beliefs about the environment do, in fact, construct the environment, as, for example, in self-fulfilling prophecies and the construction of limits through avoidance of them (Meyer and Rowan, 1977; Weick, 1977, 1979).

390

It is possible, of course, for organizations to act strategically in an environment they help create, but created environments are not ordinarily experienced in a way different from other environments. For example, the experience of learning in a situation in which the environment is simultaneously adapting to the organization is not remarkably different from the experience of learning in simpler situations. The outcomes are, however, distinctive. When environments are created, the actions taken by an organization in adapting to an environment are partly responses to previous actions by the same organization, reflected through the environment. A common result is that small signals are amplified into large ones, and the general implication is that routine adaptive processes have consequences that cannot be understood without linking them to an environment that is simultaneously, and endogenously, changing.

Individuals, Organizations, and Environments

Although it is an heroic simplification out of which theoretical mischief can come, it is possible to see an organization as the intermeshing of three systems: the individual, the organization, and the collection of organizations that can be called the environment. Many of the complications in the study of organizational change are related to the way those three systems intermesh, as is reflected in the large number of studies that discuss managing change in terms of the relations between organizations and the individuals who inhabit them (Coch and French, 1948; Burns and Stalker, 1961; Argyris, 1965), between organizations and their environment (Starbuck, 1976; Aldrich, 1979), and among organizations (Evan, 1966; Benson, 1975).

Much of classical organization theory addresses the problems of making the demands of organizations and individuals consistent (Barnard, 1938; Simon, 1947; March and Simon, 1958); the same theme is frequent in modern treatments of information (Hirschleifer and Riley, 1979) and incentives (Downs, 1967). Although it is an old problem, it continues to be interesting for the analysis of organizational change. In particular, it seems very likely that both the individuals involved in organizations and systems of organizations have different requirements for organizational change than the organization itself. For example, individual participants in an organization view their positions in the organizations, e.g., their jobs, as an important part of their milieu. They try to arrange patterns of stability and variety within the organization to meet their own desires. However, there is no particular a priori reason for assuming that individual desires for change and stability will be mutually consistent or will match requirements for organizational survival. Moreover, the survival of an organization is a more compelling requirement for the organization than it is for a system of organizations. Survival of the system of organizations may require organizational changes that are inappropriate for the individual organization; it may require greater organizational flexibility or rigidity than makes sense for the individual organization. The organizational failure rates that are optimal for systems of organizations are somewhat different from those that are optimal for individual organizations. Complications such as these are common in any combination of autonomous systems. They form a focus for some standard issues in contemporary population genetics (Wright, 1978), as well as extensions of those ideas into social science in general (Wilson, 1975; Hannan and Freeman, 1977).

391

That observed systems of individuals, organizations, and environments have evolved to an equilibrium is questionable, but it is possible that some of the features of organizations that seem particularly perverse make greater sense when considered from the point of view of the larger system of organizations.

Other illustrations of complications could easily be added, including problems introduced by the ways in which humans make inferences (Nisbet and Ross, 1980), and by the ways in which organizational demography affects regeneration (Reed, 1978). Each of the complications represents either a limitation in one of the standard models or a way in which a model of adaptation can be used to illuminate organizational change under complicated or confounding conditions. Familiar activities, rules, or procedures sometimes lead to unanticipated consequences.

FOOLISHNESS, CHANGE, AND ALTRUISM

Organizations need to maintain a balance (or dialectic) between explicitly sensible processes of change (problem-solving, learning, planning) and certain elements of foolishness that are difficult to justify locally but are important to the broader system (March, 1972, 1978a; Weick, 1979). Consider, for example, a classic complication of long-range planning. As we try to anticipate the future, we will often observe that there are many possible, but extremely unlikely, future events which would dramatically change the consequences of present actions and thus the appropriate choice to be made now. Because there are so many very unlikely future events that can be imagined, and each is so improbable, we ordinarily exclude them from our more careful forecasts, though we know that some very unlikely events will certainly occur. As a result, our plans are based on a future that we know, with certainty, will not be realized. More generally, if the most favorable outcomes of a particular choice alternative depend on the occurrence of very unlikely events, the expected value of that alternative will be low, and it would not be sensible to choose it. Thus, the best alternative after the fact is unlikely to be chosen before the fact by a rational process. For similar reasons, the prior expected value of any specific innovation is likely to be negative, and organizations are likely to resist proposals for such change. Indeed, we would expect that an institution eager to adopt innovative proposals will survive less luxuriantly and for shorter periods than others. Though some unknown change is almost certainly sensible, being the first to experiment with a new idea is not likely to be worth the risk.

The problem becomes one of introducing new ideas into organizations at a rate sufficient to sustain the larger system of organizations, when such action is not intelligent for any one organization. The conventional solution for such problems involves some kind of collaboration that pools the risk (Hirschleifer and Riley, 1979). Explicit risk-sharing agreements exist, but for the most part, organizational systems have evolved a culture of implicit altruism which introduces decentralized nonrational elements into rational choice procedures rather than relying on explicit contractual arrangements. These cultural elements of manifest foolishness have latent implications for innovation and change in organizations. New ideas are sustained in an organization by mechanisms that shield them, altruistically, from the operation of normal rationality, for example, by organizational slack, managerial incentives, symbolic action, ambiguity, and loose coupling.

Slack protects individuals and groups, who pursue change for personal or professional reasons, from normal organizational controls. As a result, it has been argued that one of the ways in which organizations search when successful is through slack (Cyert and March, 1963; Wilson, 1966). Several studies of change seem to lend support to this idea (Mansfield, 1968; Staw and Szwajkowski, 1975; Manns and March, 1978); but Kay (1979) concludes that it is hard to see consistent evidence for slack search in the data on research and development expenditures. Daft and Becker (1978) suggest that slack is associated not with excess resources but with high salaries and a consequent high level of professionalism.

Since managers and other leaders are selected by a process that is generally conservative (Cohen and March, 1974), it is probably unreasonable to see them as sources of intentional foolishness. Managerial incentives seem unlikely to stimulate managerial playfulness; incentive schemes try to tie individual rewards to organizational outcomes, so that managers help themselves by helping the organization. The ideology of good management, however, associates managers with the introduction of new ideas, new organizational forms, new technologies, new products, new slogans, or new moods. Consequently, some fraction of organizational resources is dedicated to running unlikely experiments in changes as unwitting altruistic contributions to the larger world.

Choice and decision making touch some of the more important values of modern developed cultures, and thereby become major symbolic domains in contemporary organizations. Symbolic values, including those associated with change, are important enough and pervasive enough to dominate other factors in a decision situation (Christensen, 1976; Kreiner, 1976; Feldman and March, 1981). Symbolism shades into personal motivations easily for professionals (e.g., engineers, doctors) or managers, since they express their competence and authority by the introduction of changes or symbols of changes (Daft and Becker, 1978). In a more general way, the symbolic elaboration of processes of choice becomes more important than the outcomes, and the outcomes thus reflect more foolishness than would otherwise be expected.

Organizations do not always have a well-defined set of objectives; their preferences are frequently ambiguous, imprecise, inconsistent, unstable, and affected by their choices (March, 1978a; Elster, 1979). As a result, problem solving and decision making assume some of the features of a garbage can process (Cohen, March, and Olsen, 1972), learning becomes confounded by the ambiguity of experience (Cohen and March, 1974; March and Olsen, 1976), and actions become particularly sensitive to the participation and attention patterns of organizational actors (Olsen, 1976). Moreover, the uncertainties associated with trying to guess future preferences increase considerably the variance in any estimates that might be made of the expected utility of present action and thus decrease the reliability of the process.

Finally, organizations are complex combinations of activities, purposes, and meanings; they accomplish coordinated tasks that would be inconceivable without them, and without which it is difficult to imagine a modern developed society. This impressive integration of formal organizations should not, however, obscure the many ways in which organizations are loosely coupled. Behavior is loosely coupled to intentions; actions in one part of the organization are loosely coupled to actions in another part; decisions today are loosely coupled to decisions tomorrow (Cohen and March, 1974; March and Olsen, 1976; Weick, 1976, 1979). Such loose coupling does not appear to be avoidable. Rather, limits on coordination, attention, and control are inherent restrictions on the implementation of rationality in organizational action.

These organizational phenomena ensure that some level of foolishness will occur within an organization, no matter how dedicated to rational coordination and control it may be. Although it is easy to argue that foolishness is a form of altruism by which systematic needs for change are met, it is much harder to assess whether the mixture of rationality and foolishness that we observe in organizations is optimal. The ideology underlying the development of decision engineering probably underestimates the importance of foolishness, and the ideology underlying enthusiasm for some versions of undisciplined creativity probably underestimates the importance of systematic analysis. What is much more difficult is to determine whether a particular real system errs on the side of excessive reason or excessive foolishness. We can solve the problem of appropriate foolishness within a specific model by assuming some characteristics of the environment over the future; solving the problem in a real situation, however, is not ordinarily within our ability.

Nor is it easy to devise realistic insurance, information, or contractual schemes that will reliably ensure reaching an optimum. Not only are the difficulties in analysis substantial, but, quite aside from those problems, there is also a difficulty posed by the cultural character of the existing solution. The mix of organizational foolishness and rationality is deeply embedded in the rules, incentives, and beliefs of the society and organization. It is possible to imagine changing the mix of rules, thereby changing the level of foolishness; but it is hard to imagine being able to modify broad cultural and organizational attributes with much precision or control.

DISCUSSION

The five footnotes to organizational change suggested at the outset are comments on change, not a theory of change. Nevertheless, they may have some implications for organizational leadership and for research on adaptation in organizations. The general perspective depends on the proposition that the basic processes by which organizations act, respond to their environments, and learn are quite stable, and possibly comprehensible. These stable processes of change, however, produce a great variety of action and their outcomes are sometimes surprisingly sensitive to the details of the context in which they occur.

A view of change as resulting from stable processes realized in a highly contextual and sometimes confusing world emphasizes the idea that things happen in organizations because most of the time organizational participants respond in elementary ways to the environment, including that part of the environment that might be called management or leadership. Managers and leaders propose changes, including foolish ones; they try to cope with the environment and to control it; they respond to other members of the organization; they issue orders and manipulate incentives. Since they play conventional roles, organizational leaders are not likely to behave in strikingly unusual ways. And if a leader tries to march toward strange destinations, an organization is likely to deflect the effort. Simply to describe leadership as conventional and constrained by organizational realities, however, is to risk misunderstanding its importance. Neither success nor change requires dramatic action. The conventional, routine activities that produce most organizational change require ordinary people to do ordinary things in a competent way (March, 1978b). Moreover, within some broad constraints, the adaptiveness of organizations can be managed. Typically, it is not possible to lead an organization in any arbitrary direction that might be desired, but it is possible to influence the course of events by managing the process of change, and particularly by stimulating or inhibiting predictable complications and anomalous dynamics.

Such a view of managing organizations assumes that the effectiveness of leadership often depends on being able to time small interventions so that the force of natural organizational processes amplifies the interventions. It is possible to identify a few minor rules for such actions (Cohen and March, 1974), but a comprehensive development of managerial strategies (as well as of effective strategies for frustrating managers) requires a more thorough understanding of change in organizations, not a theory of how to introduce any arbitrary change, but a theory of how to direct somewhat the conventional ways in which an organization responds to its environment, experiences, and anticipations. The footnotes to change elaborated in this paper are much too fragmentary for such a task, but they indicate a possible way of understanding change. They argue for considering the fundamental adaptive processes by which change occurs, in terms of broader theoretical ideas about organizational action. They direct attention particularly to how substantial changes occur, as the routine consequence of standard procedures or as the unintended consequence of ordinary adaptation. And they suggest that understanding organizational change requires discovering the connections between the apparently prosaic and the apparently poetic in organizational life.

REFERENCES

Aldrich, Howard E.
1979 Organizations and Environments. Englewood Cliffs, NJ: Prentice-Hall.

Argyris, Chris
1965 Organization and Innovation. Homewood, IL: Irwin-Dorsey.

Attewell, Paul, and Dean R. Gerstein
1979 "Government policy and local practice." American Sociological Review, 44: 311–327.

Bardach, Eugene
1977 The Implementation Game. Cambridge, MA: MIT Press.

Barnard, Chester I.
1938 Functions of the Executive. Cambridge, MA: Harvard University Press.

Benson, J. Kenneth
1975 "The interorganizational network as political economy." Administrative Science Quarterly 20: 229–249.

Brewer, Garry D.
1973 Politicians, Bureaucrats and the Consultant: A Critique of Urban Problem Solving. New York: Basic Books.

Browning, Rufus P.
1968 "Innovation and non-innovation decision processes in government budgeting." In Robert T. Golembiewski (ed.), Public Budgeting and Finance: 128–145. Itasca, IL: F. E. Peacock.

Burns, Tom, and G. M. Stalker
1961 The Management of Innovation. London: Tavistock.

Christensen, Soren
1976 "Decision making and socialization." In James G. March and Johan P. Olsen (eds.), Ambiguity and Choice in Organizations: 351–385. Bergen, Norway: Universitetsforlaget.

Coch, Lester, and John R. P. French, Jr.
1948 "Overcoming resistance to change." Human Relations, 1: 512–532.

Cohen, Michael D., and James G. March
1974 Leadership and Ambiguity: The American College President. New York: McGraw-Hill.

Cohen, Michael D., James G. March, and Johan P. Olsen
1972 "A garbage can model of organizational choice." Administrative Science Quarterly, 17: 1–25.

Crozier, Michel
1979 On ne Change pas la Société par Décret. Paris: Grasset.

Cyert, Richard M., William Dill, and James G. March
1958 "The role of expectations in business decision making." Administrative Science Quarterly, 3: 307–340.

Cyert, Richard M., and James G. March
1963 A Behavioral Theory of the Firm. Englewood Cliffs, NJ: Prentice-Hall.

Daft, Richard L., and Selwyn W. Becker
1978 The Innovative Organization. New York: Elsevier.

Day, R. H., and T. Groves, eds.
1975 Adaptive Economic Models. New York: Academic Press.

Downs, Anthony
1967 Inside Bureaucracy. Boston: Little, Brown.

Elster, Jon
1979 Ulysses and the Sirens. Cambridge: Cambridge University Press.

Evan, William M.
1966 "The organization set: Toward a theory of interorganizational relations." In James D. Thompson (ed.), Approaches to Organizational Design: 173–191. Pittsburgh: University of Pittsburgh Press.

Feldman, Martha S., and James G. March
1981 "Information in organizations as signal and symbol." Administrative Science Quarterly, 26: 171–186.

Gamson, William A.
1968 Power and Discontent. Homewood, IL: Dorsey.

Gross, Neal, Joseph B. Giaquinta, and Marilyn Bernstein
1971 Implementing Organizational Innovations: A Sociological Analysis of Planned Educational Change. New York: Basic Books.

Hannan, Michael T., and John Freeman
1977 "The population ecology of organizations." American Journal of Sociology, 82: 929–966.

Hedberg, Bo L. T., Paul C. Nystrom, and William H. Starbuck
1976 "Camping on seesaws: Prescriptions for a self-designing organization." Administrative Science Quarterly, 21: 41–65.

Hermann, Charles F.
1963 "Some consequences of crisis which limit the viability of organizations." Administrative Science Quarterly 8: 61–82.

Hirschleifer, J., and John G. Riley
1979 "The analytics of uncertainty and information — An expository survey." Journal of Economic Literature, 17: 1375–1421.

Hirschman, Albert O.
1979 Exit, Voice, and Loyalty. Cambridge, MA: Harvard University Press.

Hyman, Herbert H., ed.
1973 The Politics of Health Care: Nine Case Studies of Innovative Planning in New York City. New York: Praeger.

Kamien, Morton I., and Nancy L. Schwartz
1975 "Market structure and innovation: A survey." Journal of Economic Literature, 13: 1–37.

Kay, Neil M.
1979 The Innovating Firm: A Behavioral Theory of Corporate R & D. New York: St. Martin's.

Kreiner, Kristian
1976 "Ideology and management in a garbage can situation." In James G. March and Johan P. Olsen (eds.), Ambiguity and Choice in Organizations: 156–173. Bergen, Norway: Universitetsforlaget.

Krieger, Susan
1979 Hip Capitalism. Beverly Hills, CA: Sage.

Lave, Charles A., and James G. March
1975 An Introduction to Models in the Social Sciences. New York: Harper and Row.

Lindblom, Charles E.
1958 "The science of muddling through." Public Administration Review, 19: 79–88.

Manns, Curtis L., and James G. March
1978 "Financial adversity, internal competition, and curriculum change in a university." Administrative Science Quarterly, 23: 541–552.

Mansfield, Edwin
1968 The Economics of Technological Change. New York: Norton.

March, James G.
1962 "The business firm as a political coalition." Journal of Politics, 24: 662–678.
1972 "Model bias in social action." Review of Educational Research, 42: 413–429.
1978a "Bounded rationality, ambiguity, and the engineering of choice." Bell Journal of Economics, 9: 587–608.
1978b "American public school administration: A short analysis." School Review, 86: 217–250.

March, James G., and Johan P. Olsen
1975 "The uncertainty of the past: Organizational learning under ambiguity." European Journal of Political Research, 3: 147–171.
1976 Ambiguity and Choice in Organizations. Bergen, Norway: Universitetsforlaget.

March, James G., and Pierre J. Romelaer
1976 "Position and presence in the drift of decisions." In James G. March and Johan P. Olsen, (eds.), Ambiguity and Choice in Organizations: 251–276. Bergen, Norway: Universitetsforlaget.

Footnotes to Change

March, James G., and Herbert A. Simon
1958 Organizations. New York: Wiley.

Mayhew, Lewis B.
1979 Surviving the Eighties. San Francisco: Jossey-Bass.

Mayr, Ernst
1963 Population, Species, and Evolution. Cambridge, MA: Harvard University Press.

McNeil, Kenneth, and James D. Thompson
1971 "The regeneration of social organizations." American Sociological Review, 36: 624–637.

Messinger, Sheldon L.
1955 "Organizational transformation: A case study of a declining social movement." American Sociological Review, 20: 3–10.

Meyer, John W., and Brian Rowan
1977 "Institutionalized organizations: Formal structure as myth and ceremony." American Journal of Sociology, 83: 340–360.

Nelson, Richard R., and Sidney G. Winter
1974 "Neoclassical vs. evolutionary theories of economic growth: Critique and prospectus." Economic Journal, 84: 886–905.

Nelson, Richard R., and Douglas Yates, eds.
1978 Innovation and Implementation in Public Organizations. Lexington, MA: D. C. Heath.

Nisbet, Richard, and Lee Ross
1980 Human inference: Strategies and Shortcomings of Social Judgment. Englewood Cliffs, NJ: Prentice-Hall.

Olsen, Johan P.
1976 "Reorganization as a garbage can." In James G. March and Johan P. Olsen (eds.), Ambiguity and Choice in Organizations: 314–337. Bergen, Norway: Universitetsforlaget.

Pfeffer, Jeffrey
1981 Power in Organizations. Marshfield, MA: Pitman.

Pressman, Jeffrey, and Aaron Wildavsky
1973 Implementation. Berkeley, CA: University of California Press.

Reed, Theodore L.
1978 "Organizational change in the American foreign service, 1925–1965: The utility of cohort analysis." American Sociological Review, 43: 404–421.

Rogers, Everett M.
1962 Diffusion of Innovations. New York: Free Press.

Rogers, Everett M., and F. Floyd Shoemaker
1971 Communication of Innovations. New York: Free Press.

Schelling, Thomas C.
1978 Micromotives and Macrobehavior. New York: Norton.

Selznick, Philip
1949 TVA and the Grass Roots. Berkeley, CA: University of California Press.

Sills, David L.
1957 The Volunteers. New York: Free Press.

Simon, Herbert A.
1947 Administrative Behavior. New York: Macmillan.

Slovic, Paul, Bernard Fischhoff, and Sarah Lichtenstein
1977 "Behavioral decision theory." Annual Review of Psychology, 28: 1–39.

Sproull, Lee S., Stephen S. Weiner, and David Wolf
1978 Organizing an Anarchy. Chicago: University of Chicago Press.

Starbuck, William H.
1976 "Organizations and their environments." In Marvin D. Dunnette (ed.), Handbook of Industrial and Organizational Psychology: 1069–1124. Chicago: Rand McNally.

Staw, Barry M., and Eugene Szwajkowski
1975 "The scarcity-munificence component of organizational environments and the commission of illegal acts." Administrative Science Quarterly, 20: 345–354.

Stinchcombe, Arthur L., Mary Sexton McDill, and Dollie R. Walker
1968 "Demography of organizations." American Journal of Sociology, 74: 221–229.

Tversky, Amos, and Daniel Kahneman
1974 "Judgment under uncertainty: Heuristics and biases." Science, 185: 1124–1131.

Walker, Jack L.
1969 "The diffusion of innovations among the American states." American Political Science Review, 63: 880–899.

Weick, Karl E.
1976 "Educational organizations as loosely-coupled systems." Administrative Science Quarterly, 21: 1–19.
1977 "Enactment processes in organizations." In Barry M. Staw and Gerald R. Salancik (eds.), New Directions in Organizational Behavior: 267–300. Chicago: St. Clair.
1979 The Social Psychology of Organizing, 2d ed. Reading, MA: Addison-Wesley.

Weiner, Stephen S.
1976 "Participation, deadlines, and choice." In James G. March and Johan P. Olsen (eds.), Ambiguity and Choice in Organizations: 225–250. Bergen, Norway: Universitetsforlaget.

White, Harison C.
1970 Chains of Opportunity: System Models of Mobility in Organizations. Cambridge, MA: Harvard University Press.

Wilson, Edward O.
1975 Sociobiology: The New Synthesis. Cambridge, MA: Harvard University Press.

Wilson, James Q.
1966 "Innovation in organizations: Notes toward a theory." In James D. Thompson (ed.), Approaches to Organizational Design: 193–218. Pittsburgh: University of Pittsburgh Press.

Wright, Sewall
1978 Evolution and Genetics of Populations, Vol. 4. Chicago: University of Chicago Press.

Zald, Mayer N., and Patricia Denton
1963 "From evangelism to general service: The transformation of the YMCA." Administrative Science Quarterly, 8: 214–234.

Can Organizations
Be Effective?

Measuring Organizational Effectiveness in Institutions of Higher Education

Kim Cameron

This study examines the concept of organizational effectiveness in institutions of higher education. Some obstacles to the assessment of organizational effectiveness in higher education are discussed, namely criteria problems and the unique organizational attributes of colleges and universities, and criteria choices addressing these issues are outlined. Criteria were generated from dominant coalition members in six institutions, and nine dimensions of organizational effectiveness were derived. Reliability and validity of the dimensions were tested, and evidence was found for certain patterns of effectiveness across the nine dimensions.•

For the past 50 years, organizational researchers have been concerned with the "effectiveness" of organizations, yet confusion persists regarding what organizational effectiveness is. It has rarely been possible to compare studies of effectiveness, since few have used common criteria for indicating effectiveness (Campbell, 1973; Steers, 1975), and effectiveness has been a label pinned on a wide variety of organizational phenomena from a wide variety of perspectives. Difficulty in empirically assessing organizational effectiveness has arisen because no one ultimate criterion of effectiveness exists. Instead, organizations may pursue multiple and often contradictory goals (Warner, 1967; Perrow, 1970; Hall, 1972, 1978; Dubin, 1976), relevant effectiveness criteria may change over the life cycle of an organization (Yuchtman and Seashore, 1967; Kimberly, 1976; Miles and Cameron, 1977), different constituencies may have particular importance at one time or with regard to certain organizational aspects and not others (Friedlander and Pickle, 1968; Scott, 1977; Barney, 1978), criteria at one organizational level may not be the same as those at another organizational level (Price, 1972; Weick, 1977), and the relationships among various effectiveness dimensions may be difficult to discover (Seashore, Indik, and Georgopolous, 1960; Mahoney and Weitzel, 1969; Kirchhoff, 1975). In short, organizational effectiveness may be typified as being mutable (composed of different criteria at different life stages), comprehensive (including a multiplicity of dimensions), divergent (relating to different constituencies), transpositive (altering relevant criteria when different levels of analysis are used), and complex (having nonparsimonious relationships among dimensions).

A number of excellent papers have recently been published which outline many of the inadequacies and complexities of organizational effectiveness research, especially Goodman and Pennings (1977), and which also provide helpful suggestions for improving research methodology. Fewer empirical studies have been reported, however, which explicitly address those issues. The purpose of this paper is to present the results of an empirical study that attempts to deal directly with several of the important problems currently plaguing organizational effectiveness research.

PROBLEMS IN ASSESSING ORGANIZATIONAL EFFECTIVENESS

Criteria problems are the major obstacles to the empirical assessment of organizational effectiveness, and they are of

•

Special thanks is given to Richard Hackman, Bob Miles, John Kimberly, and Larry Cummings as well as to the ASQ reviewers for their helpful comments and suggestions on earlier versions of this paper. Financial support from the Richard D. Irwin Foundation is also gratefully acknowledged.

1
The following are some of the criticisms which have been advanced concerning the goal approach to effectiveness: (1) There is a focus on official or management goals to the exclusion of the organizational member, organizational constituency, and societal goals (Blau and Scott, 1961; Scriven, 1967). (2) There is neglect of implicit, latent, or informal procedures and goals (Merton, 1957). (3) There is neglect of the multiple and contradictory nature of organizational goals (Rice, 1963). (4) Environmental influences on the organization and its goals are ignored (Lawrence and Lorsch, 1969). (5) Organizational goals are retrospective and serve to justify organizational action, not to direct it (Weich, 1969). (6) Organizational goals change as contextual factors and organizational behavior change (Warner, 1967; Pfiffner, 1977).

604/**Administrative Science Quarterly**

two general kinds. The first relates to the selection of the *type* of criteria indicating effectiveness, and the second relates to the *sources* or originators of the criteria. Problems of criteria type generally focus on (1) the aspect of the organization being considered, e.g., goal accomplishment, resource acquisition, internal processes, (2) the universality or specificity of criteria, (3) the normative or descriptive character of criteria, and (4) the static or dynamic quality of criteria.

Organizational Aspects

Outputs and goal accomplishment are probably the most widely used criteria of effectiveness (Georgopolous and Tannenbaum, 1957; Etzioni, 1964; Price, 1972; Hall, 1978). Not only were the earliest approaches to effectiveness guided by a rationalistic goal model, but recent writers (Price, 1968; Campbell, 1977; Scott, 1977) have continued to advocate accomplishment of goals as the defining characteristic of organizational effectiveness.

Others, however, have pointed out problems with specifying goal accomplishment as the criterion for effectiveness[1] (Merton, 1957; Blau and Scott, 1962; Rice, 1963; Scriven, 1967; Warner, 1967; Pfeffer, 1977). Consequently, alternatives to the goal approach have been proposed.

One alternative to the goal model — the system resource model or the natural systems approach — was introduced by Yuchtman and Seashore (1967). This approach focuses on the interaction of the organization with its environment, and defines organizational effectiveness as the ability of the organization to exploit its environment in the acquisition of scarce and valued resources. Organizational inputs and acquisition of resources replace goals as the primary criteria of effectiveness.[2]

Another approach relies on internal organizational processes as the defining characteristics of effectiveness. Steers (1977: 7), for example, stated, "One solution that at least minimizes many of the obstacles to addressing effectiveness is to view effectiveness in terms of a process instead of an end state." Similarly, Pfeffer (1977) suggested that to study organizational effectiveness, it was necessary to consider the process by which organizations articulate preferences, perceive demands, and make decisions. Organizational development approaches (Beckhard, 1969), organizational health models (Bennis, 1966) or Likert's (1967) "system 4" are variations on the process model in that each uses internal organizational activities or practices as the dominant criteria of effectiveness.[3]

Universality of Criteria

Georgopolous and Tannenbaum (1957), Caplow (1964), Friedlander and Pickle (1968), Mott (1972), and Duncan (1973) are among those who suggest that effective organizations are typified largely by the same criteria (e.g., adaptivity, flexibility, sense of identity, absence of strain, capacity for reality testing capacity) and that research on effectiveness should include the appropriate universal indicators. Others point out that organizations have different characteristics, goals, and constituencies, and that each organization (or each type of organization) requires a unique set of effectiveness criteria

[2]
Criticisms of the system-resource approach include the following: (1) Efficiency and effectiveness are not separated under this approach (Price, 1972). (2) Focusing only on inputs may have damaging effects on outputs (Scott, 1977). (3) This approach assumes that the only valuable aspects of organizations are those which aid further input acquisition (Scott, 1977). (4) Only the organizational directors' viewpoint is taken (Scott, 1977). (5) It is really the same as the goal model since increasing inputs is an organizational operative goal (Kirchhoff, 1977). (6) This approach is inappropriate when considering nonprofit organizations (Molnar and Rogers, 1976).

[3]
Criticisms of the process model include the difficulty of monitoring organizational processes (Dornbusch and Scott, 1975), the expense of gathering data on processes (Scott, 1977), the focus on means to the neglect of ends (Campbell, 1977), and the inaccuracy of most process data. "Almost every individual instance of [process data] reporting has something wrong with it" (Haberstroh, 1965: 182).

(Rice, 1961; Hall, 1972; Scott, 1977). The researcher, in other words, must choose a level of specificity for criteria.

Normative/Descriptive Criteria

A related problem refers to the extent to which the research selects derived or prescribed criteria (Price, 1972). McGregor (1960), Argyris (1962), Bennis (1966), Likert (1967), and others have all indicated what qualities effective organizations should possess, and they approach the problem of effectiveness deductively by stating that the organization must meet these standards to be effective. Other writers have used a descriptive approach in which organizational characteristics or criteria are described (inductively derived) and a priori evaluative standards are avoided (Mahoney et al., 1967, 1969, 1974; Price, 1972 ; Webb, 1974; Steers, 1977). Thompson (1967) has suggested that the difference may be typified as goals for the organization versus goals of the organization.

Dynamic/Static Nature of Criteria

A fourth problem refers to static versus dynamic variables. Most studies of organizational effectiveness include static views of inputs, processes, or outcomes (Mahoney, 1967; Seashore and Yuchtman, 1967; Negandhi and.Reimann, 1973; Hall, 1978) although a few use criteria indicating changes over time (Webb, 1974; Pennings, 1975, 1976). Even when change criteria are included, however, the approach is generally analogous to a blurred snapshot in which indications of movement can be detected than to a motion picture in which the criteria changes can be tracked as they occur. Research conducted by Kimberly (1976) and by Miles and Cameron (1977) are among the few examples of studies in which longitudinal data on effectiveness have been gathered and monitored over time.[4]

Sources of Criteria

Organizational effectiveness criteria are also likely to differ depending on whose viewpoint is taken, that is, on their sources. For example, the appropriate organizational constituency, the level of analysis specified by the criteria, and the use of organizational records versus perceptual reports are all choices facing the researcher.

Constituencies. Effectiveness criteria always represent someone's values and biases, but there are conflicting opinions about who should determine effectiveness criteria and who should provide data for their measurement. Some investigators advocate relying on major decision makers and directors, or the organization's dominant coalition, to generate the criteria and to supply effectiveness information (Yuchtman and Seashore, 1967; Gross 1968; Price, 1968; Pennings and Goodman, 1977). Others suggested that these top administrators or managers have narrow and biased perceptions, so that a broad range of constituencies should be tapped (Pfiffner and Sherwood, 1960; Steers, 1975; Katz and Kahn, 1978). Still another group (Bass, 1952; Friedlander and Pickle, 1968; Reinhardt, 1973; Scott, 1977) points out that constituencies outside the organization are relevant for generating criteria inasmuch as derived goals (Perrow, 1961), "macroquality" criteria (Reinhardt, 1973), or information con-

[4]
Miles and Cameron (1977) in their study of the U.S. tobacco industry, for example, found that one firm, R. J. Reynolds, was most effective if static criteria were used, whereas another firm, Philip Morris, was most effective when dynamic criteria were considered.

cerning the organization's contribution to the supersystem (Katz and Kahn, 1978) are obtained from that group. Cameron (1978a) and Miles (1979) point out that various strategic constituencies exist for every organization, and that ratings from different constituencies may be more or less appropriate depending on the purpose of the evaluation and the domain of effectiveness.

Seashore (1976) and Scott (1977) both suggest that effectiveness criteria differ among separate constituencies because each constituency perpetuates criteria in its own self interest. Friedlander and Pickle (1968) and Molnar and Rogers (1976) found empirical evidence supporting this view.

Level of analysis. Bidwell and Kasarda (1975), Hirsch (1975), and Katz and Kahn (1978) are among those who advocate relying on the supersystem or the external organizational set to determine effectiveness criteria (they define effectiveness as the ability of the organization to adapt to, manipulate, or fulfill expectations of the external environment); whereas writers such as Webb (1974), Scott (1977), Steers (1977), and Weick (1977) suggest that criteria should relate to the organization as a unit (they see effectiveness related to the goals, processes, or characteristics of the organization itself). Pennings and Goodman (1977) propose an approach to effectiveness which focuses on organization subunits (organizational effectiveness is associated with the contributions of and the coordination among subunits), and Kaufman (1960), Argyris (1962), Lawler, Hall, and Oldham (1974) and others, focus on individual performance as criteria of organization effectiveness (organizational effectiveness is assumed to be indicated by individual behaviors and/or satisfaction).

Organizational records versus perceptual criteria. A third source of criteria concerns the use of organizational records instead of personal perceptions. Records are sources in which information concerning effectiveness criteria may be obtained with no direct involvement by organizational members (e.g., archival records such as organizational histories, changes in personnel, stock price changes) whereas personal perceptions are criteria collected directly from organizational members (generally through questionnaires, interviews, or direct observation). Campbell (1977) labeled criteria obtained from organizational records "objective criteria" and asserted that such measures are inappropriate and "preordained to fail in the end." Effectiveness criteria, according to him, should always be subjective. On the other hand, Seashore and Yuchtman (1967) relied totally on organizational records and argued that these were the most appropriate sources. Economists have generally relied on objective sources for criteria, whereas industrial and organizational psychologists have more often used perceptions. Studies such as those done by Pennings (1975, 1976) have included both objective and perceptual indicators.

Figure 1 compares the types and sources of effectiveness criteria which were selected in 20 recent empirical studies of organizational effectiveness. Empirical studies have been plotted in the figure based on the sources used to assess criteria and the types of criteria included in the investigation. The figure points out the variety of criteria choices made by researchers, since only 9 of 43 cells contain overlapping choices. Most empirical investigations, in other words, have used sources and types of effectiveness criteria which are not comparable with other empirical investigations. Furthermore, the large number of blank cells in the figure illustrates the difficulty of providing a complete picture of organizational effectiveness in any one study as well as the lack of information on a large number of possible criteria types. Organizational effectiveness criteria on one level of analysis, for example, may be different from criteria on other levels. Not only do the pragmatics of research constrain the types and sources of criteria that can be considered, but some choices of criteria may be more appropriate in one type of organization than in another (Molnar and Rogers, 1976).

In institutions of higher education, for example, unique organizational characteristics have presented special problems

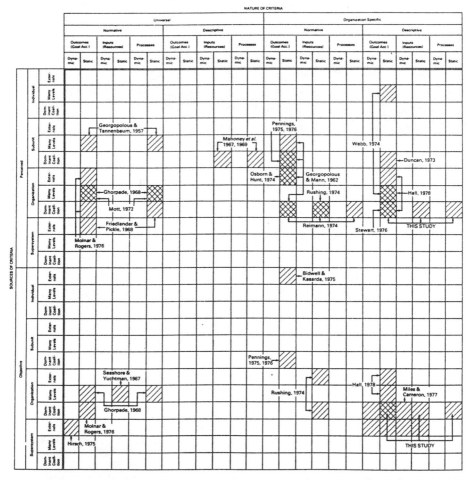

Figure 1. Selections of sources and types of criteria for 21 emperical studies of organizational effectiveness.

404

for researchers in selecting and assessing criteria for organizational effectiveness. Choices regarding the types and sources of criteria illustrated in Figure 1 have been particularly difficult to make in studying these organizations, so that the characteristics of the institutions as well as problems associated with the concept of organizational effectiveness have served as obstacles to empirical assessment of effectiveness in colleges and universities. In fact, almost no studies have been conducted to measure organizational effectiveness in institutions of higher education.

Although some instruments, such as the Educational Testing Service's *Institutional Functioning Inventory* (1970), Pace's *College and University Environment Scales* (1969), or WICHE's Management Information System materials have been widely distributed and used, none of these instruments purported to assess criteria of organizational effectiveness. Several researchers have conducted studies of quality of graduate programs (Cartter 1966, 1977; Blau and Margulis, 1973), while others have investigated objective correlates of those quality ratings (Beyer and Snipper, 1974). Still other researchers have focused on individual variables such as student achievement, teaching processes, and learning climates (Astin, 1968, 1971, 1977; Feldman and Newcomb, 1969; Bowen, 1977), but colleges and universities as organizations were not the primary focus in these studies. Clark (1970) and Blau (1973) reported two important empirical studies of colleges as organizations, but neither was interested in assessments of effectiveness per se.

Problems in Assessing Effectiveness in Higher Education

Some formidable problems stand as obstacles to the selection and assessment of criteria of effectiveness in institutions of higher education. First, it is difficult to specify concrete, measurable goals and outcomes. Some researchers have lamented the "complexity, diffuseness, ambiguity, and changeability" and typify educational goals and outcomes (National Institute of Education, 1975), and some have suggested that without meaningful and measurable objectives, it is impossible to assess the effectiveness of higher education (Warner and Havens, 1968; Chickering, 1971; Hayman and Stenner, 1971). Barro (1973), for example, stated that because information on effectiveness is not usually collected by colleges and universities, prospects for the evaluation of effectiveness "do not seem very good," and Hutchins (1977: 5) asserted:

The only way you can criticize a university, the only way you can appraise it, the only way you can determine whether it's good or bad or medium or indifferent, is to know what it's about, what it's supposed to be, what it's supposed to be doing. If you don't know these things, you haven't any standards of criticism . . . [Universities] haven't any very clear ideas of what they're doing or why. They don't even know what they are.

Second, the evaluation of institutional effectiveness engenders skepticism and defensiveness in the academic community. Several commentators (Dressel, 1972; Barro, 1973; Bowen, 1973) hypothesized that calls for evaluations of effectiveness or institutional accountability are seen as the public trying to scrutinize and control higher education, or as the existence of defects that need to be corrected. The

405

implication of pressures to evaluate seems to be that freedom to experiment and innovate, to risk failure, or to establish unique quality standards is no longer the prerogative
of the institution and that evaluations restrict academic
freedom.

Individual institutions, furthermore, tend to view themselves
as having unique characteristics and goals, and as not being
comparable to other institutions. Dressel's (1971: 6, 7) report of an administrator's position on evaluation is illustrative
of the approach taken by many administrators in higher
education:

This evaluation will be a waste of time, for either it will demonstrate that the program is excellent or that it is defective in some
sense. In the first case it is a waste of time because we already
know that it's a good program, and in the second, it's a waste of
time because we would not believe any evidence of weakness.

Third, the financial concerns of colleges and universities
have led to research on efficiency rather than on effectiveness. Meeth (1974) suggested that the central concern of
higher education in the 1970s has been how to provide
quality education for less money by focusing on efficiency.
Efficiency has generally been defined as the ratio of costs
to some output, or as the amount of energy lost in the
production of organizational output (Katz and Kahn, 1978). In
higher education, efficiency has most often been measured
by indicators such as costs per student, student-faculty
ratios, costs per faculty member, costs per square foot, etc.
(Bowen and Douglas, 1971; O'Neill, 1971; Mood et al.,
1972; Meeth, 1974; Hartmark, 1975). These criteria of efficiency, while being well used, are not sufficient for understanding institutional success inasmuch as educational institutions must not only demonstrate efficiency, i.e., using
resources with little waste, but they must also be able to
demonstrate the effective use of resources as well. Fincher
(1972) pointed out that efficiency and effectiveness could
not be assessed by the same criteria, and more emphasis
was needed on criteria of effectiveness.

Finally, even the applicability of the concept of organizational
effectiveness to colleges and universities has been questioned, as by writers who have applied the terms "organized
anarchy" or "loosely coupled system" to colleges and universities (Cohen and March, 1974; Weick, 1976). March and
Olson (1976: 176), for example, have suggested that organizations in higher education are "complex 'garbage cans' into
which a striking variety of problems, solutions, and participants may be dumped." Any attempt to make statements
about the effectiveness of such organizations, therefore, is
seen as tenuous, since the rules, goals, and choices operating within these organizations are ambiguous, changing, and
often not recognized.

It has been found (Cameron, 1978b), however, that institutions of higher education vary on a continuum from loose
coupling, i.e., organized anarchies, to tight coupling i.e.,
structured bureaucracies. Some colleges for example, maintain a relatively homogeneous structure and operation with
many effectiveness criteria being relevant for the subsystems within the institution. In others, common criteria are
difficult to find since subsystems are mostly autonomous.

The problem of studying organizational effectiveness in organizations which vary on the loosely coupled to tightly coupled continuum lies in identifying a core group of effectiveness criteria that are relevant to organizational members, applicable across subunits, and comparable across institutions. The criteria choices made in this study were oriented toward identifying such criteria.

CRITERIA CHOICES

Selections of Criteria

The problem of ambiguity and diffuseness of goals in colleges and universities was addressed by focusing on organizational characteristics rather than on goals, since it seemed unlikely that goals or outcomes were made operational in most institutions. Both objective and perceptual criteria were obtained from some institutions of higher education, and anonymity for both institutions and individuals was guaranteed in an attempt to reduce defensiveness and reporting bias. The study focused on the organizational level, since it has been the most neglected in research on higher education, and because it would allow for comparisons among institutions. Criteria specifically related to institutions of higher education were used instead of universal criteria applicable to all types of organizations. The generality of criteria often resulting from a universalistic approach and the unique organizational features of colleges and universities made this choice seem reasonable. Since there is no precedent for criteria of effectiveness in institutions of higher education, this study used an inductive approach in generating them rather than prescribing a priori standards. And, although indications of organizational change over time were sought as criteria, the study was not longitudinal, and the effectiveness indicators are best typified as static rather than dynamic. Figure 1 points out where this study falls in relation to other empirical investigations of effectiveness.

Many of the criteria used to assess organizational effectiveness were initially generated from a search of the literature.[5] Approximately 130 variables emerged from examining this literature, and they provided a framework from which interviews were later conducted with individuals at several colleges and universities.

Selections of Constituency

The strategic constituency chosen to be interviewed in deriving the effectiveness criteria for this study was the internal dominant coalition. The internal dominant coalition refers to representatives of the major subunits or interest groups within the college or university, who influence the direction and functioning of the organization (Thompson, 1967). In the institutions in this study, this included academic, financial, general, and student affairs administrators, deans, and heads of academic departments.[6] Only formal position holders or formal representatives were included in defining the dominant coalition. Whereas informal leaders or charismatic personalities may have an influence on organizational direction, resource allocation, or functioning, it is extremely difficult to identify who those individuals are; therefore, formal position

[5]
Several sources of organizational effectiveness criteria proved to be of particular value, among which were Price (1968), Pace (1969), the *Institutional Functioning Inventory* (1970), Mott (1972), Blau (1973), Campbell (1973, 1974), Balderston (1974), Micek and Wallhaus (1974), Hartmark (1975), the *Michigan Survey Research Center Assessment Package* (1975), National Institute of Education Reports (1975), and Steers (1975).

[6]
Student representatives were not included in the study's dominant coalition because (1) students are not generally in a position to directly influence the direction and functioning of the institution; (2) they generally have more limited information about the overall institution than do other dominant coalition members; (3) they have been found in other studies not to differ significantly in their perceptions of the institution from faculty members or administrators (Educational Testing Service, 1970); and most importantly, (4) constraints on time and money prohibited a representative sample from being gathered from relevant student groups on various campuses.

holders were relied upon as being representative.

The dominant coalition was selected first because several writers (Yuchtman and Seashore, 1967; Price, 1972; Pennings and Goodman, 1977) argued that the organization's major decision makers or the dominant coalition should be the sources of criteria for organizational effectiveness and their measurement, since they comprised the resource allocators, the determiners of organizational policy, and the explicators of organizational goals. Thompson (1967) suggested that the dominant coalition was the most likely group to make specific both the cause and effect relationships within an organization and the hierarchy of outcomes to be preferred. Furthermore, as Pennings and Goodman (1977:152) noted, because members of the dominant coalition served as the representatives in the bargaining process within an organization, "consensus among members of the dominant coalition can be employed as a vehicle for obtaining effectiveness data." Van de Ven (1977) suggested, further, that solving the wrong problem with the right methods can be avoided only if users of information about organizational effectiveness are included as sources. Members of the dominant coalition are among the major users of information about organizational effectiveness.

Second, members of the dominant coalition were assumed to be a knowledgeable source about each of the organizational aspects under investigation at the institutional level. The mutability, comprehensiveness, divergence, transpositiveness, and complexity of organizational effectiveness require that a limited domain of effectiveness be specified in evaluations, or that a specific operationalization of the concept be determined. This domain of effectiveness is defined by the aspects of the organization being studied coupled with the level of analysis used (Cameron, 1978a). In this study, the focus was limited to institutional characteristics relating to acquisition of resources, the vitality and viablility of internal processes and practices, and organizational outcomes and emphases. The dominant coalition is likely to be a more reliable source of information for these organizational aspects than other constituencies — for example, most external constituencies.

Selections of Institutions

It was assumed that in large, diverse institutions, dominant coalition members had less college-wide information than in smaller institutions because of the size and autonomy of departments and programs. Thompson (1967) argued that dominant coalition members, as representatives in the internal organizational negotiations, became exposed to organization-wide information as they functioned in their roles, and he suggested that more information was available to them when the dominant coalition was smaller.

The size of the institutions included was therefore limited to those with under 10,000 undergraduate students, and the focus of the study was the *undergraduate* part of the institutions. These constraints eliminated from consideration large, loosely coupled universities having many semi-autonomous professional schools from the study and helped increase the likelihood that respondents would have information related to the overall organizational level.

METHOD

Interviews were conducted with individuals associated with a variety of institutions of higher education to ensure that the effectiveness criteria had relevance for colleges and universities and that the criteria could be measured. Separate date were collected in two studies. The first study represented an initial attempt to assess the reliability and validity of the effectiveness criteria through questionnaires and interviews. The second study was designed primarily to effect refinements and improvements in the instruments and to improve their psychometric properties.

Institutional Sample

The first study included four colleges in New England with two more schools added in the second study. Two institutions were public and four were private, and their undergraduate enrollments ranged from approximately 1,000 to approximately 10,000. Two institutions were primarily commuter schools, with the others being mostly residential; four had unionized faculties, while two did not; and one of the institutions was in a rural setting, while the other five were in or near cities with a population of over 100,000.

Interviews to Derive Dimensions

Four or five top administrators at six colleges in the northeastern United States along with about ten faculty members were interviewed. They were usually the provost or academic vice-president, the president, the financial or administrative vice-president, the dean of student affairs, an assistant to the president or a director of institutional research and one or two department heads on each campus. Individuals were asked to respond to questions, including the following:

1. What organizational characteristics do effective colleges possess?

2. What is it at this institution that makes a difference in terms of its effectiveness?

3. What would have to change in order to make this institution more effective?

4. Think of an institution of higher education that you judge to be effective. What is it that makes that institution effective?

5. Of the 130 or so items generated from the literature, which ones are not relevant to the effectiveness of this school?

6. Of the 130 items, which ones are not measurable or for which are data not available?

Interviews lasted from one and one half to four hours, and special emphasis was placed on criteria relating to the organizational level of analysis. For example, references to individuals or to specific departments or programs were avoided; instead, criteria were sought that characterized the entire institution. Therefore, the success of the president's personal leadership style or the characteristics of a unique program in one department were not generally included, whereas the institution's orientation toward participatory decision making involving the faculty, or the emphasis it placed on developing community-oriented programs were. Some of the effectiveness criteria resulting from the interviews did relate to *aggregates* of individuals, e.g., student educational satisfaction, but the focus in these criteria tended to be on the entire organization rather than on one institutional subunit.

Certain clusters of items became apparent as the criteria emerged from the interviews, and on an a priori, intuitive basis, nine separate groupings of criteria were formed. As a rationale for this strategy of combining criteria into dimensions on an intuitive basis, Campbell (1977: 23) stated, "Criterion combination quite properly is based on value judgments, and there is no algorithm or higher order truth to which we can appeal." Several alternative groupings were tried but the one used here represents the only grouping that encompassed all the effectiveness criteria generated from the interviews.

These nine dimensions represented conceptually different constructs, although they were not assumed to be independent. The nine effectiveness dimensions and the criteria they encompassed were:

1. Student educational satisfaction — criteria indicated the degree of satisfaction of students with their educational experiences at the institution.

2. Student academic development — criteria indicated the extent of academic attainment, growth, and progress of students at the institution.

3. Student career development — criteria indicated the extent of occupational development of students, and the emphasis on career development and the opportunities for career development provided by the institution.

4. Student personal development — criteria indicated student development in nonacademic, noncareer oriented areas, e.g., socially, emotionally, or culturally, and the emphasis on personal development and opportunities provided by the institution for personal development.

5. Faculty and administrator employment satisfaction — criteria indicated satisfaction of faculty members and administrators with jobs and employment at the institution.

6. Professional development and quality of the faculty — criteria indicated the extent of professional attainment and development of the faculty, and the amount of stimulation toward professional development provided by the institution.

7. Systems openness and community interaction — criteria indicated the emphasis placed on interaction with, adaptation to, and service in the external environment.

8. Ability to acquire resources — criteria indicated the ability of the institution to acquire resources from the external environment, such as good students and faculty, financial support, etc.

9. Organizational health — criteria indicated benevolence, vitality, and viability in the internal processes and practices at the institution.

Instruments

Two types of instruments were developed to measure the criteria in the nine dimensions. The first was a questionnaire asking respondents to describe the extent to which their college possessed certain organizational characteristics (effectiveness criteria). Questionnaire items centered mostly on ratings of organizational traits (e.g., how much emphasis was given to college-community relations?) rather than on personal feelings or affect (e.g., how do you like this school?), in order to reduce the possibility of obtaining highly intercorrelated perceptions all related to the general satisfaction of respondents. Appendix A lists the questionnaire items assessing the effectiveness dimensions.

The second instrument included a set of questions designed to obtain objective data from the records of each institution. Appendix A also lists these items for the eight dimensions measured. These objective data were provided by the academic vice-president or provost, the financial vice-president, the dean of students, the director of institutional research, the director of development, or other appropriate administrators at each institution. The reason for developing both objective and perceived instruments was to provide data for testing the external validity of the dimensions, since there was no way to determine the amount of bias existing in the ratings of the dominant coalition members without such a test.

A modified form of Cattell's (1966) "marker item" procedure was used to guide the additions and refinements made to the questionnaire items for the second study. This procedure suggests that items be chosen which have meaning central to the concept being measured, i.e., face validity, and that overlap should occur with other criteria known to be indicators of the concept. Items were added to several of the scales, consequently, in order to make certain that the central concept indicated by the title of the effectiveness dimension was being measured. These new items were similar to Cattell's marker items. Mean within-dimension correlations ranged from .491 to .636 for the marker items, providing evidence that the central meanings of the dimensions, as specified by their titles, were being tapped.

Respondent Sample

The questionnaires were mailed, under a covering letter signed by the president or academic vice-president, to approximately 75 administrators and academic department heads at each of the six institutions. Anonymity for all respondents and institutions was guaranteed. Reports of the results of the study were promised to each participating institution, but respondents and institutional names were kept confidential. Respondents to the questionnaire were divided into five job categories: general, academic, financial, and student affairs administrators, and academic department heads. About half of the respondents were faculty members and about half were administrators. Usable questionnaires returned in the first study were 191 (70 percent); 134 (72 percent) were returned in the second study. The frequencies of returns for the five respondent categories are shown in Table 1.

Analysis

At least two different strategies were possible for analyzing the data obtained from these dominant coalition members. One was to emphasize the reliability or internal consistency of measures of the central concepts in the nine effectiveness dimensions, and the other was to ensure the inclusion

411

Table 1

Response Rates for Five Categories of Respondents in Six Institutions

| | Responses* | | | |
| | Study 1 | | Study 2 | |
Job Category	N	%	N	%
Administrators				
General	23	82	20	77
Academic	37	70	15	68
Financial	16	70	7	54
Student affairs	34	85	32	70
Academic department head	81	62	60	77
Total	191	70	134	72

*
Responses across institutions ranged from 54% to 84%.

of all variables generated by the interviews regardless of their relationships to the nine central concepts. The former strategy was adopted because, first, inasmuch as reliability is a prerequisite for validity (Nunnally, 1967; Kerlinger, 1973), it was important for the internal consistency (reliability) of the criteria to be demonstrated in order that the effectiveness dimensions could be validated. Since the questionnaire items were constructed to assess the criteria comprising the dimensions, if it was found that one of the items had low internal consistency in relation to other items thought to measure the same dimension, the item was dropped since there was no way to determine whether the variance in the item was attributable to another construct being assessed (trait variance) or to method or to random error. It was thought more important to demonstrate the reliability of the measures than to focus solely on the comprehensiveness of the criteria. This is similar to the strategies used by Mahoney (1967) and by Seashore and Yuchtman (1967) in the generation of their effectiveness criteria.

Second, it had been determined that institutional data were not available for every single criterion that emerged from the interviews. Therefore, unless a large number of questionnaire items turned out to be unrelated to the nine underlying dimensions, it was appropriate for reasons of meaningfulness and parsimony to concentrate on the nine central concepts indicated by the dimension titles.

RESULTS

Internal Consistency and Discriminant Validity

Eight of the questionnaire items in the first study were found to have low correlations within their own effectiveness dimension as well as with items from the other eight effectiveness dimensions. These eight items, which had an average intrascale correlation below .20, included quality of written work of students, attrition of students because of too few extracurricular activities, faculty grievances, attrition of faculty because of dissatisfaction, proportion of the budget available for professional development, work efficiency, and pay satisfaction. Moreover, there were no high intercorrelations among the eight items themselves; consequently, they were not included in other statistical

Table 2

Between-Dimension and Between-Item Correlations for the Nine Effectiveness Dimensions

	No. of items	$\bar{x}$	s.d.	Mean Item Correlations Inside	Outside	Dimensions† 1	2	3	4	5	6	7	8	9
†1.	4	3.78	.8	.37	.23•	(.70)‡								
	3	2.84	.7	.36	.29	(.63)								
2.	3	4.79	1.0	.38	.20•	.37	(.65)							
	5	3.79	1.0	.40	.26	.56	(.77)							
3.	4	3.65	.9	.27	.14	.33	.22	(.60)						
	5	4.27	1.0	.33	−.01•••	.05	−.20	(.71)						
4.	3	4.24	.9	.63	.13•••	.40	.54	.23	(.66)					
	4	3.23	1.2	.61	.29•••	.56	.39	−.02	(.86)					
5.	6	3.94	1.1	.40	.21••	.49	.36	.31	.34	(.91)				
	6	4.74	1.5	.57	.30•••	.60	.39	.05	.36	(.89)				
6.	4	4.62	.9	.31	.17•	.31	.32	.25	.32	.47	(.73)			
	5	4.48	1.1	.50	.24••	.42	.43	.02	.37	.37	(.83)			
7.	5	3.52	1.2	.47	.24••	.41	.33	.28	.34	.50	.46	(.90)		
	5	3.96	1.2	.51	.27••	.44	.46	.13	.55	.43	.45	(.84)		
8.	5	4.79	1.0	.46	.26••	.57	.56	.33	.46	.54	.42	.47	(.81)	
	6	4.49	1.1	.50	.33•	.68	.66	−.04	.59	.58	.55	.59	(.86)	
9.	15	3.79	1.0	.46	.23•••	.48	.28	.34	.39	.59	.41	.55	.50	(.92)
	17	3.91	1.2	.40	.30	.65	.57	−.10	.52	.69	.49	.56	.69	(.93)

•
Significant differences between inside and outside correlations at the $p<.05$ level.
••
Significant differences between inside and outside correlations at the $p<.01$ level.
•••
Significant differences between inside and outside correlations at the $p<.001$ level.

†
1. Student Educational Satisfaction; 2. Student Academic Development; 3. Student Career Development; 4. Student Personal Development; 5. Faculty and Administrator Employment Satisfaction; 6. Professional Development and Quality of the Faculty; 7. System Openness and Community Interaction; 8. Ability to Acquire Resources; 9. Organizational Health.

‡
Numbers in parentheses are reliability coefficients.

Note: The top numbers for each dimension refer to the first study, and the bottom numbers refer to the second study.

analyses of the dimensions. Coefficient alpha was applied to test the internal consistency reliability of the effectiveness dimensions and acceptable levels of reliability were found for each of them. Nunnally (1967) suggested that for exploratory research, a reliability of between .50 and .60 was acceptable, and in the first study the lowest reliability coefficient among the nine effectiveness dimensions was .601, while the highest was .928. In the second study, reliability coefficients ranged from .628 to .924. The relatively high correlations of the marker items in the second study with the appropriate effectiveness dimensions also provided some evidence for the face validity of the dimensions. The internal consistency reliability for each of the dimensions is shown in Table 2.

Factor analytic procedures also largely confirmed the existence of the dimensions. Oblique, varimax, and quartimax rotations were used in both studies, and the number of factors was limited to between six and twelve to try to uncover any underlying dimensions. Appendices B and C contain the factors produced by an orthogonal rotation pattern in which an eigenvalue of 1.0 specified the number of factors. In the first study, two of the effectiveness dimensions loaded on the same factor and two other dimensions split into two factors. After several questionnaire items were reworded to improve their meaningfulness and clarity for respondents, the second study produced a single factor for each of the dimensions except Student Educational Satisfaction, which did not load on any of the factors. Furthermore, a nine-factor rotation still did not produce a factor for this dimension.

Average within-dimensions correlations for each item were compared to the mean correlations of each item with all items outside its own effectiveness dimension as one test of the discriminant validity of the items. It was found that within-dimension mean correlations were higher than the mean outside correlations for every item except one in the first study and for all items in the second study. The single item in the first study (opportunities for personal development) was eliminated from further analysis. As Table 2 indicates, this finding confirmed that the dimensions were composed of items with high internal consistency and that they were distinguishable one from another. Also, after the median correlation coefficient for all items within a dimension was computed, correlations between the dimension and all outside items were inspected to determine overlapping among items. The purpose was to uncover the effectiveness items that correlated highly with more than one dimension and to determine which dimensions had overlapping items. Several items were slightly reworded prior to the second study as a result of this analysis in order to help clarify the conceptual differences among the effectiveness dimensions for future respondents.

The Student Educational Satisfaction dimension and the Organizational Health dimension in the second study were found to contain discriminating items, but the dimensions taken as a whole were weak in discriminant validity. Table 2 demonstrates, for example, that mean within-dimension correlations were not significantly higher than were correlations outside the dimension for either Student Educational Satisfaction or for Organizational Health. Whereas correlations within dimensions were higher in value for each of these two dimensions, an insignificant t-test indicated a relatively high intercorrelation between these two dimensions and others.

Between-School and Between-Job Differences

Analyses of variance were performed to determine whether the effectiveness dimensions differentiated among the schools and among the respondent groups. For the scales to be employable in assessments of effectiveness, there needed to be some significant differences among the institutions. If all institutions scored the same on the nine effectiveness dimensions, the instruments would be of no use in assessing relative effectiveness in institutions of higher education. Furthermore, one method of testing construct validity is to demonstrate differences among groups expected to score differently on a measure (Cronbach and Meehl, 1955).

The five respondent job categories were also analyzed to determine if differences among them existed. Multivariate and univariate analysis of variance procedures were used to test for significant effects.

The results, summarized in Table 3, suggest that institutional affiliations do have a significant effect on responses for combined organizational effectiveness (MANOVA $p < .001$), but that the job or position held is not as important. That is, in both studies, the differences are significant among the means of the institutions but not for the five job categories. In the first study, the MANOVA F-test based on Wilks' lambda for job resulted in a significance level of $p < .03$ while the theta (θ) value, normally a more conservative test, resulted in a significance level of greater than .05. No statistical significance for job resulted in the second study.

Table 3

Multivariate and Univariate Analysis of Variance for the Effectiveness Dimensions

		Institution		Job		Interaction Institution X Job	
		F	θ	F	θ	F	θ
MANOVA†		4.76•••	.281•••	1.50•	.156	1.06	.174
		19.06•••	.282•••	1.08	.127	1.37	.228

Dimension	Multiple R^2	Institution		Job		Interaction Institution X Job
		F	η^2	F	η^2	F
1. Student educational satisfaction	.124	6.08•••	.09	1.71	.04	1.29
	.478	23.97•••	.39	3.38••	.30	4.34
2. Student academic development	.185	9.73•••	.13	3.39•	.06	1.51
	.517	44.55•••	.50	.75	.12	2.50•
3 Student career development	.159	9.18•••	.12	2.01	.03	.91
	.609	70.34•••	.60	.32	.15	1.98
4. Student personal development	.087	2.61•	.03	2.91•	.05	2.05
	.366	12.56•••	.60	1.24	.22	2.53•
5. Faculty and administrator employment satisfaction	.082	4.11••	.07	.62	.02	1.41
	4.080	18.34•••	.37	1.24	.22	2.53•
6. Professional development and quality of faculty	.162	9.00•••	.14	1.81	.03	.43
	.349	15.70•••	.34	.20	.11	1.53
7. System openness and community interaction	.229	14.73•••	.20	1.52	.05	1.57
	.282	3.54•	.15	2.04	.23	2.23
8. Ability to acquire resources	.207	11.53•••	.17	2.19	.06	1.06
	.552	52.65•••	.54	.51	.14	2.18
9. Organizational health	.223	13.38•••	.18	2.31	.05	1.00
	.559	51.41•••	.52	4.79•••	.35	4.89•••

•
$p<.05$
••
$p<.01$
•••
$p<.001$
†
Degrees of freedom were 27 and 476 for institution, 36 and 612 for job, and 108 and 1199 for the interaction in the first study, and 9 and 111 for institution, 36 and 417 for job, and 36 and 417 for the interaction in the second study.
Note: The top numbers for each dimension refer to the first study, and the bottom numbers refer to the second study.

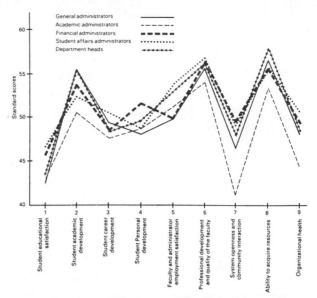

Figure 2. Organizational effectiveness profiles for the 5 job categories.

Using univariate ANOVA procedures for each separate effectiveness dimension showed that the employing institution had a significant effect in determining the perceptions of the respondents for every dimension ($p < .01$). The amount of variance accounted for among the dimensions by this institutional factor (η^2) ranged from 3 percent to 20 percent in the first study and 15 percent to 60 percent in the second

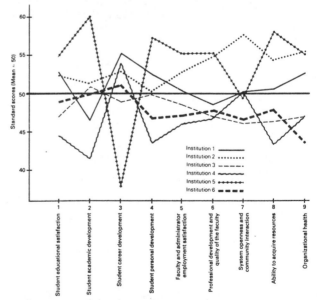

Figure 3. Organizational effectiveness profiles for the 6 institutions.

416

study. On the other hand, the job or position of the respondent had significant effects at the $p < .05$ level for only two effectiveness dimensions: Student Academic Development and Student Personal Development in the first study, and Student Education Satisfaction and Organizational Health in the second study. The interaction of the school and the job category was significant ($p < .05$) only for Student Personal Development in the first study and for four dimensions in the second study.

A profile analysis, shown in Figure 2, also confirmed the similarity of the different job categories. Mean scores for each respondent group included in the six institutions were plotted across the nine dimensions of effectiveness and tested for differences in levels (Nunnally, 1967). According to Van de Geer (1971), the MANOVA procedure had already tested for differences in parallelism. None of the respondent group pairs differed significantly (.50) in the levels of their ratings, so that it can be concluded that the dominant coalition members in these institutions had similar perceptions of effectiveness.

A second profile analysis plotting institutional means on the nine effectiveness dimensions revealed that the institutions not only varied significantly in their effectiveness profiles (significant differences exist among at least two of the institutions on every dimension), but that certain patterns of organizational effectiveness could be distinguished. Institution 5, for example, showed high effectiveness on all the dimensions except Student Career Development and System Openness and Community Interaction. This may indicate a tendency away from occupational and community involvement — an external emphasis — by this institution. Instituteness was achieved in the career and community oriented dimensions with low effectiveness scores on other dimensions. This occupational and community-oriented success may be somewhat surprising to the institution since the catalogues of each of all six institutions claimed a liberal arts undergraduate emphasis.

Institution 1 showed relatively high effectiveness on dimensions related to satisfaction and organizational morale, i.e., Student Educational Satisfaction, Faculty and Administrator Employment Satisfaction, and Organizational Health, while the academically oriented dimensions tended to be low, i.e., Student Academic Development and Professional Development and Quality of the Faculty. Institution 3, on the other hand, had relatively high effectiveness in Student Academic Development but was less effective in most other areas. Institution 2 had consistently high scores on the dimensions with the highest relative effectiveness being on the nonstudent-oriented dimensions. Institution 6 was almost exactly opposite to that pattern by being consistently low on the effectiveness dimensions but with the highest relative effectiveness being on the student oriented dimensions.

These results suggest that the institutions can be distinguished, on the basis of their effectiveness profiles, as those having very high or very low effectiveness on external dimensions (institutions 4 and 5), those with very high or low effectiveness on morale dimensions (institutions 1 and 3),

417

and as those having high or low effectiveness on student oriented dimensions (institutions 2 and 6). Furthermore, whereas institutional effectiveness profiles differ significantly from one another and relative strengths and weaknesses are evident, some institutions do achieve higher overall effectiveness than others.

The analyses of these two studies indicated that the hypothesized dimensions had acceptable reliability and that they were useful in differentiating among colleges and universities for organizational effectiveness. Each institution was found to vary uniquely across the nine effectiveness dimensions, although certain patterns of effectiveness seemed to emerge. Furthermore, scores on the dimension were generally not significantly affected by different respondent categories.

Evidence for Validity

Supporting evidence for internal consistency and discriminant validity in these studies still left questions unanswered about the external validity and construct validity of the effectiveness dimensions. There was a dilemma, however, in attempting to deal with validity. On the one hand, no generally accepted criteria exist against which to compare these perceptual dimensions; therefore, testing for concurrent or criterion validity was impossible. On the other hand, construct validity — an approach to validity used when no valid external criteria are available (Cronbach and Meehl, 1955) — was similarly questionable since, as Nunnally (1967) indicated, proof of construct validity comes from determining the extent to which measures of a construct fit into a network of expected relations. Inasmuch as organizational effectiveness in institutions of higher education has never been measured, no theoretical or predictable network of relationships has been possible between effectiveness of colleges and universities — particularly these nine dimensions — and other constructs. Campbell (1973) pointed out that much of the explanatory research on organizational effectiveness had been done using individual behavior or performance. Very few studies have used organizational units as degrees of freedom. Consequently, there is no well-defined nomological network for organizational effectiveness in general, let alone college and university effectiveness. This study was designed to begin the development of a network.

Some indications of validity in this research project were needed, nevertheless, in order that followup research, in which explanatory data could be obtained and related to the effectiveness constructs, would prove meaningful and worthwhile. Two separate pieces of evidence were found which suggested that the effectiveness dimensions had some external and construct validity.

Objective indicators of the effectiveness dimensions had been obtained from each of the six institutions, and it was hypothesized that positive correlations between the two sets of data would provide some evidence for the external validity of the perceptual measures. Table 4 reports the nonparametric rank order correlations between the objective data and the perceptual ratings.

Table 4

Rank-Order Correlations Between Objective and Perceptual Measures of the Effectiveness Dimensions

Dimension	r	$p<$
1. Student educational satisfaction	.600	.10
2. Student academic development	.829	.02
3. Student career development	−.657	.08
4. Student personal development	.771	.04
5. Faculty and administrator employment satisfaction	.314	.27
6. Professional development and quality of the faculty	.943	.002
7. System openness and community interaction	−.600	.10
8. Ability to acquire resources	.714	.05
9. Organizational health	No objective data collected	

Moderate to high positive correlations for all but two of the effectiveness dimensions provided some support for external validity, although two of the dimensions had, unexpectedly, negative correlations indicating that either the objectives measures or the perceptual measures were faulty, that different and negatively correlated concepts were being assessed, that the concepts being measured were not unidimensional and had complex relationships with each other, or that the constructs being measured in the two effectiveness dimensions were confusing to respondents.

There was no sure way to determine the reason for the negative correlations in these two studies, particularly given the small sample, but a close examination of the objective and perceptual items for the eight dimensions did suggest that two separate concepts may have been assessed. In the case of Student Career Development, objective items focused on vocational counseling and work study, whereas the perceived items emphasized successful placement of students in desired post-college employment and the offering of a career oriented curriculum. The perceived items relating to Systems Openness and Community Interaction dealt mainly with community and professional activities of employees, whereas the objective items focused on continuing education and extension programs. Close examination of the items also revealed, however, that other dimensions had the same problem. That is, differences in objective and perceptual concepts could be hypothesized for almost all of the dimensions. For example, the objective measures for the Student Academic Development dimension seemed to emphasize continued academic attainment after leaving the institution whereas the perceptual measures emphasized academic development of students within the institution. Yet, the correlation coefficient for that dimension was high and positive.

This is not an unusual difficulty when comparing objective and perceptual measures, and similar problems have been found in relation to other concepts, most notably environmental uncertainty (Tosi, Aldag, and Storey, 1973; Downey, Hellreigel, and Slocum, 1975). Researchers on environmental

419

uncertainty have generally concluded that a choice should be made between the two types of measures and comparisons between them avoided. The dilemma in this study was that some evidence of external validity was needed to help determine the amount of bias existing in the perceptual ratings, yet comparisons with the objective data was tenuous. Limited support for external validity seemed to be justified for some of the dimensions since what appeared to be related concepts were being assessed by two types of measures, but no definitive conclusions can be drawn.

There is evidence that the objective measures of effectiveness in this research, furthermore, were not as reliable as would have been desirable. It was found, for example, that relatively little objective data were available on inputs, processes, and outcomes at the six institutions studied. Data were often in confidential files, in several offices, or unavailable altogether. Answers to many of the items, consequently, were guesses by the responding administrator, particularly when the data were not readily available or had not been centrally compiled. This objective data gathering made it understandable, in fact, why most studies of higher education avoid multivariate objective data on effectiveness and rely instead on cost ratios.

A second indication of validity was found by comparing scores on the nine effectiveness dimensions of institutions with unionized faculties and those without a union. Figure 3 shows that the institutions with a faculty union (institutions 1, 3, 4, and 6) scored lower than each institution without a unionized faculty (institutions 2 and 5) on four of the effectiveness dimensions: Faculty and Administrator Employment Satisfaction, Professional Development and Quality of the Faculty, Ability to Acquire Resources, and Organizational Health. These findings are consistent with research conducted by Duryea et al. (1973), Hedgepeth (1974), Garbarino (1975), Kemerer and Baldridge (1975), and others, which found lower faculty satisfaction, more emphasis on collective bargaining issues and less on faculty concerns, feelings of powerlessness or of being externally controlled, and less collegiality and organizational benevolence in unionized institutions. In terms of construct validity, these relationships between the effectiveness dimensions and other external concepts, i.e., faculty unionism, in predictable directions provides the beginnings of a nomological network that can be expanded with additional research.

CONCLUSION

Multidomain Character of Effectiveness.

Much of the lack of cumulativeness in past effectiveness research has resulted from confusion over what conceptual referent or effectiveness domain has been applied when referring to organizational effectiveness, and from the wide variety of types and sources of criteria used to indicate effectiveness. The emphasis on one best definition of organizational effectiveness that has been common in past literature has not advanced the development of studies of organizational effectiveness either theoretically or empirically. While acknowledging the multidimensional character of organizational effectiveness, researchers continue to write as if a unitary concept is being considered (Hall, 1972; Mott, 1972; Child, 1974; Hannan and Freeman, 1977; Weick, 1977). In this study it is proposed that since the concept of organizational effectiveness differs with different constituencies, different levels of analysis, different aspects of the organization, and different research or evaluation purposes, effectiveness not only possesses multiple dimensions, but it is not a unitary concept. Rather it is a construct composed of multiple domains which are therefore operationalized in different ways. Effectiveness in one domain may not necessarily relate to effectiveness in another domain. For example, maximizing the satisfaction and growth of individuals in an organization, the domain of effectiveness for Argyris (1962), Likert (1967), Cummings (1977), and others, may be negatively related to high levels of subunit output and coordination, the domain of effectiveness for Pennings and Goodman (1977). Specifically, publishing a large number of research reports may be a goal indicating high effectiveness to faculty members (on an individual level) while indicating low effectiveness at the subunit or organizational level (e.g., poor teaching quality, little time with students, little personal attention for students, graduate student teaching instead of professors) to legislators and parents of undergraduates.

Application of the Approach

This approach to the study of organizational effectiveness is probably most useful as a first step in approaching a fine-grained analysis of effectiveness in colleges and universities. Weick (1974: 366) pointed out that:

We treat effects more crudely than we do causes. If we tried obsessively to discriminant subtle differences in effects, we would probably find more single-cause, single-effect relationships than we now see.

That is, one of the reasons for the lack of theoretical and methodological development in studies of organizational effectiveness is the tendency of researchers to do a fine-grained analysis of causes but a coarse-grained analysis of effects.

It has been discovered that no institution operates effectively on all effectiveness dimensions, but that certain effectiveness profiles are developed in which particular dimensions are emphasized. No single profile is necessarily better than any other, since strategic constituencies, environmental domain, contextual factors, etc., help determine what combination is most appropriate for the institution. Once a profile of effectiveness is identified for an institution, however, a fine-grained analysis of effectiveness can then really be made. That is, once a particular college or university is found to have high effectiveness in Organizational Health and the Ability to Acquire Resources, for example, and low effectiveness in Student Academic Development and in faculty satisfaction, detailed examinations of the causes, correlates, and components of its strengths and weaknesses are possible, whereas no such analyses can be made when general prestige rankings (Cartter, 1966) or internal efficiency ratios (Mood et al., 1972) are relied on.

The instrument used in assessing these nine dimensions of

organizational effectiveness can be the first step in a fine-grained analysis of effectiveness on the institutional level in identifying relevant effectiveness dimensions. The instrument could now be developed into at least nine separate instruments in a fine-grained analysis of each of the nine dimensions in colleges and universities.

This approach to assessing organizational effectiveness also appears applicable to other types of loosely coupled organizations, particularly in the non-profit or public sectors. Rainey, Backoff, and Levine (1976), in reviewing differences between public and private organizations, suggested that one major difference lies in the availability of tangible, specifiable goals. In the private sector, goal accomplishment is more easily recognized, agreed upon, and quantifiable than in the public sector. It is suggested that by inductively deriving criteria, by focusing on organizational attributes rather than operationalized goals, and by carefully selecting sources and types of criteria to indicate effectiveness, important dimensions of effectiveness can be identified which can lead to more fine-grained analyses of public sector organizations.

REFERENCES

Argyris, Chris
1962 Interpersonal Competence and Organizational Effectiveness. Homewood, IL: Irwin.

Astin, Alexander W.
1968 The College Environment. Washington: American Council on Education.
1971 Predicting Academic Performance in College. Riverside, NJ: Free Press.
1977 Four Critical Years. San Francisco: Jossey-Bass.

Balderston, Frederick E.
1974 Managing Today's Universities. San Francisco: Jossey-Bass.

Barney, Jay
1978 "The electronic revolution in the watch industry: a decade of environmental changes and corporate strategies." In Robert H. Miles (ed.), Organizational Adaptation to Environment: 1–63. Working Paper No. 7, Government and Business Relations Series. New Haven, CT: Yale University.

Barro, Stephen M.
1973 "Toward operational accountability systems for colleges and universities." In Addresses and Proceedings: 32–47. Oakland, CA: Western College Association.

Bass, Bernard M.
1952 "Ultimate criteria of organizational worth." Personnel Psychology, 5: 157–173.

Beckhard, Richard
1969 Organizational Development. Reading, MA: Addison-Wesley.

Bennis, Warren G.
1966 "The concept of organizational health." In Warren G. Bennis (ed.), Changing Organizations. New York: McGraw-Hill.

Beyer, Janice M., and Reuben Snipper
1974 "Objective versus subjective indicators of quality in graduate education." Sociology of Education, 47: 541–557.

Bidwell, Charles E., and John D. Kasarda
1975 "School district organization and student achievement." American Sociological Review, 40: 55–70.

Blau, Peter M.
1973 The Organization of Academic Work. New York: Wiley.

Blau, Peter M., and Rebecca Z. Margulis
1973 "America's leading professional schools." Change, 5: 21–27.

Blau, Peter M., and W. Richard Scott
1962 Formal Organizations. San Francisco: Chandler.

Bowen, Howard R.
1973 "Holding colleges accountable." The Chronicle of Higher Education, March 12: 28.
1977 Investment in Learning, San Francisco: Jossey-Bass.

Bowen, Howard R., and Gordon K. Douglas
1971 Efficiency in Liberal Education: A Study of Comparative Instructional Costs for Different Ways of Organizing Teaching-Learning in a Liberal Arts College. New York: McGraw-Hill.

Cameron, Kim
1978a "On the domains of organizational effectiveness." Working paper, School of Business, University of Wisconsin.
1978b Organizational Effectiveness: Its Measurement and Prediction in Higher Education. Doctoral dissertation, Department of Administrative Science, Yale University.

Campbell, John P.
1973 "Research into the nature of organizational effectiveness: an endangered species?" Working paper, Department of Psychology, University of Minnesota.
1974 "Sources of organizational indicators." Proceedings from the Symposium on the Utilization of Indicator Data, Institute for Social Research, University of Michigan.
1977 "On the nature of organizational effectiveness." In Paul S. Goodman and Johannes M. Pennings (eds), New Perspectives on Organizational Effectiveness: 13–55. San Francisco: Jossey-Bass.

Caplow, Theodore
1964 Principles of Organization. New York: Harcourt Brace Jovanovich.

Cartter, Allan M.
1966 An Assessment of Quality in Graduate Education. Washington: American Council on Education.
1977 "The Cartter report on the leading schools of education, law, and business." Change, 9: 44–48.

Cattell, Raymond B.
1966 "The meaning and strategic use of factor analysis." In Raymond Cattell (ed.), Handbook of Multivariate Experimental Psychology: 174–243. Chicago: Rand McNally.

Chickering, Arthur W.
1971 "Research in action." In Paul Dressel (ed.), The New Colleges: 25–52. Iowa City, IA: College Testing Program and the American Association of Higher Education.

Child, John
1974 "What determines organizational performance?" Organizational Dynamics (Summer): 2–18.

Clark, Burton R.
1970 The Distinctive College. Chicago: Aldine.

Cohen, Michael, and James G. March
1974 Leadership and Ambiguity: The American College President. New York: McGraw-Hill, Carnegie Commission for the Future of Higher Education.

Cronbach, Lee J., and Paul E. Meehl
1955 "Construct validity in psychological tests." Psychological Bulletin, 52: 281–302.

Cummings, Larry L.
1977 "Emergence of the instrumental organization." In Paul S. Goodman and Johannes M. Pennings (eds.), New Perspectives on Organizational Effectiveness: 56–62. San Francisco: Jossey-Bass.

Dornbusch, Sanford M., and William R. Scott
1975 Evaluation and the Exercise of Authority. San Francisco: Jossey-Bass.

Downey, Kirk, Don Hellreigel, and John Slocum
1975 "Environmental uncertainty: the concept and its operationalization." Administrative Science Quarterly, 20: 613–629.

Dressel, Paul L.
1971 The New Colleges: Toward an Appraisal. Iowa City, IA: American College Testing Program and the American Association of Higher Education.
1972 Return to Responsibility: Constraints on Autonomy in Higher Education. San Francisco: Jossey-Bass.

Dubin, Robert
1976 "Organizational effectiveness: some dilemmas of perspective." Organization and Administrative Sciences, 7: 7–14.

Duncan, Robert B.
1973 "Multiple decision-making structures in adapting to environmental uncertainty: the impact on organizational effectiveness." Human Relations, 26: 273–291.

Duryea, E. D., R. S. Fisk, and Associates
1973 Faculty Unions and Collective Bargaining. San Francisco: Jossey-Bass.

Educational Testing Service
1970 Institutional Functioning Inventory. Princeton, NJ: Educational Testing Service.

Etzioni, Amitai
1964 Modern Organizations. Englewood Cliffs, NJ: Prentice-Hall.

Feldman, Kenneth A., and Theodore M. Newcomb
1969 The Impact of College on Students. San Francisco: Jossey-Bass.

Fincher, Cameron
1972 "Planning models and paradigms in higher education." Journal of Higher Education, 43: 754–767.

Friedlander, Frank, and Hal Pickle
1968 "Components of effectiveness in small organizations." Administrative Science Quarterly, 13: 289–304.

Garbarino, Joseph W.
1975 Faculty Bargaining: Change and Conflict. New York: McGraw-Hill.

Georgopolous, Basil S., and Floyd C. Mann
1962 The Community General Hospital. New York: MacMillan.

Georgopolous, Basil S., and Arnold S. Tannenbaum
1957 "The study of organizational effectiveness." American Sociological Review, 22: 534–540.

Ghorpade, Jaisingh V.
1968 Study of Relative Effectiveness of Joint Stock and Cooperative Sugar Factories. Doctoral dissertation, Graduate School, University of California, Los Angeles.

Goodman, Paul S., and Johannes M. Pennings, editors
1977 New Perspectives on Organizational Effectiveness. San Francisco: Jossey-Bass.

Gross, Edward
1968 "Universities as organizations: a research approach." American Sociological Review, 33: 518–544.

Haberstroh, Chadwick J.
1965 "Organizational design and systems analysis." In James G. March (ed.), Handbook of Organizations: 1171–1211. Chicago: Rand McNally.

Hall, Richard P.
1972 Organizations: Structures and Process. Englewood Cliffs, NJ: Prentice-Hall.
1978 "Conceptual, methodological, and moral issues in the study of organizational effectiveness." Working Paper, Department of Sociology, SUNY-Albany.

Hannan, Michael T., and John Freeman
1977 "Obstacles to comparative studies." In Paul S. Goodman and Johannes M. Pennings (eds.), New Perspectives on Organizational Effectiveness: 106–131. San Francisco: Jossey-Bass.

Hartmark, Leif
1975 Accountability, Efficiency, and Effectiveness in the State University of New York. SUNY-Albany: Comparative Development Studies Center.

Hayman, John, and Jack Stenner
1971 "Student performance." In Darrell Bushnell (ed.), Planned Change in Education: 47–62. New York: Harcourt Brace Jovanovich.

Hedgepeth, Royster C.
1974 "Consequences of collective bargaining in higher education." Journal of Higher Education, 45: 691–705.

Hirsch, Paul M.
1975 "Organizational effectiveness and the institutional environment." Administrative Science Quarterly, 20: 327–344.

Hutchins, Robert Maynard
1977 "Interview with Robert Maynard Hutchins." The Chronicle of Higher Education, 14: 5.

Katz, Daniel, and Robert L. Kahn
1978 The Social Psychology of Organizations. NY: Wiley.

Kaufman, Herbert
1960 The Forest Ranger. Baltimore: Johns Hopkins Press.

Kemerer, Frank R., and J. Victor Baldridge
1975 Unions on Campus: A National Study of the Consequences of Faculty Bargaining. San Francisco: Jossey-Bass.

423

Kerlinger, Fred N.
1973 Foundations of Behavioral Research. NY: Holt, Rinehart and Winston.

Kimberly, John R.
1976 "Contingencies in the creation of organizations: an example from medical education." New Haven: School of Organization and Management, Yale University.

Kirchhoff, Bruce A.
1975 "Examination of a factor analysis as a technique for determining organizational effectiveness." Proceedings: Midwest AIDS Conference, 6: 56–59.
1977 "Organizational effectiveness measurement and policy research." Academy of Management Review, 1: 347–355.

Lawler, Edward E., Douglas T. Hall, and Greg R. Oldham
1974 "Organizational climate: relationship to organizational structure, process, and performance." Organizational Behavior and Human Performance, 11: 139–155.

Lawrence, Paul R., and Jay W. Lorsch
1969 Organization and Environment. Homewood, IL: Irwin.

Likert, Rensis
1967 The Human Organization. New York: McGraw-Hill.

Mahoney, Thomas A.
1967 "Managerial perceptions of organizational effectiveness." Administrative Science Quarterly, 14: 357–365.

Mahoney, Thomas A., and William Weitzel
1969 "Managerial models of organizational effectiveness." Administrative Science Quarterly, 14: 357–365.

Mahoney, Thomas A., and Peter J. Frost
1974 "The role of technology in models of organizational effectiveness." Organizational Behavior and Human Performance, 11: 122–138.

March, James G., and Johan P. Olsen
1976 Ambiguity and Choice in Organizations. Oslo: Univesitetsforlaget.

McGregor, Douglas
1960 The Human Side of Enterprise, New York: McGraw-Hill.

Meeth, Richard L.
1974 Quality Education for Less Money. San Francisco: Jossey-Bass.

Merton, Robert K
1957 Social Theory and Social Structure. New York: Free Press.

Micek, Sidney S., and Robert A. Wallhaus
1974 An Introduction to the Identification and Uses of Higher Education Outcome Information. Boulder, CO: Western Interstate Commission on Higher Education.

Miles, Robert H.
1979 Macro Organizational Behavior. Santa Monica, CA: Goodyear (in press).

Miles, Robert H., and Kim Cameron
1977 Coffin Nails and Corporate Strategies: A Quarter Century View of Organizational Adaptation to Environment in the U.S. Tobacco Industry. Working Paper No. 3, Business-Government Relations Series. New Haven, CT: Yale University.

Molnar, Joseph J., and David C. Rogers
1976 "Organizational effectiveness: an empirical comparison of the goal and system resource approaches." Sociological Quarterly, 17: 401–413.

Mood, Alexander M., Colin Bell, Lawrence Bogard, Helen Brownlee, and Joseph J. McCloskey
1972 Papers on Efficiency in the Management of Higher Education. New York: McGraw-Hill.

Mott, Paul E.
1972 The Characteristics of Effective Organizations. New York: Harper & Row.

National Institute of Education
1975 Administration and Management in Educational Organizations: A Proposal for Research. Watsonville, CA: National Institute of Education.

Negandhi, Anant, and Bernard Reimann
1973 "Task environment, decentralization, and organizational effectiveness." Human Relations, 26: 203–214.

Nunnally, Jum C.
1967 Psychometric Theory. New York: McGraw-Hill.

O'Neill, June
1971 Resource Use in Higher Education: Trends in Outputs and Inputs. New York: McGraw Hill.

Osborn, Richard N., and James C. Hunt
1974 "Environment and organizational effectiveness." Administrative Science Quarterly, 19: 231–246.

Pace, C. R.
1969 College and University Environment Scales: Technical Manual. Princeton, NJ: Educational Testing Service.

Pennings, Johannes M.
1975 "The relevance of the structure-contingency model for organizational effectiveness." Administrative Science Quarterly, 20: 393–410.
1976 "Dimensions of organizational influence and their effectiveness correlates." Administrative Science Quarterly, 21: 688–699.

Pennings, Johannes M., and Paul S. Goodman
1977 "Toward a workable framework." In Paul S. Goodman and Johannes M. Pennings (eds.), New Perspectives on Organizational Effectiveness: 146–184. San Francisco: Jossey-Bass.

Perrow, Charles
1961 "Goals in complex organizations." American Sociological Review, 6: 854–865.
1970 Organizational Analysis: A Sociological View. Belmont, CA: Brooks/Cole.

Pfeffer, Jeffrey
1977 "Usefulness of the concept." In Paul S. Goodman and Johannes M. Pennings (eds.), New Perspectives on Organizational Effectiveness: 132–143. San Francisco: Jossey-Bass.

Pfiffner, John M., and Frank P. Sherwood
1960 Administrative Organization. Englewood Cliffs, NJ: Prentice-Hall.

Price, James L.
1968 Organizational Effectiveness: An Inventory of Propositions. Homewood, IL: Irwin.
1972 "The study of organizational effectiveness." Sociological Quarterly, 13: 3–15.

Rainey, Hal, Robert Backoff, and Charles Levine
1976 "Comparing public and private organizations." Public Administration Review, 36: 233–244.

Reimann, Bernard C.
1974 "Dimensions of structure in effective organizations." Academy of Management Journal, 17: 693–708.

Reinhardt, Uwe E.
1973 "Proposed changes in the organization of health care delivery: an overview and critique." Milbank Memorial Fund Quarterly, 51: 169–222.

Rice, A. K.
1963 The Enterprise and Its Environment. London: Tavistock.

Rice, Charles E.
1961 "A model for the empirical study of large social organizations." General Systems Yearbook, 6: 101–106.

Rushing, William
1974 "Differences in profit and non-profit organizations." Administrative Science Quarterly, 19: 474–484.

Scott, W. Richard
1977 "Effectiveness of organizational effectiveness studies." In Paul S. Goodman and Johannes Pennings (eds.), New Perspectives on Organizational Effectiveness: 63–95. San Francisco: Jossey-Bass.

Scriven, Michael
1967 "The methodology of evaluation." In Ralph W. Tyler, Robert W. Gagne, and Michael Scriven (eds.), Perspectives in Curriculum Evaluation: 39–83. Chicago: Rand McNally.

Seashore, Stanley E.
1976 "Defining and measuring the quality of working life." In Louis E. Davis, Albert B. Cherns, and Associates (eds.), The Quality of Working Life: 105–118. New York: Free Press.

Seashore, Stanley E., B. P. Indik, and Basil S. Georgopolous
1960 "Relationships among criteria of job performance." Journal of Applied Psychology, 44: 195–202.

Seashore, Stanley E., and Ephraim Yuchtman
1967 "Factorial analysis of organizational performance." Administrative Science Quarterly, 12: 377–395.

Steers, Richard M.
1975 "Problems in measurement of organizational effectiveness." Administrative Science Quarterly, 20: 546–558.
1977 Organizational Effectiveness: A Behavioral View. Santa Monica, CA: Goodyear.

Stewart, James H.
1976 "Factors accounting for goal effectiveness." Organization and Administrative Sciences, 7: 109–121.

Survey Research Center
1975 Michigan Organizational Assessment Package. Ann Arbor: University of Michigan.

Thompson, James D.
1967 Organizations in Action. New York: McGraw-Hill.

Tosi, Henry, Ramon Aldag, and Ronald Storey
1973 "On the measurement of the environment: an assessment of the Lawrence and Lorsch environmental uncertainty scales." Administrative Science Quarterly, 18: 27–36.

Van de Geer, John P.
1971 Introduction to Multivariate Analysis. San Francisco: Freeman.

Van de Ven, Andrew
1977 "A process for organizational assessment." Working Paper, Wharton School, University of Pennsylvania.

Warner, W. Keith
1967 "Problems in measuring the goal attainment of voluntary organizations." Journal of Adult Education, 19: 3–14.

Warner, W. Keith, and A. Eugene Havens
1968 "Goal displacement and the intangibility of organizational goals." Administrative Science Quarterly, 12: 539–555.

Webb, Ronald J.
1974 "Organizational effectiveness and the voluntary organization." Academy of Management Journal, 17: 663–677.

Weick, Karl E.
1969 The Social Psychology of Organizing. Reading, MA: Addison-Wesley.
1974 "Middle range theories of social systems." Behavioral Science, 19: 357–367.
1976 "Educational organizations as loosely coupled systems." Administrative Science Quarterly, 21: 1–19.
1977 "Re-punctuating the problem." In Paul S. Goodman and Johannes M. Pennings (eds.), New Perspectives on Organizational Effectiveness: 193–225. San Francisco: Jossey-Bass.

Yuchtman, Ephraim, and Stanley E. Seashore
1967 "A system resource approach to organizational effectiveness." American Sociological Review, 32: 891–903.

APPENDIX A: Objective and perceptual items measuring the nine organizational effectiveness dimensions

Dimension   Perceived Items   Objective Items

1. Student educational satisfaction
   Manifested student dissatisfaction   Number of student terminations
   Received student complaints   Number of counseling center visits for problems
   Attrition resulting from dissatisfaction
   School spirit displayed

2. Student academic development
   Amount of extra work and study by students   Percentage going on to graduate schools
   Level of academic attainment   Number of library books checked out
   Number going on to graduate school   Percentage of alumni holding graduate degrees
   Amount of academic development*
   Emphasis on outside academic activities*

3. Student career development
   Number employed in major field   Number receiving vocational or career counseling
   Extent to which career goals are met   Number involved in work study
   Number of career oriented courses
   Number obtaining jobs of first choice
   Importance of career education and job attainment at
   school*

4. Student personal development
   Opportunities for personal development   Number of weekly extracurricular activities
   Nonacademic growth*   Number in extramurals or intramurals
   Emphasis on nonacademic activities*   Number in student government
   Importance of personal development*   Number in drama, music, art or dance presentations

5. Faculty and administrator employment satisfaction
   Faculty preference for this institution over others   Number of faculty members leaving
   Administrator preference for this institution over others   Number of administrators leaving
   Faculty satisfaction with employment*   Percentage of faculty on policy-making boards or
   Administrator satisfaction with employment*   committees
   Faculty satisfaction with the school*
   Administrator satisfaction with the school*

6. Professional development and quality of the faculty
   Faculty attendance at professional conferences   Percentage of faculty earning a degree after being hired
   Faculty publications   Percentage of budget for professional development
   Teaching at the cutting edge   Number of new courses taught
   Awards received by faculty   Percentage of faculty with doctorates
   Amount of professional development*   Percentage of administrators with doctorates

7. System openness and community interaction
   Community service of employees   Number of continuing education courses
   Professional activities outside the institution   Number of conferences and workshops for nonstudents
   Emphasis on community relations   Attendance at extension courses
   Community programs sponsored   Percentage of students with jobs in the community
   Adaptiveness to environment*

8. Ability to acquire resources
   National reputation of faculty   Amount of general funds raised
   Drawing power for local students   Previously tenured faculty hired
   Drawing power for national students   Average student high school rank
   Drawing power for faculty   Athletic teams placing first
   Drawing power for financial resources   Number of transfer students
   Ability to acquire resources*   Number of students holding outside scholarships

9. Organizational health
   Student-faculty relations   None obtained
   Interdepartment relations
   Amount of feedback obtained
   Typical communication type
   Presence of cooperative environment
   Flexibility of the administration
   Levels of trust
   Amount of conflict and frustration   •
   Problem-solving styles used   Items used in the second study but not in
   Use of talents and expertise   the first.
   Types of supervision and control
   Types and adequacy of recognition and rewards   Note: Actual questions are not listed to
   Decision-making styles   conserve space. Objective items were not
   Amount of power associated with participation   used unless all institutions provided data for
   Equity of treatment and rewards   them, therefore several items are not listed
   Organizational health*   here. The actual questionnaire and the
   Long-term planning and goal setting*   complete list of objective items are
   Intellectual orientation*   630/ASQ   available from the author.

APPENDIX B: Orthogonal factor analysis of the nine effectiveness dimensions — first study

Dimensions	Items	Factors 1	2	3	4	5	6	7	8	9	10
Student educational satisfaction	X_{11}	**.414**	.331	.012	.208	.281	.215	.144	.112	.046	-.018
	X_{12}	**.686**	.122	.109	.013	.040	.007	.277	.068	.102	.040
	X_{13}	**.656**	.199	.065	.100	-.188	-.072	-.027	-.066	.077	.158
	X_{14}	**.419**	.292	.108	.221	.385	-.065	.232	.128	.146	.138
Student academic development	X_{21}	-.052	**.496**	.230	-.161	.004	.079	.232	.072	.020	-.067
	X_{22}	.250	**.469**	.160	.001	.058	.247	-.108	.250	.030	.118
	X_{23}	-.171	**.387**	.093	-.115	.240	-.020	.031	.001	-.078	-.078
Student career development	X_{31}	.160	.087	**.472**	**.470**	.141	.178	.001	-.082	.205	.038
	X_{32}	.160	.011	**.748**	**.039**	-.026	.050	.163	.016	-.004	.253
	X_{33}	-.180	.175	**.728**	**.089**	.080	-.112	-.027	.079	.087	-.073
	X_{34}	.098	.073	**.099**	**.848**	.065	.064	.028	.073	.032	.073
Student personal development	X_{41}	-.003	.095	.047	.069	**.829**	-.008	.153	-.008	.123	.098
	X_{43}	-.028	.059	.014	.035	**.818**	-.017	-.056	.056	-.068	.005
Faculty and administrator employment satisfaction	X_{51}	.018	.133	-.043	.046	-.010	**.872**	**-.016**	.071	.129	.097
	X_{52}	-.025	.146	.028	.081	-.019	**.872**	**.154**	.072	-.039	.109
	X_{53}	.251	.208	.095	-.068	.124	**.196**	**.358**	.119	.234	.078
	X_{54}	.110	.349	.065	-.080	.159	**.230**	**.472**	-.231	.150	.225
	X_{55}	.237	.211	.118	.126	-.066	**.111**	**.513**	.072	.396	.058
	X_{56}	.134	.093	.097	.060	.016	**.115**	**.661**	.145	.274	.228
Professional development and quality of faculty	X_{61}	-.021	-.101	.052	-.010	.279	.124	.118	**.464**	.416	.012
	X_{62}	-.058	.195	.061	-.053	-.061	-.058	.146	**.745**	.073	-.008
	X_{63}	.300	.128	-.028	.114	.074	.184	-.056	**.680**	.121	.084
	X_{64}	-.180	.129	.023	.360	.127	.196	.238	**.471**	.034	.203
System openness and community interaction	X_{71}	.106	.006	.015	.045	.165	.112	.089	.166	**.403**	.039
	X_{72}	.122	.049	.194	.140	-.039	-.004	.030	.034	**.533**	.208
	X_{73}	.117	.113	.096	-.109	-.004	.086	.228	.075	**.780**	.219
	X_{74}	.111	.050	-.038	.167	.135	.163	.147	.153	**.692**	.099
	X_{75}	.098	-.002	.018	.213	-.089	-.055	.072	.008	**.677**	.235
Ability to acquire resources	X_{81}	.186	**.513**	-.048	-.075	-.022	-.097	.081	.268	.083	.107
	X_{82}	.280	**.625**	.144	.113	.058	.088	.073	-.038	.102	.304
	X_{84}	.040	**.788**	.061	.116	.089	.125	.183	.071	.126	.160
	X_{83}	.211	**.759**	-.026	.104	.051	.144	.078	.154	.111	.092
	X_{85}	-.044	**.383**	.017	.161	.139	-.048	-.001	.090	.639	.075
Organizational health	X_{91}	.395	.208	.187	-.133	.243	.072	.042	.092	.288	**.387**
	X_{92}	.196	.201	.014	-.022	.142	.079	.127	.000	.130	**.142**
	X_{93}	.168	.111	.089	.126	.007	.126	.113	.066	.139	**.451**
	X_{94}	.168	-.095	.064	.092	.087	.136	.055	.167	.077	**.512**
	X_{95}	.120	.155	.084	.041	.140	.006	.025	.101	.157	**.336**
	X_{96}	-.044	.113	-.082	.148	-.026	-.074	.202	.020	.329	**.532**
	X_{97}	.040	.037	.138	.138	.027	.035	.089	.136	.106	**.316**
	X_{98}	.024	.181	-.074	-.003	-.010	.091	.100	.135	.140	**.314**
	X_{99}	.058	.168	-.005	-.018	-.085	.069	.190	.073	.162	**.604**
	X_{910}	-.033	.212	-.083	.258	-.051	-.093	.249	-.009	.359	**.349**
	X_{911}	-.015	.012	-.032	-.059	.026	.054	.036	.186	.026	**.735**
	X_{912}	.035	.006	.105	.033	-.005	.031	-.029	.200	.215	**.315**
	X_{913}	.112	.094	.058	.054	.134	.100	.068	-.163	.085	**.801**
	X_{914}	.039	.177	.102	.121	.005	.107	.059	-.014	.214	**.745**
	X_{915}	.052	.053	.077	.048	.037	.050	.086	.024	.021	**.529**
Variance (%)		1.9	3.5	1.2	1.1	2.0	1.9	1.4	1.6	2.3	14.2
Eigenvalues		3.6	6.8	2.4	2.1	4.0	3.7	2.8	3.1	4.5	27.8

APPENDIX C: Orthogonal factor analysis of the nine effectiveness dimensions — second study

Dimensions	Items	Factors 1	2	3	4	5	6	7	8
Student educational satisfaction	X_{11}	.591	.175	.222	.283	.112	.055	.069	.339
	X_{12}	.123	−.017	.063	.350	.224	−.038	.174	.218
	X_{14}	.169	.175	.422	.341	.056	.153	.263	.218
Student academic development	X_{21}	**.613**	−.061	.088	.005	.139	.011	.159	.153
	X_{22}	**.624**	−.359	.283	.175	.152	.000	.047	.224
	X_{23}	**.231**	−.025	.188	−.027	.070	.095	.072	−.033
	X_{24}	**.693**	−.090	.272	.103	.117	.029	.234	.268
	X_{25}	**.581**	−.035	.066	.233	.118	.405	.029	.186
Student career development	X_{31}	.017	**.702**	.185	.084	.122	.011	−.020	.014
	X_{32}	−.201	**.764**	−.117	.003	−.088	.095	−.092	−.044
	X_{33}	−.294	**.509**	−.295	−.044	−.052	.237	−.188	−.228
	X_{34}	.122	**.467**	.186	.209	.117	−.099	.192	−.149
	X_{35}	.033	**.675**	.004	−.023	.016	.080	.066	−.023
Student personal development	X_{42}	.267	.034	**.707**	.056	.096	.110	.093	.171
	X_{43}	.035	−.028	**.380**	.199	.008	.308	.065	.201
	X_{41}	.182	−.125	**.563**	.177	.096	.348	.178	.302
	X_{44}	.173	.013	**.766**	−.022	.132	.139	.100	.010
Faculty and administrator employment satisfaction	X_{51}	.130	−.119	−.103	**.809**	.046	.108	−.032	.122
	X_{52}	.069	.035	.242	**.696**	.039	−.016	.197	.197
	X_{53}	.058	−.029	.004	**.728**	.145	.133	.028	.379
	X_{54}	.178	.098	.075	**.720**	.007	.092	.065	.341
	X_{55}	.126	.168	.026	**.590**	.177	.150	.230	.481
	X_{56}	.060	.171	.227	**.471**	.115	−.011	.396	.368
Professional development and quality of faculty	X_{61}	.021	.036	.220	.139	**.649**	.176	.016	.209
	X_{62}	.155	−.032	.177	.056	**.750**	.022	.218	.091
	X_{63}	.273	−.022	−.062	.200	**.706**	.103	−.205	.213
	X_{64}	.074	.095	.202	−.006	**.707**	.100	.118	.113
	X_{65}	.086	−.028	−.088	.071	**.728**	.096	.230	.144
System openness and community interaction	X_{71}	−.164	.047	.070	.043	.175	**.735**	.020	−.010
	X_{72}	.204	−.029	.166	.190	.232	**.551**	.222	.407
	X_{73}	.211	.100	.097	.083	.072	**.577**	.297	.142
	X_{74}	.292	−.015	.122	.034	.136	**.579**	.289	.242
	X_{75}	.135	.096	.164	.202	.119	**.670**	−.061	.309
Ability to acquire resources	X_{85}	.133	−.207	.252	.151	.145	.178	**.634**	.253
	X_{81}	.344	.138	.327	.119	.274	.162	**.120**	.140
	X_{82}	.276	.175	−.054	.149	.162	.237	**.392**	.082
	X_{83}	.207	.079	.156	.176	.247	.212	**.498**	.323
	X_{84}	.370	.040	.130	.340	.163	.119	**.432**	.332
	X_{86}	.274	−.196	.307	.168	.202	.092	**.649**	.265
Organizational health	X_{91}	.474	−.117	.106	.218	.135	.017	.108	**.432**
	X_{92}	.059	.079	.079	.246	.236	.084	.174	**.377**
	X_{914}	.234	−.132	.080	.080	.005	−.041	−.064	**.735**
	X_{915}	.219	.124	−.060	.185	.139	.190	.024	**.561**
	X_{912}	.069	.198	−.024	.258	.096	.169	.081	**.650**
	X_{913}	.176	−.123	.050	.098	.014	.110	.090	**.740**
	X_{93}	.089	−.058	.138	.060	.179	−.069	.187	**.646**
	X_{94}	.135	−.055	.001	.276	.129	.049	.083	**.739**
	X_{95}	.060	−.038	.093	.303	.101	.035	.021	**.489**
	X_{96}	.005	−.144	.065	.026	.127	.114	.258	**.741**
	X_{97}	.138	−.062	.129	.314	.131	.149	.030	**.662**
	X_{98}	.129	−.020	.121	.447	.105	.149	−.033	**.610**
	X_{99}	.177	−.016	.110	.250	.131	.156	.050	**.771**
	X_{910}	.089	.055	.376	.199	.171	.171	.147	**.611**
	X_{916}	.182	.065	.350	.246	.062	.346	.221	**.537**
	X_{917}	.238	−.048	.515	.185	.143	.115	.208	**.428**
	X_{918}	.449	−.046	.207	.192	.246	.139	.285	**.525**
	Variance (%)	3.7	2.8	2.4	2.8	5.7	3.1	1.9	34.3
	Eigenvalues	2.56	1.99	1.66	1.94	4.00	2.17	1.32	24.03

428

Q. Then How Do Long-Lived Organizations Attain Old Age?
A. They're Lucky.

The logic of the argument thus far leads me to the conclusion that the survival of some organizations for great lengths of time is largely a matter of luck. It seems to me such longevity comes about through the workings of chance.[1]

Why Chance Seems to Be the Answer

Speaking metaphorically, you might liken the environment to a reticular pattern of incessant waves constituting a perpetually varying net or screen sweeping continuously through the total aggregation of interlocked organizations that form in the human population.[2] The openings in the ever-changing screen constantly assume different shapes and sizes. At the same time, the organizations themselves are always changing as they try to avoid being swept away. If the two sets of changes are such that an organization can "fit" through the "holes" when the screen passes, the organization survives; if not, it is carried off. (Frequently the holes are so large that an organization will pass through no matter what it does or does not do; the efforts it makes in such instances are largely irrelevant, though it would be hard to convince the people making the efforts that this is the case. At times the mesh is so fine that nothing an organization does to save itself can succeed. At still other times, however, the actions of the organizations *are* the reason it is not swept away; it fits itself through the net. Accident may contribute as much as planning does to such happy outcomes; we un-

67

derstand very little about the screen, so our most ingenious strategies often lead to disaster instead of to good fortune.)

Let me stress again that this characterization of the relationship between organization and environment is purely metaphorical. It is not meant as a literal description of physical reality; no actual filter really sweeps through the world of organizations. The parallel is merely a literary device to suggest how environmental selection works, to make it easier to understand. It is a figure of speech that points up the apparently perpetual agitation of the surroundings in which organizations find themselves, and of the consequences of this condition for organizational survival. I would not bleed and die for this metaphor; I insist only that no portrayal, however vivid, can be accurate unless it captures the endless challenges to organizational existence and depicts the root causes of those challenges. And when it does, it makes survival and extinction matters of chance.

The result is a frequency distribution of organizational life spans, ranging from very brief existence to extremely long life. That is because some organizations would doubtless be carried off by the first environmental challenge they encounter; fewer would get through several waves of environmental pressure before succumbing; a smaller number would find themselves unscathed after many passes of the environmental filter; only a tiny handful would be fortunate enough to survive the countless sweeps of the metaphorical net to which they would be exposed in the course of extended life. The probability that the uninterrupted string of favorable outcomes necessary to produce an extremely long-lived organization willl occur must be reckoned as very low. But in a very large number of occasions (and the number of organizations forming, living, and dissolving in the world must be very great),[3] a rare low-probability event is not only possible; it should be expected. If, as I have suggested, there is no inherent reason why organizations should not continue indefinitely except for their extinguishment by the turbulence of their environment, one here and there could very well have the good fortune to escape every environmental hazard over protracted periods, and therefore to achieve extremely old age. If *many* did so, this explanation would not hold.

68

If an infinitesimal proportion of the whole population does, that is quite in accord with the laws of probability.

The leaders and members of surviving organizations are usually disposed to attribute the endurance of their organizations to their personal virtues and gifts rather than to the laws of chance. They are not guilty of hubris; they want their organizations to endure, they labor hard in that cause, they are rational, analytical creatures who can plan and calculate and learn, and so their belief that their efforts are responsible for their success is appealing. If I am right, however, we will find evidence inconsistent with this thesis when we gather and examine data of the following kind.

Why Skill Is Not the Answer

I anticipate, on grounds that I will get to shortly, that comparisons between organizations that survive and those that expire will in the vast majority of instances disclose no significant differences in their respective levels of ability, intelligence, or leadership talents. I don't *know* this to be the case; I am merely tracing out the logic of my argument. This proposition is advanced as part of my hypothesis, not as established fact. If the surmise turns out to be in accord with the facts, however, it will cast serious doubt on the belief that the cleverness of the people in long-lived organizations rather than the laws of probability account for the age of these structures.

The measures of ability, intelligence, and leadership in organizations must, of course, be independent of longevity itself. That is, we are not justified in concluding that surviving organizations are superior in these respects to those that die if we use survival as the evidence of superiority. That is circular reasoning. But if we can contrive independent indicia of the allegedly critical qualities, I predict that we will discover the failures and successes are very much alike in these regards. And if they are, if level of quality is not correlated with organizations' survival and extinction, the differences in their fates must be the result of something else. I think that "something else" will prove to be a probability function. This means that any individual

69

organization's experience may be unique and puzzling, but as a member of a population of organizations, its mystery dissipates.

My grounds for expecting probability rather than skill to govern are twofold. One is that no two organizations, no matter how closely they resemble each other, are exactly alike. Nor are the conditions of their existence exactly alike. So the factors that impede adjustment to the volatile environment operate a little differently in each one, producing a range of responses to the same stimuli even when levels of ability are equal in the organizations affected. Indeed, even when organizations try to emulate each other, their endeavors come out differently.[4]

In the second place, much change in organizations is not consciously willed and may even be opposed by members and leaders.[5] Since organizations do not live in isolation but are involved in continuous commerce across their boundaries — commerce in people, ideas, information, and materiel — new concepts and outlooks invade them willy-nilly; they cannot be kept out. Moreover, new values, ways of thinking, and patterns of behavior also develop spontaneously inside organization boundaries as a result of specialization of skills and knowledge, shifts of power when individuals move within the formal and informal structures, and alterations of relationships when groups break up and assemble in new combinations and alliances. Consequently, organizations are likely to behave differently even if they are equally gifted and are confronted by the same problems.

Much of the time, I suppose, these differences between organizations may have little effect on their survival. At other times, however, even small differences may constitute the margin between survival and extinction when the environmental "network" of changes impinges on them. Thus, not only may organizations of comparable talent fare very differently from one another; logically, it would not be surprising if organizations blessed with outstanding gifts were sometimes extinguished while mediocre ones come through and flourish. If such things are not uncommon, as I postulate, chance must be the mechanism of selection.

70

What is more, chance could be the mechanism of selection even if talent plays a larger part than my speculation's credit it with. For talent itself may be randomly distributed. Randomly does not mean evenly distributed, or that no organization is ever systematically and consistently more adept than most others at acquiring and developing talent. Rather, it implies that first-rate people can emerge from relatively obscure or undistinguished surroundings, rising to the occasion when dangers loom or opportunities beckon, furnishing an impetus or an innovation or the charisma that saves a threatened organization or lifts a hitherto mediocre one to great heights. By the same token, in a world where randomness reigns, great organizations may find themselves poorly led or badly mobilized at critical junctures and therefore unequal to the demands of the environment at a given moment, with fatal results. Thus, if I am right, the observer who bets on previously demonstrated quality of personnel to assure long organizational life or early death will often be surprised — more often than the observer who bets on sheer luck, good and bad.[6]

Perhaps the comparative data on organizational deaths and survival will not uphold this impression. If, however, survivors and succumbers are for the most part at much the same level of quality, claims for level of talent as the determinant of organizational endurance will have to give way to the statistics of probability.

Why Organizational Flexibility Is Not the Answer

Another explanation of notable organizational longevity is that organizational flexibility — the ability of organizations to change their structure or behavior or both, readily — permits the organizations endowed with it to cope with the dangers of the volatile environment and thus to survive indefinitely. They are the ones, according to this view of things, that are able to adapt easily whenever conditions warrant, to fit themselves through the environmental net, so to speak, regardless of the shape and size of its openings and the frequency of its passages. Highly flexible organizations could thus carry on for long periods, and, conversely, all long-lived organizations would turn out on close examination to be highly flexible.

Of course, flexibility itself could be the outcome of chance, a quality randomly distributed through the world population of organizations, the outcome of a host of fortuitous circumstances. The alleged advantages conferred on its possessors would then be nothing more than a fortunate break.

But it might also be portrayed as the product of organizational design. The leaders and members of any organization, aware of the great survival advantages of a generalized ability to respond to a host of environmental challenges, including unforeseen ones, would presumably strive to build this capability into their organization. Even if they were only partially successful, the likelihood of extended survival would seemingly be improved.

The trouble with flexibility as an explanation, regardless of its origins, is that it does *not* seem to me to assure long life for organizations. For one thing, flexibility is not costless; other organizational properties that also contribute to long life tend to diminish as it increases, so the *net* probabilities of long duration are not necessarily elevated when flexibility is maximized. For another thing, attributing organizational durability to flexibility implies that flexibility must remain at a fairly high level throughout the organization's existence (or else the organization would have been done in by the environment before it could attain old age), yet there is good reason to believe that flexibility *does* decline with age. Consider each point in turn.

THE COSTS OF FLEXIBILITY

As I see it, the costs of flexibility are of two kinds. One is its frequently perverse effect on the use of organizational resources. The other is its negative impact on the unifying power of internal organizational bonds.

Resource Costs. Flexibility implies the maintenance of the capacity to act in many different ways on short notice. To achieve this capacity, resources that might otherwise be fully employed in a particular immediately successful, rewarding fash-

72

ion are partly withheld, or at least less than fully engaged, so that they can be shifted, restructured, and put to alternative and maybe previously unforeseeable uses. Once they are committed to a single option, switching to other options becomes extremely difficult.[7] The fear that such commitment may thus reduce adjustment capabilities is what leads to strategies meant to preserve flexibility, and the survival of many organizations possessed of flexibility is what keeps the fear of commitment alive in the population of organizations in the world.

Yet under certain conditions concentration of resources and wholehearted commitment to a single option may be advantageous. For example, specialty stores may be able to provide better service, higher quality products, and/or lower prices than general stores as long as the demand for their specialties holds up. (Of course, when fashions and tastes change rapidly, the general stores may be better off because they are equipped to satisfy a variety of demands rather than just one or a few.) Farmers who concentrate on one crop may get higher yields and superior returns while that product commands a good market; farmers who produce a variety of commodities in order to be prepared for shifts in markets may have difficulty competing. (But if shifts do occur, because supplies of the specialty crop go up or demand goes down, the diversified producers may be better able to withstand the new conditions.) Diversification increases flexibility, but it is not invariably an assurance of advantage. Sometimes the environment supports and rewards it; at other times, intense specialization, which implies less flexibility, may fare better.

Indeed, it is a paradox that maintaining flexibility can itself shut off options and impose limits on flexibility. An organization determined to maximize its fluidity locks itself into a circumscribed set of behaviors; it cannot do all sorts of things because they would be commitments and therefore would reduce its freedom of action.[8] It is not unconstrained; it merely subjects itself to self-imposed constraints. Since some of the potential uses of resources, foreclosed by emphasis on flexibility, may improve the chances of survival under some conditions, unyielding determination to preserve flexibility can be a cause of rigidity.

73

Costs in Disunity. Just as the preservation of flexibility sometimes leads to ineffectual employment of resources in response to environmental pressures, so also it can weaken the internal unity of organizations that is sometimes a key factor in triumphs over environmental adversity. Organizations are held together by forces that may poetically be compared to magnetism in the physical world.[9] That is, people contribute their time and energy, comply with directives and informal norms, and assist one another because of attractions to one another, to the collectivity, or both, and because they are repelled by possible alternative ways of life outside the collectivity. The bonds may be emotional, including love (of all by each, of a common leader, a common symbol, a common idea), hate, and fear; moral (the feeling that one *ought* to belong and obey and conform); expedient (self-interested calculation of the value of inducements offered by the organization as compared with the contributions asked of the individual and with inducements available elsewhere); habitual (behavior without emotional or moral roots, without any thought of alternatives, resulting from inertia and organizational indoctrination, training, and other forms of "brainwashing"); and physical (the walls of a prison, for instance). The mix and strength of the bonds vary from organization to organization, and even in a given organization over time. (In general, organizations united by a mixture of the first three seem likely to be more unified than those held together primarily by the last two, but perhaps a convergence of all the bonds produces the strongest union; these are empirical matters yet to be explored.)

Maximizing flexibility is likely to weaken many of the bonds, for the following reasons: It can weaken unity because it clashes with the cathexis strong bonds require. For example, the identification with a group or a symbol or an idea or a leader binding the members of an organization together may prevent shifts to new organizational patterns or practices or leaders when new conditions render the old features dysfunctional; hence, to preserve flexibility, an organization dare not let such attachments grow too strong. If the moral grounds of membership are stressed, changes of direction or practice for pragmatic

74

reasons may be regarded as immoral and lead to wholesale desertions; to stay loose, organizations have to be cautious about invoking moral commitments. If expediential bonds are the main ones holding an organization together, they would be weakened by the obstacles to long-term contracts imposed by the demands of flexibility, even when such contracts are needed to keep key members from leaving. Similarly, the psychological conditioning that ties people to an organization is not easily undone when changed behavior is called for; organizations therefore do not always dare to ingrain habits as deeply as they might. So if an organization strives for flexibility, it frequently must eschew unifying devices that might otherwise be employed.

Admittedly, strong bonds are sometimes correlated *positively* with flexibility. For example, the organization members emotionally committed to a particular leader will follow him through occasional twists, turns, and even reversals of policy— through changes of structure, process, activity, product, and the formation or dissolution of alliances.[10] Similarly, people who join an organization mostly for the material rewards it offers will generally be relatively unconcerned about what the organization does as long as it continues to pay off.[11]

Even in such cases, however, flexibility is limited because leaders who make changes frequently are apt to exceed the tolerances of at least some of their followers, and the intensity of the commitment on the part of others will be diminished. Gradually there is an erosion of the bonds that permitted the freedom of action. A leader who keeps revising things may find his or her leadership challenged by a rebellious minority or weakened by increasing reluctance on the part of the majority to continue supporting the group at the top.[12]

Consequently, prudence constrains the most powerful leaders. Their ability to alter the structure or behavior of their organizations is an asset that can be used up. Thus they tend to draw on it sparingly. For them, too, flexibility can endanger organizational unity. For them, too, it is not a free good.

There may be times when the sacrifice of unity for flexibility is beneficial for an organization; I do not mean to suggest that the tradeoff always runs in one direction. But strong

75

bonds could conceivably allow an organization to stay together through heavy weather that overwhelms organizations that opted for flexibility at the expense of cohesion; the power of nationalism, of family ties, of esprit de corps, and of romantic love, for example, is legendary.[13] Great cohesiveness can have great survival value; renouncing it for the sake of flexibility or anything else may cost an organization dear. Clearly, maximum flexibility is *not* an assurance of long life.

THE RAVAGES OF TIME

Nor is it plausible that organizational flexibility remains constant as organizations age (which the attribution of longevity to flexibility implies it would have had to do in order to keep old organizations viable for so long). The proposition has intuitive appeal if one assumes organizations accumulate experience and wisdom in the course of their long lives, thereby learning to dodge environmental bullets. But there are still stronger reasons for expecting organizations to grow more rigid, not more flexible, with time. The longer an organization has existed, the *smaller* its ability to change ought to be.

One reason for this correlation was mentioned in the preceding chapter: Over time, people develop vested interests in the status quo and therefore tend to resist change.[14] They exhibit proprietary attitudes toward the activities they perform, and oppose structural and operational modifications they perceive as reductions in the scope of their little empires. They become fearful of possible threats to the tangible and intangible rewards of their work. They get attached to, and comfortable with, what is familiar. They therefore do not shift readily. Time locks them into established modes of behavior.

In addition, precedents accumulate over time. Most organizations are not absolutely bound by precedent, but when they confront a problem they have a tendency to see how it or similar problems were handled in the past and to take those solutions as guides to current challenges. Folk wisdom, after all, is full of injunctions to stay on course: "Leave well enough alone." "If it is not necessary to change, it is necessary not to change." "If it ain't broke, don't fix it." True, aphorisms tend

76

to come in mutually contradictory pairs; there are proverbs recommending innovation, too.[15] But as precedents pile up in organizations with the passage of the years, the forces of stability are likely to gain strength.

Indeed, organizations themselves generate such forces by training and indoctrinating their leaders and members to behave in organizationally prescribed ways.[16] Carried to the extreme, these endeavors would assure not only that their people conform to organizational commands and norms but that they are conditioned to act of their own volition, on their own impulses, in organizationally specified ways. Activities become routinized, automatic, ingrained. The more successful training and indoctrination are, the smoother, more reliable, more cooperative the organization is. At the same time, the more deeply implanted, the more thoroughly instilled, and the more completely programmed these behavior patterns are, the harder it is for the organization to change in response to environmental changes. For some reason, uprooting what has been learned often seems to be more difficult than implanting the original patterns.[17] So organizations often contribute to their own inflexibility.

Like individuals, organizations also amass sunk costs through past investments, future commitments based on past experience, and specialized knowledge and techniques. And since they contain organizations within their boundaries, and overlap other organizations, the veto points, accommodations, and negotiations that must be worked through grow more formidable with time.

That is why an organization's flexibility seems likely to decline as it gets older.[18] Along with the costs of flexibility, this tendency casts serious doubt on inherent flexibility as an explanation of the long life of old organizations.

Are Stable Ecological Niches the Answer?

Another possible explanation for the long persistence of a few organizations in the face of incessant environmental hazards is that pockets or pools of relative stability, like the backwaters

77

of turbulent rivers, may develop here and there in the environment and sustain unchanging organizations that form in, or migrate into, them. This explanation would be consistent with the observation that older organizations tend to be more inflexible than younger ones; rigidity would not be a liability in a stable setting. (Indeed, rigidity would be more advantageous than flexibility in a constant setting.)

This hypothesis presents serious difficulties, however. While it cannot be ruled out on logical grounds, invariance in a specific local environment in a world otherwise marked by continuous change is hard to imagine.

To be sure, such refuges might be chance phenomena, rare occurrences of exceedingly low probability among a great number of distinctive local environments; probability theory alone could be invoked to explain them. In that case, luck would be the chief factor in long organizational life, just as I have postulated. The stable pool hypothesis would not be identical with the version I have proposed because my version does not assume or require any islands of tranquility in the environment to explain longevity; the instability of the environment everywhere is there taken as a premise. Conceivably, then, the two explanations might ultimately diverge. It appears, however, that if they both rest primarily on chance, there are really no significant differences between them. Surviving for extremely long periods would be a matter of chance in either case.

On the other hand, they would be qualitatively different if stable niches are interpreted as functions essential to the very existence of every social system. Organizations performing such functions would naturally receive a large measure of support and protection from the other elements of the system and would therefore enjoy a high degree of security as long as the encompassing system as a whole continues, thus attaining a ripe old age. One could then argue that long organizational life is not a chance occurrence but a fixed requisite of the circumstances. The first organizations to acquire these responsibilities, or to have them thrust upon them, would not be easily displaced unless they experienced some exceptional internal failure. Hence, they could go on indefinitely.

78

A model of this sort would be determinate; long-lived organizations of specifiable traits would form inevitably, predictably. Perhaps when we know more about the organizational world, the existence of these inevitable, permanent niches will be obvious and undeniable. At the present stage of our knowledge, a probabilistic approach seems more fitting. The evidence that stable niches provide explanations of long-lived organizations often consists of the very existence of the organizations in question; the reasoning is frequently circular. If the circularity is to be avoided, independent methods of identifying stable organizational niches must be devised, and that is far from simple. Maybe long organizational life is *not* a product of chance, but if it is not, the specific causes have not been isolated. Unless and until they are, I shall construe it as a result of sheer good fortune.

Organizational Biology?

This interpretation of organizational experience bears certain resemblances to parts of the prevailing theory of organismic evolution. True, the approaches to the respective subjects come from different directions. Darwinian theory introduced the idea of species mutability into a body of thought that treated species as immutable; my contention is that organizations are frequently treated as highly plastic when their capacity for change is tightly constrained. But random variation and environmental selection figure prominently in both. One might therefore be tempted to infer that the same model is applicable to both. Are the mechanisms of biological and organizational evolution identical? Is the dynamics of the organizational world the same as the dynamics of the biological world? To these questions I turn next.

NOTES

1. See Armen A. Alchian, "Uncertainty, Evolution, and Economic Theory," *Journal of Political Economy* 58, no. 3 (June 1950): 211-21. The role

79

of chance in evolution, however, does not rule out the possibility of trends in the evolutionary process; see chapter 6.

2. The sieve metaphor did not find favor with one of the authorities on evolution, George Gaylord Simpson; see *The Meaning of Evolution: A Study of the History of Life and of Its Significance for Man* (New Haven: Yale University Press, 1949), 223. "It was a crude concept of natural selection," he wrote, "to think of it simply as something imposed on the species from the outside. It is not, as in the metaphor often used with reference to Darwinian selection, a sieve through which organisms are sifted. . . . It is rather a process intricately woven into the whole life of the group, equally present in the life and death of the individuals, in the associative relationships of the population, and in their extraspecific adaptations." I hope my characterization of the process of organizational selection, in which the properties of organizations themselves are important determinants of the environment and of adjustments to it, is not construed as a purely mechanistic concept of the kind Simpson deplores. I try to use it to suggest the striking variability and uncertainty of the organizational world, and the frustrations and disappointments associated with the efforts of organizations to cope with their situation. I do not mean to portray organizations and their environment as separate, independent forces, one active and the other passive. They are both part of the same fabric, the same intricate tapestry, which is why I resort to the network-of-waves metaphor. At any rate, it is only a point of departure for the discussion in the chapters that follow.

3. See page 45.

4. Richard R. Nelson and Sidney G. Winter, *An Evolutionary Theory of Economic Change* (Cambridge: Harvard University Press, 1982), 123-24, 267-68.

5. Herbert Kaufman, *The Limits of Organizational Change* (University, Ala.: University of Alabama Press, 1971), 41-44.

6. This position is akin to that described by Sidney Hook in his *The Hero in History: A Study in Limitation and Possibility* (Boston: Beacon Press, 1955), in which he says, at 14-15: "The role of the great man in history is not only a practical problem but one of the most fascinating theoretical questions of historical analysis. Ever since Carlyle, a century ago, proclaimed in his *Heroes and Hero-Worship* that, 'Universal History, the history of what man has accomplished in this world, is at bottom the History of the Great Men who have worked here,' the problem has intrigued historians, social theorists, and philosophers. . . . The Spencerians, the Hegelians, and the Marxists of every political persuasion — to mention only the most important schools of thought that have considered the problem — had a field day with Carlylean formulations. But in repudiating his extravagance, these critics substituted another doctrine which was just as extravagant although stated in lan-

80

guage more prosaic and dull. Great men were interpreted as colorful nodes and points on the curve of social evolution to which no tangents could be drawn. What is more significant, they overlooked a possible position which was not merely an intermediate one between two over-simplified contraries, but which sought to apply one of Darwin's key concepts to the problem; namely, *variation.* According to this view, the great men were thrown up by 'chance' in the processes of natural variation while the social environment served as a selective agency in providing them with the opportunities to get their work done." (Copyright 1943, by Sidney Hook. Reprinted in 1950 by Humanities Press by special arrangement with Sidney Hook. Excerpt reprinted by permission of Humanities Press Inc., Atlantic Highlands, N.J. 07716.) See also Kenneth E. Boulding, *Ecodynamics: A New Theory of Societal Evolution* (Beverly Hills, Calif.: Sage, 1978), 218-19, 238-40.

7. Herbert A. Simon, *Administrative Behavior: A Study of Decision-Making Processes in Administrative Organization* (New York: Macmillan, 1947), 66, 95-96, 120; Herbert A. Simon, Donald W. Smithburg, and Victor A. Thompson, *Public Administration* (New York: Knopf, 1950), 427-28; and Kaufman, *The Limits of Organizational Change,* 29-30.

8. Kaufman, *The Limits of Organizational Change,* 71.

9. Ibid., 116-17. See also E. Wight Bakke, *Bonds of Organization: An Appraisal of Corporate Human Relations* (New York: Harper, 1950), p. 8, chap. 7, and Appendix C for a different approach.

10. For example, many members of the Communist Party of the United States, whose ideology held that the policies of the Soviet Union were good for working people throughout the world, followed Soviet leadership through switches from attacks on liberal reformers to efforts to make common cause with them; then, during the period of the Hitler-Stalin nonaggression treaty, back to attacks on liberal supporters of the Allies in Europe; followed by alliance with them when the Soviet Union was invaded by Germany; and once again back to hostility when the cold war began. See Earl Latham, "Communist Party, United States of America," in *Dictionary of American History,* rev. ed. (New York: Scribner's, 1976), 3:143-46, esp. 144-45.

By the same token, nationalist considerations have permitted millions of citizens to follow their governments through alliances with recent enemies and hostilities with recent allies.

11. The things about which they don't care were said by Chester I. Barnard to fall in their "zone of indifference"; see *The Functions of the Executive* (Cambridge: Harvard University Press, 1938), 168-69. Economists have developed formal models of indifference curves and indifference maps; Paul A. Samuelson, *Economics,* 11th ed. (New York: McGraw-Hill, 1980), 416-23.

12. Eventually, the frequent changes in policy by the Communist Party of the United States alienated most of its erstwhile members; see Latham,

81

"Communist Party, United States of America." And more than two millennia earlier, even the mighty Alexander the Great, whose troops worshiped him, had to abandon his conquest of India when the weary, homesick soldiers simply declined to go on; see R. Ernest Dupuy and Trevor N. Dupuy, *The Encyclopedia of Military History from 3500 B.C. to the Present* (New York: Harper & Row, 1970), 52. That is why Herbert A. Simon, emphasizing the power of subordinates, preferred to call their willingness to obey orders their "zone of acceptance" rather than their "zone of indifference" as Barnard did (see note 11); *Administrative Behavior,* 12.

13. Perhaps this is one of the reasons that recent empires—which were presumably more diversified than individual nations—were disrupted by economic, social, and political changes that nations managed to survive, and why the immensely versatile armies of powerful nations have often had difficulties in dealing with guerrilla forces specialized to the local environment and motivated by intensely held, shared beliefs.

14. Gerald Zaltman and Robert Duncan, *Strategies for Planned Change* (New York: Wiley, 1977), chap. 3. See also chapter 3, note 36, in this volume.

15. "Nothing ventured, nothing gained." "Opportunity knocks but once." "Build a better mousetrap, and the world will beat a path to your door." "Strike while the iron is hot." "He who hesitates is lost."

16. A number of students of human behavior have remarked on this phenomenon; see Robert K. Merton, *Social Theory and Social Structure,* rev. and enlarged ed. (New York: Free Press, 1957), 197-98. For a recent illustration, see Herbert Kaufman, *The Administrative Behavior of Federal Bureau Chiefs* (Washington, D.C.: Brookings Institution, 1981), 118-22 and, more generally, 91-124.

17. The difficulty is especially acute when "the new situation presents stimuli that are similar or identical to those in a previous learning situation but demands dissimilar or opposite responses . . . ; the previous response persists and retards acquisition of the new one.

"Furthermore, the old responses are likely to reappear even after the new ones have been mastered and under the worst possible circumstances. Thus, in times of crisis or under stress, people may abandon present or new modes of coping with problems and revert to earlier patterns." Bernard Berelson and Gary A. Steiner, *Human Behavior: An Inventory of Scientific Findings* (New York: Harcourt, Brace and World, 1964), 161.

18. This position reverses my suggestion in an earlier work that age and flexibility in organizations are probably correlated positively rather than inversely; see Kaufman, *The Limits of Organizational Change,* 98-99. At the time, I could think of no other explanation for the long life expectancy of older organizations as compared with younger ones (see chapter 2, note 4, in this volume), in a volatile environment. But the proposition that flexibility grows with age appears to be contravened

82

by evidence, logic, and authority. Therefore, I abandon the initial position in favor of the one presented in this chapter. (Note, however, the recent finding in Thomas W. Casstevens, "Population Dynamics of Governmental Bureaus," *The UMAP Journal* 5 [1984]: 194, that age and survival are unrelated. This finding implies that age and flexibility are unrelated or, if they *are* related, that flexibility and survival are unrelated. The question remains open.)

Acknowledgments

Clark, Burton R. and Ted I.K. Youn. "Continental and British Modes of Academic Organization," "The Historical Emergence of American Academic Organization," "Organizational Levels in the American National System," "Academic Power: Concepts and Perspectives," and "Consequences of Different National Structures." In *Academic Power in the United States: Comparative Historic and Structural Perspectives*, AAHE-ERIC Higher Education Research Report No.3, 1976 (Washington, D.C.: American Association for Higher Education, 1976): 3–53. Reprinted with the permission of the ASHE/ERIC. Please call the ERIC Clearinghouse at 1-800-773-3742 for a complementary Publication Catalog of other titles available in the ASHE-ERIC Higher Education Report Series.

Duryea, E.D. "Evolution of University Organization." In *The University as an Organization*, edited by James A. Perkins (New York: McGraw-Hill, 1973): 15–37. Reprinted with the permission of The Carnegie Foundation for the Advancement of Teaching.

March, James G. "Emerging Developments in the Study of Organizations." *Review of Higher Education* 6 (1982): 1–17. Reprinted with the permission of the *Review of Higher Education*.

Weick, Karl E. "Educational Organizations as Loosely Coupled Systems." *Administrative Science Quarterly* 21 (1976): 1–19. Reprinted with the permission of the *Administrative Science Quarterly*.

Clark, Burton R. "Belief and Loyalty in College Organization," with Comment by Richard C. Richardson Jr. *Journal of Higher Education* 42 (1971): 499–520. Reprinted with the permission of Ohio State University Press.

Masland, Andrew T. "Organizational Culture in the Study of Higher Education." *Review of Higher Education* 8 (1985): 157–68. Reprinted with the permission of the *Review of Higher Education*.

Dahl, Robert A. "The Concept of Power." *Behavioral Science* 2 (1957): 201–15. Reprinted with the permission of the General Systems Science Foundation.

Pfeffer, Jeffrey. "Assessing Power in Organizations." In *Power in Organizations* (Marshfield, Mass.: Pitman Publishing Inc., 1981): 35–65. Reprinted with the permission of the author.

Pfeffer, Jeffrey and William L. Moore. "Power in University Budgeting: A Replication and Extension." *Administrative Science Quarterly* 25 (1980): 637–53. Reprinted with the permission of the *Administrative Science Quarterly*.

Cohen, Michael D. and James G. March. "Decisions, Presidents, and Status." In *Ambiguity and Choice in Organizations*, edited by James G. March and Johan P. Olsen (Bergen, Norway: Universitetsforlaget, 1976): 174–205. Reprinted with the permission of Universitetsforlaget.

Cameron, Kim S. "Organizational Adaptation and Higher Education." *Journal of Higher Education* 55 (1989): 122–44. Reprinted with the permission of Ohio State University Press.

Tolbert, Pamela S. "Institutional Environments and Resource Dependence: Sources of Administrative Structure in Institutions of Higher Education." *Administrative Science Quarterly* 30 (1985): 1–13. Reprinted with the permission of the *Administrative Science Quarterly*.

Youn, Ted I.K. and Karyn A. Loscocco. "Institutional History and Ideology: The Evolution of Two Women's Colleges." *History of Higher Education Annual* 11 (1991): 21–44. Reprinted with the permission of Pennsylvania State University.

Kaufman, Herbert. "Introduction to the Transaction Edition." In *The Limits of Organizational Change* (New Brunswick, N.J.: Transaction Publishers, 1995): ix–xix. Reprinted with the permission of the author and Transaction Publishers.

———. "But Organizations Do Change." In *The Limits of Organizational Change* (Mobile, Ala.: The University of Alabama Press, 1971): 41–67. Reprinted with the permission of the author and the University of Alabama Press.

———. "Some Theoretical Implications of the Argument." In *The Limits of Organizational Change* (Mobile, Ala.: University of Alabama Press, 1971): 92–113. Reprinted with the permission of the author and the University of Alabama Press.

March, James G. "Footnotes to Organizational Change." *Administrative Science Quarterly* 26 (1981): 563–77. Reprinted with the permission of the *Administrative Science Quarterly*.

Cameron, Kim. "Measuring Organizational Effectiveness in Institutions of Higher Education." *Administrative Science Quarterly* 23 (1978): 604–32. Reprinted with the permission of the *Administrative Science Quarterly*.

Kaufman, Herbert. "Then How Do Long-Lived Organizations Attain Old Age? They're Lucky." In *Time, Chance, and Organizations: Natural Selection in a Perilous Environment* (Chatham, N.J.:Chatham House Publishers, 1985): 65–84. Reprinted with the permission of Chatham House Publishers, Inc. and the author.